Karoo Morning

KAROO MORNING

GUY BUTLER

An Autobiography (1918-35)

Guy Butler

DAVID PHILIP   PUBLISHER   CAPE TOWN

OTHER BOOKS BY THE SAME AUTHOR

POETRY

Stranger to Europe. Cape Town: Balkema, 1952.
Stranger to Europe with additional poems. Cape Town: Balkema, 1960.
South of the Zambezi. London and New York: Abelard-Schuman, 1966.
Selected Poems. Johannesburg: Donker, 1975.
Songs and Ballads (Mantis Poets). Cape Town: David Philip, 1978.

PLAYS

The Dam. Cape Town: Balkema, 1953.
The Dove Returns. London: The Fortune Press, 1956.
Cape Charade. Cape Town: Balkema, 1968.
Take Root or Die. Cape Town: Balkema, 1970.

EDITED WORKS

A Book of South African Verse, with critical introduction. London: Oxford
University Press, 1958.
When Boys Were Men. Extracts from South African Diaries, 1795–1870,
with introduction and notes. Cape Town: Oxford University Press, 1969.
The 1820 Settlers. Cape Town: Human & Rousseau, 1974.

First published in 1977 by David Philip, Publisher (Pty) Ltd, P.O. Box 408,
Claremont, Cape, South Africa

Second impression (with corrections) 1978

© Guy Butler 1977

ISBN 0 949968 76 5

Printed and bound by Printpak (Cape) Ltd, Epping, Cape Town, South Africa

Contents

Illustrations

TO MY PARENTS ALICE & ERNEST

Preface

When I doubt my ability to write a book that will rise above self-indulgence, or when the pressure of the present time paralyses my right hand and leaves me staring unfocused at the paper in front of me, I take heart from what my heart insists on. As I was given a good life in a lovable world among remarkable people, mere politeness requires that I should leave a note of thanks behind. There must be a grateful record. Much of the literature by white South Africans is guilt-laden and self-condemnatory, and there are good reasons why it should be so; but where praise is possible it should be uttered. The man who has known joy and keeps it to himself is a miser.

The origins of this joy are manifold, but their main source is my parents, and their fathers before them. The conviction has grown in me that much goodness is being starved to death in the name of individual freedom; that the increasing cynicism about even the possibility of lasting human relationships, and the elevation of sexual attraction above loyalty and affection, are leading to a loss of faith in the family — the most important of human institutions.

In most families the feeling of kinship is strengthened by a body of anecdotes, stories, pictures, letters — half history, half folklore — a warm if vague awareness of many kindred moving in company through time. Children are born into its ambience, and the old do not necessarily leave it when they die.

I have lived my life on the marches of a great empire in its decline. I could also say that I have spent it on a great continent in the century of its awakening. And it is proper and inevitable that my life should be scrutinised from both points of view.

I have heard some very neat historical formulae applied to white South Africans. We are all alienated bourgeois; and we are all impermanent settlers. With these labels round our necks, 'history' knows what we deserve, and will see to it that we get it.

I wonder.

My family was certainly middle-class by white South African standards — but alienated? I don't think so. They were also settlers and settler descendants — but impermanent? I don't think so. They settled in the Eastern Cape well before the Ndebele settled in Rhodesia, before the Americans settled the Pacific Coast or the Russians settled Eastern Siberia. They share with the blacks a disgraceful record of conquest and extirpation of the original occupants of much of Southern Africa — the Khoi-Khoi and the San: almost as bad as that of the Americans and Australians with regard to the Redskins and the Aborigines.

But as this book deals with a period before these issues became a matter of polemic, let me admit frankly that I grew up inside the settler myth, which according to Monica Wilson, can usually take two forms of justification: 'We came first' or else 'We brought civilisation'. As white South Africans, we knew that the land had been occupied by Khoi-Khoi, San or Xhosa before we came; so we chose the civilisation option, i.e. we had brought reading, mathematics, writing, horses, irrigation, wheels, Christianity, fire-arms and brandy. Now no one will dispute the fact that 'we' were the first to bring these things, and a great deal more, to Southern Africa: but whether in our hands they added up to civilisation or constituted a permanent charter for power and privilege was a matter about which there was room for doubt, even in the 'twenties and 'thirties.

Any white South African who has retained old-fashioned feelings of kin will sooner or later respond appreciatively to black South Africans with similar feelings. Most blacks do not abandon their old people merely because they have died. They have a proper piety towards their shades, and dread the alienation of being deserted by them. Their feeling for their *amathongo, amadlozi* or *izinyanya* has affinities with the communion of the saints.

In Cape Town recently, staying with a friend whom we have visited regularly during the past fifteen years, I asked Angelina Hintsho, the cook, whether she did not feel cut off from her *izinyanya,* six hundred miles away in the Transkei. 'No,' she said, 'my *izinyanya* come with me from Qumbu. They are with me, here, and in Langa too.'

Then later, shortly before we left, she volunteered:

'It has been nice to see you. It is always nice to see old friends.'

And then the obvious, unabashed truth:

'With friends we are rich. Without friends we are poor. Money can't buy them.'

Which reminded me of the final sentence of a letter of childhood reminiscences from my eldest sister, Joan: 'We had everything except money.'

Two points about the nature of autobiography.

First, its main source is the writer's memory, which is soon discovered to be highly temperamental in what portions of the past it selects for conscious attention, and what portions it leaves in the limbo of its idiosyncratic amnesia.

One can, of course, supplement one's memory by appeals to members of one's family, friends, and contemporaries, and to written records: history books, newspapers, photographs, family papers, particularly old letters — all of which I have done, with great interest and considerable profit. By

such means, faces, incidents, scenes which seemed partially or entirely forgotten, have been swept clean of oblivion's dust; others, which the memory
of reliable witnesses and the written record insist were there, remain stub-
bornly obscure.

Second, while making every effort to get the facts right, one's main concern is not with truth to fact and measurement, but to character, feeling,
mood and vision. Autobiography, which would seem to be so close a cousin
to history, is less an objective record of a life than an attempt to communicate the writer's feeling for his life as lived.

'High Corner',
Grahamstown

My thanks are due to:

David Philip for encouraging me to write this book.

David Butler for permission to use material from my letters to him,
written while he was serving his year in the army in 1975.

My sisters and brother, who not only read the entire typescript, but gave
me valuable advice on what to leave out, and suggestions for additions: Miss
Joan Butler; Mrs Dorothy Murray; Mrs Christine Moys; and Professor Jeffrey
Butler.

Godfrey and Joan Collett, Professor W.A. Maxwell, Professor Ian Bunting,
Ian MacDonald, Associate Professor and Mrs M. van Wyk Smith, and Guy
Stringer, who read portions of the draft.

Miss Mary Butler, and her sisters Mrs Josie Biggs, Mrs Alice Biggs and Mrs
Kathleen Vorster, for answering innumerable questions. Mary Butler also
made available her considerable collection of Butler papers.

Professor Jeffrey Butler for coming to light with fascinating fresh material
four weeks before going to press.

Mr R.B. Wells for Butler papers preserved by his grandmother.

All those acknowledged in the List of Illustrations on pages vi and vii, for
the loan of photographs; also Joyce Townsend, Rex and Barbara Reynolds,
and my brother and sisters.

Mrs P. Driver, Mrs H. Bladen, Keith Cremer, and others who knew Cradock
in the 'twenties and 'thirties, for information.

Professor J.B.McI.Daniel of the Geography Department, Rhodes University; the Cory Library of Rhodes University, and Mr J. Walters of its photographic section; the Department of Water Affairs; and the Cape Archives.

The patient typists who converted my scrawl into legible form: Mrs Elsie
Banwell, Mrs Norma McFarlane, Mrs Priscilla Hall, and Mrs Yvonne White.

My immediate family, who endured six months of mild monomania
induced by this book; and especially my wife, Jean, whose contribution
is incalculable.

The names of some characters have been changed.

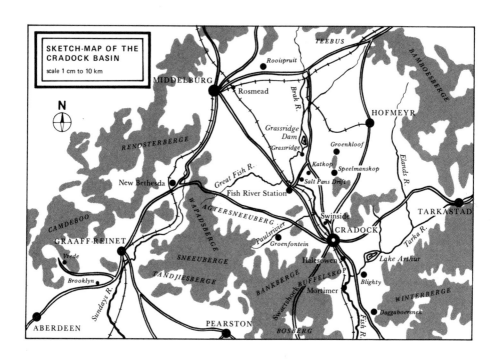

SKETCH-MAP OF THE
CRADOCK BASIN

scale 1 cm to 10 km

N

TEEBUS

BAMBOESBERGE

Rooispruit

MIDDELBURG

Rosmead

Brak R.

HOFMEYR

RENOSTERBERGE

Grassridge
Dam

Grassridge

Groenkloof

Katkop

Speelmanskop

Elands R.

New Bethesda

Great Fish R.

Salt Pans Drift

Fish River Station

WAPADSBERGE

AGTERSNEEUBERGE

Swinside

TARKASTAD

CAMDEBOO

Paulsrivier

CRADOCK

Tarka R.

GRAAFF-REINET

Groenfontein

Vrede

SNEEUBERGE

Halesowen

Lake Arthur

TANDJIESBERGE

BANKBERGE

BUFFELSKOP

Blighty

Brooklyn

Sweershoek

Mortimer

WINTERBERGE

Sundays R.

Daggaboersnek

ABERDEEN

PEARSTON

BOSBERG

Fish R.

1

Beginnings

The marriage between my mother, Alice Eyre Stringer, and my father, Ernest Collett Butler, took place in her home town, Stoke-on-Trent, Staffordshire, in 1914. After a brief spring honeymoon in Switzerland, they embarked for his home town, Cradock, in the Karoo. Europe crashed into war behind them.

60 Bree Street, to which my father took my mother, was a miserably cramped cottage right on the street, with a very small walled garden at the back. Aunt Mary, Ernest's eldest sister, now 92, remarked recently: 'Alice was always so game. When your father, apologising, showed her the place, she said, laughing, "I can be happy anywhere." That is true. No matter what life flung at Alice, she never lost her talent for happiness — in spite of the fact that she had come to South Africa with a broken heart.'

We never learnt who broke it, or how often. She was very reticent about such things.

Her broken heart had been responsible for her spending two years as a governess to a German family in Nuremberg (a city about which she rhapsodised all her life). She had then taken a teachers' course in eurythmics at the London Polytechnic. Living in Chelsea, she had been much influenced by her uncle John Eyre, an artist, who had introduced her to the women's liberation movements of those days. I recall her boasting, with lifted head, of marching in suffragette demonstrations.

She had come to South Africa in 1907 to teach gymnastics at Rocklands Girls' High School, Cradock. The notion that young ladies actually possessed bodies which should be exercised and kept fit was of course very advanced, and it is surprising to find such pedagogical venturesomeness in the heart of the Karoo in the first decade of this century. The originator of the idea seems to have been her future father-in-law, James Butler, the local newspaper editor, and a keen member of the school committee.

Before leaving England for Africa, Alice was asked what on earth she would do with her spare time in Cradock. Her reply is a measure of her ignorance of what awaited her: 'Oh, I'll go fishing and punting on the Great Fish River.'

Her first impressions of Cradock had not been favourable. She'd made the mistake of arriving on a Sunday morning at the time when everybody was at church: the grey, dusty streets were deserted. Alice walked through the empty town up the hill to the new Rocklands buildings, only to find every door locked. So much, she thought, for the famous South African hospitality. Her quick blue eyes noticed an open window on the first floor; also a large packing-case, and a drainpipe. Once inside, the gymnastic intruder inspected the deserted hostel at leisure, and was on the doorstep to welcome Miss Hockly, the principal, to her own school, when she returned from church.

She soon settled in, finding that most of her pupils 'were strong, healthy-looking girls, and saw in them excellent material for games and gymnastics'. She had to struggle hard for sports facilities — the tennis courts were in poor condition, and one end of the hockey field needed to be raised six feet.

But as the mistress of 60 Bree Street, she was engaged in a struggle of a very different and far more exacting kind. Number 60 had one great advantage for her children: it was directly opposite number 63, the large house and enormous garden of Grandma and Grandpa Butler. But whether Alice enjoyed the almost total immersion in the Butler clan which this must have entailed, I do not know.

Nine years and five children later, in 1923 when I was 5, the household moved farther up Bree Street to number 93, called 'The Poplars'.

Miserable and cramped as number 60 was, my recollections of those first five years of life are happy. Many may contain a twinge of danger or of guilt, some of sheer delighted surprise; none of desolation or anguish. Whatever anxieties or differences Alice or Ernest may have experienced, they never allowed them to disturb the confidence we felt in the little world of our home. To us number 60 was a safe, warm place.

I have learnt since that it was not so for Alice and Ernest. The post-war depression hit Cradock hard; the family firm, The Midland Printing and Publishing Company, always on the edge of a financial precipice, was threatening to crash into the disgraceful abyss of bankruptcy; and the rapid arrival of five children strained Alice's robust physique and nerves to something near breaking-point.

The rains came, and the winds blew and beat upon the house of their marriage, but, being founded on a rock, it did not fall. The nature of that rock remains a mystery to me, but it is of all the blessed mysteries the one for which I give most praise.

My earliest memory, however, dates from a holiday at the sea. I am kicking and screaming in the arms of my father, who is carrying me into a huge, hissing blue noise. To my utter relief, he relents, turns round, and deposits me on the warm sand among human shapes and sounds I know. One of them helps to build a high wall of damp yellow sand all round me. I sit there safe in the cool brightness, playing with the clean, damp grit. Suddenly, frothy and bubbling, hissing and cold, a long slither of sea leaps over the wall and swallows me whole. I scream. Someone laughs and makes reassuring noises. Quickly my dread dissolves into delight as the wave withdraws, leaving me to splash about in the sparkling pool which my fortress has become.

Many of these recollections, I note, relate to the elements: earth, water, air, fire.

We are playing in the small backyard, in the cool dust under the pear tree. I fill my cupped hands with it; I let it trickle away by spreading my fingers. On and on. When I add water from the watering-can, dust changes from silver-fawn to dark brown, and becomes as sticky as plum jam. A baby, my youngest sister Christine, is sitting opposite me, eating a fallen pear, so over-ripe that it is brown. She gets more of it on to her face and romper than into her mouth. We are blissfully happy. Suddenly angry shouts fill the air and we are jerked away to be cleaned up with a roughly handled cold wet rag.

'Don't play in the furrow.'
   The furrow, old, stone-lined, ran in front of Grannie's house. When full, it was frightening, and we obeyed; but when almost empty, who could obey? Little blue-gill fish in the puddles; not-too-frightening hard-shelled crabs, their swivel eyes on stalks, many legs moving sideways, big pincers at the ready; or soft-skinned, flabby frogs, solemn, mysterious, impassive, who would suddenly leap beyond your reach as you stretched out your hands towards them. The sun could be blazing on Bree Street, but the furrow under the beefwood trees would be cool. So one naturally took one's playthings into the furrow with one. There is a family story of Grannie pulling a sopping Butler grandchild out of the half-full furrow, both its chubby fists full of her silver teaspoons. How many she lost is not recorded.

'Don't play with the matches.'
   I recall three children, of whom I was one, playing with matches, conspiratorially, near the rubbish bin in the lane down the side of the house which led to the street gate. I remember the forbidden little flame suddenly turning wild, very big and burning; loud screaming; Christine had caught alight. A bucket of water. Tears of solicitude and wrath. And then, when my father arrived home from work, terrible deliberate investigation.
   'Who stole the matches? Come on now, own up.'
   One of us invented a lie: we had been quietly playing round the rubbish bin when a drunk Coloured man had thrown a lighted match through the palings of the gate. An icy tone entered Father's voice. How we were punished I do not recall, but he left me with no doubt that he regarded

the lie blaming the Coloured man as more serious than our other crime.

I am playing alone in Grandpa's garden, under the vine. My contentment is absolute. I have my hands round a smooth metal upright, and am swinging from side to side, looking up at the green leaves against the vast blue sky. I start moving round the pole, faster and faster. At a certain point in each circuit, I have to close my eyes because the blue changes into blinding light. Although I know what my body is doing, I am moving outside my body, high up in the boundless air, freer than any bird could be, round and round and round. My first experience of disembodiment.

It is dusk, and we are already in our flannel nightgowns. Someone is rehearsing us in the welcome we are to give our father, who is about to return from a business trip. She claps her hands and stamps her feet, and we have to do the same, to get the beat:

Clap handies, clap handies,
For Daddy's come home

This is my earliest recollection of learning to co-ordinate words and bodily movement. The quality of the verse leaves much to be desired, but we enjoyed it.

When Father arrived at last, and embraced Alice, we burst into our hand-clapping, just like a clutch of Xhosa children, but excitement broke the rhythm almost at once as each child in turn was swept aloft and hugged long and hard. I liked the sandpapery texture of my father's stubbled cheek.

Off the dining-room, there was a small forbidden room called Dad's workshop. It was never opened, except by him when he returned from work, or at weekends. When Ernest had had as much as he could bear of his four children, he would lock himself in, and square his conscience by making furniture for Alice. Strange sounds and stranger scents of teak or pine shavings or glue would steal into the household from that quarter. Very occasionally one was allowed to watch Father at work — on one condition: not to touch any of his tools. Of these, the hammer struck me as the most wonderful.

One night after I had lain awake so long that it seemed I would never fall asleep, I climbed out of my cot and made for the dining-room. Mother was holding a long piece of teak horizontally in her hands, and Father was painting one end of it with glue. They were busy assembling the back of the bench which was to grace our household for a generation. I was ordered back to bed most peremptorily, without so much as a pat; all four parental hands were busy; once glueing-up started, interruptions could not be tolerated.

Some time later, after this bench was in use, my father left a medium-sized hammer at large. It fell into my avid hands. At last I was free to put in some work of my own. Alas, I was interrupted just as I was starting to enjoy myself, but not before I had left three or four moon-shaped bruises on one of the arm-rests of the completed bench. For years afterwards whenever I indulged in moral one-upmanship, these would be pointed to by my senior sisters, Joan and Dorothy, as eternal evidence of my fallen nature.

Grannie's garden is huge — full of trees, big and small, grape vines, pampas grass, lucerne and cabbage patches, chickens, and a big animal called a cow, from which foaming warm milk is squirted into a bucket. From the bottom of the garden one can see the mimosa trees that fringe the invisible river; and beyond them the railway line, up and down which trains move. The engine is in front, it is black, and sends out great clouds of smoke and steam; it whistles sharply, the hills whistle back exactly the same note, only softly — the echo. The engine makes other noises. When it moves slowly it says: Choof; choof; choof; choof. When it moves more quickly, it says: Choof-chif, choof-chif, choof-chif; when it moves fast it goes: Chifity-chifity-chifity-chifity. On the other side of the railway a row of red-brown iron-stone hills rise; and beyond them the dark blue and purple mountains; and then the sky, nearly always blue.

Any miracle could happen in Grannie's garden. A big grey bird, standing in the lucerne, very still; suddenly it launches forward; when it straightens up, the hind legs of a frog are kicking the air outside its beak. The next moment a lump travels down the heron's long silver neck.

For what seems like an age we are told to hush. Our mother is locked up in her room. Someone in white, I presume Aunt Mary, ushers us in after our evening wash, to say goodnight. Then we are permitted to tip-toe into a room and told to peer into a basket-cot at something we can't see properly, which is our brand-new brother. He has no name yet — strange, to be without a name. In due course he is called Jeffrey with a Jay not a Gee.

Nearly all the wheeled traffic in Bree Street — apart from prams with high wicker-work bodies — is animal-drawn: horse cabs, driven by friendly old men in frock coats and top hats; horse buggies belonging to uncles and aunts from the farms; and, every so often, a huge laden oxwagon, drawn by sixteen redskinned oxen, their terrifying horned and heavy heads swaying from side to side — dragging a scent of lucerne or wool along the street. Alongside saunters a gigantic black man with a twelve-foot bamboo over his shoulder, the long whip-thong hanging in a loop from it. This magnificent procession is led by one small barefooted boy in scant and dusty clothes carelessly holding a 'riem' attached to the nose-rings of the leading oxen.

Then there are men who ride high in the sky, on horses of their own.
They are the Heathcote men, next door to Grannie's; and the house next
to them is visited by Mr Alfred Metcalf, who is always beautifully erect,
mounted on a sprightly glossy animal. Sometimes flocks of sheep or goats,
bleating, drift slowly up the street in a nimbus of sunlit dust. Their feet
make a rustling sound as they rub out all wagon and other tracks, leaving
hundreds of little heart shapes, on which the shepherd's footprints show
large and clear: and one's own feet do the same, if one looks back as one
crosses the street. A footmark is something that stays behind, not like
one's always twisted shadow that never leaves one as long as the sun or the
moon or a lamp is shining.

I do recall a few cars and lorries with brass radiators and lamps — but
they did not penetrate the quiet purlieus of lower Bree Street very often.

My sister Dorothy has vivid recollections of 63 Bree Street:

'Grandfather James was very kind, and used to smile in a happy way, and
let me ride on his shiny black boot. He taught me the text from Ephesians:
"Be ye kind one to another, tenderhearted, forgiving one another, even as
God for Christ's sake hath forgiven you." Grannie was a rather sterner
figure, and yet I was fond of her — in spite of repeatedly having to return
a little copper kettle which I used to steal when we visited her on Sundays.
She made me sit beside her and crochet a chain, but the cotton soon became
black with my clumsy efforts to manipulate the hook in the approved fashion.
While I sat on the stool she made me memorise part of St Matthew's gospel,
chapter 1.

' "And Rachel weeping for her children would not be comforted, because
they are not."

' "But Grannie, why *are* not? It ought to be *were* not."

' "Be still," said Grannie, rapping me on the head with her thimble, "you
talk too much." '

Thus Dorothy.

Why, I ask myself in 1977, should Grannie's mind have been running on
the desolation of mothers deprived of their children?

In 1923 she was 67, her lonely firstborn, my aunt Mary, was 39, and
practising as a midwife, and becoming increasingly involved with social and
political issues, particularly as they affected black people; my father Ernest
was engrossed in the family newspaper and bookshop and in his ebullient,
forceful Anglican wife and clamorous family of five; his sisters, Florence,
Alice and Josephine had married Frank, Alan and Dan Biggs; two of these
were farming up at Louisvale on the Orange River, as was her son, James;
and her youngest, Kathleen, only appeared from time to time during holidays. Number 63 Bree Street, the Sunday playground of Ernest's brood,

must at times have been a desolate place of echoing memories to her.

If you are taken for a walk in the early morning, northwards, up Bree Street, the sun is on your right and the blue shadows of beefwood tree-trunks across the street look like the rungs of a huge ladder reaching into the pure light at the end of it. And if you are taken for a walk in the afternoon, southwards, down Bree Street, the same thing happens, except that it does not end in the same happy way: for at that end, beyond the fine old houses, is the gaol; and no one likes that place. It is always better to go up Bree Street. First, a little beyond number 60 on the right, is the playing-field of the Boys' High School — where huge chaps from all over the town shout and run about in a way that fills one with envy and fear. On the tinkling of a small bell, they all troop into a big red-brick building.

A little farther up, on the left, is Mother's church, St Peter's. It is set back from the road, surrounded by tall, dark evergreen cypress trees and hundreds of different-shaped gravestones with writing on them, on the side that faces the East. None of our nursemaids will ever take us to play there. Joan tries to explain in a whisper: under the stones are dead people six foot down in the ground. Dead people are people who stop breathing, or speaking; and they are deaf and blind, and they have to be buried, other-wise they will go bad, and smell like other dead things do — lizards and mice. But Mother says, No, it's only their bodies which lie in the graves. Their souls are not there, they have flown to a happy place called heaven. Later some moralist adds, 'Not always. If they've been wicked, they go to a very hot and unhappy place, called hell.'

Beyond St Peter's, separated from the dead by laden quince and pome-granate hedges, is Parson Wallace's house. Then comes Hare Street, which runs down to the river on the left, and up to the Market Square on the right — areas of natural and human activity as yet far beyond my ken. Across Hare Street on the left is the hostel of the Boys' High School. We are always hearing stories of how naughty those big boys are. They are supposed to frequent the pepper trees at the junction of Hare Street and River Street, in order to smoke and fight. That is 'Rookers' Hoek', a spot which shares something sinister with the gaol and the graves.

Then comes a big hall, called the Kindergarten, to which I know I am destined to go one day; and then the second of the churches: the Metho-dist, which is attended by all the Butlers, and Grannie's people, the Col-letts. It is much bigger than St Peter's where my mother goes, and there are no graves around it. I am puzzled whether it's good to have graves round a church or not.

Outside the Anglican or the Methodist Church, at a respectable distance, our nursemaid will stop on certain weekdays to watch: something is going on inside — that one can hear from the organ; and there are many horse cabs and cars waiting on both sides of the street. Joan and Dorothy debate whether it will be a wedding or a funeral.

At weddings everybody, in smart and brightly coloured clothes, is in a laughing whirl around a beautiful young lady dressed in a long white dress. People throw fistfuls of tiny circles of coloured paper at her, which seem to sparkle as they fall. She holds a beautiful bunch of flowers in her hands. Joan says, 'It's not a bunch of flowers, it's a bow-kay; and the young man is the bridegroom.' Only then does one notice the shy young man on whose arm the bride moves.

If weddings are white and gay, funerals are black and sad; everything moves slowly; all speak in whispers; fists are clenched, or held behind backs. Some people look at their shoes; some up at the sky; some ladies are crying into their hankies; some men blow their noses more often than usual. And instead of laughter and shouted greetings directed at the bride and groom, a dark silence spreads from a long box heaped with flowers. It is carried from the church by six men in black suits; they are all pulled slightly out of upright by that weight which they are carrying by fine silver handles; they slip it awkwardly into a glittering glass case on wheels, with a fine pair of shining black horses to pull it. Some of the chief mourners who walk behind, carry circles of flowers in their stiff hands. 'No', says Joan, 'those aren't bow-kays, you silly; they're wreaths.'

Once, we are mystified by a rather different sort of funeral. A black man with a long black dress to his ankles, and a white smock over it, walks in front. Next comes a rickety green handcart, on which is a small black coffin, so small it must be someone not much bigger than me. Then come the mourners; the mother, with her sisters all round her; and then the husband, with his brothers and friends. All the women are in black, with shiny black shawls; and the men in the darkest clothes they have: most are barefoot, and many are ragged. This black procession from the location through the white town is explained by the nursemaid. The river has come down; and as there is no bridge from location to graveyard, they have to walk to the only bridge across the river.

Who has died?

'Small child. Throat all white inside.' This means death by diphtheria, a disease spread by flies, which we are taught to hate and swot.

Beyond the Methodist Church, parsonage and Sunday school one comes to a big house with a green and white wooden verandah called 'The Poplars', which is right on the corner of Bree and Church streets. Church Street joins the town to the railway station. It runs over the Fish River on the Gilfillan Bridge, the only means of crossing during floods, up to the Dutch Reformed Church, which has a very tall steeple.

We are always imploring our nursemaids to take us up to The Poplars corner. Church Street is busy; it always has at least one vehicle moving between the church and the station. We are particularly partial to flat wagons with small wooden wheels pulled by magnificent heavy horses with enormous white fetlocks called Clydesdales, belonging to Knight's

Cartage who move goods into the town from the goods sheds; oxwagons; cars and lorries; droves of cattle and sheep moving to and from the stock fair pens near the goods sheds.

One day, I am terrified by an unusual sight. It seems that an engine has gone wild and is blundering across the bridge towards us, sending out black smoke and white steam. As it draws closer, I see it is like a small house on wheels, roaring and rumbling, and shaking the ground under my feet. I clutch the knees of the nursemaid, and try to climb to safety. She lifts me up, and her boyfriend puts me on his shoulder. Safe now, I look at the monster once more. There is a marvellous chain connecting a small wheel under the driver's seat to the big back wheels. I am told that it is a steam lorry. It is taking cement to build a dam called Lake Arthur on the Tarka River.

On the other side of Church Street opposite The Poplars, was the wicked South African Hotel; and then a row of fascinating small shops called: N.C. Rogers, general dealers; then two Indians, one Mr Casavan, who sold vegetables and sweets, the other Mr Ranchod, who mended shoes; and then the premises of *The Midland News* — 'the Works' — where Grandpa and Father worked; and then Mr Smythe's garage; and then J.W. Stevens, big general dealers, where our farmer uncles bought gates and windmills, and mowers to cut down whole fields of lucerne, and bales for the wool from their sheep. Farther up the town was the shop Butler Bros., also a place of work for Father.

Bree Street changed its name to Dundas on the other side of Church Street. At the far end of it was the Park; and beyond the Park the Rugby Field; and beyond the Rugby Field, the Cemetery; and beyond the Cemetery, mystery.

Sometimes as a great treat Mother would take us for our walk — always to the Park, at the far end of Dundas Street: a long, long way to the end of the world, and then a great adventure through the iron gates into the tall world of trees. The baby, Jeffrey, and the toddler, Christine, if they came at all, must have been pushed there in a pram. Alice would take trouble to see that we were dressed smartly for those gala occasions.

While Alice slowly paged through *The Ladies' Home Journal* or *The Queen* or re-read *Elizabeth in Her German Garden,* we made free of the tall presence of the trees — trees whose colours and shapes were already beginning to impress us with their differences: cypresses, shaped like upside-down carrots, only blue-green, with dense, rough foliage usually full of dust, totally hiding the stems for most of their length; bluegums, with smooth white limbs spread high and wide, their leaves hanging loose and glinting, and letting the sun and sky through; and spreading oaks, not nearly as tall, with dark-green leaves, much softer in texture than cypress or bluegum leaves, which would all fall down in the winter. And then the seeds of each: the small, hard, round cone of the cypress, like a rough brown marble, with markings like a tortoise shell; the bell-shaped seeds of the bluegum, in clusters; the golden, smooth egg of the acorn in its corrugated cup; and each with its distinctive scent. Like squirrels, we collected and hoarded these in secret places.

Then there was the large, raised, round pond in the park. Into this we stared entranced at upside-down trees and sky, and also, under the mirror surface, at the tadpoles swimming through delicate water weeds, which were not upside-down.

On one occasion when Alice was staring into her own pool, her book, deeply engrossed in the double images she found there, Dorothy and I clambered up on to the rim of the pond and started running round it. All would have been well had we run in the same direction. The inevitable head-on collision took place. It was my lot to fall, hard but silently, on to dry land, Dorothy's to splash loudly into yielding water. Alice was jerked back to reality. Red-faced, humiliated, she dragged us home, all down Dundas and Bree streets. It was a miserable return journey, particularly for Dorothy, squelching along in her bedraggled best dress.

Sometimes I'd sit on the brass double-bed while Mother combed her thick, long hair with a big white coarse-toothed comb — from which it was a strange pleasure afterwards to remove the strands caught round the teeth, and wind them round one's left index finger.

On the dressing-table among the embossed silver-backed brushes stood several photographs, including two of men in uniform wearing soldier's caps: my mother's brothers, uncles Guy and George.

I was named after Guy. He was dead. What that meant I did not know, but he'd been killed in France shortly before I was born. France was a long way away, and most of the Great War had taken place there.

At one stage each year, early in November, I resented that dead man in France whose name I had been obliged to carry. Possibly the first bit of poetry turned to the purposes of contempt and attack that I heard was:

Guy Fawkes Guy,
Stick him in the eye,
Hang him on the lamp post
And there let him die.

While crackers were detonating, and rockets rising above the beefwood trees, five or six cruel boys, circling me, chanted this jingle over and over again — normally my friends, now inexplicably threatening and exultant. From the same source came my nickname Foxy.

Later, I heard that Uncle Guy had gone to Malaya 'to plant rubber'. This took some explaining, but I grasped it at last. When the Great War broke out (all sorts of other things 'broke out', like chicken pox, and prisoners from the gaol), he went back to England to fight in the war to end all wars. I gather from my cousin Guy Stringer, who also has the honour of carrying his name, that he was a difficult customer, whom old Frederick Septimus Stringer, his father, had placed in the bank or business, without success; indeed with such non-success that he was 'sent out to the colonies to make good'. He was killed by a shell near Ypres, a direct hit, all to himself, in 1915, aged 29.

Mother's other soldier brother was Uncle George. He was not dead. He had recovered from his war wounds and was now managing director of a pottery called Newhall. 'George is such a dear,' Mother would say over and over, whenever she received a letter from him.

When she received letters from her eldest brother, Harold, she never said, 'Harold is such a dear.' Harold was very clever; he'd been to Cambridge, and had built railways — imagine that! — in Angola. He was now in China, building more railways. Once or twice parcels arrived from Shanghai, containing beautiful scarlet silks, with terrifying dragons embroidered upon them, and gentle ducks, herons, and bending bamboos.

Then one of her family came to stay with us — her sister Janet.

My one clear recollection of Aunt Janet is frightening and portentous: she was crying uncontrollably, for what cause I cannot say. This upset us all, because no Butler, Biggs or Collett adult female ever cried 'in front of the children'. Extreme displays of emotion of any kind were taboo. We were already dimly aware that our mother permitted herself to express much more emotion than our Butler aunts — she played about ten more octaves on the emotional scale than they did.

She never lost control as Janet did. Highly intelligent, Janet had been sent to Cambridge like Harold; but after a year at Newnham she had succumbed to some sort of breakdown. She spent several years with her mother — also a highly strung woman, who 'took to her chaise longue early on in life' — on whose death she was sent to her eldest sister in South Africa to recover her spirits. According to Guy Stringer, she was suffering from a permanently broken heart. She taught for some time at Ellerslie School in Cape Town. In Cradock, when not with Alice, she stayed with the Hilton Barbers at Halesowen, as a governess, I think.

Aunt Janet seems to have had a strong romantic streak in her, which the people of Cradock did their best to gratify. For instance, she expressed a keen longing to experience a trek by oxwagon — the whole slow ritual of inspanning and outspanning, of moving over vast spaces by sunlight or moonlight, of the huge patient beasts, the straining trek chain, the rifle-cracking whip, the intimate campfire, and of crunching biscuits and sipping aromatic coffee. Aunt Mary tells me that 'dear old Ted Gilfillan laid on a little trek especially to gratify this whim of the poor suffering Janet'. Perhaps she was hoping desperately for some healing from this exposure to the wide open spaces.

One day she decided to do a watercolour sketch of the town from an ironstone hill on the outskirts, known as the Slippery Rocks — so named after the exposed domes of dolerite down which the children of Cradock of all races used to toboggan on flattened paraffin tins or old scraps of sacking — a forbidden activity, since one usually slipped off one's skid, to the detriment of one's knickers or shorts.

Alice no doubt encouraged this exercise, and deputed Dorothy to carry the artist's bottle of water. 'Being me,' says Dorothy, 'I spilt it just as we arrived.' Janet did not handle the situation well. Instead of asking for a bottle of water at any of the houses at the upper end of town, she abandoned the attempt and walked the humiliated child all the way back to Bree Street.

Of Mother's other sisters, May and Dorothy, I was but dimly aware. If her mother was dead, her father was very much alive — particularly at Christmas time, when he sent money all the way from England for presents for us all.

But of all the memories of this early era, the one which captures best my joyful coming into consciousness of the marvellous world is this. We are standing in number 63 round a piano which is being played by my father's youngest sister Aunt Kathleen. We are learning music and words at one and the same time. The song seems to sing my entire world; I have not had to struggle to find either note or word; it has all been done for me.

> *All things bright and beautiful,*
> *All creatures great and small,*
> *All things wise and wonderful,*
> *The Lord God made them all. . . .*
>
> *The purple-headed mountain,*
> *The river running by,*
> *The sunset and the morning,*
> *That brightens up the sky; . . .*
>
> *He gave us eyes to see them,*
> *And lips that we might tell*
> *How great is God Almighty,*
> *Who has made all things well.*

Then we moved from 60 Bree Street to The Poplars, the house with the wooden lace verandah and palings at the corner of Bree and Church streets.

I remember walking behind an old handcart loaded to the sky with furniture. Its tall wheels seemed to waver, and the whole load to reel from side to side. To be moving house was an exciting and frightening thing. I had been given a basket to carry, to make me feel important, I suppose. I clung to it for dear life. Joan, three years older, was of far greater use. She had baby Jeffrey strapped on her back; and, as if that were not responsibility enough, she'd been entrusted with Father's favourite picture — a blind-folded lady, sitting on a ball which we were told was the world, trying to extract music from a harp which has only one string — G.F. Watts's 'Hope'.

Tradition says that when we reached The Poplars, Alice relieved Joan of Jeffrey, while Ernest took the picture, and nailed it up in the hallway at once.

2

My Grandfather James

The Poplars (number 93) seemed paradise after number 60 Bree Street: not only did the house contain many more rooms, but they were large, with high ceilings, and connected by a long, wide passage. And the garden! It was as big as Grandpa's, but neglected and wild, with remnants of gnarled old orchards, and huge pear trees, and orange trees, and lemons, and scented lavender, and Adam figs, and Spanish reeds, and lucerne patches shimmering with butterflies — 'a small farm', said a visitor. But the garden did not start from the back of the kitchen doors. They opened on to the back yard — where it was not cobbled, it consisted of bare dusty earth, with two huge pepper trees, its limits confined by an L-shaped group of very old out-buildings, stables and coach houses dating from the old Kimberley days. Indeed, there were worn old yellowwood cribs in some of them, supported by sneezewood posts. 'They're worn smooth', said Father, 'from the horses rubbing themselves against them.' The tall wall which ran along the Church Street boundary was pierced by two handsome archways — through which the jingling coaches used to arrive and depart when The Poplars was an inn.

There was a curiously close bond between my mother Alice and her father-in-law. According to Aunt Kathleen, he loved talking to her about the old country, the English Lakes, and historic London; and she enjoyed his yearly planting of English trees in his vast garden — lilac, cherry, apple, pear, laburnum, hawthorn and eglantine — not all of which would survive the terrible heat of summer. They were both essentially townspeople with an idealised love for the countryside. Our grandmother Lettie Butler by contrast was the countrywoman in town, practical and efficient to a degree: a garden for her was less a romantic and nostalgic pleasance in which to refresh one's tired and exiled spirit than a useful extension of the kitchen, dining-room and nursery, yielding fresh vegetables and fruit in season, and food for the Swiss goat or cow which provided milk for her seven children.

This seems the appropriate point to sketch the life of James Butler, the founder of the family, whose spiritual and economic struggles provide many of the themes of this book.

In May 1820, the very month during which transports were putting other

ancestors of ours ashore in Port Elizabeth, John Butler (1792–1830), a
brush and bellows maker, married Philippa Norman (1794–1867) in the
Quaker Meeting of Bristol. In 1827, bad times led the young couple to
emigrate to New York. There three years later John died of consumption.
Philippa returned to England with her two small children, Philip John
(1826–90) and Harriet. Philip seems to have inherited his father's suscep-
tibility, and suffered from tuberculosis of the spine as a child, which left
him with a slight hump. He was self-conscious of this as an adult, always
insisting that he should be photographed at an angle in order to hide it.

His beautiful, courageous mother brought him up well. After various
touching trials and vicissitudes he entered the employ of Poole's, chrono-
meter makers of Fenchurch Street, where he rose to be manager. He sent
his seven children to Quaker schools. A superb clock and instrument maker,
he also studied zoology, published papers on such topics as 'Flies in Amber',
and connected the summerhouse to the drawing-room of De Beauvoir Road
by means of a primitive telegraph — and retained the affection of all his
family.

After a period at Croydon School, James (b. 1854) was apprenticed to
Poole's for five years on 28 November 1870. For a period it was his task to
visit the ships as they docked, to collect the chronometers, bring them to
Poole's for checking and servicing, and then return them to the captains.
In this way he imbibed some knowledge of the human race as seen through
the eyes of nineteenth-century British traders, seamen and missionaries;
and he witnessed the degradation of poverty and drink in Dockland. At
one time he and two of his brothers worked among the slum children at
the Bedford Institute in the East End. Aunt Mary recalls, as a small girl,
being shown a photograph of James surrounded by a group of his charges.

'How ugly they are!' she exclaimed.

'No, they're just poor,' was his reply.

The London image of my grandfather James which I like best concerns
Greenwich Observatory: the place which regulated all the chronometers
and clocks in the world on land or sea, from 'Big Ben' itself to my lady's
jewelled watch, clocks on the bridges of battleships, cathedral towers,
railway stations, hospitals, grandfather clocks in suburban hallways — all,
ultimately, taking their time from the golden instruments of Greenwich,
which, with some help from men, took it from the great sun itself. Once a
week in order to service the chronometers, the young Quaker visited the
place where time was tamed and taught to be tidy.

He might in due course have followed his father as manager of Poole's,
but alas, tuberculosis, the family curse, struck again so severely that in
1876, at the age of 22, he was shipped off to the ends of the earth — like
Cecil John Rhodes a few years before — in search of health.

For reasons I cannot establish, he was sent to Grahamstown — not the
best place for consumptives or asthmatics. He endured the interminable,

boring, idle days under the suspended death sentence which tuberculosis
then imposed, marking time, as best he could, hoping for his condition to
improve.

His letters home, packed as they are with detailed observations on people
and places, on natural history, on farming, on politics, free as they are from
self-pity and introspection, cannot conceal his longing for England and his
own people. Apart from his old school friend, Robert Wilkie, similarly
afflicted and similarly unoccupied in South Africa, he seemed incapable
of finding congenial company.

Early in May 1877, after visits to a variety of farms in Albany, the two
young consumptives took stock of their condition, and came to a crucial
decision.

'Much as we have been favoured in the past and thankful that we have
not got worse, we think we ought to try some fresh place, and, as Cradock
has been so highly spoken of by so many as possessing such a health-
restoring climate, we are moving up there to see if it will benefit us.'

The mode of travel, oxwagon, was hard on near-invalids.

'7.v.1878 . . . *bump,* bump – bump – bump, bump, *bump* – bump
– bump, *B UMP, B UMP,* bump, bump – and so on mile after mile, hour
after hour. We were tired of the exertion and manoeuvring requisite to
gain even a sitting posture. Even the inducement of viewing fresh scenery
did not make us change our recumbent positions. After five hours of this,
at last we stopped.

'8.v.78. At what time last night we were again on the move I cannot say,
but I remember waking up with the too familiar bump, bump, dozing off
again only to be aroused by an extra heavy bump. . . . How I longed for
daylight . . . by dint of considerable fumbling I found some matches, and
then by skilful scheming got at my watch and found the time was only
1.40 a.m. Presently we discovered we were crossing a bridge . . . and outspanned. We had been lying down for the space of seventeen hours.'

They had reached Carlisle Bridge – half an hour's easy run by car today.

'. . . I wanted a wash, so made my way down to the water – a little
stream that I could almost jump over, and this the "Great Fish River"!
If you venture to laugh at the colonial rivers in the presence of a Colonist,
you are soon met with "I wish that you might be there when the river
comes down". No doubt this is a "great" river when it does come down,
but what is the use of it? It is no use for navigation and little for irrigation.
When it comes down it carries away thousands of tons of soil to the sea,
washes away bridges, etc., floods houses, and generally destroys many lives
of stock and human beings. . . . I saw one immense block of timber that
must have been the stem of some giant tree which, after luxuriating all its
life on the banks of the river, must have been uprooted by some great
torrent and carried down; now it lies high and dry until the next flood
comes. . . .'

He is talking of the river where it runs parallel to the Winterberg Mountains, some fifty miles to the north; the Winterberg Mountains, which,
with the Bosberge and Tandjiesberge form a great barrier of bare flank and
high rock running east and west, protecting the elevated semi-deserts
beyond them from too easy access from the gentler grass and bush lands
to the south. He is talking of the river before it turns north and cuts its way
between the Winter- and Bosberge at East Poort and Daggaboersnek, before
it enters a great basin of some 16 600 square kilometres which its upper
reaches and tributaries have carved from iron and sandstone over a period
of some 200 million years. In the southern half of that basin lies his destination, Cradock, a small market village on the same river, some sixty-five
years old. On an erratic radius, the mountains ring it round: close in, the
Bankberge, extending west into the Sneeuberge, drained by Paulsrivier;
then the Wapadsberge, and Renosterberge, running west and north, drained
by the Fish itself; to the north the Stormberge, drained by the Brak; to
north-east and east, the Bamboes and Tarka mountains, drained by the
Elands and Tarka rivers, and so back to join the Winterberge in the south.

Once you top the escarpment at Daggaboersnek and enter the basin, the
climate, the landscape and the vegetation undergo a dramatic change:
Cradock has a rainfall of 330 mm per annum, Grahamstown 675 mm;
Cradock is 920 metres above sea level, Grahamstown 570 metres; except
in good seasons, there is little grass; the characteristic colours are browns,
blues, slate-greens. The sense of space is enormously expanded by the
clarity of the dry air, and by the presence of successive ridges and mountain
silhouettes receding one behind the other towards a usually remote horizon.
Most European travellers experience something of a shock on their first
exposure to the dwarfing scale of the Karoo: the inability of the thin vegetation to disguise the elemental rock; the severity; the silence; and, depending on the season, the heat, or the cold.

Two days later their wagon wound its way up Daggaboersnek, turned the
corner and started to descend into the Cradock district.

On the left 'I saw a house, and on enquiry found it belonged to a Mr
John Trollip to whom we had some goods to deliver and to whom we had
a letter of introduction from Mrs Chapman'. They were set down to a good
breakfast and entertained with intelligent conversation.

But outside the friendly homestead was 'a waste howling wilderness
beyond which again mountains rise in grand style. A waste howling wilderness does not, I think, overstate the case; stones and scrubby bush are
spread about in equal quantities over an immense tract through which a
road runs, which road is inches deep in dust, which dust with the howling
wind is spread in clouds over the wilderness. Not another house in sight
. . .'

In the small cemetery he finds the tombs of two brothers who during the last Kaffir War (1850-1) were waylaid on returning home and both killed. The inscription reads: 'They were lovely in their lives and in their death they were not divided.' These were the brothers of their host, the story of whose death in ambush within sight of their home was still being told and retold in my boyhood.

After a day's rest 'we were sent on our way rejoicing with an open invitation (from Mr Trollip) to return and spend a week or two as soon as we are tired of Cradock — which we were told we would be very soon'. And then significantly, 'I slept well tonight. With sunset came a more breathable air. . . .'

After a journey of six days they jolted into Cradock. '. . . We were disappointed. Our broad dusty road was indefinitely bounded by a stony, dusty waste; there seemed an incompleteness, a neglected unfinished appearance about the place as if . . . a plan had been stopped when only partially carried out.' They went in search of the boarding house of Mrs Rhoda Saunders, recommended by Mrs Trollip. The first street consisted of 'low white-washed single storey houses, without front gardens or anything to break their sudden out-step on to the wilderness'. They note, however, the handsome Dutch Reformed Church on the Market Square, 'almost the finest building I have seen in the Colony', a modest public library and then 'a good broad street, plenty of trees . . . and what rejoiced our eyes most of all, running water in channels at the sides of the roads'. They have entered the old town — the Cradock of my childhood — which lies below the furrow, where the gardens are large, and each erf-owner has his turn when water is available.

Mrs Saunders of The Poplars, Bree Street, had accommodation for them — the best they had experienced anywhere — but 'we are warned not to expect to keep them beyond the end of the month'. This limit, according to family tradition, was imposed because Mrs John Collett of Grassridge had booked the room for her twelfth lying-in. They went for a ramble after breakfast next morning and 'brought back a glowing opinion of the air — a light, free freshness such as we have not known hitherto.' But they soon discover that there is little to attract them beyond the oasis below the furrows.

If the town is surrounded by desert, its intellectual life is barren. So, on the 18th: 'It is rather rare to find anybody who cares to talk about anything sensible, if indeed they are sufficiently well informed to be able to.' On the 22nd he called on the watchmaker: 'I pity him,' said the young man from Poole's of Fenchurch Street. 'Correctly speaking he is not a watch*maker;* scarcely can he be called a watch *seller,* but he has the drudgery of watch *jobbing;* and oh! such watches! The greater part of them, had they been handed to me in former days, I should probably have politely handed back and declined to have anything to do with them. Smousers sell them. . . . I was shown one, a wretched Geneva watch in metal-gilt case that a Dutchman had been induced to give £25 for. . . . In buying it he asked:"Is it gold?" The smouser blandly replies: "You can see for yourself!" It is not worth as many shillings.'

On the 27th it was the local newspaper's turn to come in for criticism. 'The Cradock Register . . . is published weekly, and for a single copy we had to pay sixpence. . . . The Editor is rather a comical customer. . . . He rides a bicycle which is much too high for him.' On the 31st the two exiles 'walked on to a fresh desolate hill and amused ourselves aiming stones at a prickly pear — What we are driven to!'

It is no surprise that they took the Trollips at their word, and returned to Daggaboer. They stayed eight weeks. Hospitable people, the Trollips of Daggaboer. As they felt they might be overstaying their welcome, and as the Karoo air was indubitably doing them good, they returned to Cradock, James on a horse called Moscow, which he had bought from Mr Trollip for £16.

Moscow marks the first stage in the liberation of James. He began to expand with the freedom of movement which his steed provided. On 26 August he spent four-and-a-half hours in the saddle in order to visit Mrs Trollip's brother, John Collett at Grassridge — a ride that was probably the most important in his life. There he found a large, close-knit, devout Victorian family, which, in spite of many differences, had much in common with the family in De Beauvoir Road for whom he longed so intensely. Philip John Butler in London and John Collett in the Karoo were splendid patriarchs, and their wives, both Marys, rejoiced in their many children.

'Mr Collett's property, consisting of several farms, stretches about an hour's ride each side of the homestead — about sixteen miles in all, and some four miles wide.' John Collett's family was also large: twelve — five daughters, and seven sons. Only one son, Walter, had left home, and was farming at Groenkloof among the reddish ironstone hills to the east. The rest ranged at an average interval of two years from Annie Letitia, aged 22, through Herbert, Jessie, Emma, Rose, Owen, Agnes, Bertie, Gervase, Norman (aged 1) to the as yet nameless baby. (All the boys became Karoo farmers in the Fish River catchment, and all the girls married Karoo farmers or spent their lives on Karoo farms, except Annie Letitia and Emma, who married editors of Karoo or Kalahari newspapers. Except for Rose, I have vivid recollections of them all. They lasted well. Only one of them died under the age of 80 — Herbert, at 79.)

On the 27th the infant whose impending arrival had limited James's tenure of the room at The Poplars, was given his names, Dudley Templeton, at a christening conducted in the home. 'He did not cry during the ceremony,' notes the observant young Quaker, 'because his thoughtful sisters had warmed the water beforehand.' James stayed a month at Grassridge — driving cattle with Herbert, riding up to Walter's with Miss Collett (Letitia), making pancakes and tea there, playing croquet, reading, visiting different farms. Congenial people were dispelling the desolation of the veld. He then made an excursion north, beyond Middelburg, to the farms of James Collett's brothers, William and Joseph (who also left substantial clans) returning to Cradock on 7 December.

He found it 'the same dead-alive place'.

He was not entirely correct about Cradock, as his kind friends Mrs Grey and Mrs Cawood could have told him. The small library — under the stimulus of Dr Grey — had expanded sufficiently to supply the needs of a moody, beautiful, peripatetic governess, one year junior to James, who moved from post to post, tutoring children on Boer farms called Ganna Hoek, Leliefontein, Kat Kop, Ratel Hoek. In 1875–6 she had devoured Spencer's *First Principles,* J.S. Mill's *Logic,* John Ruskin's *Crown of Wild Olives,* Shelley's *Prometheus Unbound,* T.H. Huxley's *Lay Sermons,* and Darwin's *Plants and Animals.* Her bedside reading was Gibbon's *Decline and Fall of the Roman Empire.*

At this very moment she was at Kat Kop (a farm which will feature again in this book), where old Mr van Heerden, the father-in-law of her present employer Mr Martin of Ratel Hoek, was dying. She was more miserable and self-conscious than usual — the impending death and funeral may have caused her to worry whether mourning would suit her or not. The only diary entry for this period (2 December 1878) reads:

'. . . I mean to sit up far into the night and write. I have done nothing all day. Vanity is the root of all evil; I have been troubled about clothes. Oh, for a large, true, strong soul! Why should not mine be such?'

Then, the sudden change after the catharsis of creation.

'. . . Had very happy time tonight, writing Waldo's letter. I think it must be one o'clock. . . .'

Olive Schreiner was finishing *The Story of an African Farm,* the first work of imaginative power in South African literature.

After a month in the saddle, touring Albany and exploring the Zuurveld, James returned to Cradock ('as uninteresting and uninviting as ever'), where he planned an extensive tour of the eastern Karoo. He did not intend to go via Grassridge, but was invited to do so. There he had received 'a very cordial welcome from old and young. . . . I don't exactly know how I became so liked here, but Mr Collett said that if it had been their own brother the young people were expecting, they could not have been more excited.' On 29 November he left for his tour of the eastern Karoo.

All alone on Moscow, the young man went in a great arc: Middelburg, Hanover, Richmond, Graaff-Reinet; then south to the Hobsons, friends of the Colletts, at Ebenezer; to 'Wellfound', where he met the Biggs family, and struck up a friendship with young John Ebenezer which was to last a lifetime (three of James's daughters would in due course marry three of

John's sons); then east to Somerset East; Daggaboer once more, Cradock, Grassridge — some 700 kilometres of plain and mountain, through a landscape as different from the England he knew as the surface of the moon. He arrived at Grassridge on 21 January.

Grassridge was everything which Cradock was not: there he was made to feel that he belonged, and it is clear that he was loved. It was a restrained and difficult parting on 25 February.

'Saying goodbye to such a number of such dear friends was a hard task. . . . From now on I am on my way home.'

His exile was drawing to an end. Africa — in particular the arid Karoo — had served its purpose. When he arrived at Daggaboersnek, the hot berg wind was blowing as it had blown on his first arrival there. Robert Wilkie was there, and in very low spirits; he had not recovered as his friend had done, and was doomed to stay longer. We now find the first suggestion that James might return.

'Probably Wilkie will be somewhat guided by my own course of action — if I remain at home probably he will look to go home next year; if I come out again, we shall enter into some business together.'

On 18 April 1879 he embarked on the *Dunrobin Castle* from Port Elizabeth. On board were the Biggs brothers whom he had met during his recent tour.

What brought him back to 'dead and alive' Cradock within a year? According to Aunt Mary, the doctor was so impressed with his improvement that he advised him to make South Africa his permanent home. But a young man whose health is greatly improved does not return to a 'howling wilderness' with much alacrity. He was not driven back by considerations of health; he was drawn back by considerations of love — in particular, love for Annie Letitia, eldest daughter of John Collett of Grassridge.

Before returning to South Africa, James went on a short walking tour of the Lake District with his brother Joseph, who introduced him to the rudiments of bookkeeping while they picnicked among the fine scenery. This brief bucolic tutoring was regarded as adequate preparation for running a shop at the other end of the earth. Having returned to Cradock, he entered into a business partnership with Robert Wilkie; and into holy matrimony with Letitia Collett, in 1881.

The firm of Butler and Wilkie stocked a variety of goods: the 'lines' of which I have heard seem to have little in common except that they all came from Quaker firms. Uncle Cephas Butler of Birmingham supplied a fine range of paraffin and gas lamps. Poole's of Fenchurch Street provided clocks and watches, and Clarke's of Street, boots and shoes.

The partnership did not last very long. Robert Wilkie went farming in the Steynsburg district, and in 1887 the firm of Butler Bros. came into existence when James was joined by his younger brother Charles. Boots were replaced by books.

Both the Collett and Butler families entered into the spirit of the new venture. James's brother John, a man with some skill as a draughtsman, drew the plans for the shop. Stone-built, it proved costly, but Herbert, Lettie's brother, put up the money, while James and Charlie paid the rent. The dream of a daily newspaper — not a mere weekly like *The Cradock Register* — became fact in 1892 when the first issue of *The Midland News and Karroo Farmer* rolled off the new and expensive machines. The paper and the shop came under the umbrella of The Midland Printing and Publishing Company. Though the Butler–Collett tie had been doubled in 1891, when Charles (1864–1949) married Emma (1862–1948), one of Letitia's younger sisters, neither the brothers nor the sisters seem to have found each other altogether congenial, so that it is not surprising to find Charles going north in 1908 to establish a newspaper, *The Northern News,* and a clan of his own at Vryburg.

James Butler's editorial policy was sound: 'when in doubt, leave out'; and to ascertain facts and report them quickly in good clean prose; but his independence of thought in his editorial comment soon got him into disfavour in certain quarters. He disapproved of many imperialist acts, and said so. He condemned the Jameson Raid, as did his father-in-law and Uncle Herbert. He soon had the label pro-Boer round his neck, which did the business no good.

From the start, the paper was always on the edge of a financial precipice. Aunt Mary says that the London Butlers helped in times of crisis; and Herbert was always prepared to wait for his rent. She remembers him saying to her father, 'Well, the town must have a paper.'

'Father was such a visionary, but so impractical,' she says. 'Perhaps it would have been better if he'd been second-in-command — editor only. But who would have been found to back a man with such ideas?'

James had his sympathisers, however. There was a certain magistrate, whose first and crucial question to a man up for stock theft was, 'What wages do you get?' Few farmers liked that question. During the Anglo-Boer War, having refused point blank to appear at a flag-waving function to celebrate the relief of Mafeking or some other event, the magistrate was promptly dubbed 'mug-wump', like the editor — 'fence sitter, mug on one side, wump on the other,' explains Aunt Mary. His wife, in a ridiculous attempt to appease the jingos, strode out of the Residency singing 'Rule Britannia' all the way to the Town Hall.

This was not Lettie's style. She knew her place — by her husband's side. It must have been difficult at times. Her husband's ideas did not irritate the citizens of Cradock only: *The Midland News* became known to pro-Boers both in and outside the country as one of the very few South African papers 'not in Mr Rhodes's pocket'. In 1897 at the height of their financial troubles (which always seemed to be at the height), James and Lettie, as the chief shareholders, were approached by Mr Alfred Metcalf, the attorney, with a 'fix-your-own-price' offer from a buyer whose name he could not disclose, nor his motive for wishing to buy, nor the policies which the paper would follow in future. Grannie assured me that they turned the offer down because they were convinced that it came from C.J. Rhodes himself. 'Every man has his price' is said to have been one of Rhodes's more cynical principles; but here and there he encountered people who could not be bought.

On 17 September 1902, the offer was repeated. 'Mr Metcalf called at the M/N office: said he had been requested to ascertain whether J.B. was prepared to sell the M/N at any price.' In a letter to his brother Joseph, he adds a PS. to his memo of the conversation. It reveals his dilemma, and the character of his daughter, Mary:

'Your niece, when she heard of the fact that we had been approached with a view to selling, and that probably the reason was that it was because we were too independent for those who controlled other papers, queried would it be right to sell? And when it was explained that if we did not sell the would-be buyers might come and regardless of expense try and ruin us, she replied that we ought to be ready to suffer for what we felt to be right. Then I remarked that I had a family to consider, and it was not easy for me at my age, if I was ruined, to make a fresh start, and she replied,"We can all work. I am working; Ernest soon will be, and Florrie is coming on" ... You see that there is some of the old Quaker spirit in her, and I doubt not in others concerned.' And so they did not sell.

After the Boer War, James undertook a long journey throughout those portions of the Free State and Transvaal that had suffered most as a result of the scorched-earth policy of the British Army. He was accompanied by Lawrence Richardson, a fellow Quaker, their purpose being to discover how the Society of Friends might best use its limited resources to help and heal. It was through their efforts that an appeal was made to British soldiers to return family Bibles which they had removed from Boer farms as mementos. His letters have survived, and are being prepared for publication.

During the Great War, James, now abetted by his daughter Mary, refused to report some of the more horrific pieces of anti-German propaganda, such as Northcliffe's canard that, in order to meet a shortage of fats and other materials, the German High Command were boiling down the corpses of their own dead heroes. Things came to a head when, at the insistence of Mary, the paper carried Red Cross reports indicating that the Huns still possessed a few human traits. The Cradock Chamber of Commerce met, and threatened to boycott the editor by withdrawing their advertisements from his paper.

A strict principle governing the policy of *The Midland News* was Temperance. Throughout the two generations during which the paper was in Butler hands, it never carried an advertisement for liquor.

But there was a great deal more to James Butler than good journalism and high principles. The talent for education which he had displayed at the Bedford Institute found ample employment in Cradock, through organisations such as the Wesley Guild. Old Mr Roberts of Pietermaritzburg at the age of 104 told my sister Joan that James transformed the lives of the young people: 'He opened our minds and our hearts to the world.' James served on the Library Committee, the School Board and the Town Council, was secretary of the Cradock Farmers' Association, and successfully pressed for the planting of a park and the establishment of the Queen's Central Hospital.

Jeffrey recalls being taken by Grannie and Joan to visit our mother in this hospital in 1937. As they emerged, Grannie pointed to a brass plate on which the name of Mr Austen, an erstwhile mayor, was inscribed, and proceeded to declare with unusual vehemence that Mr Austen's name had no business to be there at all. It took all Joan's tact to get her to postpone her indictment until they were back at The Poplars.

The tension between James Butler and Mr Austen went back to the early 'eighties. Mr Austen, a large florid man, was the established chemist of Cradock, and a proud Anglican; and he did not appreciate it when a slight young Quaker started selling a line of homeopathic medicines in a shop round the corner. They found themselves opposed in principle on every issue, municipal, national, and international. Austen sought the limelight, James avoided it. Austen spoke loudly and often, James softly and seldom.

James was one of the earliest and most persistent campaigners for the hospital. Mr Austen could hardly oppose him on this issue. When, owing to opposition in Cape Town, the scheme seemed likely to come to nothing, thus exposing the promoters to loss of face, Austen turned on James and accused him of getting them all into a mess.

James decided to beard the administrative lions in their official dens in the far distant Cape. Lettie sat up late in order to finish knitting a pullover to keep him warm. When he returned from Cape Town with an assurance that the hospital would be built, Mr Alfred Metcalf, quite unconscious of the inappropriateness of the metaphor, welcomed his Quaker friend with the words: 'Well done, James! A regiment of soldiers could not have done better!'

So Grannie had a point.

During the first part of 1923 his health deteriorated, and he and Lettie went up to Jack Collett, then farming at Lion Hill, for a rest. From there he wrote to Uncle Joe in London, on 25 April. He hopes that 'absence from all regular duties will enable me to get into harness again and pull my share. At the same time I realise that I am not as young as I was and must be adapting our organisation to the inevitable future . . . prior to relinquishing the News entirely. Ernest does work that I could not do in some directions especially in the works, but on the other hand has not the journalistic instinct though he does a good deal of reporting on occasion, and does it well — better than I do when Dutch is spoken, and that is increasingly the case. . . .' The firm is suffering from the post-war slump. 'From the end of last year I had cut down my salary by ten pounds and Ernest volunteered to reduce his by five. . . .'

The holiday did not restore him. On 12 June his sister, Aunt Eliza, wrote to her sister Emmie Fear: 'Mary was in just now and she said how listless her father was, so unlike him. He did not seem to want to do anything and she remarked "the paper can never flourish while father is like this".' And then on the 17th: 'A cold bleak day. Meeting was at the Lidbetters, and James, Mary, Ernest and Alison and I all went up. I found Mary and Jim on my stoep. When I was ready to start James felt he had best rest a few minutes before toiling up the rest of the hill . . . he looks so white, but he wanted to go.'

He had been approached by one of the sons of the Methodist minister, the Rev. Mr Floweday, to speak to the young men's guild that afternoon, and had elected to speak on temperance. Aunt Mary writes:

'After dinner (i.e. at midday) he had his bath as usual and rested for about half an hour tho' I don't think he had slept when I called him at 2.30 and took him a cup of tea. He was not walking well when he came down the passage to me in the diningroom, and I asked him if he felt all right. He said "Yes" rather hesitatingly and sat down to look over his notes. I did not speak to him again leaving him to concentrate on his notes.'

He gave the promised talk to the Guild, but sat while he did so. When he had finished, a young man rose and asked a question, to which he replied, 'I think we have come to the end.' He slumped forward, lost consciousness, and died.

The first intimation of his death was a young man from the Guild knocking at the front door of The Poplars. Could Mrs Butler please lend him a blanket for Mr James Butler, who had taken a turn? Alice, with her children around her skirts, rushed down the passage, and returned with a thick woollen rug, her brow puckered, muttering, 'Oh dear, oh dear.'

'What's the matter?' we asked.

'Grandfather's ill,' she said, disappearing with the rug.

She returned later, weeping profusely. Aunt Mary was with her. Dorothy remembers her removing Alice's spectacles in order to wipe her eyes.

The funeral was fixed for Tuesday 22 June 1923. Aunt Mary's account continues: 'It was very gratifying to receive so many letters from former employees, and the present staff was most sympathetic: they all came to see Mother the evening before the funeral and to look their last on Father. Miss Loscombe, who had worked with Father for nineteen years, said, "No one could work with him without loving him." Ferreira, the senior apprentice, said, "He was a brave man — he was so brave." '

Aunt Eliza thought she 'would not see Jim in his coffin but remember him as I last saw him when I buttoned up his coat, but Mary said, "Oh, do. He looks so peaceful." So when I thought no one was in the Drawing Room I stole in, and Mary quickly followed me. . . . She uncovered his face and there he was, so calm and peaceful, pale and stiff, eyes closed, surely at rest. I said, "Poor old Jimmy . . ." and tears flowed freely.' She then describes the progress of the funeral from 60 Bree Street to the Wesleyan Church.

'By 2.30 every one of Letty's brothers was present: Walter, Owen, Herbert, Gervase, Norman, Bertie, Dudley. The room was decked with wreaths. I had one more peep at Jim's dear face — then the family gathered and about five minutes of silence in "thoughtful remembrance" and prayer. Then the coffin was lifted and we followed. Only Ernest walked, bare-headed, immediately behind, in a grey suit. In the first carriage Letty, Alice, Alison and I — Mr Metcalf, Lidbetter, G. Roberts and Coetzee were pall bearers. The Church was packed. My brother was eulogised as much as anyone can be but I don't think too much.'

The Poplars — in which he had spent his first night in Cradock forty-five years previously, in which his son and grandsons were now living — was hushed, the blinds and curtains drawn. The rooms which had filled up with relatives who had come from great distances to attend the funeral, emptied as they all went out to the Methodist Church next door, in special black clothes.

We children, dressed in our darkest and best, were taken off to the Park by the maids, with strict instructions to behave quietly. Whether it was intended that this manoeuvre would save our tender eyes from a sight which might bring our dear grandfather's death too sharply home to us, I do not know; but we watched the procession at close quarters through the wrought-iron gates at the south-east entry to the park. It seemed endless. Indeed, it was one of the longest Cradock had ever seen. All shops and offices had been closed for the occasion so that people would be free 'to pay their last respects' to our grandfather; and the flags in front of the Town Hall and the Magistrate's Court were flying at half-mast, also because of our grandfather whose body was in the hearse, drawn by two of Uncle Herbert's blackest and most beautiful horses, a hearse barely visible beneath wreaths of dark green, glossy leaves, and white and purple flowers.

Everyone we'd ever known seemed to pass slowly and solemnly before our eyes. There was our father; and his brother and five sisters — three of them with their Biggs husbands, from Graaff-Reinet and Louisvale; the Vryburg Butlers; there were the Grassridge Colletts, our great-uncles and -aunts, Grannie's brothers and sisters, and their nephews and nieces; Mother's father, Mr F.S. Stringer, Grandpa 'England', recently arrived in Cradock; three different ministers of religion, each of whom conducted a portion of the service; the whole Town Council; the Hospital Board; the

School Board; the neighbours; shopkeepers, doctors, lawyers — and many whom we did not know. There were also many black and Coloured people in the procession — something we had never seen before.

The editor of *The Middelburg Echo,* Mr Cursons, attended the funeral, and devoted three full columns to it. He also published the following:

'One of the late Mr Butler's oldest friends is Mr Alfred Metcalf, himself one of the best known and respected of Cradock citizens. In response to a question, by our representative, he said with deep feeling: "I have known James Butler over forty years. Cradock will not be the same place without him. The main object of his life was the well-being of his fellowmen. If he felt anything was likely to benefit them, discouragement was not allowed to stand in the way of its accomplishment. That was his life-long policy. Walk through Cradock and look at the fine scholastic buildings that it boasts. They are in no small measure due to James Butler, who pegged away amidst all sorts of difficulties: and today we can claim to be one of the leading educational centres in the Midlands. He was absolutely sincere, and always tried to do good in the most lowly and unobtrusive manner. And moreover it is, I think, largely due to his tact, moderate views and courtesy to his opponents, that the pleasant relationships exist today between the two political parties." '

On their way back to Louisvale, Frank, Flo, Josie and Dan Biggs had to change trains at De Aar. Dan wrote to his mother-in-law on 1 July: 'We met General Smuts at De Aar. He spoke very nicely about Father. He said among other things that Mr Butler had had more influence for good in the Midlands than any other man.'

3

Comings and Goings

Early in 1923 Mother's father, Frederick Septimus Stringer, Grandpa 'England', decided to cruise round the world in order to visit the remote members of his family: Alice and her offspring, and the distraught Janet in South Africa; and Harold and his family in China; Guy, alas, was no longer in Malaya, but buried in Flanders. For good measure, Grandpa would cross the Pacific to see his photographer brother in Portland, Oregon, then, via the U.S.A. and the Atlantic, return to The Villas, Stoke-on-Trent. He would not attempt to find another brother, Joseph Henry, who had long since 'disappeared into Australia'. The spread of his relatives indicates how much of the world had become the inheritance of the Anglo-Saxon peoples; and the fate of some of them was to prove how treacherous membership of 'an empire on which the sun never sets' could be, particularly for those in its remoter provinces.

He arrived in Cradock at a difficult time for Alice and Ernest, who had only just moved into The Poplars and whose efforts to restore Janet's morale had been to no avail. And then this sudden and unexpected death of his opposite number, James Butler, had absorbed everyone's attention, and raised speculations as to the future of the family concerns, Butler Bros., and *The Midland News* — about the finances of which he, as an experienced bank manager, knew enough to be apprehensive.

I have vivid if restricted recollections of a spruce, dignified, neatly bearded man, who wore stiff white collars, and said very little to me. He never took a child on his lap, or danced it up and down on his foot, like Grandpa James Butler had done, but he did assure me that if I behaved myself, he would take me to Hyam's Tickey Bazaar before he left for China, and buy me a present. This promise had two unfortunate consequences: I was forever pestering people to take me up to Hyam's Tickey Bazaar to spy out the land; and I was forever asking Grandpa when he was going to leave for China. This question drew forth impatient reactions from Alice. The same question may have been bothering her.

At last we were taken into Hyam's Paradise of Dainty Delights. By this time I knew exactly what I wanted — a green clockwork railway engine, price half-a-crown. It was, I think, the first object to absorb my total conscious desire. All my capacity to want — which was considerable — was focused on it.

Neither Alice nor Septimus, daughter and father, seemed to notice the anguish of hope in the young. They, in their lofty world, four foot above our heads, were not even looking at the heaped-up treasures, but talking earnestly about some common adult concern. Eventually I could bear it no longer, fetched the engine and, moving to a position more or less between them, lifted it up, hoping to catch their gaze.

No success.

So I tapped Alice in the middle with it.

'What *is* it, child?'

Without waiting for a reply, she took the toy, looked at the price and said, 'Too much. Put it back where you found it,' and turned back to her father.

I have no recollection of what happened next. I suspect I burst into an incredulous wail. I do recall other objects, at one shilling, etc., being offered to me instead. And I do remember returning home *with the engine.* So Frederick Septimus gave way, but after how long a scene I do not know.

I have no recollection of saying goodbye to Grandpa 'England'. He took Aunt Janet with him. As Alice and Africa had failed to help her, Harold and China were to see what they could do.

Grannie wasn't a memorable storyteller like her younger brother Uncle Norman Collett. She didn't change her voice, and pull her mouth into shapes, and roll her eyes, and fling her body and arms about. She was no performer. She simply added simple sentence to simple sentence, seldom taking her eyes off her crocheting. Indeed, the crocheting was priority number one. Sometimes she'd pause in the midst of the most nerve-racking tale, to count the stitches and check on the pattern, leaving us dangling off the edge of a cliff as it were. Then she'd resume in the same unemotional, laconic manner. In fact, she had been in bad health for the first fifteen years of her married life, suffering from low spirits, incapable of taking much interest in her large household and garden in the old end of Bree Street. It took a new doctor to diagnose her trouble as lack of thyroid. The cure seemed worse than the disease to us when we heard of it: to eat raw sheep's thyroid in considerable quantities. Maybe her quietness derived from that period. More likely it was just Collett taciturnity.

Before her marriage, Lettie had been sent to school in the next new village of Bedford, a mere 60 miles to the south. She used to spend weekends with her Trollip relatives at Daggaboersnek. It's a lengthy climb up the mountain pass, and then there's a long, fairly straight road down a steep incline before the turn-off up to the homestead. Again, the details escape me, but it seems that she was in charge of the buggy or trap, and possibly accompanied by other children. Somehow the reins slipped from her hands, and the next thing the horses, scenting home, were off down the slope at a break-neck speed. There was nothing, nothing they could do,

30 COMINGS AND GOINGS

but hold on to the bodywork of the trap for dear life, and pray. The light vehicle bounded from side to side, from wheel to wheel, over the humps and stones.

Then Grannie would stop and count stitches, and we'd wait, squirming with impatience. Then:

'Where was I?'

'Bounding from side to side, from wheel to wheel.'

'Well, I said to myself, if we don't turn over in the drift, it'll be a plain miracle.' (Pause.) 'Well, we got past the drift all right.' (Pause.) 'Well, I said, if we don't turn over taking the corner at the turn-off, it'll be another miracle.' (Pause.) 'Well, there in the road near the turn-off was a big flock of sheep. Of course the horses saw them, and slowed up to a walk. I jumped out, ran to the front, and stopped the horses, and told the shepherd to retrieve the reins for me. Then I took the trap up to the house.' (Pause.) 'Uncle John gave me a scolding for driving so fast down the hill. "It's dangerous," he said. "You might have had a spill." I said, "Yes, Uncle. The horses were anxious to get home." "What are reins for but to pull at the right time and slow the brutes up? Don't blame the horses, child." "Yes, Uncle John," I said.'

This Uncle John Trollip was her mother's brother. He'd had no children. He and his wife had been to England, and held advanced ideas for their time and place; and they were very hospitable to young people, particularly young people from England 'with lungs'. The phrase 'with lungs', like 'with a heart', meant troublesome or diseased lungs, or a weak heart; whereas if you said, He's got a head (for this or that), it meant nothing troublesome at all. I digress, simply to remark how the careful speech of that generation seemed loaded with delightful turns, puzzles and surprises.

This same Uncle John Trollip, before very long, would offer hospitality to a young Englishman 'with lungs'; would pass him on to his sister at Grassridge; and that would be that: he would be Lettie's 'fate'. 'I met my fate' used to be a common phrase for meeting one's life partner. It may sound rather doom-laden, but there is an acceptance of permanence in it.

There were several stories about her own practical and forthright behaviour. She stood for no nonsense. She worked hard at her father's gift of a garden, to make it yield fresh fruit, eggs and milk. She was not a farmer's daughter for nothing. There were difficulties, however. Chief of these were the neighbour's pigs, Irish of course. These Irish pigs were always finding their way into Lettie's garden, and rooting up the vegetables. Repeated remonstrances produced no results. At last Lettie said:

'Mrs Rafferty, the next time I catch your pig in my garden, I'll shoot him.'

The next time came, and she shot the pig; and told her Hottentot gardener to put it in the wheelbarrow, and deliver it at Mrs Rafferty's back door.

It was lunch time. The young Butler couple were having guests. In stormed Mrs Rafferty, swearing like ten tinkers, looking like the wrath of God and the wreck of the *Hesperus,* and calling the curse of Cromwell down on the bunch of black Protestants.

'Yis has a dacent enough Oirish name, but yis is no better than a lot o' Belfast planters.'

Lettie had risen to her feet on the first entry of the virago, and simply stared at her, silently stared at her, not deigning to speak. Mr Rafferty appeared in the unusual role of peacemaker, and seized his spouse by the arm to drag her away. Her parting shot from the door was, 'Call yerself a lidy? Oi'll kick yis in the oi.'

How we loved that punch line! It became a family legend.

Ernest, like his mother, held economic expectations of gardens. Having decided to go in for chickens, he bought a second-hand incubator, which had a mysterious lamp, and a thermometer, to keep the eggs at just the right temperature. As he ticked the days off the calendar, tension mounted; and then, at last, the first beak splintered a shell; and before the yellow ball of fluff was out of its brittle white prison, the sharp, high peep-peep sounded. And by the end of the day there were twenty! What wonder! One's hands hungered to cup the creatures – but that was seldom allowed.

The pert, cheeping, pretty scraps of life were transferred to a low pen of wire netting. They had to be properly watered and fed – on chopped-up hard-boiled eggs, meal, and fine-cut lucerne.

Father was not short of helpers. The only member of the family not allowed to participate was our rather ugly black-and-marmalade cat. In spite of his built-in murderous tendencies, he could still be cuddled or stroked – at a safe distance from the chicks. If he were seen anywhere near the coop an open season was declared, and we were allowed to chase him away with clods, if necessary. He usually shinned up the pepper tree. Father assured us that once the chickens were big enough, no cat would dare attack them. He was busy constructing a larger coop against a low wall on the west side of the yard.

One morning we woke up to Chrissie, the maid, crying disaster. Under cover of night the cat had found its way into the coop where pieces of netting overlapped. He'd killed and eaten his fill – and then found that he could not get out.

It was a dreadful scene. In one corner, the terrified survivors huddled, some of them frozen with terror, others chirping frantically; crouching in another, his tummy distended, guilt all over his ugly face, was the murderer; and strewn between were the dead and the dying – several floundering and mutilated, one with a leg missing. Father let the cat out, and promptly and quickly wrung the necks of the wounded and dying. These acts seemed suddenly terrible, but we trusted the doer when he said, 'I'm putting them out of their pain.'

We spent much of the morning burying the dead in a cemetery which we established in the shade of the scented lemon tree. We covered each little mound with flowers from the garden. Our feelings were in a strange turmoil — sorrow for our small friends, already stiff and lifeless, anger at the cat, whom we pelted whenever we caught a glimpse of his hated form. Someone said he should be killed, and have a stake driven through his heart, like a murderer.

But when Father appeared at lunch time with a borrowed .22 rifle in his hand, when he pointed it at the cat up the pepper tree, one of us started crying in protest, not against our father, but in general protest against any more death that day. But he pulled the trigger, and the cat fell out of the tree.

'Come inside and have lunch,' cried Mother, and we trooped in obediently, each with his own thoughts. Sensing the tension, Dad explained that it wasn't the cat's fault, because he was driven by instinct; it was stupid to try to keep a cat and chickens at the same time. He was very sorry about it, but . . .

Suddenly our sorrow flowed for the cat also. According to Chrissie, he was given a royal funeral. Whereas the chickens had been carried to their last resting-places in our hands, a hearse was provided (a shoe box), and a horse (me, on all fours). Joan was master of ceremonies and, as we interred him, she conducted us in the singing of the following words at the graveside, over and over, to the opening bars of 'God Save the King':

> *God save our gracious cat,*
> *Feed him on bread and fat,*
> *God save our cat.*

His grave, sited with his numerous victims under the scented lemon tree, was surmounted by a cross, and no stake was driven through his murderous heart.

He sits very still in the plumbago hedge behind The Poplars palings, looking at me suspiciously. He is small, and funny; his body is rough and ends in a curly tail. He holds on to the twig with four little hands; each hand, instead of having a thumb and four fingers, seems to have four fingers only, two on each side. His eyes are two beads, with bright black centres, protruding from his head — and they roll about independently of each other. I stretch out my hand. Unlike the crabs and the frogs he does not scuttle or jump for safety. True, he seems cross, and opens a yellow-lined mouth with an angry gasp; but as I know I intend him no harm, I capture and cage him in my two hands — run, sit on the step in triumph. I carefully open my hands to see what he will do. He rolls his eyes cautiously, and then starts walking slowly, slowly up my arm.

I decide to share my joy, and enter the house via the kitchen. Matilda, the Xhosa cook, lets out a scream, and bolts into the yard for safety. Puzzled I follow her.

But she shouts, 'Go away. He'll keel you,' and storms down the lane to the safety of the street.

I then find Alice, who looks at the little reptile and wrinkles her nose in distaste.

'Put it back where you found it,' she says.

'Why is Matilda afraid of him?' I ask.

'Some superstition or other,' she says. 'Ask Grannie.'

Grannie said that the Xhosa had some very strange ideas of God. One day in the beginning of the world God said to the chameleon, 'Go, chameleon, to men, and say to them, You will not die.' The chameleon took his time, and even stopped to eat fruit on the way. Then God had second thoughts. He said to the blue-headed lizard, 'Go, lizard, to men and say to them, You will die.' The lizard ran quickly and did not stop to eat fruit. He shouted to men, 'You will die,' and went back to God. At long last the chameleon came, and he said, 'You will not die.' But men cried, 'Alas, we cannot hear you; we have heard the word of the lizard.' Ever since then man is afraid of the messenger whose slowness brought death.

'Why did God change his mind?'

'They don't know. Who can know the mind of God?'

'Why didn't God give the good message to the quick lizard?'

'I don't know, my child. Indeed I don't know.'

After James's death, Grannie's mind must have been running much on her past. There was no point, however, in moping in 63 Bree Street. As she started dividing the furniture among her children, and making short and long term plans for her widowhood, she must have thought back to her father, old John Collett of Grassridge, who had bought 63 Bree Street for her as a wedding gift — a wise, fatherly act, not altogether unlike Frederick Septimus Stringer's later act in making it possible for his daughter to acquire The Poplars. It is always good for a woman with children to have a house in her name — particularly when the men are impractical Butlers.

Meanwhile Grandpa 'England' had reached China, and found his way inland to his son in Tientsin, busy constructing the Peking–Mukden Railway. In a letter dated 21 February 1924 he gives a vignette of Harold's highly privileged but isolated and therefore somewhat senseless life.

From the same letter it is clear that during his visit to Cradock he had not been impressed by his son-in-law Ernest, or by his daughter Alice, and least of all by their five children.

James Butler had left his frail business loaded down to the gunwales with bonds and debts, for which his son had accepted responsibility. Septimus advises his daughter that her own 'little bit of money' should 'be kept religiously free from any responsibility for liabilities'. As Ernest had not contracted these liabilities 'there can be no obligation on him to beggar himself and his wife and children' in an attempt to discharge them. 'It would be utterly Quixotic to saddle himself with any other liabilities than his own. I write strongly because I am afraid he is Quixotic himself to some extent.' One has some sympathy with the old bank manager; why should his daughter's and grandchildren's future be jeopardised because the idealistic Ernest insisted on inheriting a financial curse from an un-businesslike parent?

Having dealt with Ernest, Septimus turned his eye on to his daughter and her children. 'I want also to think that you will some day be able to give those dear children of yours the advantage of a better school, where some of the graces of education are included in the curriculum. One other thing I must say, whether I offend you or not, in the best interest of those dear children. Do let me beg of you to hammer, hammer, hammer into them orderly ways. My memory recalls such an utter want of it that I can see nothing but trouble for them in after life unless there is a change. I am fully sensible of the heavy demands on your time with so many to look after; but, apart from the children's interests, I say that, if order was established and insisted on, you would really find you had less to do. You make the mistake of taking the line of least resistance, i.e. letting them do what they wish too much, and children are quick to see how far they can go in resistance to authority. Janet has said that you have contended that my own house was just as disorderly, but this I cannot admit, and you must know it is not true. I say no more, but I commend to your earnest consideration the appeal I have made, satisfied that you will know it has proceeded from an earnest, affectionate desire for the wellbeing and happiness of you all.'

One can only guess at the impact of this rebuke on Alice and Ernest: Alice, overburdened with five young children, and an enormous new house and garden to manage, and Ernest grappling with the full responsibilities of the heavily bonded firm, and of caring for a strong-willed widowed mother. 1923 must have been an appalling year for them — as it was for me.

To moving house, Grandpa's death, the cat among the chickens, must be added my first attacks of insomnia, and then a long, long exile from everyone I knew except Grannie and my sister Dorothy.

First, insomnia. It is possible that the arrival of Christine and Jeffrey had made me feel that my mother had rejected me; and I may have been jealous of my younger siblings. Although I have no conscious recollections of such feelings, I do recall my father replacing Mother at bed-time. It seems that evenings would find her in a state of near collapse. Ernest, also under strain, attempted to simplify everybody's lives by inculcating prompt obedience in his young. He may have been reacting to Septimus's letter, 'to hammer, hammer, hammer' orderly ways into us. Various punishments of a non-violent kind were devised — for he was always a gentle if strict man. The nearest he got to corporal punishment — and then only for a very naughty child — was to demand that the culprit should put out his hands, which he would then slap with his own flat palm.

'Your mother is very tired, and so am I,' he would say, tucking us in. 'We want no noise at all.'

I'd lie awake staring into the dark, getting more and more awake and more and more lonely and anxious. I'd say such prayers as I'd been taught, over and over again. Sometimes, suddenly, it would be morning. But at other times nothing would end my awakeness-in-darkness, and I'd start whimpering to be taken into the brass double-bed, where I'd fall asleep instantly — and sometimes be carried back in that state to my own room.

Years later, in a rueful reminiscence, my father recounted how he heard me crying, and entered the nursery. There he found me, standing up in the cot, with my hands ready, stretched out in front of me, waiting to be slapped. I have no recollection of this, but it argues that I was prepared to accept the pain that would put an end to being alone in the dark.

At last Grannie intervened. She mobilised the resources of her extended family into a masterly exercise in mutual help. First, there was the impending marriage of her younger son Jamie, who was farming five hundred miles away at 'Louisvale', near Upington. His bride-to-be, a teacher, Hilda van Wyk, was a Kakamas girl, and was currently teaching in Cradock, having come to see and be seen by the family whom she was to adopt and who were to adopt her. It would make a deal of sense for Grannie to go up to Louisvale with Hilda and keep house for Jamie, and get the place ship-shape for this charming wife-to-be. Her daughters, Flo and Josie, married to Frank and Dan Biggs, were also at Louisvale. She could stay with them in turn after Jamie's wedding. By removing herself from Cradock, she'd reduce her son's responsibilities a little. Josie and Flo could put up with her for a while, and maybe she'd be useful with their new babies. In addition she'd take Dorothy and Guy with her, to give the dear but inefficient Alice a chance to get her breath back. It would also give her a change from the ubiquitous reminders of a broken pattern which could never be restored. Number 63 Bree Street, Cradock, was no longer tolerable to her.

Jamie and Hilda van Wyk were married in the Dutch Reformed Church, Cradock; Joan was their flower girl; and the reception was held at The Poplars. The time for the move had come.

Memory plays the strangest tricks. It has repressed the agony of the last hugs and kisses entirely. All I can recall is this: I am crying from the depths of my being; I am sitting in a train for the first time, and it is jerking into movement; a lady I hardly know with a lovely face is sitting opposite me, smiling and speaking kind words, but to no avail. Then she stops speaking, purses her lips, and does what no woman has ever done before: she whistles like a bird. I stop crying.

My new Aunt Hilda had no further difficulties with me on the long train journey to Louisvale.

1   The author's father, Ernest Collett Butler, about 1912.

2   The wedding of Ernest Collett Butler and Alice Eyre Stringer at 'The Villas', Stoke-on-Trent, 1914. The bride's parents, Frederick Septimus Stringer and his wife Sarah, are on her left.

3   Gilfillan Bridge, the old iron bridge at Cradock, about 1880.

4 Osborne House, Isle of Wight, was built in the 1840s for the Prince Consort, the tiles and mosaic being designed by the author's great-grandfather George Eyre (1818–87).

5 View of Cradock from the east, as it would have appeared to James Butler on arrival in 1878. Elandsberg is in the background, the Great Fish River in the foreground.

Gilfillan
Bridge

D.R.Church
Church St

roof of
'The Poplars'
Church St

6 Earthenware plaque manufactured by Josiah Wedgwood and Company and handpainted by George Eyre, who inscribed the back 'L'Amour enchainé par les Graces d'après Boucher'.

7 Royal Patriotic Jug designed by George Eyre, first sold in January 1855, the profits being used to help the widows and children of soldiers killed in the Crimean War.

Methodist
Church
Bree St

St Peter's   63 Bree St
Church
Bree St

8 The children of the author's grandparents James and Lettie Butler in their garden at 63 Bree Street, Cradock, about 1910.

9 Joan, Dorothy, Christine and Guy Butler, 1922.

10 Joan, Guy, Christine and Dorothy in their grandparents' garden, 1923.

11 Grandfather James Butler with Dorothy, Joan and Guy Butler and their cousin Honor Biggs, Christmas 1922, when Japanese parasols were given to Joan and Honor.

12 Mother's church: St Peter's (Anglican) Church, Bree Street, Cradock.

13 Father's church: Wesleyan Methodist Church, Cradock, 1899.

14 Church Street, Cradock, leading to the D.R.C. Church, centre; the bare poplar branches on right indicate the position of 'The Poplars'. The South African Hotel is on the left.

15 A typical shop in Cradock: The Midland Produce Agency, before 1900.

16 Market Square, Cradock, with the Victoria Hotel, in the early 1920s.

17 Town Hall, Cradock.

4

Louisvale and Vrede

How did it come about that four of the seven Cradock Butlers of my father's generation should land up at Louisvale, a place hardly known to the Post Office, near outlandish Upington, in the arid north-west, towards South West Africa and the Kalahari Desert?

Once more we must return to James Butler exploring the Cape Midlands on his horse Moscow in 1878. It will be recalled that south of Graaff-Reinet, on the farm 'Wellfound', he'd met a young Mr John Ebenezer Biggs, and that they'd shared a cabin in the *Dunrobin Castle* en route to England in April 1879. They struck up a lifelong friendship, having much in common: 'character', devout Protestantism (Quaker and Baptist) and a firm rejection of tobacco and alcohol.

They differed, however, on the issues of Pacifism and Vegetarianism. James Butler objected to War: men should not kill men; John Biggs objected to eating meat: men should not kill animals. Their rejection of such time-honoured human activities, of man- and animal-slaughter, singled them out as somewhat cranky, courageous men of principle, easy butts for the barbs of traditionalists.

John Ebenezer Biggs was perhaps less tolerant of worldlings than his Quaker friend. For instance, in later years something of a distance grew up between his branch of the family and another, whose meals were begun with steady courses of meat and strong drink and dissolved in tobacco clouds. John Ebenezer, asked if they were relatives, dismissed them as 'Biggses only in name'. They responded by referring to his vegetarian clan as 'those cabbage Biggses'.

In 1883 John Ebenezer married Susan, daughter of Daniel Roberts, the remarkable missionary son of an 1820 Settler.

As a girl, Susie had been with her father during the outbreak of one of the frontier wars. Their family wagon was surrounded by a small impi of Xhosa warriors. Daniel Roberts did not shoot at them, but spoke to them in a firm and confident manner, in good idiomatic Xhosa.

'If you kill me, your chief will be angry with you. Send to him; ask him if Daniel Roberts must die.'

The induna did so. For forty-eight hours the missionary and his family waited, watched by the impatient warriors. The messenger returned:

'Let Daniel Roberts go.'

After his marriage to Susie, John Ebenezer Biggs bought a farm with two names — 'Swartrivier' or 'Droëdrif' — ten miles from Graaff-Reinet on the Aberdeen road. Living frugally in an old boer dwelling, he paid off his bond in fourteen years, then built a new house for Susie and his three sons, Dan (b. 1885), Frank (b. 1887) and Alan (b. 1894). The boys were sent to Kingswood College, Grahamstown, where the cast of their intelligence and individualism made that school intolerable to them, or them intolerable to that school. So they were called back home, and placed at the mercy of a series of tutors.

After a visit to the U.S.A., John Ebenezer and Susie renamed their farm 'Brooklyn'. This was not Susie's first trip overseas; she had visited England before her marriage. As the prospective bride of John Ebenezer, James Butler provided her with an introduction to his father Philip John of De Beauvoir Road. She liked the Butlers and they liked her.

It is not surprising that the Brooklyn Biggses sympathised with the Quaker Butlers; and the bonds of friendship and shared principles which united the elder generation were soon reinforced by marriages among the younger. When John Ebenezer placed his eldest son Daniel on the farm Grootvlei in the Swaershoek, it was natural enough for the young man to visit the Butlers when in Cradock on business. Daniel promptly fell in love with Josephine, and then Frank fell in love with Florence.

As tennis was an acknowledged ploy in any courtship, they invited all the Butler girls up to Grootvlei — and their parents, of course. This was no afternoon jaunt, however. Dan arrived in town on Friday morning to fetch the entire family in his donkey wagon. It took the best part of a dreamy and somewhat hilarious day to reach Grootvlei. After several hours Dan, a great tease, said, 'We're nearly there now — the house is just otherside that big poplar bush.'

In due course the wagon pulled up in front of a ramshackle building without a swept yard, let alone the grace of a garden. Dan apologised: bachelors were not much good at keeping homesteads trim, but he was sure that all his guests would sleep comfortably enough on the mis-vloer, which had been smeared with cow-dung the day before 'to fix the fleas'.

When the party entered the front door they found it was being used to store fencing and other materials. It had been abandoned as a human habitation a decade before. After these preliminaries Grootvlei homestead seemed like a palace. For the next day and a half they all played tennis and went on picnics; then returned in the same leisurely manner, up, over and down the Swaershoek mountains to Cradock, through all of a long Sunday afternoon.

A double Biggs–Butler wedding between Dan and Josie, and Flo and Frank was celebrated in 1914. That was strong bond enough. Four years later, the bond was strengthened further: Alan returned from East Africa and, when he had recovered from malaria, married Alice.

This triple alliance could account for the migration of three Butler girls from Cradock in the Fish River Valley to Biggs territory in the Graaff-Reinet district in the Sundays River Valley; but it does not explain the presence of two of them in the back of beyond — at Louisvale on the Orange River, near the Kalahari desert.

The answer lies, most improbably, in the ostrich. Before the Great War the feathers of this outlandish giant of a bird were the farmers' shortest road to wealth. The eldest Biggs brothers, Frank and Dan, believed that effective ostrich farming needed extensive lucerne lands, which needed extensive irrigation. They went exploring, riding hundreds of miles along the banks of the Orange River, looking for dam sites. The best of all, they thought, was the site eventually chosen, many years later, for the Verwoerd Dam, and Frank made a trip to Britain to raise the million pounds sterling their scheme would need, but with no success. So Frank and Dan took their inheritances from John Ebenezer Biggs of Brooklyn and sank them partly into buying land near Upington — land across which the Orange River flowed in years of exceptional floods — and partly into building dykes and canals. The Biggs brothers and the Butler sisters lived first in tents, and then in rondavels, close to the stream, and then in houses built on hills connected by one of the dykes they had constructed.

By the time Dorothy and I arrived at Louisvale, rondavels were giving way to houses. At first we stayed at 'Virginia', Uncle Jim's new house. Grannie, as promised, looked after us and kept house for him. Jim evidently put his big brother's children to work. Both Dorothy and I have clear recollections of carrying innumerable buckets of water to young fruit trees round the house. Our feet are bare, the soil is blisteringly hot; but after two or three weeks the skin thickens, and is impervious not only to heat, but to all but the sharpest dubbeltjies.

I do not believe we stayed at Virginia very long. I suspect that, once James and Hilda were safely married, Grannie and I moved to Florrie and Frank Biggs of the 'Top House', their son John being almost exactly my age. I was parted from Dorothy who was sent to the rondavels to Josie and Dan Biggs; their eldest daughter, Honor, was more or less her age. When she returned to The Poplars, long before I did, my only remaining human link with the past was Grannie.

Life at Louisvale was very different from life at Cradock. It was a new world. The people, the plants, the very stones were all different. If you were lucky you lived in a hartbeeshuisie or rondavel rather than a bell tent pitched among the kameeldorings. Brick houses were still rare, let alone stone, which made Uncle Frank's house all the more remarkable: it was built of stone, on a hill, surrounded by a pergola of enormous concrete

pillars, a small hill temple designed to last for ever. The hill was the termi-
nus of one of the large dykes, or 'walle', by means of which the Biggs
brothers had linked two koppies, their purpose being to prevent the Orange
River from inundating the old river beds which flowed between them during
flood time. This scheme, at once daring and imaginative, had already been
put to the test in 1920, when the river rose, and rose, and rose. Whenever
grown-ups reminisced, sooner or later the saga of the flood would come up:
of working through the moonlit nights and blazing days with every 'scrop'
and wheelbarrow and spade to keep the height of the thin ribbon of earth
above the rising waters; the women running coffee and soup kitchens round
the clock for the men dizzy from want of sleep; of the collapse of rivalries
and enmities of class and race as the need to save the 'wal' infected everybody with its sober fever.

By the time I arrived, the flood was already something of a myth, but
men and women still eyed the river like an unpredictable lover: yes, it had
deposited the rich alluvial soils; yes, it provided the perennial water they
needed; but, who knows, at any time . . .

Indeed, Dorothy experienced the river's caprice. Her eighth birthday was
at hand. The day before, a shady place among the tall river trees and water-
polished rocks was cleared of scrub for the picnic; and the evening was
spent in excited preparations. But when the sun came up, the clump of
trees and rocks was a far tiny island in a sinister, slowly sliding sheet of
chocolate-coloured water.

The riverbank was alive with birds such as parakeets, which we had never
seen in Cradock, and otters, and long likkewaans. Many of the trees were
unknown to me. One tree I came to dread, a real vegetable demon. Unlike
the honest thorn tree of the Karoo, which declared its 'keep-off' intentions
by painting its straight thorns pure white, the haak-en-steek presented a
consistent friendly green. You had to walk into one to experience its camouflaged malice: not only did it have a straight thorn to prick your flesh,
but a hooked thorn to grab you and not let you go; and the more you
struggled, the harder it gripped and stabbed you. The only thing to do was
to behave with intolerable patience, and carefully unpick yourself, twig by
twig, with the help of a friend, if one was near.

A few hundred yards from the glittering shade of the river bank, just over
the earthen 'wal', the world changed to bare distances under a high sky,
and the air at noon buckled in pulsing heat. And all over the plain, men
and teams of donkeys were at work; making canals which either followed
the contours or went straight as an arrow; or ploughing, or planting their
neatly marked out plots; or 'spoeling'. This last was what John Biggs and I
loved best. A powerful stream of water from the canal is led, by skilful men
with spades, against the side of an old alluvial dune. The water erodes the
soil, eats into it; it collapses in little landslides into the stream, which
sweeps it away, and deposits it in strange fan-shapes in the hollows, so

helping to level the surface in preparation for the fields of cotton or lucerne, or orchards of apricots or citrus, or vineyards of sultana grapes. One of our main motives in watching this process was the macabre hope that a human skeleton would be washed out, as had indeed happened not so long before: the ancient bones of a Bushman or Koranna had been uncovered. The shopkeeper had assembled them, and hung them in his storeroom; since when, we were told, he had not had a single burglary.

Of the many new insects that I met at Louisvale, there was one I simply could not warm to: the koringkriek. He is corn coloured, his bloated abdomen is bigger than an acorn, he is rough and spiky all over like a lobster, he twiddles sinister feelers at you, he moves slowly, he is ugly: and worse than all these, he is a cannibal. I remember with revulsion seeing two of these creatures locked in combat, head to tail. Each gripped the other with five of its legs; each was methodically eating the other's sixth leg. Nature produces images that are as often horrible as beautiful. Sanity perhaps depends on a selective memory.

I mentioned, towards the end of chapter 1, the joy of singing what I subsequently learnt was a holy song. At Louisvale, during the New Year's dance, which took place on the river bank, I first succumbed to pagan music. A portion of earth under some old camelthorns was levelled and covered with a wagon sail: this was the dance floor. In the thickening dusk the merrymakers gathered in their donkey carts, their mouths full of watermelon or song, or both, bringing cakes or other refreshments, and stools for their old folk to sit on. Lanterns were lit and suspended from the shadowy trees. Then the musicians arrived, with a rakish confidence and glint about them, setting them apart from the innocent and simple-looking farming folk. Only two, Jan Harp, a Griqua tinker, a barrel of a man with bull shoulders and Popeye biceps, with a strange box slung over one shoulder; and Giovanni Tomaselli, a defrocked Catholic priest, tall, aquiline, a scarlet scarf round his neck, and a slender dark green bag in his hand.

At a signal from Uncle Frank, Jan Harp did something to the shoulder strap, and, seizing the handles of the box, opened his arms wide. With a terrifying discordant sound, the box stretched itself out like a gigantic caterpillar. 'That', I was reassured, 'is a concertina.'

Giovanni undid the loop on his green bag, and gently, so gently, extracted a violin, a bow, and another large silk handkerchief, which he arranged tenderly over his left shoulder. Then he gripped the violin between his jaw and collarbone, and while he adjusted the pegs, plucked the strings in turn till each was in key with a note which Jan Harp squeezed from his caterpillar. This done, they nodded to each other, and the music came singing and droning out of them into the night, and the dancing began. I was entranced. Harp's big flat fingers danced over the stops with delicate deliberation, and his whole body, responding to the movement of his arms, seemed to be breathing music, while his apricot-coloured face shone like a benign harvest moon on all. Tomaselli, on the other hand, scowled with the concentration of true genius, the fingers of his left hand quivering as they slid up and down the strings, pinning them momentarily, while the bow sailed back and forth, like a canoe over the ocean wave. Whereas Harp stood with his feet slightly apart, and seemed solid wood up to his heaving chest and shoulders, Tomaselli's entire body, from his ankles upwards, swayed and twisted like seaweed in a tidal pool. And the music they made! Its power! How it flung the people into rhythmical skipping, and whirling, and waltzing, and great gusts of singing.

Every so often the music would stop to allow the dancers to change partners, and the musicians to quench their thirst. They seemed thirstier than anyone else present. During these pauses people ate cakes, and tarts, and watermelon. Apparently I did myself justice. Years afterwards Aunt Hilda, with tears of laughter in her eyes, reported finding me — a huge sickle of watermelon in my grubby paws — between Harp and Tomaselli, who were once more quenching their thirst. She offered me a slice of cake. I shook my head and declined:

'Uh-uh. Dik.'

One of Uncle Frank's assistants who took John and me on exciting expeditions was a blue-eyed man called Barend ('Boy') Vorster. He was a fountain of stories. He had a slim, quick body, and could do anything with his strong skilful hands. In 1914, aged 17, he had been among defence force trainees at Upington, who had refused to go into rebellion with General Manie Maritz, had been handed over as a p.o.w. to the Germans in South West Africa, and had escaped with a friend. They nearly died of thirst. What saved them was the water left in the boiler of a wrecked railway engine. As if that wasn't experience enough, he'd volunteered for service in German East Africa, and there were stories about that too. He was still a bachelor, which Uncle Frank said was a useful sort of man to have at your side. Uncle Jim had just stopped being a bachelor, and Aunt Hilda had just stopped being a spinster.

Aunt Hilda's father, old Abraham van Wyk of 'Lemoendraai', was someone whose company Boy Vorster did not choose to frequent; not because he was a bad man — far from it, he was an exceptionally upright man — but he was a 'siener', a prophet, gifted or cursed with second sight, something of which he was ashamed and for which he apologised. One day he had staggered into the voorkamer, pale as a sheet, and said to his wife, 'Vrou, I've just seen the most terrible thing: a train thundering through the orange orchard, turning over, screams — then nothing.' Shortly after, news reached them of a train disaster in the western Cape in which many people were killed. The time tallied exactly with Oom Abraham's vision. Barend Vorster had already experienced enough of natural and human calamity to have no curiosity about what the future held, nor any desire to be confronted in the midst of present tasks with distracting glimpses of cataclysms elsewhere.

I have dim recollections of Grannie at the Top House — a subdued but real presence behind her dynamic daughter Flo and son-in-law Frank. Crocheting, mending clothes for her grandchildren, writing letters, keeping an eye on the kitchen, she was adjusting to her new role — no longer mistress of her own establishment, nor wife to an editor, but a homeless widow, a wandering guest in her children's establishments, mulling over her past and finding her chief delight in her grandchildren, which took the form of telling and retelling stories about them. One of these shows how successfully Aunt Mary and others had educated me into a proper dogmatic confidence about matters theological.

The concrete pillars of the Top House were massive pieces of masonry. Grannie was knitting on the stoep, while John, Katot, a little Hottentot playmate, and I were entertaining each other. It appears I was already displaying a desire to pass on knowledge to the unenlightened. I was expatiating on the attributes of the Deity.

'God is everywhere. In Louisvale. In Cradock. Overseas.'

'What about Pofadder?' asked Katot, putting in a claim for his father's birthplace.

'He's also in Pofadder. Everywhere. And he is in everything. You can never hide anything from him.'

Apparently one of the pillars was partially between the unimpressed Katot and myself.

'Katot,' I said, 'God is even in this pillar.'

That was too much for Katot, who exclaimed:

'Nou dit lieg jy! Oom Jacob het dit gemaak. Dis vol sement.'

According to Grannie this heretical rejection of sound doctrine resulted in a rough-and-tumble which ended only on Katot's admission that God could see through and be in *twenty* pillars if he chose.

When James Butler II (Jamie) returned from the war, he joined his sisters and brother-in-law in the great adventure of Louisvale; and before very long, his youngest sister, Kathleen, would find a husband there, none other than Barend Vorster (henceforward known as Uncle Boy), Uncle Frank's right-hand man.

The war spelt the doom of the ostrich. Feminine fashion found little use for feathers after the holocaust; and that new-fangled vehicle, the cramped, windy, inelegant motor car, was not as appropriate as the horse-drawn carriage for large hats with gorgeous sweeping plumes. The market in ostrich feathers collapsed. Though the Biggses, including Alan, like other farmers, still kept a few breeding-birds in the hopes that the fashion would return, they had to look to other staples. Frank decided to revert to wool.

He went to Graaff-Reinet in search of a farm; in March 1924, he bought
'Vrede' in the Camdeboo Mountains from William Collett, son of James of
'Rynheath'. He then returned to Louisvale, loaded his family and me into
the T-model Ford, and set out on the return journey in April.

Two events on the journey stick in my mind. Somewhere near Britstown,
I think, we saw a long, shining cobra writhing on the top strands of a jackal-
proof fence. A moment later the explanation was at hand: a huge grey bird
with long legs and a hawk's head came to a bouncing landing nearby,
stalked up, and proceeded to pluck the broken-backed reptile from the
wire.

Uncle Frank explained how a secretary bird flies aloft with a snake in its
claws (or beak?) and releases it from a considerable height, to kill it by
impact.

I had been taught to be afraid and indeed terrified of snakes, but I found
myself feeling sorry for this one, and mystified at a world in which big,
angry-looking birds dropped twisting golden snakes from a blue sky.

The other event was my first remembered experience of desperation.
John, Ruth and I sat in the back seat of the T-model Ford, while Flo and
Frank and the baby, Denny, sat in the front. Our function was to open
gates, of which there were hundreds in those days. There was much quarrelling as to whose turn it was. It was dusk when we drew near Vrede, the
end of the long, long journey. Not only was the light fading, but the mountains were drawing in closer, reaching higher, and growing darker, on each
side of the road; and, in place of Karoo bush, which never reaches higher
than your knees as it stretches away into open distances, there was a tall,
dense mass of thorn trees mingled with prickly pear. The road seemed like
a deep, dark furrow or trench through the bush. And it was dry and dusty.
The gate at which I knew despair is called 'Stofhek' to this day.

It was my turn; as the car stopped I clambered out and opened the gate,
and the car passed through, and I closed and fixed the catch, and turned
round. The car had not stopped, but was rapidly disappearing in a cloud of
dust, down the gloomy twilight funnel. I stood staring, not knowing what
to do. The prickly pear and thorn trees towered over me, horribly threatening and big. Their stillness was deep and terrifying. The sound of the car
grew thinner and thinner. I started to run after it in utter, hopeless panic.

No words can describe my relief when I saw the car reversing through its
own dust. In all probability the whole episode took no more than a few
seconds — before John reminded his father that he had left his gate-opener
behind. But for me, aged 6, those few seconds were filled with a sense of
desertion which fixed them as an archetype of desolation in my mind.
What permanently abandoned children must suffer!

Nearly all my first memories of Vrede centre round a double-storey outbuilding. One half housed the creamery, where Mr van Eyck, having filled a whole bath with milk, carefully added two or three drops from a small bottle which contained 'microbes', tiny little animals whose entire mission in life was to turn milk into cheese. But wonderful as it was to see Mr van Eyck take the very sour curds from the bath and squeeze the juice out of them through a cheese cloth, and shape it up to look like a cheese, which had to stand and get ripe, it was the water mill in the other half of the building that caught our imaginations. Outside there was the biggest wheel I had ever seen, made of wood; all round its rim were little boxes, their fronts set at an angle to catch the water which, shooting down from a timber flume, filled them up in rapid succession. Weighted down with the water in the top boxes, the wheel turned, emptying them as they drew near the bottom with a great sparkling and splashing. John and I would stand, small among the silver poplar saplings, watching and listening to this great black wheel whirling under the impetus of liquid silver. Inside was equally miraculous. On the same axle as the waterwheel turned a smaller cogwheel, also of timber, whose teeth, we were assured, were made of a very hard wood called stinkwood; these spun the vertical shaft, which joined the mill stones, upper and nether, one stationary, one turning. They were hidden in a circular box on a platform; above them was a shaking conical hopper into which the golden grain was fed from the timber loft. It was a marvellous dark, cool place, smelling of meal and mice. The beams of sunlight which entered it were turned into seeming solid bars of silver, so thick was the air with tiny particles. The whole building trembled and rumbled and thundered quietly; yet, if one put one's ear right against the fur of the cat that crawled into one's lap, one could hear him purring and vibrating in sympathy, as if he had his own water mill grinding away inside him.

It was at the back of the mill, between the building and the main furrow to the lands, that John and I struck gold on the very first morning. Mining operations began at once. My own sons have mined the ancient rubbish dumps of Grahamstown for bottles of ancient design and colour, and I'm prepared to pay handsomely for old stoneware ginger- or other beer-bottles with the name of a South African town on them — but John and I were not mining bottles. No, the jewels we sought were sardine-tin keys. To this day John experiences a pang when he recalls how his output for the day was handicapped by unkind fate: he was summoned by Aunt Flo to look after his baby brother, Denys.

Nearby, close to the oak and the mulberry trees, Caspar Jafta was making 'stellasies' out of reeds — trays on which de-pipped peaches and apricots were spread to dry in the sun. And under the pear tree, near the mill, his wife was busy washing mountains of linen in a series of small tin baths. The mill stream provided cold rinsing facilities; the hot water came from an enormous black vessel called a kaffir pot.

'Why's it called a kaffir pot?' I asked Uncle Frank.

He grinned wickedly and said, 'Because the kaffirs use them to boil missionaries in!'

One day, when the fire was out and the pot without water, I climbed into it. Then I knew he was only joking. A grown-up could never get into one; and all missionaries were grown-ups.

The kitchen door at Vrede opens on to a raised back stoep, on which is a Dutch oven with its own chimney. Stone steps lead down into the backyard. We liked sitting there, between the different interests of the house and yard.

It is twilight after a long, hot day, the stones of the steps are still warm. Uncle Frank is standing near the oven, looking towards Towerberg.

'Flo,' he called.

Aunt Flo appeared in the kitchen doorway.

'Yes dear?'

'It's new moon. It's a good omen. Come and look.'

She came and stood beside him.

He pointed at a thin delicate semicircle in the pale sky. She slipped her arm through his. They stood like that, staring at the new moon, the moon of good omen, for what seemed a long time, in complete silence.

Barend (Boy) Vorster had been left at Louisvale to look after Uncle Frank's affairs, and to bring the stock down when the weather was cooler. In due course he set out, with a dozen Ayrshires — a magnificent stud bull called Wonderfontein Pride, and eleven cows — two dozen donkeys, and 200 ostriches. The distance he had to drive this circus was 640 kilometres.

The ostriches and donkeys stood up to the journey well enough, but the Ayrshires' hooves gave in. He had no means of getting into touch with Frank — the 'phone had not yet reached Vrede. So at Britstown he trucked the cattle to Mr Asher of Graaff-Reinet, a big dealer in farming goods, and Frank's supplier, with a request that he should get a message to Vrede. He then continued his southward drift with his ostriches and donkeys, calling in at post offices en route for messages. In due course he received a telegram from Frank: 'Cows safe Wonderfontein Pride snuffed it.'

He arrived at Vrede with the birds and animals. The lands were suddenly full of ostriches — the black ones were men, the grey ones were ladies. Why were they different colours?

'They say it's for protection. You see, the wyfie sits on the eggs in the daytime, with her neck flat on the ground. Her grey colour makes her look just like any old bush. The mannetjie sits on the eggs at night; and because he is black, his enemies can't see him at all.'

We were warned to keep clear of these huge birds. When a male ostrich's legs went red, that meant that his wife was nesting, or had chicks, and he didn't want any interference. He could kill you with one kick, or rip you open from top to bottom with the terrible claw on his long big toe.

It was on Vrede that I had my first formal schooling from a teacher new to the school-room, Patty Bowker, fresh from the Grahamstown Training College. She had to take several standards in one classroom. We used slates, and slate pencils, and were taught how to shape letters and figures. The slate pencils kept breaking in our clumsy fists. When this happened we would ask permission to go outside and sharpen them on the sandstone steps that led up to the schoolroom stoep. Miss Watermeyer rightly suspected us of breaking our pencils deliberately, and of spending too long a time sharpening them.

Whether this produced the crisis or not, I do not know; but she summoned me to stand in the corner in front of the class. Rather than submit to this indignity I ran out of the room.

Acting on the Biblical precedent of abandoning the ninety-and-nine sheep in order to find the one that had gone astray, she followed me. As she had longer legs than I had, she would soon have run me to earth, had not salvation loomed in the form of the mulberry tree, up which I scuttled with the speed of a scared squirrel.

She ordered me to come down. I refused. Threats and promises were equally useless. No doubt thinking that her whole future control of the class might be at stake if she lost this battle of wills, she went into the classroom for reinforcements. If it was 'infra dig' for a teacher to climb a mulberry tree in pursuit of a recalcitrant boy, it was surely permissible to use other small boys for the task. She unleashed the Evans brothers after me. By this time the whole school had left its benches and was lined up on the stoep. I stopped eating mulberries, climbed as high as I could, and got ready to kick the first Evans head that dared to approach too close. It was quite a complicated campaign. Three branches soon had Evanses on them, but they were heavy boys, and the branches started bending. The whole tree was shaking as if visited by a pack of hungry baboons.

The teacher was now in a terrible dilemma — what if a branch broke? How would Mr and Mrs Biggs react to that? What if any of the children in the tree fell and broke an arm? How would she explain that? So, being a young woman of resource, she promptly rang the school bell. At which magical sound, every child, with Pavlovian promptitude, returned to his or her place in class. Only I stayed, stubborn among the leaves. She rightly calculated that in the fullness of time boredom and hunger would bring me down. They did. How she dealt with me I do not recall. But she left a very favourable impression on my mind.

I was sent back to Cradock per opportunity. An engineer of the Department of Irrigation took me back in his car. He was a strange man with a strange sense of humour. After almost a year — an eternity for a child — I was both excited and uncertain about returning home to The Poplars. I'd grown in size, of that I was sure. Would my parents recognise me? But he asked another question:

'Do you know the way to your parents' house?'

'Yes,' I said.

'Are you quite sure? I won't know where to leave you if you can't show me where it is.'

My hold on reality was loosened by this thoughtless jest from a strange adult, driving a strange car, through a landscape which also was strange. That journey was miserable for me.

At last, as we came down the old road through Moordenaar's Nek, I saw the spire of the Dutch Reformed Church. Then we drew near the station. 'You must tell me when to turn and when to stop,' he said.

We crossed the Great Fish River by the Gilfillan Bridge, and there was The Poplars garden on the right.

'You must turn right on the corner,' I said.

He did so.

'Stop!' I cried.

Opposite me stood the house with the white paling fence and the green and white wooden verandah.

According to my father, I rushed into the house, shouting, 'I'm six years old!'

5

Kindergarten

I was sent to the Kindergarten, just down the street, beyond the Methodist Church.

I remember precious little about it except that I liked both the teachers, Miss Allman and Chrissie van Heerden. I had a passion for Miss A.

They both seemed old to me — but how old I could not say. Anyone out of school was old. Of course, one did realise that there were degrees of oldness. Grey hair in women and beards in men were sure signs of age, proper old age, not mere middle age, which began in your twenties.

I remember hearing the grown-ups discussing the vexed question of whether Miss Allman should marry or not. One of the objections was that the suitor was too old. (I gather from Aunt Mary that he was a very conceited lieutenant, about 30, and Miss Allman 21 or so.) This apparently filled us with indignation. Joan, Dorothy and I lined up in the passage outside the drawing-room where Mother was entertaining Miss Allman. Somewhere or other we had picked up the words of an old song which, to my mother's shame and indignation, we sang in treble chorus:

Never marry an old man;
Now list to what I say;
For an old man he is old,
And an old man he is grey,
But a young man's heart is full of love,
Get away, Old Man, get away.

I suppose this was the first picket protest I ever took part in. I don't know whether it had any effect on Miss Allman's decision or not. She did not marry. Years later, after the opening of one of my plays in Cape Town, I received a charming letter from her.

To Miss Allman I also owe my introduction to the footlights. With the help of parents she put virtually the whole Kindergarten into costume and on to the town hall stage. I had to play the part of a grasshopper. I was not happy in the part. I would have much preferred to be an ordinary gnome. Gnomes smoked! They were issued with clay pipes, into the bowls of which a little dry flour was put. By blowing gently, gnomes could send up puffs of white smoke. If in their excitement they sucked instead of blowing, their mouths were filled with flour paste, as I discovered during the dress

rehearsal. But they didn't have to break ranks and prance and hop about in
a green outfit uttering the sublime lines:

> Grasshopper green is a comical chap,
> He lives on the best of fare;
> Bright little trousers, jacket and cap,
> These are his summer wear.

Mother struggled hard to train me into a proper speaking of the vowels
but, I gather, without success. According to an S.A.B.C. programme in the
'fifties, the Cradock rendering would have been:

> Grawshorper grin iss a cormical chep
> He lives orn the bist ov fê;
> Brart liddle trowzers, jecket end cep,
> These ore his summer wê.

Dorothy was cast as a fairy attendant to the Queen, a confident, pretty
girl called Shanie Karstaedt.

I can remember very little of what I was taught, but I can remember vividly
who taught me. My affections were always deeply involved. At the age of 7
I came out of one Sunday school class radiant, because I had at last found
my future bride — the Sunday school teacher. An elder sister scoffed
and pointed out that she was old, 19, and wouldn't look at me. I replied
that I was growing fast and would soon catch up with her. 'Oh, no, you
won't,' she said, 'she'll always be twelve years older than you.' I was
plunged into confusion and anger at the unfair way in which life was
arranged. She couldn't even wait until I caught up. So, dimly, Time began
to impress itself on my mind.

I learnt much from my elder siblings, Joan and Dorothy. Joan knew, or
was told, what ought to be done and, being eldest, had to see to it that it
was done. Dorothy had no such appalling early responsibilities, lived a rich
fantasy life and, in a manner totally incomprehensible to Joan — or me,
for that matter — could spend a whole day absorbed in a book. She was,
from very early on, the one great reader among us.

There is a legend in the family about Dorothy's addiction to reading, and
Joan's practical bent. Dorothy climbed to the top of a stepladder with her
book, to read, undistracted by the noise and business of the world below,
which consisted mainly of Joan, who kept inviting her sister to 'come down
and play'. 'Just let me finish this bit,' was the reply. But one paragraph led
to another and, finally, to a chapter, and one chapter lengthened into the
next. After a couple of days of this treatment, Joan decided to teach her
sister a lesson. Dorothy's perch was near two old water tanks at the end of
the stoep, a square iron one, reddish, and a round one, blue, galvanised and
corrugated. The latter was the taller — taller, in fact, than the stepladder.

Joan fetched the watering-can, with fine seed-rose nozzle attached, and, lifting it on to the square tank, climbed up after it.

'Dorothy, won't you come and play?' she entreated.

No reply.

Joan heaved her watering-can on to the round tank and climbed up after it.

'Dorothy, for the last time, come and play.'

But Dorothy remained totally absorbed.

So Joan stood on top of the round tank and, from her elevated vantage-point, saturated her sister.

Dorothy went on reading in the artificial rain.

Only when the shower stopped did she let out an indignant wail, which she took, dripping book in hand, inside to Grannie (who was then looking after Alice's brood for some reason).

I do not have any particularly intense recollections of my parents during the next two or three years. But I remember a lengthy debate about the name of our house.

'Why is it called The Poplars?'

'It used to have poplar trees in front of it, all along the furrow. They pulled them out when they changed the house to a single storey.'

'Why don't we plant some again?'

I supported this heartily. I'd got to know all about poplar trees at Vrede — their white and stippled stems, their scent and, above all, the conflagration of their leaves in autumn. But Dad said, 'They send their suckers everywhere. Plant a poplar and you have a problem.'

'They use poplar poles and planks a lot at Vrede,' I said, hoping to appeal to Dad's practical side, but he would have none of it.

'But if we are not going to have a single poplar tree on the place, hadn't we better change the name?' asked Alice.

'It's always been called The Poplars,' said Father, dubious.

We spent some days trying out other names. Father offered a simple, unpretentious Quaker solution: what was wrong with our house being known by its number? Alice rejected that as colourless. 'Let's stick to The Poplars,' she said. 'Not many houses are called that, and it has been, as you say, The Poplars as far back as anyone in Cradock can remember.' So the name survived without the justification of the trees.

And yet, in spite of the fact that there was no poplar among the many trees in our garden, of all trees the poplar became my favourite. There is a poplar bush or avenue on most Karoo farms; boys love climbing tall trees, trees which birds love nesting in. But, most important, its dramatic habit of changing its colour and texture every few months slowly came to symbolise for me the great mystery of the year, the tidal ebb and flow of sap in every living thing.

We watched this, marvelling each year when the first tree blossomed —

usually an almond; and we waited for the first leaves to turn red on the pear trees. Between these miracles and the marvels in books — particularly those in the Bible — there was no cleavage. Life was all of a piece. The facts we were slowly learning in school and from our environment were still particles floating in the sunlight of our happy subjectivity. Things might be removed by time or distance — as Vrede or Louisvale were — but they were not gone, never taken away. Nothing was alien and there were no exiles. The world was whole.

So it seemed, for most of the time.

I don't think my education in religion, which should have tempered this lyricism, was bad, it was merely confused: Anglican, Methodist and Quaker influences were equally strong, and often in conflict.

The historical tap-root of our family is South African Methodism. The Colletts were staunch Methodists; and when the Quakers, James and Charlie, Butler brothers, married Lettie and Emma, Collett sisters, they brought up the families in a Methodist ambience. Both James and his son Ernest held important lay offices in the Cradock Methodist Circuit. Nevertheless, we were all baptised into the Anglican Church — which did not prevent us from attending the Methodist Sunday school.

Methodists are generally modest but they are shameless singers. It's only with Methodists that an indifferent singer, who really wants to let rip, feels free to do so. In the Sunday school building adjacent to The Poplars, I recall yelling both lungs and heart out with ecstatic conviction, one of a dozen or more innocents:

> *Jesus wants me for a sunbeam*
> *a sunbeam*
> *a sunbeam*
> *I'll be a sunbeam for Him!*

I do not remember when we started going to the Anglican Sunday school, or why. It is quite possible that we attended both for a time. Father continued to go to the Methodist Church on Sunday evenings; sometimes Mother kept him company; very seldom any of the children. Father never appeared in the Anglican Church except for a wedding or a confirmation. For a time he read the Bible to his family after supper. He read well, as I recall, not being a stutterer like myself.

Of course *the* religious community of my childhood was at Fish River — that little Methodist Church, and the monthly service there. It was almost the only truly corporate worship I've ever known: everybody knew everybody; everybody talked to everybody; most were blood relatives; they belonged to a valley, a religion, a history and a God. And they sang. So that I've always listened with a residual scepticism to Anglicans when they question the validity of Methodist orders: it didn't *feel* invalid to me. And the congregation in St Peter's, Cradock never created that sense of community,

18   The author's great-great-grandparents, Philippa (née Norman) and John Butler, married in Bristol in 1820.

19   The author's great-grandparents, Philip John and Mary (née Watts) Butler, married in Bristol in 1850.

20 The author's grandparents: Annie Letitia (Lettie) Collett, shortly before her marriage in 1882; and James Butler, aged 22, in 1876.

21 The opening of the Queen's Central Hospital, Cradock, 1899.

The Midland News and Karroo Farmer

THE
MIDLAND NEWS
AND
KARROO FARMER

VOL. I.   CRADOCK, CAPE COLONY, THURSDAY, SEPTEMBER 3, 1891.   No. 1.

GARRETT BROWN & CO.,
Fashionable Supply Stores,
CRADOCK.

POSTAL ORDERS RECEIVE SPECIAL CARE AND PROMPT ATTENTION.

22 First issue of *The Midland News and Karroo Farmer*, 3 September 1891.
23 James Butler as Editor of *The Midland News*.
24 Lettie and James Butler in 1910.

25 Midland House — offices of Butler Brothers and The Midland Printing and Publishing Company — and adjacent buildings in the 1890s.

26 Midland House in 1898.

27 'Wellfound', where James Butler met John Ebenezer Biggs in 1878. Oil painting by Doke.

28 'Top House', Louisvale, home of Frank and Florrie Biggs, overlooking the Orange River.

29 'Vrede', in the Camdeboo Mountains, later home of Frank and Florrie Biggs. Watercolour by Mabel Winters.

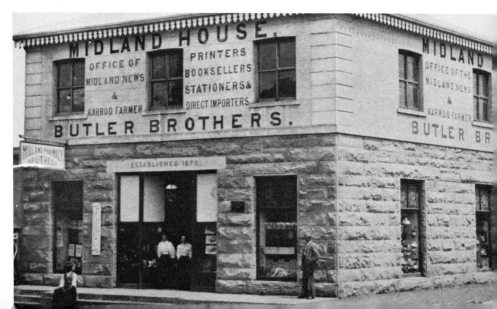

30 Setting off from 63 Bree Street for the tennis week-end at 'Grootvlei'.

31 The tennis week-end at 'Grootvlei'. Back: Frank and Dan Biggs, Clarence du Toit, Jamie Butler, Alan Biggs. Middle: Grandpa James, Flo Butler, Grannie (Lettie) Butler, Alice Butler, Josie Butler. Front: Kathleen Butler.

32 Joan, Christine, Dorothy and Guy, expecting something more terrible than a dicky bird from the camera.

33 Alice with her brood: Guy, Jeffrey, Joan, Dorothy, Christine, on the back steps of 'The Poplars' soon after moving in, 1924.

34 Guy as a grass-
hopper (back row,
left) and Dorothy
as a fairy (front row,
left) in 'A Trip to
Fairyland', 1924.

35 Guy, 1928.

36 Christine, Ernest,
Jeffrey, Dorothy,
Alice, Guy, Joan,
1924.

that sense of belonging, that warmth towards visitors. The time I felt this warmth most was at the Annual Fish River fête, held to raise funds for the church. Every farm brought of its bounty. Everything for sale on the fête was fresh or home-made: ripe fruits, skins tight with sweetness and sunlight, toning their bright cheeks down with a powder-like bloom; flowers — bunches of brassy zinnias like a committee of chairladies of ladies' committees, delicate gothic spires of delphiniums, whole Milky Ways of shasta daisies; dairy produce — newly patted butter, white, yellow and red cheeses; vegetables piled in strata on racks, a green and leafy geology — carrots as in golden nuggets, radishes as ruby clusters; sweets — home-made fudge and coconut cubes in frilly, brightly coloured paper punnets; meat — smoked hams, skeins of sausages, brawns, biltong, whole springbok shot yesterday; preserves — watermelon konfyt, apricots, pears, plums and peaches, stewed or made into jam, peach leather, dried peaches, dried apricots; honey — clear, crystallised, or in the comb; clothes — bright pinafores, floral cottons for small girls, and soft woollens for babies, pink for girls, blue for boys. No machine-made thing in sight, all given for the glory of God, the good of the church — and also perhaps, to enhance one's reputation as a master or mistress of agricultural and domestic crafts and mysteries, new or inherited. Not a till or receipt book in sight: simply an old saucer full of silver and notes at each stall. Everybody meeting everybody, from aged grandparents to the newest born; and frequently the scent of rain still in the air.

Sometimes the event was switched to the Town Hall, Cradock — presumably for the whole Methodist Circuit: it was then called a Church bazaar, not a fête. I suppose the function at Fish River was called a fête because the English ear dearly loves alliteration. Mother never missed the Fête or the Bazaar. They were for her a sort of harvest festival, a joyous gathering of everybody to celebrate the bounty of the earth and its Maker.

Everybody? Alas, no.

Only a fraction of the population of Cradock joined in these affairs. The Afrikaners kept very much to themselves, saving their produce and pennies for their own Church; as for the Coloureds and the blacks, some might be present to set up the stalls and clean up afterwards; but they were never permitted to partake. It simply did not occur to anyone as a possibility.

I must attempt to recapture the feeling between the races in my childhood. My predominant recollection is one of affection, warmth, pleasure and patronising or paternalistic tolerance and good humour: which shows how good-natured and long-suffering the blacks must have been, on the low wages they were paid and in the squalid conditions of living they had to endure.

There were, however, occasional images of dread, little seismic shocks. For instance, the name Tonjeni springs from my childhood, as a 'cheeky' black man who disturbed complacent whites with 'impossible' political demands. I don't think he got as far as Cradock, but his voice did. He was perhaps the articulate voice of the blacks all about us, who were seldom 'cheeky'. More disturbing and exciting was 'Slippery Jim', who went about burgling, stark naked, his muscular form smeared in grease, which made it impossible to grip him. He was supposed to have been in Cradock, and for a time the night shadows were sinister with his slippery nudity. Yet he was curiously unaggressive, only intent on eluding capture with his loot intact. He never carried either gun or knife, unlike the white gangsters in the films. (I do not recall a case of a black murdering a white, or raping a white woman, in Cradock in the 'twenties or 'thirties.) We used to listen to his escapades, breathless with dread and covert admiration.

Shortly after we moved to The Poplars a symbolic event occurred which left a lasting impression on my mind; so much so that, each time I recall it, it grows in power and vividness so that I cannot say just how much of it is history, and how much other experience has attached itself to the original sequence of events.

I was about 6 or 7 at the time, and had been put in charge of a Xhosa lad called Thomas, aged 10 or 12, I suppose, whose job it was to trail after me and keep me safe.

The forbidden area was River Street, which ran between the bottom of the Bree Street gardens and the mimosa-fringed bank of the Great Fish River. It was the dumping area for builders' and other rubbish, littered with cigarette boxes and empty sherry bottles left there by Coloureds who imbibed among the ash and thorn bushes nearest to the South African Hotel. River Street ran from the Gilfillan Bridge down to the point where Hare Street crossed it, and entered a very old drift through the thin stream of the river and then emerged on the other side, near the big, sinister, dirty white building called the abbatoir or 'slaghuis'. Below the drift was a concrete wall, on whose downstream side were two large, dark green pools, dreaded by my mother.

It was a sinister spot. Entire oxwagons, drivers, teams and all, had been swept away by sudden ramping walls of brown, boiling storm water. A stage coach from Kimberley, with diamonds, had been ambushed at night as it entered the drift, and the driver shot; and the murderer sentenced in Grahamstown and hung by his neck till he was dead. The area was still the haunt of tramps and loose women, where illicit deals in dagga and liquor were transacted in broad daylight. The 'broad daylight' suggested, even then, that darkness could be relied upon to cover a multitude of sins.

This eventful day was in an era before I knew that all white men, whatever their age, education or status, were superior to all Coloureds; that all Coloureds (and all whites) were superior to all black men; and that all black men (and all Coloureds and whites) were superior to all Hottentots; and that all Hottentots (and all black men, Coloureds and whites) were superior to all Bushmen; and that Bushmen had nobody to be superior to. How this simple, obvious and eternal heirarchy had not yet got through to me I do not know. My parents must have been very slack about instructing me in the sacred and essential facts of South African life.

Well, Thomas liked me, and I liked Thomas, and we were both bored with the bottom reaches of The Poplars garden; so we slipped through the fence, and in no time at all were down at the old wagon drift playing in the cool, blue-white river sand.

A funny little boy, naked but for a dirty shirt, making strange happy noises to himself, came down the cutting, driving half-a-dozen big, smelly goats. His skin was pale yellow, his cheekbones high, his eyes small and bright, and his teeth protruding beyond the line of his very flat nose; and his behind seemed much too big for the rest of him. I was entranced, but Thomas shouted:

'Haai, jou Boesman! Weg is jy!'

As the Bushman was on his way anyway, this seemed silly. To make matters worse, Thomas picked up a handful of gravel and flung it at him, hard.

The little fellow stopped and picked up a fair-sized stone; then he came dancing slowly towards Thomas, chirruping and clicking like a bunch of lady-crackers, pivoting on the points of his toes.

A goat bleated.

Thomas promptly spat, and shouted:

'Voetsek, hond!'

On being called 'dog', the dwarf flung the stone at Thomas with frightening force. Thomas ducked, and brandishing his kerrie, strode towards him, lordly and contemptuous, twice his opponent's size. The little fellow lifted his whip as if to use it to parry a blow.

They drew close together. Suddenly Thomas struck, but struck air. His opponent, casting his whip aside, had come in close, with pulled-in chin, and, leaping from the ground like a kangaroo, butted Thomas under the jaw with the top of his head.

Thomas fell over, the Bushman leapt on his chest and started trying to hammer his face with a large stone. Thomas, defending his features with widespread frantic fingers, yelled for help.

Suddenly a big man was there, a big laughing man, in a dirty old suit. He seemed in no hurry to stop the fight, but squatted on his haunches to watch the fun. He fumbled a bottle out of his pocket.

'Stop them,' I pleaded. 'Stop them!'

'Bushmen and Kaffirs always fight,' he said, chuckling, taking a swig.

'Stop them!'

'Orl right, basie,' he said.

He rose unsteadily and kicked at the Bushman for all he was worth. The little fellow slid aside and suffered only a glancing blow; the Coloured man lost his balance and almost fell. Thomas rolled away, got on to his feet and ran for about a hundred yards, then stopped and sat down to await developments. The Bushman retrieved his stick and went to gather his goats.

I was now alone with my saviour, who was smiling, wiping his hands on his hams. He had a face like a pirate and big gaps between long, yellow teeth. I was suddenly very afraid of that friendly smile, four foot above me, against the sky.

'Basie, tell your father he mustn't let you play with Kaffirs. Swartgoed is rubbish. They let a Bushman-dog give them a hiding. A Coloured boy will look after you much better. Now, Basie, I got a son . . .'

I had backed away from him during this speech, but he kept walking after me. I was terrified of the green pools at my back. Then he stopped smiling, stood still and seemed to take stock. Finally he nodded, as if to say, Yes, I'm wasting my time, turned round, retrieved his bottle and disappeared into the grey thorn bushes.

I ran to join Thomas. While he washed the blood off his face, I asked him why he called the Bushman names. He looked at me, taken aback; then, realising I was merely an ignorant white child who couldn't be expected to know any better, he said gaily, 'Because he's a Bushman.'

Years later, in the 'sixties, I gave a few extra classes to a Xhosa youth called Abel Pike, who was preparing for his Matric. One of his set books was Laurens van der Post's *Lost World of the Kalahari,* which gives a vivid and sympathetic account of Bushman people. I asked Abel whether he liked the book. 'Very much,' he said, 'except that it made me so ashamed.' Why? 'We black and you white people treated them very badly.'

There was, however, one exceptional occasion when all races were invited and present. The miracle was brought about by Edward, Prince of Wales, on a hands-across-the-ocean tour of the domains he seemed destined to rule.

For weeks we practised a song, of which His Royal Highness must have been sick to the point of nausea by the end of his tour —

From out our ancient mountains,
And from our distant Vales,
O let the hills re-echo
God bless the Prince of Wales.

In due course, breathless with excitement to see a real live Prince, we waited in neat phalanxes, school by school, below the steps to the station, between the captured German howitzer and the two Maxim guns, reminders of the Great War. Boy Scouts and Girl Guides; ex-servicemen, with their medals glinting; and a large block of African school children and adults.

'Well, you see,' explained the teacher to a puzzled child who asked why the black children were there, 'He's their prince also.'

The prince, when he did appear, was a bitter disappointment to all; a small man, with sleepy eyelids, in a crushed linen suit, with his arm in a sling. He shook hands with the mayor and ex-servicemen with his left hand. In response to a fervent speech by the mayor, he said a few words which no one could hear. His lack of interest in Cradock was evident. The white children sang, the black children sang, and it was all over.

Later that week I heard some grown-ups discussing what had happened at King William's Town. The Xhosa chieftains had asked for a chance to pay their respects to their monarch-to-be. His Highness was honoured by a praise poem written specially for him by a great imbongi, Mqhayi. It was a very fine poem, some said. Others weren't so sure. Xhosas speak in metaphors which can mean many things, and the translator found his task tricky. One old police officer, who knew Xhosa well, reckoned that, had he but known it, the prince was not only being praised but he and his kingdom were being indicted for betraying the Xhosa people.

On one of those periodic returns to home base which an adventurous child makes once or twice a day in order to reassure himself that the world is still a safe place, I run from the garden into the kitchen in search of Mother.

She is standing near the stove, a red telegram crumpled in her fist. She is without her pince-nez, weeping unrestrainedly. Chrissie, the Sotho cook, has her arms round her, and is trying to calm her, crying — 'Shame, shame, shame.' It is the first time I have seen Mother weep since Grandpa's death. Neither she nor Chrissie sees me. In a panic I rush out to announce the portent to my sisters — Mother is crying. We return to the kitchen. When she sees us, she wails, 'Your Aunt Janet's dead.' And we start crying because of her tears.

We were told that she had died of brain fever in Shanghai. After the day of the telegram, Mother spoke very little about her, and we were left to weave romantic stories around that remote death. In China, that place of appalling famines and epidemics, Aunt Janet had volunteered to nurse the afflicted, like Aunt Mary nearer home; and she had caught the fatal brain fever from her patients. Only recently I have discovered that 'died of brain fever' was a euphemism for suicide. Her brother Harold and his wife May must have found her mounting insanity and self-inflicted death terrifying. And Alice and Ernest must have thanked Heaven for delaying the climax of her tragedy until she had reached China. The old dread of insanity must have accounted for their conspiracy of silence over Janet's end, and over subsequent family tragedies.

Sunday was the great day for 'walks' or 'spins'.

Aunt Mary would sometimes take us to the cemetery, to look at Grandfather's grave. The day is hot and still. She is trying to get us to memorise a Biblical text. I had mastered it before we reached the long galvanised-iron fence of the rugby field, which lies adjacent to the cemetery. I always looked forward to that fence, because I could take a stick and make it rattle over the corrugations, the exciting sound becoming part of the pleasant vibration in my wrist. When I started rattling my stick, however, Aunt Mary told me to stop. I don't know why. Not suitable for Sunday, perhaps. Or maybe she wanted to approach James Butler's simple Quaker tombstone in fitting silence. Once there, the girls would place their posies of flowers on his grave.

Later, when our legs were longer, we would walk to the top of Ou Kop, or other hills round about. We were all more or less keen on what was known as nature study — the names and varieties of plants, the seasonal flowers, the birds and their nesting-places, their characteristic cries and flight — small buck, ground squirrels, meercats and other small mammals — reptiles, snakes, lizards and tortoises — the veld, a perennial source of delight, mainly sunlit, dry and still, sometimes overcast and damp, or windy, the shrubs shaking and cirrus clouds streaking the blue overhead.

If Aunt Mary was with us, we would sit down somewhere, usually on some big boulders (of which there was no shortage) and she would read something or other. Never the Bible. I can recall one of Olive Schreiner's allegories; or something from a Quaker magazine called *The Friend,* or a poem with a clear spiritual drift.

We went for 'spins' in the car. Alice presided, and loved them — a breath of fresh air, away from household chores. The earliest 'spins' I recall were in, or rather on, a marvellous contraption called a Humberette. This was a diminutive little vehicle, a sort of Ur-Volkswagen, more like two motor-cycles running parallel with seating between them; it was also propelled by a most unusual motorbike engine — two air-cooled cylinders in V-formation. It was bright yellow, with black trimmings. It had a copper bugle for a hooter, blown by squeezing a black rubber bulb. The front seat was high off the ground, and was designed for two. The Butlers were seven, five smalls and two large, Alice almost outsize. Ernest was never defeated by a small practical problem like that. Behind the front seat and over the back axle was a large flat-topped, shallow box, with a strong lid that could be lifted. A perfectly safe area for children, provided they didn't fall off. He attached a foot-rest to the back of the chassis. Then he went to the saddler — what a handsome old ramrod he was, white whiskers and pink face — and returned with a leather strap of a width and thickness sufficient to persuade Alice that all of us would be safe. This he attached to the front seats.

Jeffrey, then an infant, had the distinction and honour of sitting in front, on his mother's lap. Joan, Dorothy, Guy and Christine were securely strapped on the back, facing the wrong way, with strict instructions not to turn round: we'd get grit in our eyes. The dirt roads were corrugated and infernally dusty. The chief view we four got during a 'spin' was a boiling cloud of whitish powder. The taste, dust mingled with the exhaust fumes, was distinctive; not the 'breath of fresh air' that Alice was enjoying in front.

However, there were stretches of road where there was comparatively little dust. Maybe a shower had settled it and the veld was smelling sweet. Then one had a marvellous view — a view of trees and roads and huts rushing past the sides of the vehicle, gradually slowing down as they were pulled into the distance, then steadying themselves, settling down into the vast landscape.

This is a very different experience from sitting in the front seat of a car: in that position the stable landscape ahead becomes nervous as it draws nearer, breaks loose from its moorings, and then starts flying and hurtling past on either side in great fragments. One is splitting and splintering the scene, a wedge destroying the unity of things.

This movement through space has provided me with a metaphor for my sense of movement through time. If you have a feeling for the past, you have the assurance that the chaos or excitements that occur in the present will be integrated, composed and ultimately reconciled in that inevitable landscape. But if you are future-orientated, the beautiful composition breaks up as it reaches you, or you break it; and you never get into it, it is always fragmenting and falling apart. Not that I had any such high-falutin speculations at the age of 7 or 8. Everything, then, was almost always miraculously present.

So leave us there for the moment — strapped to the back of a yellow-bodied insect buzzing like a bumble-bee along a spider web of a dirt road — west, up Moordenaar's Nek, to the great vlakte under Salpeterskop and Spekboomberg; or down south towards Mortimer, along the river, where smallholders were planting orchards and vegetables under the Grassridge irrigation scheme; or east, out to the new Lake Arthur Dam on the Tarka River, the sheet of pale, purple-brown water among the ironstone hills; or north, to the Fish River Valley, up past the First Krantz, and the Second Krantz, towards Grassridge.

On two of the koppies, at some distance from each other, someone at some time in the past had selected a flat-surfaced rock and, in large clear letters, cut two quotations from the Bible. Who inscribed them? No one seems to know, but, whoever he was, his sublime graffiti are looked at endlessly by the sun, the moon and the stars, and, once in a blue moon by human eyes — surprised by the unexpected. The grandeur of the first, on Oukop, is lent a touching quaintness by a misspelt word:

What availe it a man if he gain the whole world and lose his own soul?

The second, among the black and purple boulders above First Krantz, reads in my memory as:·

The heavens declare the Glory of God and the firmament showeth His handiwork.

6

My Father and Others

From the Kindergarten in Bree Street, between the Methodist and Anglican churches, I graduated to what was known as the Little Boys' School in Cross Street, in a part of the town which bordered on the location. Several of the houses in the neighbourhood were occupied by Coloured people, and the Jewish, Indian and Chinese shops catered mainly for them and the black people. Aunt Eliza lived quite close, in Market Street, and also Aunt Mary, firstly in a very old cottage, below the ancient water furrow near the gaol (the oldest part of Cradock), and then as close to the location proper as she could get.

The school playground was a dry waste of blue-brown dolerite gravel, bare of growth except for a stunted group of pepper trees round the bucket latrines. The school's mental climate was about as barren as its setting. During break time the smaller boys were terrorised by the bigger boys, particularly by toughs from the Railway Camp, into giving up all or some of their sandwiches. There were one or two boys from poor homes who smelled so bad that it was painful to sit near them; sometimes we came home with lice in our hair. There was no uniform, but socks and shoes were required. During winter, mobile black paraffin heaters were lit in the classrooms; a small tin of water was placed on each. I used to keep glancing up until the first vague wisp of steam drifted off the surface. That was a sign that the room was warm at last, the feeling in one's toes notwithstanding.

My first teacher there was Miss Paterson, short, slight, bossy, with a very wrinkled face. The lined nature of her skin, Mother assured us all, was due to needless and excessive application of make-up in her youth. Mother scowled momentarily at Joan and Dorothy, busy with dolls, and said:

'Girls, remember that! Make-up ruins your skin!'

Mother never used make-up. She regarded it as 'fast'. It also happened to cost money. And her complexion was perfect.

Miss Paterson had a brisk, tart manner, and stood for no nonsense. While her use of English displayed nothing of the genteel formality of my later Scots mentor, Aird, it was peppered and spiced with vigorous, if crude metaphors. So, to a boy, sucking his ruler, in the first period: 'What are you trying to do with that ruler? Hook your breakfast up?'

When I relayed these verbal felicities at home, Mother would frown and shake her head in distress: 'I wish I could send you all away to decent schools,' she would say.

Most of my recollections of those years in the Little Boys' School are unpleasant. One of the worst incidents occurred when Miss Paterson required each of us to recount a recent dream to the class.

It was not during the marble season, or the 'pictures-and-blanks' season, or the 'kennetjie' season, but the silkworm season. The Poplars windowsills were cluttered with shoeboxes (lids pierced, so that the worms could breathe), in which we watched immobile white pinheads yield to tiny black grubs, which grew whiter as they grew longer and rounder, consuming a succession of mulberry leaves. Within a few weeks, when we changed the leaves, we would pick up delicate-skinned, bluish-white caterpillars, two and a half inches long, heavy with unspun liquid silk. Suddenly, one of them would seem to go to sleep, as if into a deep dream; then he would bestir himself, find a corner, and start swinging his body around in vague arcs, and begin to spin; we would watch the weird way the worm would enclose himself in an ever-darkening, narrowing, golden cocoon, spinning himself into his own coffin. Months later, he would emerge a white moth, with furry, frenetically trembling wings, unable to fly but searching until he found a member of the opposite sex; and then followed the mysterious, slightly ridiculous, protracted end-to-end attachment of the two creatures, called mating, without which, I was told, the eggs would be infertile.

One of the class was called Abbott, and his dream went like this.

'I'm good about eating my food, but there are some things I can't stand: turnips, and mutton fat. In this dream I had to eat a chop and turnips. I cut off the mutton fat, and left it in strips on the edge of my plate, and ate the red meat. My mother kept shouting, "Eat your turnips." So at last I ate them, but felt sick. Then she said, "You'll sit there till you've cleaned your plate." So one by one I had to put these bits of cold mutton fat in my mouth and eat them. It was awful.'

'I quite agree,' said Miss Paterson. 'Sit down.'

'But I'm not finished,' said Abbott. 'When I woke up, it was getting light. I found myself with my silkworm box in my lap. The silkworms were all gone.'

What the dream analysts will make of this, I don't know. I could never regard Abbott as quite normal after that. The class laughed of course, but there was a note of anxiety and horror in my mirth. Years later, when I saw Goya's horrific painting of the old god Saturn devouring his young, Abbott's dream leapt to mind.

There was one teacher in the Little Boys' School who did make a favourable impression: Miss Norman, in charge of standard 3. The classroom was on the west side of the building. From my desk I could look at the horses being driven in and outspanned at the municipal stables; occasionally one caught the sharp scent of manure — a change from the Jeyes fluid smell of the classroom. Beyond the stables in the distance, floated the flat-topped mountains to the west — Salpeterskop and Spekboomberg.

Miss Norman arranged extra voluntary classes for Art, which took place on Friday afternoons. I can remember the delightful agonies of designing and executing three pieces of work. First she set us making lampshades of yellow waxed paper, on which each boy had to stencil a design of his own devising, using a very stub brush, and oil paints. I do not recall my design at all; but cutting the stencil, with a razor blade that always slipped and cut too far, that I remember. The second task was a design for the centre of a small tray. We were told to use objects or animals from nature as our motifs. I chose two fish. By curving their spines, and taking other liberties, particularly with their fins and tails, and placing both nose to tail, I produced a pattern which pleased me and my teacher. Fifty years later, during committee meetings, I find myself producing these two happy, simple fish, swimming eternally after each other round a still centre, completing a design, filling a space of which they are unaware.

The third was a decoration for a small circular box. Each boy had to pester his Ma or Auntie or Big Sister to provide a powder box. I can recall today the delicate scent of that box, almost forbidden, taboo, magical. Having painted it white, we then had to draw our design upon it, and raise portions by successive applications of something called 'gesso'. Whether the scent was responsible, or the feminine associations of the powder, I do not know, but I produced a butterfly which I hoped would look beautiful, delicate and flamboyant. It was a total disaster. The more I laboured at this creature of colour and air, the more muddy and earthy it became. The sense of failure is still with me. As a keen insect collector I had caught the fluttering creatures, big and small, rare and common, and knew that their brilliant pigments were generated by myriads of tiny scales reflecting and refracting the light. But my miserable butterfly never got out of the gesso.

Miss Norman had to pay for being imaginative, for daring to climb out of the rut. One day 'Tiger Tim' Russell, the headmaster, came up from the Big Boys' School to inspect the Little Boys' School. He asked one of us to recite. A nervous knock-kneed boy started:

'The Hunting of Shumba' by Kingsley Fairbridge.

'The hairs about his muzzle tipped with wet,
The last sun glinting on his tawny mane
And burnishing his hide —— '

— and so on. Perhaps the reciter did not do the poem justice. Perhaps the good know-all Scot was offended at hearing a poem, unknown to him, by an unknown South African, on animals, mere animals, in the unknown bush; but for whatever reason, he told Miss Norman then and there, before us all, that the poem was unsuitable and too difficult for boys in standard 3. This outraged some: had all those hours of effort in learning the poem

been wasted? But I never regretted it. Phrases from it still leap to mind —
'night jars wing / weird in the azure dusk'. Perhaps I owe my interest in
South African poetry to a teacher who had to be publicly humiliated
for introducing South African boys to verse written in and about Africa.
I lived that poem, word by word, line by line. The detailed observations,
and the colours, bit into my memory far more deeply than most of what
we learnt subsequently. What happened to Miss Norman, I wonder?

It was during these years that I became more aware of my father, and
through him of a world that fascinated him, the world of machines, of
engines. I was already vaguely familiar with some of his close mechanical
acquaintances in the works of *The Midland News* — the 'lino', which was
always going wrong, the huge Wharfedale, which never went wrong, the
folding-machine, which turned a big sheet of paper into a booklet in no
time at all, and the terrifying guillotine, which sliced sideways through
enormous blocks of paper like butter.

Occasionally, very occasionally, Ernest would take me for a walk. These
walks were always to places where there were big machines. The first was to
the Cradock municipality's electric power station. It was then sited just
across the river, opposite the bottom of our garden. The visits were frequent
at one time — small plant was being replaced by larger plant. The power
plant performed the miracle of turning coal and water into electric current.
The S.A.R. would shunt a couple of trucks of coal to the side line, and
dump it. This would be unloaded into a sort of bunker, thence into a hopper at the end of one of the big boilers, and from the hopper on to a mobile
chain-grid under the boiler. The coal would ignite as it was drawn into the
furnace, and nothing but white ash would emerge at the other end.

The heat released by the burning coal converted the water in the boiler
into steam under pressure, and this steam was fed by pipes to the engine
room; the new turbines converted the indiscriminate pressure of steam
into energy, to be precise, a steel shaft spinning smoothly on its bearings;
and this turned the huge armature in the generators. I found it all fairly
simple up to this point. But when Dad or the electrical engineer tried to
explain what happened in the generators, about the North and the South
Poles, the electric coils, and the difference between alternating and direct
current, I gave up and took it on faith: somehow the energy of the spinning
shaft was transformed into something called an electric current, which unlike water could flow along a solid copper wire at incredible speed; it was
highly dangerous but, if used properly, could be converted into heat or
light, or made to drive electrical motors, which were generators in reverse;
and the same force or energy or waves or impulses had something to do with
wireless, then just beginning to appear in the valley.

The Electronic Age had begun. But I have remained an Early Steam Age
man.

My main recollection of the power station is coming into it out of cold dusk, my hand firmly clasped in Ernest's (no doubt on Alice's instructions) into a huge, warm, brilliantly lit hall, and standing in front of a massive polished flywheel, about eight foot in diameter. It was spinning at heaven knows how many revolutions per minute, but it looked perfectly motion-less. Long before I encountered T.S. Eliot's image of the Chinese jar, which 'moves perpetually in its stillness', and related images about the still point of the turning world, I was already happily confused on the issues of ap-pearance and reality, motion and stillness.

Another place Ernest took me to once or twice was the Railway Work-shops. Cradock was then an important point in the Eastern Cape railway system: they used to change engines there — all steam-driven, of course.

Those old dinosaurs are dying out — pistons and connecting-rods, steam hissing on alternate sides of the huge, black but shining beast, and that clean-cutting whistle sound — they are nearly all gone, driven out by brown diesels emitting self-pitying arrogant moans.

The railway workshops were vast, capable of garaging several engines at once, but unlike the power station, they were not well lit. The effect was of murky and brilliant black, wet rails glinting like swords, quicksilver pools of water, glowing coals, and polished copper pipes. And a big man in dark overalls with oily hands, the fingers slightly apart, gripping a piece of white-hot metal in black tongs; clear blue eyes looking calmly at a problem despite the gloom and the colossal din of metallic hammerings and high-pitched hisses of steam. The next time I felt awed in this way was in Pretoria at ISCOR in 1940, watching steelworkers, with the aid of an enormous roller mill, converting a blunt orange-hot steel ingot into a slender, long black railway line. Such images, quite as much as my visits to the blacksmith, were to help me with portions of Blake's poetry, particularly 'The Tyger'.

Another of my father's rare walks was to the Municipal Quarries to watch the crusher working. The loose stones, previously blasted from the rock face, were loaded by big black men into coco pans, and pushed on little railway lines to a ramp, where they were tipped, and stacked ready for my hero: the man who fed the stones into the steel mouth of the crusher — a monster purring silently, until its jaws got into a nice chunk of dolerite. Then it would emit a loud growl, with a thud, which would modulate into a pleased purr again as the last stubborn morsel was splintered into gravel. The gravel fell into rotating sorting cylinders pierced with holes increasing in size, through which the fragments would drop into appropriate bins — mechanically elementary, but with plenty of sound and action.

The irrigation canals and the dams that fed them were not machines, and did not fascinate Father as much, but he knew the importance of water in our semi-desert and we were taken to see both dams under construction. Lake Arthur relied on an overhead cable, on which the huge buckets of concrete travelled to and fro, tipping their contents into the shuttering beneath. Grassridge was mainly an earth dam; we liked it better because there were coco pans there, with diminutive steam engines, and, more important, there were relations to give us tea, and all the fascinations of farm life.

Occasionally several of one's interests were presented with a challenge which called for a co-ordinated creative response.

The challenge was presented by the silkworms. We had been so conscientious about changing the greenery, that we now had dozens of golden cocoons, I was smitten with the desire to unwind the silk of these, to produce a skein of the delicate filament. I learnt, with a little practice, how to peel off the loose outer fibres, and to find the necessary single strand. Placing the cocoon in a tumbler of water, where it would float and move with a minimum of friction, I attached the thread to a piece of cardboard. By turning this round and round, I transferred the silk from the cocoon to the card. But it was too laborious a process to perform manually. Bored, I went outside to play in the garden.

It was our turn for water-leading, and September, our Xhosa gardener, was busy with the sluices of our diminutive domestic irrigation scheme. Suddenly I recalled the water wheel at Vrede. Water power!

In a fever of inventive concentration, I manufactured a simple water wheel in the workshop. I gave it a long axle on which I fixed a light wire cradle or framework. I then found a suitable mill-site in the garden — a place where there was a change in levels — and led a small stream of water to it. It took some time to fix the axle bearings and adjust the stream of water, but by the third day I had that wheel spinning satisfactorily. Then came the great moment: I placed a cocoon in a Ball jar, and attached its thread to the wire frame; then I released the water to turn the wheel, just a little at a time, in case a sudden jerk of the frame should snap the silken thread. There followed hours of technical hitches, but at last, with the late sun glittering behind the Spanish reeds, I watched my mill unwinding an entire cocoon. I stopped my mechanical marvel, and slipped the shining silk off the wire frame, and took it inside in triumph. My sisters thought me a genius, which shows how intelligent and perceptive they were.

The next day I made a larger frame, and had five cocoons bobbing about in a line of tumblers, all being unwound at once.

But I did not tackle the next stage — the spinning of the filament into a usable thread. As suddenly as the craze had gripped me, it let me go. Two days later, September accidentally trod on my mill and broke it. He brought it apologetically to me; but I was not upset. My mind was already on something else.

Years later, in a history class, when we came to deal with the use of water power in the early industrial revolution, I realised that I had already taken part in it, personally.

These years — until the end of 1929 — were good years for The Poplars. True, there was never enough money to do things in the style that Alice would have liked; but business picked up to the point where *The Midland News* could afford a full-time editor, leaving Ernest free to build up the jobbing side of the printing, to manage the bookshop, and eventually to launch a weekly Stock and Wool Edition of the paper. Improved communications meant that papers from the big centres — in our case *The Eastern Province Herald* from Port Elizabeth — were reaching the small centres more quickly, and affecting the circulation of local papers. A Karoo paper which specialised in farming matters, however, might keep its subscribers, possibly even expand its circulation. One had to meet the challenge with an enterprising counter-attack.

And then there was The Poplars itself. Over these years my father put his practical bent to maximum use. Alice having used a small legacy to acquire an additional piece of land between the old stables and the Methodist Sunday school, Ernest set about redesigning and altering the house, adding a long back verandah, on which three children slept throughout the summer months. For several years, only one stuck it through the winter — me. I used our cats as hot-water bottles! The boys' room was simply too small for two beds. Father took off the old wooden trellis-work verandah from the front, because it was rotten and, much to Alice's delight, built a tennis court between the butt-end of the house and the Methodist Sunday school. He surfaced it with ant-heap and old unbaked bricks, employing his children as draught animals to drag a six-foot section of railway line back and forth and to and fro, to level it.

He 'got in the prisoners' to clear and reshape the garden into the beds that could be watered, making the sluice gates himself. It was a great day when September cut the first crop of barley, tied it into sheaves, and took it to the market for sale. Father put in new fruit trees and in due course Alice bottled apricots by the hundredweight. He made a long pergola out of old boiler tubing bought from the Railways, over which he grew a variety of vines. In due course we sold huge quantities of grapes at tuppence a pound, or seven pounds for one shilling. He converted some of the stables into garages, which he let; but the largest he kept for a workshop for his bench and his growing stock of equipment and tools. He continued to make furniture for his home. Alice and Ernest spent all their spare time improving the property and garden, saving a pound here, earning a few shillings there.

Alice did her best to account for every penny spent on the housekeeping, but she was not good at it. 'Bother!' she would cry. 'Was that elastic for your knickers ha'pence or three ha'pence? My mind's a positive sieve. Joan, be a brick, dear, run up to Badger's and ask them.'

She was as sociable as Ernest was shy. Ernest's lack of friends worried her. She put it down to two causes, his teetotalism and his eyes. Most men enjoyed a beer or a brandy after tennis or bowls or golf; but Ernest played none of these games, possibly because he could not enjoy 'one with the boys' afterwards. And men tend to do business with their friends, rather than with lonely, high-principled puritans.

The deeper cause was, of course, his eyes.

It happened when he was a boy on holiday at Salt Pans Drift. A crowd of youngsters are taking turns to be pulled in a small hand-cart down a path between the thorn trees. A branch is pulled forward by a passing shoulder and then whips back. A long, white thorn pierces the passenger's left eye.

James Butler was away from home at the time. His wife's letters to him over the next few weeks are a model of restraint, through which hope fights a losing battle with anguish. After weeks of medical attention her handsome boy emerges not merely blind in one eye, but disfigured for life: he has a distressing cast. He never quite recovers his social confidence.

Just as his grandfather, Philip John, sits sideways before the camera to hide his tubercular lump, so my father usually stands in profile, or three-quarter face. The devices we adopt to cover our spiritual wounds are more devious, more difficult to detect. There is Alice's broken heart, for instance. No one, to my knowledge, was ever admitted even to glimpse that scar.

Ernest and his sister Mary were sent to Britain for their education, at Sidcot, a Quaker school in Somerset, from 1897 to 1900. Coming from Africa, he was promptly nicknamed Zulu. In her old age Aunt Mary admitted that he was so difficult that the dear old Quaker headmaster was driven to the most unusual measures: he resorted to the cane. Ernest also indulged in secret feasts, one of which nearly cost him his remaining eye. The rendezvous was the lee of one of the chimneys on the roof. The day was hot, so they sat in its shade, leaving their tuck in the sun. One of the ginger beer bottles exploded, and a splinter of glass lodged in Ernest's left eyebrow. He would show the scar as he told the story. Aunt Mary also recalls being taken into the centre of London during Queen Victoria's diamond jubilee in an open carriage to see the crowds and decorations; so infected by the excitement was her brother that he lost his inhibitions and sang loudly all the way.

Back in South Africa, his self-consciousness was not ameliorated by his parents' insistence that he should attend school in his English clothes — his knickerbockers raised hoots of derision. He had started French at Sidcot and, although no good French tuition was available, he was made to continue with it, rather than switch to Nederlands. He failed French, and left school without a matriculation certificate.

He was put into the bank, and soon rose to the rank of teller; and there, say almost all his relatives, he should have stayed. He would have risen to be a manager in no time at all. But I praise God that he left the bank. The bank would have moved him on promotion to a big city, where he could have met and married someone other than the gym mistress at Rocklands Girls' High School. I cannot think of a worse thing happening to my father or to my mother.

While at Rocklands Mother used to show off her schoolgirls in an annual gym display. She also took the opportunity to show off herself. From relatives and ex-pupils, I have heard that she would wear a gold outfit hidden beneath a floor-length velvet cloak. The latter she would shed at the appropriate moment, with stunning effect. Stunned Ernest was, stunned to the point of trying to impress her by making a witty contribution to a conversation. Her reply crushed him for weeks:

'*A propos* of what was that?'

He persisted, thank God, in spite of her initial hauteur, in spite of the fact that she was six years his senior, to the point of proposal, and thank God she said yes, and they married, were fruitful and started multiplying. Within a year of their marriage Joan was born, in 1915. Dorothy followed in 1916, myself in January 1918, Christine in 1920, Jeffrey in 1922.

When I returned from my year's exile in 1924, the family circle was complete. Each child was moving up an educational ladder, demanding more attention and more space. One measure of our advance in wisdom and stature was the lateness of the hour at which we went to bed. As child after child reached the stage of being allowed to sit up after supper to do homework, it became clear that the dining-room table was too small, the more so after Godfrey and Neville Collett came to board with us in order to attend school. So we were excited when Father announced that we were to acquire a larger, new table — new to the Butlers, that is, not new from Alfred Hyam & Co., Furnishers. Father had 'picked it up for a song' at a sale.

When the table arrived we were somewhat disappointed: it was not much bigger than the old one. Father explained that it soon would be, because it was expandable: the two ends could be made to slide apart, creating a gap in the middle, into which could be slipped one, two, three or even four 'leaves'. And where were the leaves? They were missing: that was why it had gone for a song. But the provision of new leaves would be no problem at all to Ernest: he'd make them in a matter of days.

It took a trifle longer than he expected, because none of the timber merchants in Port Elizabeth stocked oak. Eventually he settled for teak, his favourite wood.

It was an exciting day when the table was expanded and the three new teak leaves slipped in. We all rejoiced in its generous expanse, but Alice lamented the piebald effect created by the different timbers. Ernest undertook to treat the teak leaves so as to make them match the ends, but he never did manage to find the time to do so during the next twenty years. Alice ceased to worry about it. After all, whenever we had guests it was covered by a huge snow-white linen cloth, her pretty china, and a bowl of roses, nasturtiums, or calendulas.

After the table had been cleared, two of the children would carry the cloth through the kitchen into the yard, taking care to keep it taut between them so that it did not touch the floor. There we would shake it out, before folding it. Later on, it was fun to get a visitor of the opposite sex whom one liked to share this chore, because one could signal one's presence by every change of tension or tug one gave the linen; and then the folding process involved a progressive decrease in the white distance between, until in the final stages one was brought face to face, possibly even touching hands.

That multi-leaved table became the heart of our family life: there we faced each other at breakfast, before we went out to face the day; there we returned for lunch, and sometimes for afternoon tea, with new experiences to share; and there we gathered for supper, and for the long evenings after it. It was large enough to give each member of the family, and our cousin boarders, a reasonable amount of work space. At one end Father would work at his books or play chess; halfway down the left side Mother would mend clothes or write letters; the rest of the frontage would be occupied by children busy with their homework or hobbies. While there were no silence rules, any distracting disturbance would soon be squashed by Father.

Christine reminds me how Mother would stop her darning about nine o'clock, saying that her eyes were tired or that she felt like forty winks. Chin in hand, she would promptly slip into a catnap of ten or twenty minutes' duration, from which she would emerge completely refreshed, and cry, 'Now let's have some fun! Dorothy, make the tea!'

Tea was everything to Alice: elixir of life, sinews of war, sedative, stimulant, social sacrament, individual rite. She would brew herself a pot at first light, and carry a cup to Ernest and to whichever child or visitor seemed to her in need of it — there was nothing predictable about this early-morning favour; then tea for breakfast, and at eleven — and at any time a visitor appeared. Somehow she managed to do without it at lunch, but she was busy brewing again by three-thirty. A tea-less supper was unthinkable, and she could not get through an evening without one other round at least.

After her 'forty winks' Alice got her second wind. While everybody drifted off to bed — or, if reluctant, was ordered to do so — she moved into action, and assaulted those household chores which she found it best to do on her own. One of these was to prepare the dough for her beautiful home-made brown bread. One stage in this process involved crushing a tough yeast-cake before mixing it into the meal. She had a short way with a yeast cake. Placing it on the pastry board, she would wham it with the rolling-pin. Sometimes — perhaps when she was getting rid of a hard day's frustrations — this single crack would jerk her entire family back into startled consciousness for a moment or two. (On one occasion a conscientious young policeman, thinking he had heard a gunshot, knocked on the front door to inquire if all was well.) Having wrapped the dough trough in an old blanket and set it on the side of the stove to rise, she would sometimes brew herself a final cuppa before consigning herself and her household to silence, darkness and sleep.

Until Godfrey and Neville Collett came to board with us, the spare room was let to a Mr Engelbrecht, who gave us boiled sweets on the sly, and spent the morning of the Sabbath in bed reading the *Sunday Times*. The huge bell of the Dutch Reformed Church could call as long and loud as it liked for him. Like Barend Vorster, he had broken away from his church. Still in candy-striped pyjamas, he would surreptitiously slip us the comics. Our parents disapproved of comics in general; comics on Sunday were a double sin. So we had to read them in secret. It is strange to think that the first person in my experience to break a ban on literature should have been an Afrikaner.

We were becoming more conscious of Afrikaners. We had already had Van Riebeeck twice and the Great Trek thrice in class. The latter saga, and its causes, seemed to be sung in and out of history class almost every year. Afrikaners presumably loved hearing about it, over and over; but it didn't fire my imagination, partly because the British were cast as villains of the piece, a disgrace they shared with the blacks.

Father was nothing if not practical, and he loved handing on his skills, of which he had taught himself many, such as cabinet making, carpentry, brick laying and simple but elementary metal work. And he was a good, patient teacher, starting his pupil off with simple tasks. If these tasks went on a bit longer than one found congenial, if one ached to go off and play with one's friends, he did not relent; tears and tantrums were of no avail. One such task was to demolish an old brick wall, built with Kimberley bricks (unfired bricks of dried mud) and plastered with lime plaster so old that it was friable. I was given a mason's hammer and chisel, and told to get on with it, and to save as many of the bricks as I could. These were to be ready stacked when Old Isak came to build the new hen coop.

It was hot and dusty work. As my hands were tender, and not yet large enough to grip a brick properly, I dropped more than one on my toes. The dust then made mud of my tears of pain and loneliness. I was only halfway through the task when Isak arrived — incredibly old, bent double, suffering from curvature of the spine.

Whether the ancient man had any inkling of the injured and rebellious frame of my young mind, I do not know. As I slowly demolished the old wall, he slowly built the new.

'Your father is a wise man to teach you a trade,' he said. Then later:

'I am very glad my father apprenticed me to learn a trade. You are always sure of work if you are a good tradesman.'

And again, much later:

'My father was born in chains; he was a slave.'

Now I knew that the slaves had been liberated in 1834. That date had cropped up twice in South African history classes, less as a laudable act of British conscience and justice to be applauded than as an act of British bungling — the compensation had been so badly managed that many otherwise happy former slave-owners trekked north in the name of liberty and efficiency.

Was it really possible that I was speaking to the son of a slave?

At lunch I asked my father how old he thought Isak was. He smiled. 'I don't know. He seemed old when I was your age, when he did odd jobs for my father. I think he'd come from the Western Cape as a young man. He used to be a marvel at plaster work — probably learnt it from the Malays who made those fancy Dutch gables.'

'He says he's the son of a slave,' I said.

'Well, if old Isak is 80, he would have been born in 1848. If his slave father was born in 1810, he would have been 24 when liberated; so he could have a son when he was 38 years old. Yes, it is clearly possible.'

The next day I watched him handling his trowel with a kind of reverence. The Malays had been brought to the Cape by the Dutch East India Company either as skilled artisan-slaves, or because they had been politically troublesome to the Dutch in their eastern empire. But none of this historical agony worried the gentle old man, exercising his skill, even allowing me to handle his trowel.

'You must skep just the right lot of dagga on to your trowel, and throw it right, like this,' he admonished me.

The act looked simple enough, but I never got near to mastering it.

One of the few Afrikaans-speaking friends I made at the Little Boys' School was Paul Michau, son of Piet, whose milk cart from his dairy farm, Braemore, five miles out of town, pulled up outside The Poplars every morning. A child or servant would be sent out with a jug of the correct size, which would be filled from a frothing tap in one or other of the two enormous milk cans strapped to the back.

Vacations, in theory, were heaven, the blessed isles. In fact, they were sometimes far too long, particularly for the parents, but also for the children. I can confess it now, in my later years, that towards the end of a holiday, I felt a pleasurable excitement at the prospect of returning to school. And I suspect that children on lonely farms felt this even more strongly.

I remember my surprise and delight at the warm welcome I got from Paul after one holiday — he flung one arm round my neck, crying, 'Once more we two together.'

A year or two later, I cycled out to their farm one Saturday afternoon, and there stood Piet Michau, burly, big in front of his door. I had never visited his farm before.

'Well,' he rumbled, 'what brings a little rooinek trespassing on my farm?'

I was petrified.

'Please, Mr Michau, I've come to play tennis with Paul.'

He put a hand the size of a spade on the back of my neck, and chuckled, 'Come inside, sonny, come inside.'

And then he bellowed 'Paul!' in a voice that shook the shutters. Paul appeared, and we went out to play game after game of indifferent tennis with his two sisters, Marie and Leta, who filled me with delight and awe.

Our friendship was interrupted when Paul was removed from the Boys' High School, Cradock, and sent to Grey College and Marie to the Collegiate, Port Elizabeth.

Yet that one brief visit endowed Braemore with a kind of enchantment; so much so that I once took myself off on a solo picnic to an ironstone koppie which overlooks it. My mother puckered her brow as she wrapped up my chop: it struck her as odd for a small boy to plan an outing for himself alone.

I climbed the koppie, gathered twigs, lit my fire, and grilled my chop. It smelt delicious. I was vaguely conscious that a car had stopped on the road below. Suddenly a huge man leapt up from behind a boulder immediately in front of me, and another to my right. They were as surprised as I was.

Having smelt grilling meat and seen a wisp of smoke they had suspected a sheep stealer. They had determined to stalk and catch the culprit red-handed. Feeling slightly foolish at their catch, they asked me what I was doing alone in the veld. I told them I liked being alone in the veld.

One said, 'Wragtig! Mooi so!' The other shook his head, grinning.

When I offered to share my one and only chop, they laughingly declined, and took their leave.

I ate my chop in the great silence, my fantasies ranging from being a Stone Age Bushman to playing tennis singles with Leta.

7

Grannie's Folk: The Colletts

In 1929 I moved from the Little Boys' School to the Boys' High School proper. For the next two years I acquired two intimate friends, my second cousins, Godfrey and Neville Collett, who came to board at The Poplars in order to attend school: Godfrey in standard 3 at the Little School, Neville with me in standard 4 at the Big. They were not strangers to me as I had already spent holidays with them at Katkop, their father's, Uncle Norman Collett's farm. For the next two years, apart from occasional visits to Vrede, nearly every holiday was spent with them, or on Blighty, the farm of Uncle George Collett on the Tarka River fourteen miles south of the town.

The twelve children of John Collett whom James Butler had met at Grassridge in 1878-9 were all still alive and well, and the Fish River basin was stippled with their children and grandchildren — nearly all of them farmers. The only exceptions were Lettie, her eldest daughter Mary, and her eldest son Ernest, and his family. Alice instinctively understood and appreciated the quiet, roomy trust and mutual acceptance which the members of all generations and branches of the clan displayed towards each other; and the Colletts knew that Ernest's wife was the sort of person they could drop in on almost any time of the day. On Stock Fair days — the second Tuesday of each month — Colletts came from all directions to take morning or afternoon tea with Alice, and exchange family news; and they usually left a pound of butter or a dozen eggs or a jar of honey behind.

It was from Grannie that we heard the great stories about James Lydford Collett, the Settler, the founder of the clan, parts of which are verifiable, parts refutable, parts dubious, but all interesting because they show what she had made of the past as told to her.

Born in the West Country in 1800, James Lydford Collett was indentured to a lawyer in Oxford. He had to work long hours for little money, and live with his master — in the attic, of course. He was doing well enough, but the lawyer was stern and James took to sleepwalking. A less sleepwalking sort of man — judging from the rest of his life — I cannot imagine. It was fine while he walked in his sleep round the attic, but one night he took to walking on to the landing, and then, believe it or not, climbed on to the banister itself, over the stairwell above the hall. He woke to find himself poised above the abyss. Appalled, he lost his balance, and plunged down. Grabbing wildly, he caught the vast glass chandelier, upon which for some magical seconds he swung amid the gentle tintinnabulation of crystals, until the chain pulled the plaster rosette out of the ceiling, and all crashed on to the Turkey carpet in a heap.

I do not recall whether he fled at once, or only after being thrashed by his cruel master, but leave he did, breaking his articles.

So in 1823 James Lydford Collett left Oxford — not yet called the City of Dreaming Spires by Matthew Arnold, nor yet the Home of Lost Causes, not yet the site of the Morris Cowley works; something closer to the Oxford of G.M. Hopkins:

> Towery city and branchy between towers;
> Cuckoo-echoing, bell-swarmed, lark-charmed, rook-racked,
>   river-rounded.

A century and more later, at least two of his numerous seed would haunt the place, serving articles of a different kind.

He made his way to the coast. Southampton? Portsmouth? Or was it London? — intending to get out of Old England, anywhere, but out. Not having a penny to bless himself with, he had to work his passage. He was lucky enough to be employed as tutor by an Indian Army officer returning to Bombay with his delicate wife and four energetic children.

James did not do well on the voyage. He was perpetually seasick; the officer was a worse tyrant than his Oxford master, his wife was a whiner, and the children were spoilt brats. On arrival at the Cape, the officer and family went ashore with their tutor. They all rejoiced in feeling the good earth beneath them, and took delight in the fine scenery and fresh food. James was allowed some time off. So enchanted was he, that he lost all sense of time. When he returned to the docks, he saw the ship already diminishing, sailing to India without him, alas — or was it hooray?

It was never quite clear whether this atypical enchantment, this loss of all sense of time, ought to be taken with a pinch of salt or not; but there he was, stranded once more; and once more without a penny. No innkeeper in the hardbitten port would give him a bed for the night. He wandered on and on into the wild continent — towards Rondebosch, I suppose — through the farms, through the deepening twilight and the sharpening cold, under threatening Devil's Peak. It came on to rain. He found somewhat original shelter for his first night in Africa in a Dutch oven, still slightly warm from the previous day's baking.

This highly symbolic incident, marking the Colletts' first identification with Africa, raises the hackles of some descendants. Gervase, one of Lettie's younger brothers, would have nothing of it.

'My grandfather never slept in any oven, least of all in a Dutchman's,' he said with crushing authority and a challenging glare. But others would say,

'Yes, in a Dutchman's oven, and without permission, what's more.'

Anyway he slept somewhere, woke up, carried on, and survived to tell a tale.

There's something curious about all this. Did he spin such yarns to delight his granddaughter Lettie? Was this the lighter side of his nature, suppressed by piety, hard times and responsibilities? I often wonder. Certainly, reading his diaries — forty years of them — no one would suspect much fancy, humour, or poetry; but then, who, reading the diaries of his fellow settler, John Ayliff, would believe him to be capable of the humour of *The Diary of Harry Hastings*?

The available facts about James Lydford's arrival in South Africa were few then. Lettie and others contended that he arrived *after* the 1820 Settlers, as late as 1823, and joined up with them in Albany. It is possible that certain Colletts invented this story bit by bit, as hard work, education and success raised them above average settlerdom. Each branch of the family has a different version of the origins and arrival of their Collett progenitor.

Professor Winifred Maxwell is currently preparing his diaries for publication, and the truth may well turn out to be stranger than the family folklore. I grew up with one volume of the diaries — presumably it reached The Poplars via Grannie. In the late 'thirties Aunt Mary, who has a proper sense of the importance of preserving records, harried Ernest into tracking down the others, and depositing them all in the Albany Museum. He had considerable difficulty in persuading some descendants to part with theirs.

In 1824 James Collett married Rhoda Trollip in Albany, where he owned a small farm near Port Alfred. When the frontier was thrown open, he became a successful trader, so much so that he was able to buy Olifantsbeen and several other farms on the Koonap River in the Fort Beaufort district. When the 1835–6 Frontier War broke out he refused to seek shelter in Grahamstown, preferring to continue on his farm. Of his grim experiences during this time I shall write more later in this chapter. A progressive stockbreeder who imported Merino rams from New South Wales and Saxony, he was able to lend £200 sterling to his brother Joseph, who had emigrated to America with sister Elizabeth — a debt which Joseph never honoured. In 1842 he bought three large farms in the Cradock district. Based on Groenfontein, west of the town, in the direction of Agtersneeuberg, he soon gained a reputation as one of the most progressive farmers in the district. He was chosen to represent the district in the first Cape Parliament in 1854, but attended one session only. In 1857 he sold Groenfontein, and moved up the valley to Dassie Kranz and Salt Pans Drift.

The tide of his fortunes now turned, and the long ebb began. Drought and recession drove him to bankruptcy in 1862. All his farms were sold and the proud old tiger had to accept the hospitality of a cottage on Mulberry Grove, the farm of his son-in-law, Joseph Trollip, who gave the old man a few fields to cultivate, but would not allow him to run a single sheep

— a limitation he deeply resented. From these humiliations he was redeemed by his most successful son, John, who had recently built a magnificent house on Grassridge, and who placed him on Dassie Kranz. Each of his nine children contributed one hundred sheep to set him up once more, but it seems that relationships were difficult and strained. How else does one explain the entry for his 65th birthday: 'Spent the day very quiet in our lonely Dassie Kranz Cottage and ate our Plumbpudding (alone) for as none were invited none came.' Several of his children were within an hour or two's ride. Once again the estimable John took pity on his isolated parents, and built them a new cottage closer to the main road, but it soon became painfully obvious that the old man's right hand had forgotten its cunning: he could no longer control his labourers or look after his flocks. After a frightening incident with a defiant servant, John intervened, and removed his parents to the old premises on Grassridge. There he died in 1875.

His patient widow Rhoda had suffered much. One cannot help sympathising with her, caught between a self-willed, dominating husband and nine energetic children. On more than one occasion, after one of his more violent bouts of buying and selling farms, of quarrelling and trekking, she collapsed into the comparative safety of temporary insanity. It is touching to observe how old James Lydford, the main cause of her distraction, suddenly ceases to be the self-willed egotist: all his care for his own concerns disappears in his great solicitude for her. After his death she went to live with her childless daughter at Daggaboer; and there James Butler met her, in 1877, a grieving old widow in need of consolation.

There is no room for the fortunes of eight of his nine children; only for the briefest of glances at John, his eldest son, the patriarch of Grassridge: a strong, steady and devout man, whose success as a farmer grew out of his close observation of the habits of his animals and of the shrubs and grasses which fed them. His observation of people was equally close, and he disapproved of impulsive expressions of ill-informed opinion. During some divisive scandal in the district he heard his wife speaking her mind with an emphasis and authority which he found unwarranted. He stopped her — and the conversation of which she was the centre — with the succinct sentence, 'Mary, you don't know All.'

Some thought him a hard man; others said that no man without a bit of ironstone in his heart could farm in the Karoo. Aunt Mary tells the following stories about him.

Someone's baby is desperately ill. Grandmother and Mother do all they can. The great encyclopaedic *Home Doctor* has been consulted. Folk remedies have been tried. At breakfast, after watching all night his wife says, 'John, the child is worse. You must send for the doctor.'

There is a pause. Then he says, softly but firmly, 'Will the child last till he comes?'

Aunt Mary explained: 'You see, there were no telephones, no trains, no cars, and a horseman would take four or five hours to reach Cradock — provided no rivers were down of course. He'd be lucky if he found that the doctor could leave at once; and the doctor would take four or five hours to get back. So the round trip was a matter of ten or twelve hours at least. If the child was past help, why bring the doctor on a futile errand? Merely to keep the young mother's hope alive when the child was past praying for?'

He expected, and would receive, considered answers to such apparently heartless questions.

A terrible storm starts building up in the late afternoon. The atmosphere darkens as for an eclipse. The sheep and cattle make for shelter — some seek it in the dongas, which will soon be drowning-deep. John orders the men (mainly his sons) to bring the stock near the homestead to shelter, and to drive the beasts out of the watercourses. One of the men is a young bywoner.

The storm, a great dark blundering beast, breaks loose. The lightning flashes and stabs, thunder cracks and rumbles, and water comes down on the roof so loud that you have to shout to be heard. Darkness closes in. Lamps are lit. One by one the men come back — except the young bywoner. An hour passes, the storm continues. His young wife in velskoens comes to the house, soaked to the skin.

'Waar is hy?' she asks.

'Ek weet nie,' says old John.

She stands in the doorway, her back to the doorpost, staring into the pouring dark; waiting; waiting; waiting. Young Mary can bear it no longer. She goes up to her grandfather and cries:

'Grandpa, why don't you send the men out to look for him?'

Softly, firmly he says:

'I'm sure he's been struck by lightning. You do not send living men to look for a dead man.'

Later, the thunder passes into the distance, the sky splits into fragments reeling across a calm, remote moon. The only sound is the sound of running water. John orders the men out. He is right. They find horse and rider dead.

Of Grannie's generation — children of John — the two who first impressed themselves upon my mind were Uncle Herbert and Aunt Jessie.

Herbert Collett of Salt Pans Drift was a quiet, short, erect bachelor with a trim white beard, who always wore a white topee. He was supposed to be enormously wealthy. He certainly never forgot to slip a tickey into each grubby Butler palm, always accidentally but punctually hovering at the wicket gate before he left The Poplars after tea with Alice. He usually came with his sister, Jessie, who kept house for him; a somewhat severe spinster, hard on pretty young nieces and their friends, but, we were always assured, with a heart of gold. To dispose of her butter, eggs and other produce she would be driven into town every Friday by one of her nieces, Enid, who had the sharp features and bright eyes of a bird.

There was one room in The Poplars which was called Aunt Jessie's room. It had a vast brass double bedstead in it, with a canopy and swinging side curtains. She never slept in it that I can remember, although she might lie down and rest there for an hour after lunch. Parcels would be left there for her to pick up, that was all. It was never used as a spare room either.

I recall this quiet reserved void in our rackety house with unease. One would occasionally steal into it. The lace bed curtains were yellow with age. The wallpaper had faded. There was nothing in any of the cupboards or drawers, except two copies of *The Sphere* of about 1908, in one of which was a gorgeous slender lady in white lace, a tight waist and a shapely bust — my first wicked pin-up. With curls piled on the top of her head, she looked at me sideways, smiling, with a fan held lightly in her hands — the kind of gear mother would have aspired to wear, I suppose. Not Jessie. Jessie would have been that age *before* the Boer War.

But why the room? I can only think that Ernest and Alice insisted on keeping it free for Jessie and Herbert because, as I was to learn much later, Herbert had come to the financial rescue of Letitia and her high-principled Quaker husband more than once. Or did Jessie hire the room to do good by stealth?

Nearly all the Colletts were men and women of few words. For instance, there is the story of Herbert and his farm manager, Nixon, an inefficient fellow, something of a blusterer. During one of the droughts, he came up to Herbert on the stoep and said:

'Mr Collett, I'm resigning.'

No response, just a nod.

'I'm trekking to Alexandria. Decent climate, good rainfall.'

A pale blue stare for reply. In a last effort to get some response, Nixon rolls his head at the boiling sun, wipes his forehead and cries:

'The Karoo's only fit for Colletts and Hottentots to farm in.'

No response.

A year passes, and Nixon is back from Alexandria, jobless. Smiling, he approaches the stoep, his story ready. He removes his hat with a little flourish, but before he can so much as utter an ingratiating word, Herbert says, deadpan, softly:

'Well, Nixon. So you're back in the Karoo. And you're not a Collett.'

And then there was a story which Uncle Jim (later Senator) Butler got from the old Boer general, Kritzinger, who had met Herbert before that tragic war. Herbert had already established himself as a fine breeder of horses. Unlike his younger brothers, Dudley and Norman, he did not join up, but bred remounts for the Army.

Salt Pans Drift is near Fish River Station. Kritzinger was coming down the valley from Teebus, I think. At some point he needed to cross the railway, to reach the Agtersneeuberg, and hole up before making for Graaff-Reinet; and he needed new horses, forage, food and clothes for his men. News of his approach was known, of course, and one of Herbert's young Afrikaner bywoners deserted.

Herbert, alone at Salt Pans, knew that the young rebel would show Kritzinger all the possible hiding-places for horses; so he drove them to a neighbouring farm, into a corral formed in the middle of a huge poplar bush.

Midnight. A half moon. Frost. The little cavalcade draws up between the farm house and the stables. Kritzinger dismounts and knocks on the door.

Herbert lights his bedside candle.

Kritzinger knocks again.

No response.

Kritzinger strides along the stoep to the glimmering window and shouts: 'If you don't open your door, I'll break it in.'

'It's open,' says Herbert.

Kritzinger strides down the passage into the bedroom.

' 'Naand, Herbert,' he says.

Herbert nods.

'Where are your horses?'

'You can find them.'

Kritzinger looks grim, gives some orders. Four or five riders on tired horses move away from the house in different directions.

'Where's the forage? My horses are hungry.'

'You can find it.'

But it seems that the Boers have found it already, and are flinging it into the yard, in heaps from the hay loft.

'My men need meal, flour, sugar, coffee. Where's your pantry?'

Herbert picks up the huge bunch of farm keys and flings it over the brass foot of the bed. The general fields it expertly.

'Which room?'

'The one that's locked, of course.'

'Which key?'

'You can find it.'

They found it.

Kritzinger went off then for a while, leaving a ragged, shivering young Boer in the bedroom to keep Herbert company. When he returned half an hour later he found the young fellow beautifully dressed in Herbert's worsted Sunday best. This was too much for Kritzinger. He demanded of the youngster how he dared to loot the wardrobe of the man he was guarding.

The young Boer stammered that he didn't mean to take the best suit,
only the corduroys and the working jacket hanging over the end of the bed,
but the oubaas had told him No, he'd better maar choose a suit from the
kas.

'Herbert, is that so?'

Herbert nods.

Kritzinger tells the young man to go and drink coffee, and turns a sharp
eye on the man in the bed.

'What's the game, Herbert?'

'A month's wages for twenty men in the trousers, that's all.'

The two smile at each other faintly. Then the general makes some observations on the weather and the war. Herbert says nothing; his only response
is a nod or a grunt.

'We'll be going now. Good night,' says the general. At last Herbert takes
the conversational initiative.

'Don't forget to shut the front door behind you.'

Kritzinger swears that Herbert had nipped the candlewick before he
closed the front door.

It sounds incredible, doesn't it? Staying in bed, while all that is going on.
But how sensible. Why, when you have to lose your forage, a good suit,
and the contents of your pantry, run the risk of catching a cold as well?

There are many many other stories in the same vein about Collett deliberation and quietness. And they've usually got a horse in them somewhere.

Norman was younger than Letitia, Jessie, or Herbert; and he had married
late, so that his children arrived more or less at the same time as his nephew
Ernest's. So we grew up with Uncle Norman's sons, who called our parents
Cousin Alice and Cousin Ernest. I count this accident of Norman's late
marriage as one of the great good fortunes of my life: having children of
the same age gave our parents common ground.

There's an old piece of Germanic wisdom that every young man needs an
uncle as a second father: an adult male sponsor who does not suffer from
the disadvantages that adhere to the mere biological begetter — or, as we
would say, someone about whom the growing boy will have no Oedipus
hang-ups. For many years Uncle Norman was my favourite uncle. That
says a great deal, for I was blessed with many uncles. Uncle Frank Biggs
may have eclipsed Norman for some time and in certain respects, but, tall,
rangy, in his dark waistcoat and khaki trousers, with a drooping moustache,
just like the Sheriff in the cowboy films, Norman was the magical man,
warm hearted, humorous, and, for a Collett, loquacious. In fact, one of his
quieter relatives once referred to him as 'that chatterbox'. This was unfair.
It suggests speaking to no effect. Norman never did. When he spoke, men
listened; and when he got into a reminiscent vein about his boyhood or the
Anglo–Boer War, he held a young audience in the palm of his hand, or,
changing his tone, he would have them rolling on the springbok mats in

mirth. He could make the most impressive bass sounds, coming deep out of his throat and chest like a 'volstruis bromming'; and he could roll his eyes for dramatic or comic effect. Also, he smelt of Magaliesberg tobacco: he wielded a pipe, that marvellous extension of masculinity. Some Colletts allowed themselves this indulgence. Butlers and Biggses never did. It was even rumoured that on rare occasions — during a campaign, or after a cold springbok hunt, or gemsbok shooting in the Kalahari during the winter — he might even take a snapsie of brandy. This may be nonsense, of course. In all my visits to Katkop down the years I never saw drink taken or offered.

What was it that differentiated Norman from his brothers and sisters? I suppose he gave his emotions a slightly freer rein than those about him on those stony vast farms, and he had a marvellous sense of humour.

As for his wife, Gladys Hart, descended from that pre-1820 settler, old Robert Hart of Glen Avon, Somerset East: slim and tall she seemed, dark haired, with a slightly sing-song voice, infinite patience with the young, and a sense of humour which matched her husband's. I do not remember her telling many stories, but rather as encouraging an intelligent interest in nature, the mysterious creatures of the veld, of the lands, the orchards, the poplar bush, the dam — all parts of that complex miraculous universe, Katkop — plants, particularly succulents; insects, animals, birds, and stones. Fossils, for instance: it was at Katkop that I was first made aware of the petrified life in the stones beneath my velskoens: fish in the recent shales; ancient lizards the size of short-legged oxen, in the older Karoo beds — 300 000 000 years old. And over them grazed the new animals, warm-blooded mammals, selectively bred by men — Norman's sheep and an ever-diminishing number of horses.

These beautiful creatures were disappearing before an invading American beast — the motor car. Norman acquired a Buick, but not before I had had sufficient experience of travelling in the buggy, high up off the ground, with the horses jogging along the two parallel footpaths through the miles of Karoo bush which constituted the road. Most frequent was the trip to and from the Fish River Station; or to Grassridge, to see Aunt Katie and Uncle Dudley and their adopted daughter; or to Groenkloof, to see Uncle Walter and Aunt Bremmie; or to Speelmanskop to see Uncle Bertie and Aunt Annie; or to Salt Pans to see Uncle Herbert and Aunt Jessie; or to Retreat to see Uncle Jack and Aunt Agnes. It seemed that at a certain distance along any road from Katkop you would find another hospitable uncle and aunt, with a different sort of house, and a different sort of orchard, and a different sort of water supply, and a different sort of afternoon tea. What more can a young child ask of life?

The longest trip I ever did in the buggy was at the end of a holiday — all of 28 miles into town. We got up before dawn. I can remember the morning star shining still and liquid above the bobbing black of the horses' heads; and the clear silhouette of the Speelmanskop mountains against the pale

dawn sky. And the ritual of opening the many gates; and one's hands
folded under the rugs, night air burning cold on one's cheeks.

Once Norman and Dudley were going to Stock Fair in the buggy along
that road — that old, old road to the north. Shortly after setting out,
Norman said to Dudley, as he dismounted to open a gate:
    'I'll give you £10 for that horse.'
He opened the gate, the buggy went through, and he resumed his seat.
Silence, immense miles of silence. Two days later, on the way back, they
came to the same gate. Norman duly opened it. The buggy drove through.
Norman resumed his seat.
    'Norman, it's a deal,' said Dudley.

Old John of Grassridge had been a great breeder of horses, and his many
sons had spent their early manhood breaking in the beautiful beasts. The
stories they told about horses were endless. One did not believe them all,
of course, but there was always something about them that made them
stick in the memory, which is the test of a good story, surely; like the one
about their grandfather James, the Settler, also a man with an interest in
good horses.
    It is 1854, and James Collett has been elected as Cradock's member of
the first Legislative Assembly, meeting in Cape Town, some 650 miles
away. On arrival in Cape Town (after how many days on the road?), he
looked for stabling for his horses, and found the price asked exorbitant.
He did a rough calculation as to how much it would cost to keep them in
Cape Town for the length of the session, and arrived at a figure which
would be sufficient to buy two new horses in Cape Town. So he took his
old horses to the outskirts of the town, and let them go. At the end of the
session he bought two new horses, inspanned them and returned. And sure
enough, he found the other horses back on his farm — after fifteen days,
according to tradition.
    Of course I didn't believe a word of it. But whichever uncle told me this,
said, 'You see, there were no fences anywhere in those days, only beacons,
and kraals, and shepherds.'
    After the Hitler war, in a second-hand bookstall off the Tottenham Court
Road in London, I picked up an 1842 edition of Captain Cornwallis Harris's
Wild Sports in Southern Africa. This engaging gentleman, an officer in the
Indian Army, feeling out of sorts and in low spirits, decided to cheer him-
self up with the healthy delights of the chase in Africa. With a friend and a
Parsee servant, he arrived in Cape Town in 1836; he was directed to Port
Elizabeth, which he reached on a small coasting-ship; thence to Grahams-
town, where he picked up some unreliable Hottentot servants; thence to
Graaff-Reinet, where he equipped himself with wagons, and bought horses,
several from the Richmond district.

Eventually we find him at Moselekatze's kraal at the very time the Matabele are attacking the Boers at Vechtkop. His hunting was almost ruined by the carelessness of his Hottentot grooms, who let some of the horses graze without knee-haltering them. Days of search failed to find them. The Hottentots did not look very hard. 'You'll find them back on the farm in Richmond,' they said laconically. And so he did, months later on his return.

This made me think again. Perhaps the story about old James Collett and the horses was not so impossible after all. So the next time I saw Uncle Norman, I asked him if he knew of any other instances of horses finding their way home across hundreds of miles of territory. He paused and said:

'Yes, Walter's horse, Prince. It was that time when Mr Rhodes was having some trouble with the Pondos. So a commando went all through the Transkei to Pondoland. I don't remember what happened there, but I think they fixed it up without fighting. Anyway, Prince cut his pastern very badly on a rock. So Walter got a remount, and let old Prince go. Just let him go.

'I was cleaning out the pig-sties with Boesak the old Hottentot. I was still quite a youngster. He said, "Luister." We could hear the odd sound of a lame horse on the road. And then we looked over the stone wall of the sty, and there was old Prince hobbling along, clippity clop.'

What horses can do in other parts of the world I don't know, but in 1837, 1854, and 1894, they knew how to find their way to the Eastern Cape from the Marico, Cape Town and Pondoland respectively, all distances in excess of 400 miles.

There is another anecdote about old James Collett's trip back from the first Cape Parliament — the same trip as when he let his horses go and bought two new ones. It is shortly after the War of Mlanjeni, the longest and toughest of the Frontier Wars — not least because many of the Hottentots (Khoikhoi) had made common cause with the Xhosa, which cast doubt upon the loyalty of the rest. (What would have happened if the Fingos, or Mfengu, had not stayed loyal to the whites, God alone knows.) Two young Trollip nephews had been ambushed by rebel Cape Corps soldiers near Daggaboers Nek, and had been killed.

En route from Cape Town, James had plenty of time to think. He was about twenty years older than the man who had gone through appalling experiences at the end of 1834 and early 1835; on one occasion he had discovered in the moonlight the body of his 'faithful Faltein', his Hottentot herdboy, lying with his throat cut in the empty cattle kraal.

It is clear from the sequel that the Hottentots were much on his mind, as were other issues likely to be discussed in Parliament: frontier defence, the Coloured franchise, the mission stations.

As I recall the story, old James, tired and harassed, experienced something of a crisis with his buggy and horses at some dry drift, with the heat blazing up from the earth and down from the sky. The nature of the difficulty needed an extra pair of hands for its solution. And there, squatting placidly in the only bit of shade for miles, was this Hottentot, who simply watched, who didn't even bother to say good day. Not even that.

The story was told me as an example of the difficulties that old British-born James had in making himself understood in Cape Dutch; I am not sure of the exact words attributed to him as he exploded, whip in fist, but they went something like this:

'Ik gaan na de Kaap, dage en dage in de son, om de groot, groot sake reg te maak vir u, en u kan niet eers seggen goedendag.'

The Hottentot is reported to have left his piece of shade in haste shouting: 'Goedendag, Baas! Goedendag!'

Who was *he*? What was *his* story?

There are other stories about Colletts and their horses.

There's the story of Dudley, for instance. Was it the Boer War or the 1914 Rebellion? Some men were mending the telephone wires which the Boers had cut. The Boers, still close at hand, shot and wounded one of them. Dudley rode in, dismounted, lifted the wounded man on to his pommel, and rode out again.

Norman was with a column chasing Smuts up the Langkloof. He was lying behind a stone during a skirmish near Haarlem. The weather was hot. He was firing away. Then he felt he was sweating abnormally. He put his hand inside his tunic — and brought it out, scarlet and sticky with blood. He had been shot through the shoulder, and had not felt a thing.

The wound was slow in healing. He spent some time on sick leave with his sister Lettie in Cradock and then went out to Grassridge. He was still in uniform, of course, and very weak, with no energy at all.

Advance news reached the homestead that a commando of Boers was approaching. His young brother Dudley took all the rifles off the rack and hid them most ingeniously in the quince hedge alongside the dry furrow — the grey slender shapes blending with grey stems, camouflaged by shadow.

Sure enough, a few minutes later the Boers cantered up to the front of the homestead. Norman, still in uniform, lost his nerve for a moment, and fled down the passage, out through the garden, and then sat down to think at the back of the kraals.

'I didn't know what to do. At last I said: No, dammit, I'm not going to let them find me hiding like this. So I got up and walked inside again. They did nothing to me.'

The Boers bivouacked for the night along the furrow. They did not spot the rifles. They left some time during the night — possibly hoping to capture Herbert's horses.

During this period one of the Butler children was being driven to Grassridge in a buggy by one of the younger Collett relatives, who had just acquired a new pair of boots for best. The old pair was in the cardboard box on the floor of the buggy. On one of the ridges, they met a buggy coming in the opposite direction, and, as is common in such cases, the two vehicles pulled up, and the occupants started to exchange items of news, particularly about the war. One of the adults pointed to the horizon, above which a feather of dust could be seen, and then a cavalcade of horses. No one made any comment, but young Mr Collett unlaced his new boots, and put on the old pair, walked thirty metres from the vehicle, hid the new boots in an antbear hole, returned, resumed his seat in the buggy, and continued the conversation. The child was totally mystified.

The cavalcade drew closer. They turned out to be Tommies, 9th Lancers, not Boers. They rode past, with an exchange of greetings. Mr Collett then retrieved his boots from the antbear hole. The buggies went their divergent ways.

'Why did you change your boots? Why — ?'

'If they'd been Boers, they'd of had them off of me for sure, you see.'

One evening at Katkop, after a story-session, either Godfrey or Neville suddenly said, 'Dad, are Quakers any use in war-time?' My stomach bunched with shame. But I needn't have worried. The dear old man puffed his pipe and said, 'Yes, man. They go into the Medical Corps, like Cousin Jamie.'

'And what use are the Medical Corps?' continued my temporary persecutor.

'Wait until you're wounded, and then you'll see,' came the reply.

When the government of the newly-formed Union of South Africa was busy drafting its Defence Act (1912), James Butler led a deputation to Cape Town to seek exemption for conscientious objectors, and was granted an interview by the Minister of Defence, J.C. Smuts. He met with partial success. As a result, Jeffrey and I, as minors, could be excused from Cadets on our father's affidavit. During Cadet periods, I sat all alone in the classroom, in fact alone in the whole school, feeling an outcast and a pariah. I *suppose* it did me good. One *can* survive alone. I doubt if it affected anyone's thinking on the topic of war.

Then came the great day — the Cadet sham-fight. Blank ammo. was issued to the 'troops'. Among the latter were Godfrey and Neville, who were boarders at The Poplars at the time. Excitement grew as the Friday drew near. I determined to take part, in secret. I found out where the 'battle' was to be fought, went early and waited in the milk bushes above the 'Slippery Rocks'. Sure enough, I was soon joined by my cousins. In due course, the shooting began. What an exciting, echoing din! And how quickly over! It takes no time at all to fire three rounds of blanks.

Godfrey and Neville, as boys familiar with rifles, had foreseen this and come with an extra supply, of live ammunition from the farm. Of course

they blazed high into the sky, but a live round gives an unmistakably different crack from a blank, and in no time a panic-stricken schoolmaster/officer
was on the scene.

'Who's firing live ammunition?'

The Defence Force officer in charge was so shaken that he called an
immediate halt to the exercise.

Godfrey and Neville returned to The Poplars, sheepish and crestfallen. I
thought Cadets was fine fun — for one afternoon.

I never told my father of this betrayal of pacifist principles.

In the late 'twenties Uncle Norman enlarged the homestead at Katkop by
two new stone-built rooms on either side of the front door. He went to
great trouble to secure yellowwood for the floor of the new sitting-room:
that honey-coloured indigenous timber had been all but forgotten in the
'twenties.

The mason was a picturesque old man called Barter, a legendary figure
who was and who wasn't part of that landscape. Born in Belfast, he had
spent the early years of his youth before the mast whaling all round the
world. He was a great dropper of place-names like Valparaiso, San Fran-
cisco, Sydney, Greenland, Singapore and the Shetlands; his vocabulary
included nautical items such as the roaring forties, halyards, southerlies,
belaying-pins, monsoons, mainsheets and doldrums; and his heroic adventures were all with blue and white whales and other coloured monsters of
the deep. Seated on a paraffin box, his rough hands dusty from trimming
a block of ironstone instead of gleaming with whale oil, he would spin
yarns that transformed the arid landscape into ocean and wave, farmers
into sailors, houses into ships.

I believe much of it was sheer fancy. According to his own account, he
and a friend had tired of a certain tyrannical captain, lowered a boat and
rowed ashore one night in 'Aligoa' Bay with a quantity of loot including
the captain's telescope. They went to earth in the dense bush, where they
nearly starved to death. Stealing into the port, they learnt that a price of
£20 had been offered for any information that might lead to their arrest.
But once their ship had left the Bay, they found a pawnbroker who gave
them a pittance for their stolen goods. They turned inland, chastened and
humiliated. Again, they nearly died of hunger. Eventually they apprenticed
themselves to master masons who were laying the railway line north of
Kommadagga. Barter built culverts and bridges from there over every gully,
sloot, donga and river as far as Fish River Station; and there old John Collett hired him to build a stone weir across the Brak River on Grassridge.
He then moved from farmer to farmer, serving in various capacities. Mr
Gilfillan of Conway sent him up to the Eastern Transvaal to look after his
game farm, whence he returned to kill jackals for the four farmers whose
boundaries converged on Doornberg. Jackal-proof fencing was still a thing

of the future. Such were the depredations of these creatures among their
flocks, that they offered him £5 per pelt. He is reported to have killed as
many as 75 in a single year. One of the farmers was Norman Collett, then
farming at Woolwyn (Botmanskop). At some time Barter had married a
Hottentot, by whom he had three children.

In 1926 Uncle Norman hired him to do the alterations to Katkop homestead necessitated by his growing family. By this time Barter's wife had
died, and he was looked after by his daughter and her husband, a handsome,
swaggering Coloured man called Kameel. His family was something of an
embarrassment to his employers. Accommodation was difficult. As he could
not properly be housed with the whites, the Coloureds or the blacks, he
usually ended up with the horses — in part of the stables, or, if the farm
had one, in the chapel.

He'd been so long with Afrikaans-speaking Coloured people that he sometimes thought in Afrikaans and then translated his thought literally into
English, e.g. to set something alight was always 'to stick it on the brand'
(iets aan die brand te steek).

I recall him as a gentle, fanciful old fellow, whom Uncle Norman liked
except for one trait: he and his family had a taste for turtle soup — a taste
no doubt deriving from his nautical days. As there were no turtles in the
Karoo, he used tortoises instead — the grand old mountain tortoises. Uncle
Norman told him that he must not poach his tortoises, and was furious
when he found one of the creatures — no doubt being saved for a week-end
party — scraping its way round and round the dry inside of a large soap pot
under the blistering sun.

On one occasion at Katkop during this time, when Aunt Gladys was absent,
the weather turned bitterly cold.

'It'll snow tonight on the Renosterberg,' said Uncle Norman. After supper
he and Jimmy Lister, a young man who was learning to farm, and the children, all gathered round the fire for a talk. All males together. The hearth
held a generous blaze, and Uncle Norman was in fine narrative form. Suddenly there was a loud knocking on the door and shouting outside.

'Seer, seer, die huis die brand,' cried a panting Coloured man who had
seen the blaze from the other side of the river.

We rushed outside. The chimney was on fire. Barter had but recently
finished plastering it and, in the careful manner of old-fashioned masons,
he had covered it with sacks to let it dry out slowly. The only real danger
was that the heat of the blazing sacks might set fire to roof timbers. I recall
the flame-lit shape of a man on the top of a ladder against the black sky,
with a long pole in his hands prizing the sacks loose — and their smoking,
blazing descent to earth. Then the knife-cold wind drove us inside once
more.

The time has come for the lambs' tails to be docked. Uncle Norman and one of the old shepherds stand behind a table at the exit to the kraal. With a very sharp knife he cuts the tail off. He does something else to them, which I am told turns them into hamels. Shy of betraying my ignorance, I do not press my question. (The nature and necessity of castration in animal husbandry remained a mystery to me for another season, until Neville pointed out the difference between a bull and an ox. 'And', he added, 'you couldn't inspan sixteen bulls.')

The docked lambs do not seem to complain any more loudly than those still to be done, and I am relieved to see that they do not bleed much. Reassured, I find Godfrey and Neville who have taken shelter out of the cold wind on the other side of the kraal. They have made a roaring fire of mimosa branches. Into this they cast lambs' tails. The smell of burning wool mingles with the mimosa scent, soon to be followed by the smell of roasting fat. They hook the now-thin black tails out of the fire. As soon as these are cool enough, they seize the tip of the spine in one hand and grip the skin in the other, and pull them apart: a long silver morsel appears from the black sheath, juicy and delicious. The black and the yellow children join us and we all gormandise. Our faces, forearms, shirts, knees are shining with fat until dust and ash darken them.

Suddenly I feel nauseous. Maybe my dislike of mutton fat dates from the next half hour, spent heaving behind a wolwedoring. The farm-bred boys laughed at my weak stomach.

Normally we were saved from excesses of this kind by Tembile Mtoybile, a Xhosa lad a few years older than Neville, whose double duty it was to amuse us and keep us out of trouble. He was a wizard at both. He bore the badge of being Tambukie (Tembu): the third finger of his right hand was short of the final nail section. Tambukies are thus deprived in infancy, for mysterious reasons.

There was on Katkop a small-scale ox-wagon — its bed was a mere six foot long. The wheels were exactly like those of a real big wagon, so was the undercarriage, the 'voortang' and the 'agtertang' — everything authentic from the brake to the disselboom. It had been made to scale by Uncle Norman and old Langjan Mafilika, who was a skilled tinsmith and blacksmith. (Old Langjan was one of the few blacks in the neighbourhood who had the vote — the old Cape franchise had not yet been abolished.) Since this wagon was too small for any draught-animal to pull, you might be tempted to say, What a useless object, but you would be wrong. It was designed to be drawn by four big boer goats. True, the goats, being clever, could not be subdued to the yoke, but special suits of harness, not unlike a horse's, had been made for them from leather cured by old Langjan himself, who used pounded mesembrianthemum to remove the hair, and rooibos for tanning. The whole exercise had no other purpose than to amuse Norman's sons: the small-size wagon was a large-size toy.

The goats — those aromatic, horned old gentlemen of the veld — did not take kindly to their transformation into draught-animals; and they made their resentment known by butting us hard into the dust whenever they could. Having managed to inspan the two agterosse after half an hour's battle, we would turn our attention to the voorosse; but by the time these were under control the agterosse had wriggled free or broken their traces or tied themselves and the harness into inextricable knots. In due course under Tembile's tutelage, man triumphed over the brute creation; I and the younger boys would pile on to the wagon, with a large picnic basket, Tembile would act as voorloper, Neville would work the whip and Godfrey the brake. 'Trek!' shouted Neville, and we would be off along the road that led to the river. The journey was never without its mishaps and adventures. The goats saw to that.

At our destination we would outspan the goats in a small camp, and enter the deep river bed. There we would find a long, deep pool with clean river sand on one side, strip to the skin, rush in and swim till the dust and smell of goat disappeared in cool sparkles and rings and splashes of water. Then we would find long water-polished boulders, and fry on them like kippers; then back into the water, ducking about like coots or otters.

Suddenly we would all change direction at once — as pigeons in flight seem to do — into the reeds to rifle the vinks' nests; then back to our clothes, where we would find Tembile already busy frying our chops; then up to the weir to inspect the great iron wheels that worked the sluices; and so across the fine wire suspension bridge above the dark water, one by one, in case it snapped under our weight — adventure upon adventure, hour after hour, until the setting sun and weariness told us that it was time to return to the wagon, and to the glowering goats.

This was the critical moment. By now, after all our labours, we were exhausted, but the goats had spent the entire day renewing their strength.

The battle of the morning had to be refought under a sunset sky. The greatest dangers to success were human impatience and frayed tempers. Quarrels were imminent. Again, it was the tactful Tembile who maintained our discipline and morale.

The defeated goats had a hard pull back. Godfrey and Neville, deciding that the whip and brake were redundant, had climbed on with the rest of us. Tembile the voorloper remained on the job, and brought his charges safely home.

A stranger on a Karoo farm suffers various handicaps, not least of which is the size of the establishment. In small stone or brick huts of various vintage, and frequently sited at some distance from each other, dwell the labourers and their families, as many as a dozen households with innumerable children. They are likely to consist of two main groups: Hottentots (Khoi-khoi) with a greater or lesser mixture of white blood, the descendants of peoples who had been here long before the black or the white men arrived. They have lost their language and speak Afrikaans; they have lost their religion and are Christians of various shades. Their features are sharp and wizened, their hands small, their skins range from apricot through dusty yellow to leather brown. Their women are small boned and shrill voiced, and seldom put on weight.

Then there are the heavier, handsomer blacks, whose families had arrived in the valley at various times since the Difaqane of the early nineteenth century. Some of them still have links with relatives in the Transkei or Lesotho, and visit them.

Aunt Gladys made her kitchen oven available to Sanna the cook, to bake bread for her family. To her surprise, she did not take the trouble to mix yeast into her batch of dough the evening before, with the result that her baking was sad — real doodgooi. She reprimanded Sanna sharply. The cook replied, 'Ag, Miesies, they're just a lot of Kaffirs'. She may have meant they preferred their bread unleavened or she may have lost heart and interest, having just produced her twelfth and thirteenth children — a boy and a girl twin, whom she asked Uncle Norman to supply with additional names which white people could pronounce. He obliged with Max and Climax.

Amongst the Xhosa themselves there were clear distinctions between Tembu (Tambuki), Gaika and other tribes. Most of them were Christians, but they clung to many old customs and beliefs. They still spoke Xhosa amongst themselves, but the day-to-day business of the farm was conducted in Afrikaans. Indeed, few farmers liked to be addressed in English by a black man: it upset them, signalling a mission background, education, attitudes and expectations which were not suited to their humble, unskilled status on the farms. Most farmers found it difficult to imagine — let alone accept — a black man outside the master-servant relationship. The lingua franca of the Karoo farms is Afrikaans to this day.

Then there were the animals: thousands of sheep and goats; cattle — many cows and oxen and maybe one lonely, morose bull; and, of course, the horses. The horses all had names, and so did the bull and the milch cows and the trek oxen. Some of them, as the result of intimate association with men in the work of the farm, assumed almost human dimensions: every quirk of their individuality was known and commented upon, their strengths and weaknesses discussed. A particular ox who worked well on the left of the disselboom might be useless on the right. This horse was best for a long canter, that for a tripple.

The townee would sometimes be at a loss to follow an evening's discussion of the day's activities. He would hear that Daisy's baby was sick with the croup, and then that Daffodil's new calf was pretty. A name like Prins could signify a Coloured man or a stallion. Was 'Old Jacob with the ewes in the top camp' a Wanganella ram or a shepherd?

The mechanisation of farming has destroyed something of this close association of men and beasts.

An old horse that had served Uncle Norman for many years was allowed
to range freely, and never required to work. He enjoyed his retirement for
several years. After a severe winter his old master said sadly, 'I saw old
Wellington today. His rheumatism is really bad.' And a year later, 'It's
time to shoot old Wellington. The poor chap's getting no pleasure out of
life any more.'

The next morning a group of horses, old Wellington among them, were
driven on the gravel patch near the wagon house. The men stood at a distance round the animals, who moved about a little, as they waited patiently
to be harnessed. We stood behind Uncle Norman. When the other horses
had moved so that he had a clear view of his old steed, he lifted the .303
up to his shoulder.

I had never been so close to a rifle shot. I was doubly shocked: by the
loud detonation; and by the sight of Wellington, who seemed to be standing
deaf and still among the other now excited horses. Had Uncle Norman
missed? Suddenly the old horse crumbled in a heap. The clean *coup de
grâce* had found his brain.

His kind executioner strode into the house to put the rifle on the rack,
leaving a sharp whiff of cordite in the air.

In the 'fifties, when I was trying to write a play about the Anglo-Boer War,
in which a colonial Englishman appears as a scout with the British army, I
asked:

'Uncle Norman, how did you chaps get on with the Tommies?'

He looked at me a moment, and then said:

'Guy, those fellows was always getting lawst.'

And he proceeded to give some hilarious and some pathetic accounts of
Tommies stolidly marching, in terrible conditions of heat and cold, under
enormous packs, miles off course — as many as twenty miles wrong. Instead
of marching due east, the subaltern had marched them due west. Things
like that.

'Those poor Tommies. Those poor foot soldiers. Mind you,' he said, 'it
was the horses I felt sorriest for. Ridden into the ground. Broken. Horse
after horse.' He paused. Obviously some recollection which he could not
put into adequate words was upon him. He lifted a bony hand and pointed
into the west: 'The finest horse I ever had — his bones lie there, on the top
of the Naude's berg.'

I said nothing. After a moment or two he knocked out his pipe, got up,
and walked inside.

8

Boys' High School

Few boyhood autobiographies are complete without at least one beating from a brute of a master and a vicious fight with another boy. This chapter disposes of both. I don't believe that they differ markedly from the usual except perhaps in their social and political ambience.

In 1929 the Cradock Boys' High was still in its old premises between High and Bree Streets, an unloved red-brick barracks smelling of disinfectant and dust. Although below the furrow, the site was without lawns or gardens of any kind. The playground was a bare expanse of gravel, with some dolerite boulders here and there, flanked on the north by a row of twisted and gnarled bluegums.

To the south ran a long quince hedge. Real intelligent planting, those quinces. A 'kweper-lat' was the sanctified instrument of correction for Karoo boys, and every school of any pretensions grew its own supply of 'latte'.

We had already heard how one of the senior masters used that hedge. When an offender stood in front of him he would say, bending the stick between his hands, 'Buk!' Then before striking the expectant victim, he would deliberately snap the stick, and cry in mock surprise:

'Dried out! No pliability. Here, take my knife, and go and cut me another.'

So the offender would go out, with the master's pocket knife, and cut another 'cane'. On his return, his offering would be inspected by a professional eye.

'No, man, this is no good. Too thin. It will cut right through your skin. It must be just about the thickness of your little finger. Try again.'

The matric class called this master a 'real psychologist'.

But to return to the 'playground'. 'No-man's-land' would be a better name for that unpredictable desert. The most dangerous spot of all was the oasis — the one water tap. Here the trouble makers would wait, the predators, the dinosaurs — boys, from 15 to 19, who found immense satisfaction in pinching you violently in the buttocks, or 'screwing your neck' as you bent over the tap, or throwing a fist-full of dust into your cupped hands just as you were about to sip the water. But these primitive beasts were comparatively innocent and tolerable. The real devils were the Machiavellis who liked violence but always at second-hand. They didn't want to fight themselves, but it amused them to see others maul each other. The more blood streaming from faces on to fists, on to shirts, on to shoes, on to the soil, the better they liked it.

Their classic war-mongering gambit was perfectly simple. All you have to do is persuade peace-loving A to kick B's grandmother. Then B simply has to defend the family honour, and not only kick the other fellow's grandmother, but punch him hard, preferably on the nose.

Now, any boy who ever got within kicking distance of my real grandmother, and who so much as looked her straight in the eye — why, he'd be worthy of the V.C. But the cunning devils did not bring our real grandmothers on to the playground at all. The dear old ladies were left to their tea parties, ignorant of how the blood of their descendants was being spilt into the dolerite grit in defence of the family name. These Machiavellis were symbolists. They provided grandmother-substitutes.

You would be standing there talking to your friend, when suddenly the two of you would be totally surrounded by four bland, smiling, big fellows. One would bend, and make two little heaps of sand between the two of you.

'Butler,' he'd say, 'that's your grandmother; and Knaggs, that's your grandmother.'

If there was any scepticism or delay in acknowledging your sandy progenetrix, he would grip the tendons behind your neck, and say, smiling:

'It *is* your grannie, isn't it now?'

Having tortured us into accepting our descent from the heaps of dust at our feet, the master of ceremonies would continue:

'Tell me, Knaggs, are you afraid of Butler?'

'Of course not.'

'We don't believe you,' and 'Prove it!' the big chaps would shout.

By this time a crowd would have gathered.

'Knaggs is "bang" of Butler!'

'I'm not.'

'If you're not, kick his grandmother!'

And Knaggs, being a fellow whose reputation as a man of courage was at stake, would kick Butler's grandmother. And Butler would have to retaliate and kick Knaggs's grandmother flat. There was nothing for it then but fisticuffs and blood.

There were no prefects at that school. But, from what I hear of some prefect systems, I am not sure if it would have helped very much. We would have had organised, semi-official gangsterdom, instead of free-enterprise. Boys have a need to be aggressive somewhere, sometime, somehow. It's one of the few justifications for organised sport, which might be described as controlled catharsis of the aggressive instinct. Or does it encourage it?

In standard 4 or 5 we had a geography teacher called Olkers — powerfully built, with heavy features. He never explained anything. He would start a ninety-minute afternoon session by saying, 'Learn Japan.' He would then take out a newspaper and swot the sports page before turning to politics. After an hour and a quarter he would fire questions at us; and if we had not committed all the facts about Japan to memory, we would be caned. He loved the cane.

In most classes there is a lightly built, intelligent fellow, who loves excitement, but is clever enough to persuade others to create it for him. When the explosion occurs, he is the innocent spectator. Such an honest Iago in embryo was Bobby Thornton.

Three o'clock on a Thursday afternoon. The chapter on Turkey having no further charms for me, I was busy practising my Boy Scout knots on a fine piece of whipcord under my desk. Olkers was dozing on his dais, head on his folded forearms, which in turn lay on the newspaper spread on the table. Very hot and somnolent it was. The boredom was thick as lard. Then Thornton slipped a note to me.

'Do you think Hough is asleep?' it read.

Hough, a clumsy, fat fellow, was sitting in front under Olkers's nose, head on his arms, almost a replica of his schoolmaster.

'Yes,' I scrawled, and returned the note. The reply came back.

'Bet you won't tie his foot to his desk.'

Hough's right foot was stretched backwards, and perfectly aligned with the iron support of the desk seat.

I crawled along the aisle; no one reacted in too noisy a way; but by the time I got back to my desk almost the whole class was awake and watching. Only Olkers and Hough dozed on. The tension mounted as the minutes ticked by, and back in my seat I began to wonder how it was going to work out. Thornton was hugging himself.

Olkers woke up, and glanced around. He was no doubt alerted into suspicion by the watchful, expectant faces in front of him. All except Hough.

Olkers stood up, and bellowed down:

'Hough! Staan op!'

Hough woke up, and stared up at the giant towering above him, mouth open, goggling.

'Staan op!'

Hough leapt to it. The result was that he fell into the aisle, and pulled the desk over on top of himself. Amidst roars of laughter and exclamations of delight the class rose to get a better view, the chaps at the back of the room climbing onto their desks. Poor Hough took some time to discover that his foot was attached to the desk. He was in such a state of terror that he couldn't undo the knot.

'Who did this?' thundered Olkers.

'Me, Sir,' I admitted, genuinely surprised at what practising my Boy Scout knots had led to. Olkers, enraged, gave me three violent cuts across each palm, and three across the buttocks..I went back to my desk, wondering how on earth I could have been so stupid. And there, ahead of me, was

Thornton with a grin on his face. What happened in my mind at this point I do not know, but I grinned back.

The grin was clearly of that unfunny kind that sticks to one's face like a mask long after it should have left it. Olkers saw it as I sat down.

'So you think it's funny? Come here!' he bellowed.

Then with icy fury, he repeated the caning in full.

I didn't cry. But my mind was screaming.

Even Thornton stopped smiling.

Olkers started his questions on Turkey. I was the only one whom he questioned.

I wonder what would have happened if I had answered incorrectly. He was clearly looking for an excuse to thrash me again. Had he done so, I suspect that I would have attacked him like a mad dog. Buttocks and hands burning and throbbing, trembling from head to foot, I had to speak through gasps for breath.

Good schoolmaster, Olkers. He knew how to keep discipline and got us to respect facts.

Afrikaans in the junior school was taught by 'Buggie' du Toit — who made no effort to disguise his strong Nationalistic convictions. We had to choose a poem from our poetry book, and learn it off by heart. I selected a simple ballad about a small thorn tree growing alongside the road. One day a heavy oxwagon tramples it; but it is resilient, recovers and grows into a big tree; but the scar left on its stem grows bigger with the years.

I recited this with great enjoyment:

Daar het 'n doring boompie
Vlak by die pad gestaan
Waar lange osse spanne
Met sware vragte gaan.

I sat down, expecting a word of approval. I had completed it without a stumble. But Buggie was glowering at me, in a puzzled way.

'Butler, you chose a poem which no Englishman should ever recite. I hate people who side with the enemies of their own people.'

It then dawned on him that I was blissfully unaware of the allegorical meaning of the piece: so he had to spell it out. The little thorn tree was the Afrikaner volk; the oxwagon was the British Empire. The Afrikaner thorn tree could forgive, but it could not forget the injury inflicted: it was part of the very fibre of the people. I told my father about this. And he said that the Anglo–Boer War was the worst mistake the British ever made, and that people had long memories for injuries and short memories for benefits.

Buggie was not a bad old chap. He took us for singing. There was a part-song which went:

List to the bells,
Beautiful bells,
Bim, Bom,
Beautiful bells,
Rhyming and chiming their melody swells,
Bim, Bom,
Beautiful bells.

And so on *ad infinitum.*

The carillon of our treble voices on a weekday was very different from the solemn iron tongue of the single bell in the D.R.C. steeple, summoning the people to service on the Sabbath; a bell so much more powerful than the bell of St Peter's Anglican church, or the Angelus of the Convent to the north near the Park, or the distant forlorn tinkles down in the location: if not the King of Cradock bells, it was their President. An Oom Paul of a bell. Particularly on winter evenings, at dusk, it filled the whole valley for miles with a grand, cold resonance.

Buggie was a man of principle all right, and my father respected him. There was a crisis when a fiat went out from the Director General of Education for the Cape Province that all the schools should learn 'Land of Hope and Glory, Mother of the Free', to be sung on the King's Jubilee, or some such occasion. Buggie refused to teach it. Feeling ran high, and he had plenty of supporters. He stuck to his guns.

There was no music whatever in the senior school.

National and political tensions seeped into us from all directions, and from none more memorably than from the songs we were required to learn and sing. I have already referred to 'God bless the Prince of Wales'. 'God Save the King', at that time the only national anthem, would be sung on public occasions — with many Afrikaans people standing silent as posts. Every cinema performance ended with this imperial reminder, and great would be the outcry if a Nationalist refused to stand for 'The King', or walked out during the playing of that indifferent tune.

'The King' would sometimes have to keep company with 'Afrikaners, landgenote', whose tune I preferred, though I dared admit this to none. The latter was gradually replaced by a new patriotic song called 'Die Stem' — words by C.J. Langenhoven, music by the Rev. M.L. de Villiers and Stephen H. Eyssen (1919). We learnt it, and sang it with varying degrees of enthusiasm. We approved of the evocation of our country in images of deep seas, blue skies, desolate plains, but we did not respond particularly to the creaking of oxwagons; and we were not sure whether our patriotic sentiments had penetrated to the marrow of our bones. 'Die Stem' had two great disadvantages: it was much longer than 'The King', and its assertive, even jaunty tune demanded far more of the human voice.

It was said of one of the less musical Bowkers that he knew only two tunes: 'The King' and 'Rule Britannia'. He sang both with patriotic verve, but no bystander could tell the difference.

Many years later I sat on a committee appointed by the Minister of the Interior, Dr Dönges, to establish the text of an official English version of 'Die Stem'. It proved to be untranslatable, but all things are possible to committees. 'Die Stem', with an awkward English version, was officially recognised as the national anthem in 1957.

There was, however, another patriotic South African song, which one heard with increasing frequency, usually in Aunt Mary's company. It was written by a schoolmaster in a Methodist mission school, in a poor African township called Nancefield or Klipspruit, eleven miles west of Johannesburg, in 1897 — before the Anglo–Boer War. Enoch Sontanga was his name, of the Mpinga clan of the Tembu. Unlike 'The King', which is a prayer to God to save the monarch, to give him victory, glory, happiness and a long reign; unlike 'Die Stem', which is a thoroughly secular and romantic promise to respond to the call of personalised South Africa and to live and die for her; 'Nkosi, Sikelel 'i Afrika' is a devout prayer to a Holy Spirit to descend and bless Africa.

Lord, bless Africa;
May her horn increase;
Hear Thou our prayers,
And bless us.
Descend, O Spirit,
Descend, O Holy Spirit.

Mqhayi, the great Xhosa poet, by adding seven stanzas to Sontanga's single plangent cry, converted it into a litany. The prayers become specific: for our chiefs; for our public men and our young men; for matrons and maidens; for ministers of religion; for crops and herds; for education and understanding; for an obliteration of iniquity; and each stanza ends with the choric plea for the Spirit's descent. The African National Congress adopted it as a closing anthem for its meetings. Its impeccable Christian credentials were established by its inclusion in the Presbyterian Xhosa Hymn Book of 1929.

It is not the words, not even the tune, that move me; it is the manner in which it is sung: the reciprocity of trebles and bases, men to women; lyrical cry and lament in flight over a great epic surge and throb. It marries agony and aspiration, blood and spirit, as only the greatest hymns of Christendom can.

Every few years the spiritual climate of the Boys' High School would change for the better. If a fight should be deemed necessary to liven up the tea break, no one needed the pretext of kicking grandmothers. The adult world, as the result of a mysterious activity called politics, was working itself up to a crisis called an election, in which we felt totally involved. In our experience, political humanity at this time was entirely white, and was divided into two species or races: Nats and Saps. Nats were all Afrikaners; Saps were mostly English, plus Jews, and some very brave Afrikaners. If you were a Nat it was your sacred duty to fight for your language and the Vierkleur; if a Sap, you knew you were fighting for Britain, the Union Jack, and progress. The Anglo–Boer War was refought on the playing-fields of the B.H.S.

It was the 'swart gevaar' election, but the flag issue was still much in our minds. The papers came out at intervals with coloured supplements illustrating designs which might solve the knotty problem. But the extremists in Cradock would settle for nothing but the Union Jack or the Vierkleur.

Those flags were as provocative as the grandmothers. You could draw them, for instance, in a subversive way, on the cover of your enemy's scribble pad, or on the blackboard before the class entered. And they encouraged our appreciation of the metaphor of insult. To call the Union Jack a 'rooi spinnekop' was definitely cleverer, but was it more, or less, insulting than 'die rooi vaddoek'? The Sappe found no metaphors as vivid as these.

The nastiest nickname we found for the Vierkleur was 'Kruger se sakdoek'. That a Rooinek should suggest that the great President would blow his nose on those sacred colours unleashed a retaliatory stroke of near genius in a big stoker's son. He produced a small Union Jack at tea break, waved it over his head, and invited all and sundry to follow him to the latrines, where he would show them what it was fit for. This was more than the Heathcote twins could stand.

George and Charlie Heathcote, aged about 11, took on this giant, whose face they could barely reach with their fists. He was so confident that he said he would clean them up with one fist tied behind his back. It was a terrible fight, two fox-terriers versus a lion. As I recall, it was a draw. As the crowd dwindled on the summons of the bell, another fight started, but was immediately postponed till 'after school at Rookers' Hoek'.

At Rookers' Hoek, the illicit smokers' site within easy distance of both the school and the boys' hostel, one could fight without hindrance from the school authorities, who were legally entitled to stop brawls in the school grounds only — a right they never exercised, to my knowledge.

This contest was between 'Bul' Kotze (Nat) and Dick Stone (Sap). It did not last long. Bul was an impetuous, powerful boy, who stormed on to Stone like a bulldozer out of control. Stone attempted a crafty piece of footwork — a sidestep, and a duck; but he tripped and fell, spraining his right wrist. (Some say he was tripped by a boy with the sinister name of Marx.) When he regained his feet it was clear that he was in great pain. After receiving two black eyes and a bloody nose the sensible fellow gave up. Amid roars of triumph, Kotze was carried shoulder high up Hare Street by the victorious Republicans, leaving the Royalists to mutter and sulk in the shade of the pepper trees — which, incidentally, provided a dangerous grandstand from which dozens of smaller boys could stare down into the shifting hole in the human crowd below, which formed the ring.

The next day Stone appeared at school with his wrist bandaged and his arm in a sling. His desk happened to be close to Bul's in class. By lunch time Stone was near to tears. I asked him, 'What's up?'

'He says my arm makeers niks.'

So I told Bul if he said that again, I'd be happy to donner him up 'into a raw sosatie'. Before you could say knife, everybody knew that there was another date with destiny at Rookers' Hoek.

Now, my father was a Quaker, and a man of peace, and he strictly forbade us to settle disputes by violence. Disarmament was an ominous issue in the early 'thirties, when Italy and Germany started rearming, and Britain and France were trying to keep out of the arms race. Our home was full of pacifist literature, some of it containing horrific photographs of corpses in dugouts, rags and bones on barbed wire in no-man's-land. My father frequently expressed his contempt for two ancient militaristic clichés which his non-pacifist friends kept using:

'If you wish for peace, prepare for war.'

'The best defence is attack.'

Father pointed out that the first piece of advice simply encouraged militarism and the arms race, and the second invited any powerful state to invade its neighbours on the pretext that it was doing so in self-defence. But while I had a certain theoretical grasp of some of the philosophies of pacifism, I was deficient as a peacemaker. I should have said to Bul, in a gentle voice, after offering him half a tomato sandwich at tea break, 'Bul, you won your fight with Dick. Why don't you leave him alone?'

But I was also very confused about the whole philosophy of conflict, armed, bare-fisted, or what-have-you. For instance, chess. Father was a keen chess player and often exacted a game or two from me in the evenings. There you have them, two medieval states at war, a war to the finish: castles for square defence, knights for a crooked flank attack, bishops for long-range influence; and there was Ernest, a real general, preparing for war on all fronts, supporting all his pieces in case of attack, building Maginot Lines which I found impenetrable; and while I was still timidly getting familiar with the shoe-maker's opening (beyond which I have not advanced) and looking in dread at his serried ranks, he would detect aggressive intent in me, and launch one of his devastating defensive attacks.

Apart from well-supervised bouts, with huge gloves, in the Scout Hall, I knew nothing about boxing. The idea of hitting anyone in the face, with the naked fist, horrified me. I did not know what to do with my arms, except that one ought to push one's 'left' out in front, and keep the right for two deadly strokes — the uppercut and the right hook. A proper uppercut was supposed to connect with your foe's chin; this would lift him clean off his feet, his eyes would close, and sparks and stars appear all round his head. This was common knowledge, from the comics. The right hook was not quite as spectacular; it simply propelled your foe sideways through the ropes.

So I decided to finish Kotze off quickly. The best defence is attack; a right hook followed by an uppercut should do the trick.

Kotze had similar ideas. The upshot of the first contact was this: the two right hooks embraced the two heads; there we were, having missed each other's ears, locked in an unholy embrace. My mouth was full of Bul's brilliantined hair.

One of the big boys separated us, and we tried again. Every time I defended myself by attacking, I got a swipe on the left ear or the right ear, and none of my uppercuts or hooks connected. I didn't sail through the ropes, because there were no ropes, but I was twice floored on the gravel, with a fine view of spectators' knees and boots. It was all very unexpected and humiliating. My mouth was full of the taste of blood. As I was being lifted to my feet for the third time by one of the big boys, he hissed:

'Lead with your left. Put your weight behind it.'

I heard Bul's friends shouting:

'Hy's klaar! Moor hom!'

Which he came on in fine style to do. I advanced with what little strength I had left, and thrust out my left fist, fast, straight from the shoulder. It met the advancing Bul full between the eyes. The shock almost dislocated my shoulder. Bul swayed, his knees turned to putty, and he sank on to the gravel, 'lights out'.

Now my real troubles began. There I was, being carried shoulder high along River Street towards Church Street, my swelling lips cut to pieces, and eyes, it seemed, fast closing. I was far more scared of my father's reaction than I had been of Bul. It took much kicking and shouting to persuade my friends to put me down, and leave me alone.

I crawled through the hedge at the bottom of our garden, found the nearest garden tap and tenderly washed my aching face. My head was buzzing inside like a swarm of bees.

September, our garden boy, came up, looked at my face and bloody shirt, cried out 'Kwok!' and made sympathetic clicking noises with his tongue. It was now about a quarter to four. Father usually got home about five-thirty. Supper was at seven. Three hours to remove all evidence of the fight. How quickly would my eyes go blue? I asked September to call Chrissie, our cook. Somewhere I had heard that raw steak applied to the face was good in such cases; and also a liberal application of Reckitts blue.

Having exacted an oath from a very distressed Chrissie that she would tell no one, I persuaded her to bring these medicaments and a clean shirt to my hide-out behind the lucerne stack.

And there I lay, waiting in the afternoon sun for the muti to work. I must have looked a sight — like an ancient Briton, my face woad-blue; on top of which lay the steaks, which I kept moving about.

Raw steak has a tiresome smell after an hour and a half. I heard five strike, and then six. I got up, stripped, and washed myself very tenderly. No mother ever washed her first baby with more care. Then I put on the clean shirt.

How to make a suitably casual approach? Take it from the front gate. Come down Bree Street, whistling. I tried to whistle. My bruised lips refused to co-operate. So I came in down the passage, which was dark.

Nobody seemed to notice anything. Why should they? In a routine home-situation people do not continually inspect each other for battle scars and scratches, because, perhaps, they are too preoccupied with their own.

Eating my boiled egg I said to myself, 'What are you afraid of? As a pacifist, Dad can't resort to violence. He's never touched you — well, not in years.' Then it dawned on me that my greatest dread was his disapproval. He would be angry. His moral force was enormous. Perhaps, perhaps I would get through supper. And perhaps there would be no black eyes at breakfast.

In the detective stories, the criminal is frequently caught out by the last person he thinks capable of doing so; and usually by means of a clue he had not considered. Sitting opposite me was Christine, the most placid, least troublesome of my three sisters. In a pause in the conversation, she said:

'What's the matter with your hands?'

I looked at them, guiltily. They were swollen, and had a couple of cuts on the knuckles. Bul's teeth, no doubt. I slipped them under the table.

'Nothing,' I said, too late. Mother was staring straight at me.

'My boy,' she exclaimed, rising, and moving to my chair. 'Ernest, just look at the child's face! Who's been bullying you? Ernest, some beastly brute has been beating your boy!'

'Calm down, Alice,' he said. Alice did her best, trying in vain to lift me, big as I was, on to her lap. I felt a real fool, and infinitely reassured.

'What have you been up to?' Father demanded, looking at me hard. There was no option but to tell the unvarnished truth. Well, perhaps a *little* varnish remained on it. For example I omitted my threat to turn Bul into a raw sosatie. My speech had been reason, sweetness and light, all along.

'Well,' he said, 'it could be worse. You got involved on behalf of a friend. You didn't get violently engaged on the political issue.'

But Alice exploded. 'Ernest! The boy has been hurt. Look at him. He's been beaten!' Then Ernest: 'I gather he's beaten someone else.' And then: 'Come, dear, don't take it to heart so. Boys will be boys.'

He never took the matter further. He had bigger worries, which he was at pains to conceal from us.

A note on Bul Kotze. We got on well after the fight — never friends, but mutually tolerant. He left Cradock before senior school, I think.

During the autumn of 1944, in the Apennines, the Sixth South African Division was fighting a grim set of battles for the possession of a series of high points along a ridge commanding two highways into the Po valley near Bologna. One of these high points was Monte Stanco.

I was up on one of the roads, watching one of our regiments filing up a steep track through the cold, dripping, golden chestnut woods. There were three faces that stay with me: one of a boy I had taught at St John's College four years before, pale, abstracted expression, his Bren across his shoulders; another of a happy-go-lucky Rhodian who had introduced my bigoted mind to the real meaning of Jazz; and the third of Bul Kotze, sweating under the base plate of a mortar. They had a rendezvouz, were already in a dream, a nightmare, where the past was irrelevant. They counter-attacked that night, for possession of a hilltop already strewn with the bodies of South Africans, Sikhs, Germans; a hilltop under heavy, cold mist.

A little more than a week before — 29, 30 September and 1 October — on the other side of the ridge for which we were fighting, the German S.S. Command had gone mad, morally mad, and committed atrocities of an horrific kind, slaughtering about two thousand men, women and children in what has been described as one of the most gruesome episodes in Italian history.

There is a difference between the proper use of force, and indulgence in the heady drug of violence and revenge. I often ponder the words of Pascal (*Pensées*, 285):

Justice without power is powerless;
power without justice is tyranny.
Justice without power is defied,
for there are always wicked men;
power without justice is condemned.
Justice and power should therefore be combined,
and to this end the just should be made strong,
or the strong be made just.

9

Settlers, New and Old

Life in Cradock during the 'twenties and 'thirties was deeply affected by the building of two dams, both on tributaries of the Great Fish River: Grassridge, on the Brak River, on Uncle Dudley's farm; and Lake Arthur (named after Prince Arthur of Connaught, the Governor General), on the Tarka. Grassridge water was responsible for feeding the weirs and canals all down the valley — Baroda, Marlowe, Cradock, Scanlen, Halesowen — as far as Mortimer; Lake Arthur water took over after the confluence of the Tarka and the Fish.

The prospect of permanent water raised hopes in thousands of hearts, and millions of pounds went into surveying, levelling lands, building fences, sheds, houses. It was Louisvale on a titanic scale.

But there was a major difference: Louisvale was not named after the Prime Minister Louis Botha for nothing. Dan and Frank Biggs were selective about those to whom they sold holdings. There were a few British exservicemen, a handful of South African English speakers; but the vast majority were Afrikaans-speaking supporters of Botha and Smuts.

What made the Cradock scene different was the large number of new settlers from Great Britain itself. Many of them came under the aegis of the 1820 Settlers Memorial Association — a body founded in Grahamstown during the centenary celebrations of the landing of the 1820 Settlers. Its main brief was, and is, to bring British settlers to South Africa. The association went further: it established the Tarka training farm, to teach young settlers the rudiments of farming in Africa. We saw very little of these gay bachelors, most of whom were more interested in horses than farming. Our contact was mainly with the children who came, and more rarely with their parents.

First, a general observation about the nature of the English-speaking community in Cradock — which was probably typical enough of most East Cape towns. Most families were descended from 1820 stock, with some admixture of post-Kimberley arrivals. All were aware of Britain: it was a perpetual point of reference, the touchstone, if you like, on almost every issue. To quote a few examples: few English-speaking South Africans felt the need for a South African flag, let alone a national anthem other than 'God Save the King'. It was only on Father's insistence that we were polite about the first and learnt to sing the second with a good grace. When the

Nationalist government decided to establish ISCOR, I can recall something of an outcry: the steel would be more costly and less good than British steel. Those were the great days of 'Buy British' campaigns. The Union Jack appeared stamped on countless articles; and if possible one avoided articles made in Germany, and more particularly Japan. As for America, there was a curious attitude of superiority towards the U.S.A. — in spite of the American films, American music, and American cars, which between them were changing the external and internal behaviour patterns of life in the valley. Some — including Father — observed these changes with dismay: particularly the courting habits of young people. A dashing young man in an American coupé was obviously better equipped for the seduction of innocent Karoo maidens than a dashing young man on a horse; the horseman could only sit in the front parlour, or in the summer-house, subject to inhibiting interruptions.

What kept Britain close was not politics or economics; it was people. I think it would be true to say that every English-speaking child in the town had at least one parent or grandparent who had been born in Great Britain. A high percentage of the parsons and ministers were English or Scots; and then there were these new arrivals, whole families of settlers.

Down the valley, at Mortimer, were several such households; and up the valley too, for instance at 'Swinside', where the Bladens farmed. Most of the families that we came to know were Anglicans: they used to come into Cradock for evensong, and always for the eucharist at Christmas and Easter; if for the former, they would have supper at The Poplars; if for the latter, breakfast. Real feast days they were, greatly enjoyed by all except Ernest, who, although always impeccably polite and courteous, never 'clicked' with Alice's English middle class and Tory friends — mostly ex-army and -navy people.

The family I recall best were the Winters: they had two girls and a boy. Even then I recognised that girls from other families had a kind of interest for me that my sisters, those girls indigenous to The Poplars, could not match. The Winter girls were fair, pink, romping, laughing. One was not inappropriately named Felicity. We would play 'ghosts' in the darkened house, and other spooky games after church — and those girls screamed with excitement and delicious terror.

One of the highlights of Cradock's social season was the Red Cross Ball. It was followed the next evening by the Junior Red Cross Ball, when the young fry were treated to the stale trifles and wilting jellies left over by their elders and betters. Some elders and betters came, of course, to cluck over their daughters and to see that their boys behaved themselves.

It was at the 1929 Junior Ball that two such mothers, both new to Cradock, found themselves in conversation: Mrs Winter, wife of Colonel Winter, D.S.O.; and Mrs Gould, wife of the new Anglican Minister, the

Rev. Charles Gould, M.A. (Cantab.). The Goulds had been in South Africa some time; indeed, all their children had been born in the country. Their previous parish had been Cathcart.

The evening started badly for the Winter family. The son Peter had been forced into a very pretty Fauntleroy outfit, with frills all down the front, and silver buckles on his slipper shoes. He took one look at the off-the-peg serge suits of his colonial coevals, and fled to the gents', whither he knew that not even his redoubtable mother would follow him. His sisters, Felicity and Angela, whose dresses were equally out of key, having sat expectantly for the best part of an hour, were beginning to droop. On the other side of the hall sat the two Gould boys, Charlie and Astley, doing absolutely nothing.

'Aren't your boys ever going to ask my dear girls to dance?' asked Mrs Winter.

'I'm sure they will,' said Mrs Gould, rising and walking across to them.

'Charlie, Astley, please get up and ask the Winter girls to dance.'

'She's too big,' said Charlie, eyeing Felicity.

'You're quite as tall as she is!'

But Charlie replied: 'She's too big sideways. And one leg of her frilly knickers is showing.'

'Well,' said Mrs Gould, 'her mother can get her to rectify that, I'm sure.'

But Charlie had disappeared into the gents', where he struck up a friendship with the other refugee from the terrors of high society.

Mrs Gould turned an imploring eye on Astley.

'Please,' she pleaded.

'How much?' he answered.

'Threepence a dance.'

'Double it, and it's on,' he said.

Astley danced alternatively with Felicity and Angela for the rest of the evening. Mrs Winter declared, over the many cups of tea which she had occasion to sip during the next month, that the youngest of the parson's sons was a perfectly charming young man. Astley bought cigarettes, and held smoking parties in the hayloft of the old rectory stables.

Colonel Winter did not survive as a settler: the irrigation scheme failed to produce the promised water; he lacked experience in farming; and Mrs Winter no doubt looked on the social life of the valley with horror. But there were other families that stuck it, although the dice seemed loaded against them. I think particularly of the Bladens.

Harold Bladen went up to Jesus College, Cambridge, at a more mature age than most, and read history. He joined the educational branch of the Indian Civil Service, became headmaster of a college in Gwalior, and later was tutor to the eldest son of the Nawab of Junagadh. There he stayed from 1909 to 1920, when the Prince reached his majority. Harold was now just 40, and had recently married. He had no desire to continue teaching. In India he had grown to love animals, particularly cattle, and his instruction of the Prince had given him considerable theoretical knowledge of agriculture, but both he and his wife Nell were townsfolk with no practical experience of farming.

En route to England via the Cape, he made tentative inquiries about farming possibilities in South Africa. Sir Thomas Smartt, the Minister of Lands, gave him a glowing account of developments in the Fish River valley. The Bladens continued their voyage to England, but after a decade in India Harold found he could not endure the English cold, and decided to go farming in South Africa. After arriving with his expectant wife and baby daughter, Joan, in Grahamstown, he went on by himself to Cradock, where he bought a piece of land 'below the furrow' from Mr Willie van Rensburg. He named it 'Swinside' because the shape of the ironstone hill on the farm reminded him of that feature in the Lake District.

In due course his wife Nell arrived with her firstborn, Joan, and the new arrival, David, by Cape cart. The drought was severe, and many cattle had died. She approached her new home through a black confetti of crows and a stench of carcasses.

Harold put in 900 apple trees and 600 walnuts, but it was a bad farm for fruit, being subject to late frost, and many trees died because Grassridge dam failed to supply the promised regular water. But they did not give up; they diversified their farming, grew lucerne for cows, made butter, ran poultry, produced vegetables for the local market, and bred pigs.

For the first few years their transport consisted of a buggy. Nell would come into town, with eggs and cream, with potatoes and apples, and deliver them herself to private customers. When Aunt Mary asked her why she did not employ a kwedien to lug the provender from car to kitchen, she would say, 'That would eat up the little profit.'

Aunt Mary had got to know Nell in 1923. In conversation she spoke of her sister-in-law, who had come from Stone, Staffordshire — the very place from which Harold Bladen came. Inquiries established that Harold had been on walking tours of the Lakes with Alice's brothers.

A visit to the Bladens was always memorable. There was a kind of holy poverty there. The little house may have needed plastering and a coat of whitewash, but inside one was given a feast of apple tarts (home made), walnuts (home grown), or date biscuits and small sandwiches daintily served by Nell. Nell, said my mother, was 'an absolute saint'. Everyone deferred to Harold, whom Alice once affectionately referred to as an 'old tyrant'. Deep in his Morris chair, his bald, sunburnt head shining like polished mahogany, he seldom smiled; but he spoke incisively and interestingly. He knew a great deal about economics and agriculture, and from his firm if limited base of Swinside wrote letters to the press, telling all the successful and rich farmers in the district how mistaken their farming methods were. Those letters! In them one felt the triumph of the intellect and the English language over alien landscape and circumstance.

One day, out at Swinside, Harold said, 'Do you know anything about Rupert Brooke?' Dorothy lit up, ready to quote 'If I should die, think only this of me,' but his pale-blue-eyed glare cut the sonnet short. 'I knew him at Cambridge. An evil man.' This startled us. We knew, of course, that poets like Shelley and Byron had been gloriously guilty of romantic irregularities, and perhaps we hoped he would hint at elevating agonies of that kind. But all he would add by way of explanation was, 'He was diabolical. He had a devil.' What did he mean? A less demonic poet it is hard to imagine. Had Rupert stolen Harold's girl? We were left guessing, hanging over the fence, looking at a farrow of pink piglets greedily imbibing from a happily grunting sow.

Swinside was good to experience: it showed how manners and cultivation can triumph over hardship. For instance, birds. That family knew about birds like no other family in the district, except perhaps the Jameses, down at Halesowen. And through their knowledge of birds — their calls, nesting habits, number and colour of eggs in a clutch, migrations — they had an intimate entrée to the seasons, the cycles of weather and growth. By following the flick of a hedgebird's wing or by noting the first arrivals or departures of distant migrants, the Swinside people grew to know the natural life of the valley in a way many older families never achieved.

As birds were to the Bladens, so bees were to the Airds, who had a small farm below the Scanlan weir. The Airds were Scots, both teachers, who had come out to South Africa shortly after the Anglo–Boer War in response to Lord Milner's appeal for teachers prepared to civilise and anglicise the land.

William Alexander Aird was a tall, thin man, with a small sandy head, perched on a long wrinkled neck, up and down which his Adam's apple danced like a yo-yo to the mellow tune of his Lowland voice. Maggie was small, shrivelled, and tense. When they came to dinner at The Poplars, she flatly contradicted everything he said — when she allowed him to finish a sentence. Report said that William lived in mortal terror of Maggie. They had no children, and by some fiendish instinct for irony the school had found the one nickname for him which could hurt: Papa. If he read derision into the name, he was mistaken: we used it with affection.

The Airds did not depend financially on their little farm: the Cape Education Department provided their source of income. They lived out of town, about five miles, under the furrow, among lucerne lands and orchards, because they were country people by origin, and because of his bees. His bees produced tons of lucerne honey, samples of which won him prizes on agricultural shows up and down the land. We never visited his little Eden, because Maggie never invited anyone; but we heard all about it in class. Those talks of his, the talks of the informed enthusiast, talks that had nothing whatever to do with the syllabus: the political organisation of the hive; the fantastic instinctual engineering and mathematics contained in a common piece of honeycomb; the feeding-habits of the various orders of bees; the pollination process; the variety of willing flowers they violated and the quality and colour of the nectar, and hence the honey (aloe honey gathered in winter was dark and bitter); the life-cycle of the bee; the mysterious selection and special dieting of the grub destined to be the queen; and, how desperately sad, the limited, so limited love-life of the bee! That perfect state-organisation almost totally sexless.

So Papa made us aware of other creatures with utterly different modes of existence; and of man's ability to understand them, and collaborate with them. The perfect comity of the hive had been evolved perhaps fifty million years ago; and here was the parvenu monkey, Man, using its produce to gratify his sweet tooth, and to delight his curiosity.

On more than one occasion, Papa Aird recited:

When Mrs Gorm, Aunt Heloise,
Was stung to death by a swarm of bees,
Her husband, Prebendary Gorm,
Fetched his veil and took the swarm;
He's publishing a book next May
How to Make Beekeeping Pay.

Papa came to town in an ancient Armstrong Siddeley car, a dark green affair, riding fairly high off the ground.

Twice during the period I knew him, he and Maggie took leave and went to Britain. For weeks after his return, the bees took second place as classroom distraction number one, and he would tell us endlessly of abbeys, and battlefields, and Burns's cottage, and war-memorials (in which he specialised) and folk customs, and the history of Great Britain as it affected Scotland; and how sensible and tolerant the Scots had been to accept military defeat (but no other), and to collaborate with the Sassenachs; and — he virtually spelt it out for the Afrikaans members of the class — it was time the Nationalist politicians in South Africa adopted the same policy.

Gentle, always gentle. Like all the good schoolmasters I have sat under, he never found it necessary to use a cane.

And then there were the Robertsons, straight from Scotland, who arrived about 1930, and bought a small farm at Limebank. He was a retired marine engineer. They had two daughters, Nell and Jean, and a powerful son, Bob, who did most of the farming. We first heard of them through Joan and Dorothy, who reported the arrival at Rocklands of a pretty Scots girl with a delightful accent, and a blissful ignorance of South African politics and the current flag and language tensions. She had spent the first few weeks in her new country on the farm, where she heard two new languages, Xhosa and Afrikaans. She had heard Afrikaans spoken only as a means of commu-

nication between Coloured and black labourers; and her menfolk were
struggling to learn it in order to be able to instruct their dark-skinned work
force in its tasks. She had no idea that it was the home language of more
than half the whites in the country.

At school she was acutely self-conscious of her broad Scots accent, and
spoke as little as possible; but it was precisely her accent that intrigued her
classmates, who would surround her at tea break, and tease her into breaking her silence. An Afrikaans-speaking child asked her:

'Why can't you speak Afrikaans?'

'We've got no black people in Sco'land,' she replied in all innocence.

One third of the town was shaken with indignation; one third smirked
with covert pleasure; one third smiled, sadly.

Father and Mr Robertson struck up a strong friendship — they had
machines in common; and Mrs Robertson and Mother warmed to each
other.

The Robertsons were befriended also by the Airds, whose plot was no
more than three miles away. Recently Jean Robertson gave me two touching facts about Maggie Aird. When brother Bob was sent over with the
horse-drawn rake to help stook and stack the Airds' lucerne, Maggie, well
into middle age, no doubt re-living her country girlhood in a remote northern world, followed slowly behind the rake, hand-gleaning under the blazing African sun.

Even more touching was Jean's revelation of Maggie's dangerous suscepti-
bility to bee stings. A single sting could bring her near to suffocation, and
she would have to be rushed to the doctor. But she tolerated her husband's
passion, and lived her life among endless talk of bees, beehives, wax and
honey.

I remember a tall, dignified man, always impeccably dressed in a suit;
straight hair, regular features; straight back, with a fine black Kitchener
moustache. He spoke good English. His skin was walnut coloured. He was
messenger and mail-man to *The Midland News,* and his name was Dohman.
One frequently encountered Dohman in our kitchen, having coffee, but
one never got on to the terms of ease that one achieved with Dumpy, our
man-of-all-work, during the Sunday silver-cleaning sessions. Dohman suffered from a compulsion to tell about his trip overseas with the Army during
the Great War. What he told us about was not his adventures in the trenches
of Flanders, nor guarding ammunition dumps, nor bearing stretchers, but
about London — not the Tower, nor London Bridge, nor Buckingham
Palace, but about Uncle Joe, James Butler's brother, who had him to
meals in his dining-room on two separate occasions. He would tell this in
our kitchen.

The third time he told me this, the penny dropped, and I asked Mother
why we never had Dohman to a meal. 'One doesn't have one's servants to

meals. Uncle Joe in England, I am sure, would never have *his* messenger to a meal.'

'Then are all black and Coloured people servants? We never have any of them to meals, ever.'

'One only has one's friends to meals. Besides, it's not done to have Coloured or black friends.'

'Why?'

Alice's brow furrowed with puzzlement.

'They're different. What have we in common with white people of the poorer class? We don't have them to meals.'

The 'poorer classes', for my mother, were not measured by their incomes. If they had been, in the early 'thirties, the inhabitants of The Poplars would have been right down among them. Poverty in this sense had something to do with what she called culture — interests, values, wide horizons, background. To be without background was a great social handicap. 'Mother's attitude towards the poorer classes', says Dorothy, 'was a curious combination of Edwardian awareness of social differences and a hint of compassion conveyed in the phrase she applied to them — "poor things". Her snobbishness was of a venial kind. Her warmth and generosity in fact always transcended her awareness of class.' I don't think she worried much about pigmentation. I'm not saying that she was entirely free of colour prejudice — how many are? She did show some anxiety when the girls expressed vague admiration for two handsome young men who were supposed to have a touch of colour. But she knew what was proper and civilised behaviour, and would break the racial taboos with very little sign of strain, in full view of the D.R.C. pastorie opposite, the Methodist manse to the right, and the South African Hotel to the left. In the early 'thirties, in the shadow of the 'swart gevaar' election, during the depression when blacks and whites were competing for the same pick-and-shovel jobs, she would have the priest in charge of the black Anglican parish, the Rev. James Calata to tea. I don't think she was even aware of the gauntlet she was throwing down. How else should a well-bred woman entertain a priest of her own church? Send him to the back door? Give him a rusk in the kitchen? A puzzled Chrissie or Susan would have to prepare a tray with the silver teapot and the Spode, and a plate of thin lettuce and cucumber sandwiches, as if for Mrs Jim Metcalf.

The winters on the Karoo plateaux are severe and dry. Sometimes soft, low, grey clouds would settle and sag over our world, making us huddle closer to our fires; sometimes we would wake to a cold crystal morning with the mountaintops miraculously white with snow. In my recollection, that mysterious powder never fell in the town itself. But the river took little notice of snow, it waited, like everything in the valley, for the thunder to speak in late October or November.

No one who has not lived in a semi-desert can imagine the annual hope and anxiety with which the inhabitants wait through days of intensifying heat for the rains to come. Our eyes are on the look-out for the appearance of the first cumulus cloud, the cloud no bigger than a man's hand, which grows, and is joined by other presences, impenetrably purple below, rising through thousands of feet to their rounded heads, each head a white cerebellum, a tumultuous brain churning its intentions over and over. Then these giants step between us and the sun, the shadows disappear, earth darkens. A gust of wind bends trees, whips up dust, rattles the windows. Birds, sheep, cattle, make for shelter. The twilight is lit alternately by great aluminium flashes of sheet lightning or splintered by vicious stabs at the earth. The first thunder comes like a sinister drumroll mustering a barbarous host in the remote hills; then much closer, a growling lion's roar. Drops of water smack into the dust, making small craters like bullets, more and more, faster and faster. A hissing, swishing sound surrounds us; the yard, the street, the veld, are all awash with sliding sheets whose surface is continuously riddled and dimpled with innumerable globules of water. Gutters, runnels, sluits, dongas, rivers, receive the fluid which has cut and carved them, which is cutting and carving them now. Unpredictably, the thunder wields his club, and earth and air shake and reverberate with crashing cymbals and deep, subterranean gongs. We are in the heart of the scented storm: the water has released a fragrance from the earth.

A few hours later we hear that the river has come down — a strange paradoxical phrase, quite inadequate to describe what has happened. The little trickle that connects the silver pools has disappeared under a cataract of dark brown, rough-backed water stampeding to the sea. Mingled with the intoxicating scent which the dry earth has released is the related but different flood smell of silty waters. But, as James Butler observed at Carlisle Bridge, if that water is our lifeblood, it is given indiscriminately, with a force which carries millions upon millions of tons of topsoil to the sea. From the grandstand of the Gilfillan Bridge one may see occasional drowned sheep and other animals, and great logs of dead trees, and trees with green leaves still on them, rolling and plunging downstream.

The people of Cradock would come to watch this great performance of their old river, and also the performance of those who had not come to watch but to work: the wood fishermen, who took up their positions between the bridge and the old weir near the Abattoir, where the stream flows with less speed and turbulence, and the shelving banks are favourable to their work.

The equipment of a wood fisherman is simple: a long, strong, light rope with a three-pronged grapple attached to one end of it. His eyes scan the waters upstream. When he sees a large log or uprooted tree approaching within reasonable distance of his bank, he starts whirling the anchor round and round his head, then releases it so that it splashes down just beyond his prize; then immediately he starts hauling in, hand over hand. If he has judged and thrown well, and the grapple does not slip, he will pull his plunder into shore: firewood to be stored for the winter or to be chopped up and sold on the morning market.

Anyone — whites, Coloureds, blacks — could be a wood fisherman. Sometimes a man would harpoon such a whale of a tree that it would threaten to drag him downstream unless he abandoned his precious line and grapple. Then he would sing out for help. Fellow fishermen and bystanders would rush to his aid, determined not to let the old river defeat that man. You would find all races and generations pulling on one rope then.

During one particularly big flood, I met Cradock's photographer Mr William Lidbetter setting up his camera to record the sight. He was one of the most cultivated and intelligent men in Cradock. Born among the English Lakes, he was driven into exile by bad asthma. He tried Tasmania, but ended up in Cradock, possibly because he had heard of the wonders it had worked for a fellow Quaker. He made a modest living as a family photographer and recorder of local events. He was bearded and wheezy, Dorothy reminds me, and 'had a deep chuckling laugh which seemed to struggle upwards from subterranean depths and emerge gasping and heaving'. He served on the Library Committee, and on the Joint Council. Gentle, and deeply concerned with social justice, he did not have the impact on the community which one might have expected. Possibly the stress and tension of civic debate would bring on attacks of asthma, so that he limited himself to humour, irony, and sad shrugging of shoulders at the private or public vanities which he observed with a focus sharper and deeper than any lens.

A large log came plunging and leaping down. A fisherman caught it, and started hauling. He cried for help and I ran to join the polyglot tug-of-war. When I got back to him, Mr Lidbetter was packing up his camera, having taken three shots.

'Did you enjoy landing that tree?'

'It was great fun.'

Then his shoulders started to shrug. Through his despairing little chuckle came the words:

'Give the Nats time and they'll make a law against it.'

10

The Muses in Rags

Saturday night was big bath night. Electrical geysers and piped hot water were not common in Cradock households in the 'twenties. Relays of hot water in large pots and paraffin tins had to be carried from the kitchen through the dining-room and down the passage to the bathroom, where Alice would see to it that each member of her brood was thoroughly scrubbed with a stiff bristled brush and red carbolic soap. (On one occasion when Grannie was looking after us, and we had to put ourselves through this ritual of purgation, we incurred her displeasure by using two four-gallon tins of water-glass mixture, in which she had intended to preserve a substantial stock of eggs which were cheap at the time.)

In nightgowns and pyjamas we would gather in the drawing-room, where a fire would be blazing in the old Victorian iron grate, if it was winter. Father would enter, and the fun would begin. Where was the slab of chocolate? On his person, or hidden somewhere in the room? The child who found it would get an extra square.

Then came the concert. Each child in turn, standing on the small oak table, had to tell a story, or sing a song, or recite a poem. I had discovered Macaulay's *Lays of Ancient Rome,* and secretly mastered 'How well Horatius kept the bridge'. One evening when my turn came, I declaimed it from beginning to end. In spite of my father's pacifist teaching, I revelled in the heroic violence. One verse in particular thrilled me: I could use bad language in public and escape scot free.

At Picus brave Horatius
Darted one fiery thrust,
And the proud Umbrian's gilded arms
Clashed in the bloody dust.

The servants went off in the afternoon, and supper was prepared by Alice and the girls. We all helped lay and clear the table, and took turns at washing up. When Dorothy and I were on duty we took a long time over it. She had a good poetry teacher, and could recite and discuss poem after poem, with a cup in one hand and a dishcloth in the other. I learnt more poetry from her than all my teachers until I entered Mr Aird's class. I had no thought of trying to write poems myself.

The Poplars could not be called a musical household; but when we were still young, Alice used to sit down at the piano, and sing sentimental Edwardian songs: 'She is far from the land', 'Less than the dust', and 'Pale hands I loved beside the Shalimar'. I found it distinctly unnerving — to hear such unashamed emotion pouring from the person whose business it was to be a loving but calm island in my chaotic world. Apparently she overheard me saying something uncomplimentary about her singing to one of my friends. Years later she told me of it, how it hurt her, and how she never sang at the piano again. The power of egocentric boys to silence their mothers is frightening.

Joan, Dorothy, and Christine were given piano lessons. No girl from a decent home could be expected to brave the wicked world without having 'done the piano'. They tried. Joan got farthest up the musical ladder. About the second rung, I think.

I used to sit at the instrument with a beginner's piece of sheet music in front of me, trying to teach myself the rudiments. Mother caught me at it one day, smiled wistfully, and shook her head. The prospect of four bills for piano lessons was not to be contemplated.

Neville and Godfrey Collett had good 'ears'. They would sit down at the keyboard, and in a matter of minutes pick out any tune in the world, and 'vamp' in some kind of a bass for it. How I envied them!

It was at Katkop that the God of Music was on his most familiar terms with mankind. You know those classical fables where some god or other, bored no doubt with the perpetual gossip and in-fighting on Olympus, assumes the impenetrable disguise of a peasant or traveller, and wanders among men, testing their hospitality. If he is treated well, he blesses the habitation and all who dwell therein. I don't know if the Greek gods ever came as far south as the Karoo, though; maybe some Bushman, Hottentot or Xhosa spirit had done the trick.

I speak from faulty memory, of course; but I don't think anyone could read music in the Katkop household, though several could make it.

On Sunday evenings after supper a regular sacred concert would take place round the piano — but before it began, Uncle Norman would say:

'Godfrey, phone your Uncle Dudley, and tell him we're going to begin.'

Uncle Dudley on Grassridge, eight miles away on the party line, would pull his chair to the phone, and light his pipe. The Katkop receiver would be left dangling off the hook. None of the neighbours on that party line ever objected to this procedure. This national hook-up having taken place, the singing would commence. The orchestra consisted of Uncle Norman at the piano, Neville with the fiddle, and Godfrey on the concertina. Of these, only Neville could not sing, his chin being clamped to the fiddle.

It was a very democratic programme. Each child was allowed to suggest a hymn. The favourite opening number, as I recall, was:

Now the day is over
Night is drawing nigh,
Shadows of the evening
Steal across the sky.

Now the darkness gathers
Stars begin to peep,
Birds and beasts and flowers
Soon will be asleep.

It was followed by 'Stand up, stand up for Jesus' and 'Rock of Ages',
and, if there had been a disaster or a big thunderstorm, 'For those in peril
on the sea'. Some of the smaller children, who had not yet grasped   the
difference between sacred and secular, would demand 'Wrap me up in my
old tarpaulin jacket' too soon — which was tantamount to asking for the
sweets before the main dish had been served. But sooner or later, almost
unnoticed, we would slip from the love of God to the love of man, either
by way of a soldier lamenting for his dead comrade, or a dying warrior
asking his chum to 'Break the news to Mother', and from there to 'A Spanish Cavalier' and 'Nita Juanita' — both favourites of Uncle Norman's. We
would usually stop in about 1910, I think. I can't recall singing 'Pack up
your troubles in your old kit bag' or 'Tipperary' on these Sunday evenings.
I do have a dim recollection of Godfrey being allowed to sing, in a clear
treble voice:

You're the cream in my cof—fee,
You're the lace in my shoe,
You will always be
My necessittee,
I'd be lost without you —

The fact that I had no instrument galled me. True, I could do as well as
most on a mouth-organ — and could look with contempt on those who had
to make do with humming against a piece of tissue paper wrapped round a
comb. Enviously I watched fellows at campfire singsongs strumming guitars
and banjos. During one camp, I was shown the rudiments of playing, but
knew within ten minutes that I would never master the fingering with my
short digits. Worse, I couldn't tune the strings, my ear was too poor.

It was at Katkop that Uncle Norman told us stories of a genre difficult
to define, but they were clearly related to old Boer 'jag stories'. They always
involved man and the animal kingdom. The observation of details had to be
exact and circumstantial, so that the audience was at a loss to know at what
precise point the narrator had left the realm of probability for the realm of
fantasy.

Many of these stories started with the formula, 'One day a fellow was
walking (or riding) in the veld'.

Well, this fellow was a transport rider, and he'd outspanned at Salt Pans Drift. Looking over his wagon gear, he saw it was time to renew the stroppe.

('What's a strop, Uncle Norman?' 'Man, it's a thick thong that hooks into the notches of the jukskeis under the ox's neck. It keeps the yoke in place.')

Now the best skin for stroppe comes from the skin of the old aardvark — very tough, and so strong you don't need to plait it.

So he got on his horse, and rode up towards Rhebokberg looking for an aardvark. Just as he got over a rise, there he saw him, waddling along. He put the old voorlaaier to his shoulder, and pulled the trigger. Nothing happened. The flint had fallen out of the old snaphaan. But the fellow was determined not to let the old aardvark get away. So he put his dogs on to him. They caught him, one on each ear, but he just dragged them along like two feathers of klitsgras towards a shallow hole which he had started digging the day before. Now you must know that once he starts in a hole an aardvark can dig himself right out of sight in no time.

So this fellow jumped off his horse, and ran up to help his dogs. He caught hold of the aardvark's tail; but the old creature just dragged him along with the dogs towards the hole, which was now very close.

So this smart fellow tied his horse's tail to the aardvark's tail, hoping that he'd be able to drag the animal backwards to the outspan and fix him there. Not a bit of it. It was all that the horse and dogs could do to keep up their end of the tug-o'-war.

So this fellow ran back to his outspan, inspanned the sixteen oxen, and came hot-foot over the veld, ready to tie the trek tow to the aardvark's tail.

But he was disappointed. For when he got to the crest of the rise, what did he see? His poor old horse was sitting upright on his bottom, whinnying like mad. Where were his dogs? Still holding on to the aardvark's ears, they had been dragged into the hole. But when the horse's bottom came down on the hole like a cork and shut out the light, they lost their nerve in the dark, and let go, and started to bark and bite the poor old horse's bottom.

So this fellow had a problem. How to connect the trek tow to the aardvark's tail? He dug a small hole alongside the horse's bottom, and put his arm in to see if he could reach the knot; but his own dogs bit his hand. There was nothing for it but to cut off his horse's tail.

The moral of the story is that if you go hunting with a voorlaaier you must always carry a spare flint.

The other sort of story purported to be verifiable history.

You know that mountain with the two domes of ironstone on top? Aasvogelskop, not far from Speelmanskop. Well in 1857 at the foot of it young P.J. Bezuidenhout and P.Z. his brother had a hartbeeshuisie. They were supposed to be looking after their father's sheep, but they spent most of their time hunting. This meant that the aasvogels did just what they liked with the poor lambing ewes. The birds were particularly greedy, because they had to feed their hungry chicks in their nests on the ironstone crags of Aasvogelskop.

When P.J. Bezuidenhout senior came out to inspect and count the spring lambs he found it necessary to reprimand his sons more severely than usual.

Old P.J. Bezuidenhout senior was a devout man, who never spared the sjambok lest he should spoil his two children. When he'd satisfied himself that he had not fallen into the trap of spoiling them, he put the sjambok aside, and talked to them gently about the end of the world, the day of judgement, and all the strange portents that would announce those events: and that they must now pull themselves together, so that when the trumpets of doomsday sounded, and the seals were broken and the books were opened, they could face their Maker with a clear conscience, particularly on this matter of protecting their father's ewes from the aasvogels. He then rode back to Cradock, to which place he had retired to be closer to the church, and the morning market.

Well, P.J. junior and P.Z. made a plan. First they fitted themselves out with gauntlets made of rhino skin so thick that not even an aasvogel's beak could penetrate them. Then they shot two zebras, skinned them, and left the carcasses to the aasvogels. When the aasvogels had picked them clean, they sewed the skeletons into their skins again, except for a hole for themselves to crawl into.

Well, sure enough, the old aasvogels spotted these zebras lying still near the water hole, and came down to inspect. And as they ripped the hide open, they were caught by their naked necks. In no time the brothers tied their beaks up, and put a thong round their wings.

The next step was to get the pith of a big dead aloe, the kokerboom: two pieces about four inches thick and two feet long, and tinder-dry. These they attached with three-foot thongs to the birds' legs. When the right moment came, they would set them alight. Kokerboom fibre does not flame, it smoulders like an enormous cigarette.

The plan was very clever. The birds when released would of course fly straight up to Aasvogelskop, and the smouldering pith would set alight to the nests, and burn the whole colony of wicked birds to ashes, just as they deserved. They decided to release the birds at nightfall, so that the fire would show up better. To give some idea how godless P.J. junior and P.Z. were, they worked all Sunday catching those birds.

Their plan didn't work out as expected. These aasvogels didn't come from Aasvogelskop at all, but from Babylonstoren in the Agtersneeuberg. They flew right over Cradock just as the people were going into church, P.J. Bezuidenhout senior along with the rest. The sight of two comets moving across the sky had a strange effect on Cradock. Everyone was riveted to the ground; and the people already in the church came pouring out in order not to miss the start of the Apocalypse.

Strange things began to happen. On P.J. senior's right hand the lawyer turned to one of his clients and asked to be forgiven for having taken more than his due in fees; on his left the dominee's daughter assured her mother that she would pray all night for her and for her father because now all their secret hypocrisy was going to be shouted from the rooftops of Cradock.

P.J. senior was smitten in his conscience. The market had preoccupied him so much during the past few days that he'd forgotten all about P.J. junior and P.Z. Perhaps they'd not seen the comets; perhaps they'd turned in early and were thus at a disadvantage, not having had proper warning of the wrath to come.

P.J. junior and P.Z. had taken their setback philosophically. Maybe they'd be lucky and catch aasvogels with the right address the next day. Meanwhile it was important to save their decoy zebras from the hyenas. They found the easiest way to carry them was to get inside them and walk back to the hartbeeshuisie. This caused a sensation among the rest of the animal kingdom. Responsible baboon patriarchs harried their families to safety deep into the Tarkastad district. A water-tortoise buried himself in the mud and wished he were a barbel. Hundreds of dassies lined the route, their inquisitive natures quite overcoming their sense of danger. A katlagter died of laughter.

Safely back at the hartbeeshuisie P.J. junior and P.Z. decided to make an early start the next morning.

P.J. senior was up with the morning star. If he had any doubts about the proximity of the day of wrath, these were dispelled by the sight of two zebras walking upright, like chessmen, through the melk- and gannabos. He put the spurs into his horse and made a dash for the hartbeeshuisie. It was empty. He was plunged into even deeper remorse. Here was clear evidence that P.J. junior and P.Z. were not lay-abouts or lie-abeds. The dutiful lads had risen before dawn to guard their father's ewes from the aasvogels — and were even now somewhere in the veld quite unaware that two of the Horses of the Apocalypse were in the neighbourhood. P.J. senior decided to stay where he was, reciting all the psalms and hymns he knew.

It was a long, long day. Some time in the afternoon, exhausted with hunger and emotion, he fell asleep. When he awoke he went outside. There he collapsed on his knees in terror. The general conflagration had begun. Aasvogelskop was burning.

It was in this condition that P.J. junior and P.Z. found their father when they returned from their highly gratifying day. Pointing wildly, shouting incoherently, ordering them to fall on their knees, P.J. senior begged their forgiveness, which he hoped they would give because they also probably had things on their minds.

It took P.J. junior and P.Z. the best part of an hour, and half a bottle of witblitz, to explain how they had been the unwitting bringers-on of the day of wrath, which was merely the first Wednesday in October 1857.

When he grasped this, old P.J. senior was sorry he'd left his sjambok behind. He had no option but to spare it on this occasion. Would they be spoilt by its non-application? He took another swig of brandy. No, perhaps not.

By the time the moon came up, P.J. senior had his right arm over P.J. junior's shoulders, and his left over the shoulders of P.Z. And he was saying, 'We Bezuidenhouts aren't bred under a turkey hen. It takes Bezuidenhouts to send two comets over Cradock and burn up Aasvogelskop.'

There was no Dramatic Society in Cradock during this period, and no school teacher, after Miss Allman, attempted to get drama into the schools. There were occasional performances in the town hall by touring companies. I recall two — one, the last flicker of vaudeville, the other, a pioneer piece of Afrikaans theatre. We were allowed to attend by virtue of the complimentary tickets which the managers had sent to the editor of the paper.

The first was a one-man show. He was a sad middle-aged man, in an illfitting dress suit, who kept six plates rotating in the air for a long, long time; he had a piece of folded parchment, which, at the flick of a hand, became a fan, a geisha's headgear, a king's crown, a concertina. The second half was devoted to a recitation of a plangent poem by Alfred Lord Tennyson called 'Enoch Arden'. It moved me deeply.

The other show was a stage version of Jochem van Bruggen's pioneer Afrikaans novel about a poor-white called *Ampie*. The production was nothing if not realistic. When the squatting, barefoot hero stretched and broke his piece of liquorice by hooking it round his big toe, the audience wept with laughter; and when he brought on to the stage his one true friend, his donkey — a real live dusty moke — our bliss was measureless.

But we were occasionally privileged to see the celluloid surrogates for legitimate drama — from the jittery black-and-white silent films to the first raw-colour talkies. This great technical development in popular entertainment was much discussed in the dorp. Ernest and Alice, particularly Ernest, had reservations about letting their offspring haunt the 'bio'; for what was the 'bio' after all, but a mass-produced version of the theatre; and the theatre, all good Quakers knew or suspected, was a corrupt concern, financed and staffed by pretty but naughty ladies and handsome but nefarious gentlemen, all bred in the suburbs of Sodom and Gomorrah. The lives of modern film stars confirmed this ancient view. Very occasionally we would be allowed to enter the stuffy palace of suspect pleasures, situated opposite the post office. A tickey for the under-10s, and Coloured people upstairs. To my knowledge there was never any difficulty about the admission of Coloured people. If only it had been allowed to continue, by now we would be agitating to allow them to sit anywhere, instead of struggling to get them back into the building.

The first 'bio' I saw was 'Charlie's Aunt'. I was completely confused, because I did not understand that the funny old lady was really the young hero in disguise. I think the next was 'The Massacre of Glencoe'. Father would relent if he could be persuaded that the film was innocent comedy, like 'Charlie's Aunt', or educational or historical, like this depiction of Scots treachery and massacre. I remember little beyond hairy men in yards of tartan, and a feasting scene in which Douglas Fairbanks (was it?) drank thirstily, nay greedily, from a goblet, tilting his head back until the wicked fire-water spilt into his beard and trickled down the tendons of his manly neck, much to the secret delight of the heroine. The table manners at The Poplars were better than those of Glencoe.

This was the first occasion on which the importance of a suitable musical accompaniment was discussed. In those days the sound track differed from cinema to cinema, dorp to dorp. It was provided by an industrious lady at a piano up front, who had to slide cleverly from tune to tune in order to keep in emotional key with the shifting drama before her. Well, this Scots epic put our accompanist to the test, and the town was divided sharply as to whether she should be given a fail, a pass, or a distinction. Those 'for', pointed out that she had not used anything but traditional Scots tunes for the entire one and a half hours. Others maintained that her knowledge of Scots folk music was exiguous and undiscriminating, that Scots music was not limited to 'Annie Laurie', 'Scots wha hae wi' Wallace bled', 'Loch Lomond', and 'Auld lang syne'. During the tender scenes she would give us 'Loch Lomond'; but as soon as the mood had more Mars than Venus in it, she would start vamping 'Scots wha hae'. This was confusing, because she used the same tune no matter which of the opponents were arming to battle, or swinging their claymores. On the other hand, what chance had she to prepare her score? I am sure she was never given a preview of the celluloid epics for which she had to improvise these instantaneous musical obligatos.

A challenging job, one of the few openings for dorp musicians; it was soon to disappear with the advent of talkies.

Graaff-Reinet was the scene of my next disconcerting experience of the equivocal nature of artistic illusion. The film was none other than that masterpiece of the British middle-class domestic muse, J.M. Barrie's 'Peter Pan and Wendy'. You will recall the nauseating fairy in this tender drama called Tinkerbell, who on the point of dying can only be brought back to life if sufficient people in the audience, in response to the hero's tearful pleas across the curtain line, shout out that they believe in fairies. The children would never have fallen for it but for their dear Mums shouting like maniacs to resuscitate Tinkerbell. And the Mums were only doing it to maintain the children's belief in fairies.

Admittedly I saw the piece under conditions unfavourable to a willing suspension of disbelief. Some good citizen (was it Mrs Asher?) used to arrange cinema shows, in the open, in the Location. A portable projector would fling its nervous images on to the white external wall of the school-room; and the populace would gather out of their little houses and shanties to witness it — mainly Afrikaans-speaking Coloureds and Xhosas, and perhaps a sprinkling of whites who had brought their canvas chairs. All very relaxed in the warm air. No one felt that they were making an heroic social gesture; and no one believed that a sacred taboo was being broken.

Nevertheless the credibility gap between that audience and 'Peter Pan and Wendy' must have been astronomical. While I was still wondering why on earth a female actress, called Mary Pickford, was playing the male part of Peter, she started her passionate plea to us to restore the dying Tinkerbell by declaring that we believed in fairies. Her light was growing dimmer and dimmer. The film being silent, her words appeared in print at the bottom of the screen. It was quite clear, however, from her mime and her facial contortions, that she was extremely distressed because no one in the Graaff-Reinet Location that night was prepared to believe in fairies. This was too much for Uncle Frank, a man of imagination and gentle chivalry. He sudden-ly appeared in front of the wall, and shouted out Miss Pickford's pleas, first in English and then in Afrikaans, his shadow a dizzy black hole in the screen-picture behind him. His wife, Aunt Flo, and Mrs Asher responded loyally, and others followed their example. Tinkerbell was saved. But, I asked myself on the way back to the car, if Uncle Frank hadn't got up, would not Tinker-bell have been saved anyway?

I mustn't be too sceptical about audience participation. Occasionally I would be allowed to see a Tom Mix or a Buck Jones cowboy film. The lady accompanist had an easy task with these. As soon as the tension reached a sufficient pitch, usually within five minutes, someone would put two grubby fingers between his missing front teeth and let out a whistle like a steam ex-press emerging from a tunnel. From then on life was aurally unpredictable: shouts, particularly from the gallery, of encouragement to the hero; cries of 'Shame' when a child or the heroine was being bullied by the villain; groans; boos; hisses; peals of demonic laughter, in the middle of which you might find time to swop chewing-gum with your neighbour, or pull a girl's plait. But when it came to the final shoot-out, we were ducking for cover behind the chairs, jumping up for heroic open shots at the crooks, falling dead in the aisles, whistling, banging, yelling, groaning, and using forbidden and un-genteel language such as The Poplars had not heard since it was a staging-hotel in the diamond days.

The Butler children did not enjoy this emotional catharsis very often. We were, however, kept up to date with all the films by Dumpy, our gentle Coloured male servant, who never missed a change of programme.

On Sunday mornings his task was to polish the family E.P.N.S. The polish, a pink substance in a white box called 'Goddard's Plate Powder', was applied as a thin paste, allowed to dry, and then rubbed off with a yellow flannel duster. We would sit round him under the pepper tree, and he'd give us a methodical, blow-by-blow, kiss-by-kiss, shot-by-shot, miss-by-miss, hit-by-hit account of what had happened in the Saturday afternoon matinée, including the serial. But he didn't lay much store by the serials. He was a main features man; and he could hold us fascinated on such absorbing questions as: who is the best cowboy — Tom Mix or Buck Jones? And which is the best cowboy's horse — Tom Mix's horse, or Buck Jones's? And which is the best cowboy's girl? In fact, he related the stories so vividly, with a true balladist's sense of the telling detail, the one necessary gesture, that I soon found the 'bio' itself a let-down. A good prose narrative, with gesture and changes of pace, calls for a degree of imaginative collaboration which may leave a deeper impression than the Turkish-bath immersion of the cinema.

Alice had a horror of Horrors. She dutifully took Joan and Christine to see 'The Tale of Two Cities' (educational and historical). But Christine says that she forced each child's head into her lap as soon as anything nasty appeared, allowing them to surface for air only when the climate was safe. Chris says she was left with the impression from the little she saw that 'The Tale of Two Cities' was a rather sweet story.

Then there was 'Helen of Troy' (educational and historical). We had already read Kingsley's *Heroes* and other scraps of Greek mythology; so, after the film, we entered a rich world of fantasy in which the Owen boys and girls from the Methodist parsonage next door eagerly participated, and the Goulds from the Anglican rectory, and many others. There were just enough males to man the walls of Troy, and enough to attack them. But there were too many girls, not one of whom was prepared to settle long for any role less than Helen; who, as a result, had so many understudies that she never mastered her part. It became so bad that Dorothy got bored and went and played Florence Nightingale all by herself.

We built Troy in two and a half days flat, out of a pile of packing-cases belonging to the Works but stored in The Poplars backyard. Troy had a grand main gate, plus medieval drawbridge. The Wooden Horse took shape in a single morning. We fixed a cunning superstructure on to Grannie Leppan's bath chair. Meanwhile the armourers were not idle. Shields were made from the ends of Laurel paraffin boxes; kitchenware served for helmets; and Spanish reeds for javelins and spears.

We did not quite grasp all the nuances of that classical story, nor the changes in word usage. I remember a particular afternoon, when I was playing Menelaus opposite Libby, whose turn it was to do Helen. Libby did not have a classical cast of mind. She would have been perfectly content to stay with me in Argos (under the fig tree) all afternoon. So when Paris (a minor part, handed out to the bank manager's 7-year-old son) appeared and said, 'Libby, you must come now,' she said she wouldn't.

News got back to Troy that Helen had snubbed Paris. This was too much of a liberty to take with the sacred text of Homer; so the most authoritative girl involved, Hecuba, appeared in Argos, with Paris in tow, and said, 'Libby, if you want to be Helen, you've just got to let Paris rape you.'

Helen went off like a lamb with the diminutive seducer, and I started working on my brother Agamemnon's sense of family honour. We did the round of the Greek islands and states together, picking up Ulysses, who was only too happy to leave Penelope (his sister) knitting. We had to sacrifice Iphigenia several times because nearly all the girls wanted a turn. Then we got a fair wind and sailed for Troy. The Aegean was black with our ships.

Ten years is a long time to conduct a siege in your own backyard; but time passes quickly if you can change sides often enough, and take a shift as Hector if you are bored with being Achilles.

We were, of course, delaying what we knew was the inevitable end. The Wooden Horse was all ready, but we were reluctant to use it, because it had to be preceded by the final meeting of Hector and Achilles, and no one wanted to play Hector *that* day. At last — possibly under pressure from a parental ultimatum to clean up the backyard — we drew lots for it. Fate decreed that I should play Hector opposite Dennis Owen's Achilles.

It was strange playing Hector, when, unlike the real Hector, you knew in advance what the Gods had decided, and what the outcome had to be. I didn't relish being dragged behind Achilles' chariot wheels at all.

Achilles took up his stance at the corner of the chicken run, and Hector walked by Scamander's stream (the gully that took the bath water on to the vegetable garden), and, with proud challenges and boastings, we started hurling far-shadowing spears at each other. It was Achilles' turn. He took a longish run, like a fast bowler or a polevaulter, before letting fly. The fearless Hector did not flinch, but thrust forth his shield to fend off the missile. Unfortunately it glanced off the paraffin box-end into his right eye.

Two things saved my eye. The first was Ernest's emphatic insistence that no sword, spear or other weapon, Grecian or Trojan, should have a sharp point on it; the spear's point was the butt end of a reed, about an inch and a half in diameter. The second was the decree of fate that the rim of this reed should be prevented from crushing the eyeball by encountering the lower rim of the eye socket. It cut the flesh of the cheek right through to the bone.

I lay in a dark room for several days. The incident must have had a strange effect on Ernest, who had gone through life with his impaired vision and cast as the result of a childish accident.

When I returned to the world, with a black patch over my right eye, I noticed that Troy had disappeared, for ever. So I arranged for a fortnight of Pirates, in which the handicap of an eye-patch could be converted into a distinct asset.

If the weekly cinema was under a partial ban, the annual visits of the migratory amusement parks were absolute anathema. We had to content ourselves with watching the erection of the gaily painted booths and engines of delight from a distance. On one occasion I stole forth at dead of night, crossed the bridge and, wandering among the motley crowd, inspected marvel after marvel. Unable to pay for a turn on anything, I eventually took up my stand near a gaudily painted hurdy-gurdy. It was near midnight when I stole back to bed on uncertain feet, drunk with its barbarous noise, dizzy with watching the whirling horses and abandoned riders of the merry-go-round.

As for Pagel's or Boswell's Circuses, how any responsible parent could allow a child near them was incomprehensible to Father. First, circuses carried diseases from one town to the next. 'But we've had measles and chickenpox,' we would cry. 'Much worse diseases than those' was the response. Second, what joy could be got out of mangy caged animals, whose tricks had been so cruelly taught? And third, the prices were ridiculously high. (I did not enter a big top until I took two small god-daughters to Boswell & Wilkie's Circus in Johannesburg in the 'fifties.)

But we would hang around on the fringes, and watch the cages of lions and tigers being wheeled into position, and the enormous tent rise into the sky.

Once the circus brought us a marvel which no audience in a big top has ever seen. Four huge dusty grey elephants processed solemnly down to the river to bathe. That was a sight in itself — great beasts as tall as the thorn trees. They entered the pool, lay down in it, rolled over, stood up, lay down again. They sucked water into their trunks, and squirted their own backs and one another's. Their hides now almost black, crinkled, semi-silvered, they trumpeted their huge delight in unforgettable falsetto screams.

The river had seen nothing like it in how many years? Half-fossilised tusks of elephants had been found when excavating the hole for the swimming-baths round the eye of the hot springs three miles to the north; and more recent tusks had been found in the alluvial soil elsewhere. 'It's not exactly elephant country,' said one of the uncles, 'although they're mighty fond of young mimosa — they root them up with their trunks and chew the roots, you see. There are still some down in the Addo Bush, so I suppose it's safe to reckon they'd drift up the river beds for a treat — until the white hunters put a stop to it.' That would have been toward the end of the eighteenth century, when the first Boers penetrated the Sneeuberge, into the huge basin of the Fish River valley — one of the last resorts of the Bushmen.

The Poplars was known for a variety of peculiarities, not least of which was the number of plates hanging on the walls of the drawing-room, the passages, the dining-room, even the bedrooms; and for other pieces of pottery or china — what Mother called 'crocks'.

The finer pieces were in a display cabinet made by Ernest; and every corridor sill, mantelpiece, table, side-table and ledge supported a jug, bowl, vase, or teapot of some charm or interest. Here and there were decorative plates that had been hand-painted by Mother's mother's father, George Eyre: charming pieces, of pink nude goddesses, smiling at us as though it was quite normal for ladies to go around naked; or plump cupids handling bows and arrows, or mathematical instruments, in a totally trivial and in-expert manner — with the same inane smiles as the goddesses. Then there was the large plate, about fifteen inches across, depicting a roundfaced handsome lady, in Tudor headgear, looking straight at one, goodnaturedly enough, but with only a trace of smile — very Holbein — against a back-ground of apple or pear blossom.

If the Stringers represented the financial competence which was so im-portant in the development of the potteries, the Eyres embodied the arts and crafts. The key figure among them is George Eyre (1818-87). His grandson, George Stringer, states that 'it was at the instance of Herbert Minton that George Eyre came into the district. Herbert had applied to Somerset House for an artist to design tiles, and the principal picked out George Eyre for the job.' In addition to his job at Minton's, he was one of the early pupil teachers at the Stoke School of Art, and member of the executive committee of the Potteries Mechanics Institute. How did he come to decorate china?

'There was, I suggest,' (says Uncle George) 'less process work in the days of our Victorian forebears, and thus many more artists in the industry, and, like all artists, they were underpaid. It was, however, customary for the artists to work at home on ware which they had purchased. Their employers allowed them to have their pieces fixed in their kilns, and the artist then sold them for his own benefit.'

When I was in England in 1974 George's son, Guy, gave me 'an oval dish in earthenware manufactured by Harding's (W. & J. Harding Bros at New Hall, 1864-1869), painted by George Eyre, with a scene from Don Quixote after Gustave Doré. Size 6" x 9".'

George Eyre was not merely an artist and designer, but 'a wonderful craftsman in wood, as witness the inlay work on the cabinet now in the possession of his granddaugher Alice Butler of Cradock C.P.' This arrived in Cradock in 1936, with his chisels, a fine set, still in my possession.

George's daughter, Sarah, married Frederick Septimus Stringer. His son inherited his father's interests. John Eyre, R.I., R.B.A., Hon. A.R.C.A., added painting in watercolours to ceramic design. He spent most of his life in London, and died in 1927.

Shortly after his death a crate of unframed pictures arrived at The Pop-lars. Many and anguished were Mother's deliberations as to which should be framed, and how; but in due course, after equally nerve-racking decisions as to where to hang them, during which Ernest scaled the heights of patience as well as the stepladder, the pictures were hung and The Poplars transformed.

The English pastoral scene, gentle, moist, was now available as never before to the eye of Alice when she came indoors from the harsh light: crumbling Harlech Castle; ruined Buildwas Abbey; a half-timbered house; a village church; a group of red-tiled farm buildings with sheep in the foreground; fields with stooks of golden corn. But she gave us to understand that these were mere sketches, or less successful efforts which hadn't sold; that he had done much painting in London and made a special study of the old soldiers of the Empire, the Chelsea Pensioners, and painted them in the quadrangle of their Hospital, or playing at cards, or staring at the Thames, or parading with their medals, or dining in their hall. One of his pictures, his most ambitious, had been hung on the line, and been acquired by Her Majesty the Queen, Victoria herself.

It never occurred to us to ask whether Queen Victoria had had any judgement in pictures. It was sufficient glory to have had a great-uncle who had been an Associate of the Royal Academy, and whose picture had pleased the Queen.

There were other originals, too: a little French oil, of a road through a grey wood — obviously influenced by Corot; and a tall Madonna of the Rocks. She stands barefoot, a trifle stiff, on brown crags in the midst of very formalised waves. She is erect, unafraid; in one arm is the Christ child, in the other a toy sailing-ship. I never discovered the myth behind the picture.

Where had these pictures come from? Admirers of Alice?

Alice's art interests showed in the bookshelves too: neat little introductory volumes to the painters of the Renaissance and the Pre-Raphaelites. These art books stood cheek by jowl with Father's Quaker books, the History of Sidcot School, and, later, volumes of the Left Book Club, such as Edgar Snow's *Red Star over China*.

There was another, somewhat incongruous stratum of pictures, in the passage near the bathroom: good, largish photographs of pieces of sculpture, the Venus de Milo, the Apollo Belvedere, and Rodin's 'Der Denker'. We called them the bath queue: Venus, with her towel slipping off her ample hips, but, alas, no arms to pull it up; she's not unduly worried, though. Apollo, naked, has his towel spread out and draped from one arm; he's not worried either, because he's got that fig leaf. But poor old Der Denker — no towel at all! He has sat himself down to hide his nakedness, and is pretending to be looking for something he's dropped on the passage floor — 'Where's that ruddy soap?'

One might joke, of course. But we all knew perfectly well that nudity was no joking matter. And there was a sublime severity of form, a singing, naked clarity in these statues, that showed itself nowhere else on our walls. Curiously enough that dimension found its nearest echo in the touches of Quaker asceticism in Ernest, and in Mary.

John Eyre's presence on the walls encouraged me to think that I might paint. Esoteric activities have only to be mastered by one relative to raise hopes of competence in the entire cousinage. But Uncle John was dead and I had never met him. My main source of encouragement was Frank Biggs of Vrede. Whenever I went over there for a holiday I would look at the paintings he had done. How different from Uncle John Eyre's! No soft water-colours for him. Oils applied, not with a brush, but a palette knife. And of scenes one knew, mountains outside the house, particular trees in particular fields at particular times of the year. And a world of colour and light not yet encountered in pictures.

Of course I had no idea of composition, but somewhere I acquired a drawing-block and a box of Reeves water-colour paints, and attempted a picture from the backyard of Vrede house, looking toward the pear trees. There was a bull in the field over the fence; he fascinated me — something about the hump, and the low-hanging dewlap. Trembling with the excitement of having tried and achieved, I returned to the house and, greatly daring, propped my masterpiece on the dining-room sideboard. Aunt Flo made kind remarks, and so did Ruth. John said nothing. He has always been a man of few words. Would Uncle Frank even notice it?

Well, he did. He had a marvellous grin, and he grinned at me. 'I particularly like the bull,' he said. 'That hump — it's alive.' I lived on that hump for years. But he never had time to tell me to try this or that, or that my skies were too dark. The fact that he was an adult, a farmer who found time to paint — that was the inestimable example.

There was Aunt Josie too, who, I knew from her daughter Honor, loved crafts and drew in pastels, and was sympathetic to such activities, but she was 600 miles away at Upington.

Back in Cradock an unexpected thing happened. In the good old tradition that Cradock's dry air was good for lungs, a Mr Thomas, a bad asthmatic, arrived to stay as a paying guest with Aunt Eliza in Market Street. He had been a Vickers Gunner during the Great War, and had been caught without a mask in a gas attack. He became manager of Butler Bros Book Shop, and attended Quaker meetings, although I doubt if he became one. In Meeting sometimes he would start breathing so that everyone could hear him, the muscles in his neck straining, fine sweat beads forming on his brow. And then in my mind's eye I would see the Vickers gun in front of him, chewing its belts of bullets, steam coiling out of the water jacket, as it pumped lead into a gap in the wire in no-man's-land, towards the hated Huns.

He was a difficult customer, but he sensed my hunger for the arts. After one Quaker meeting — or was it near my birthday? — he gave me a little book on how to paint in water-colours. It helped me considerably. It is amazing what leaps forward one can take by learning a few elementary techniques which one would perhaps never hit on alone.

I was also becoming increasingly aware of a school of indigenous artists that had disappeared suddenly in the late eighteenth and early nineteenth century: the Bushmen. Aunt Mary and a retired missionary from Healdtown, Mr Kissack, aroused my interest in the Stone Age. Mr Kissack specialised in large artefacts found in the open veld, so old that the flakings had weathered to a uniform brown. Aunt Mary would take us to recent Bushman sites along the river bank, where we would hunt for stone scrapers and arrowheads, for shards of broken pots, and for beads which the little huntsmen made from scraps of ostrich eggshell, while waiting for the game to come down to the water. It was a great day when Aunt Olive of Groenkloof brought me a Bushman stone — a beautifully shaped object with a hole bored through it — the first of my collection of seven. From the start these were pieces of sculpture to me, not mere tools.

Then came my first view of Bushman paintings, on 'Blighty', on the Tarka River. The irrigation canal had to negotiate a bottleneck between the river bed and a small cliff, in which was a cave. The blasting had in part removed the overhanging rock, but the paintings were still clearly visible. One enjoyed looking at those strong monochrome cutouts of elephants, rhino, eland, all the more for having had to crawl through prickly pears and mimosas to reach them, and at the risk of slipping into the muddy canal. Sitting there, staring at those strong, simple images, evoked many thoughts: the artist is dead, his subject matter is dead, the whites and the blacks exterminated both him and the game, but neither the whites nor the blacks have left their signatures on millions of small stones along the river banks, nor such a loving record of the other creatures who shared the land with them. The Bushman had chipped and shaped his existence out of stone; he had left shaped stones behind him; and on stone he had set down the shapes of the great beasts before bullets sent them into oblivion.

That eland's hump: I understood all about it from the bull I had painted at Vrede.

11

Realities and Fantasies

Two causes for anxiety invaded my life at the same time: the Great Depression, and puberty. And I do not pretend to understand more about the mysteries of economics and sex now than I did in 1930, when I was 12 years old. This chapter deals with the first of these mysteries.

The advent of the Great Depression is associated in my mind with the acquisition of a brand-new car called an Overland Whippet. The radiator cap, in silver, was surmounted by an elegant greyhound leaping ahead into the blue. Business was good early in 1929 — wool prices were satisfactory. To make his weekly Stock and Wool Edition financially viable, my father needed to persuade farmers and agricultural merchants to advertise in it. It was essential to visit them personally and sell the new idea. The old second-hand Essex, which had replaced the Humberette, would not impress prospective clients. A new image, a new car was called for. Hence the Whippet. Hence long journeys to stud farmers N, S, E, and W of Cradock; over corrugated dirt roads, through countless cattle gates. Hence those meals on farms strange to me, a self-conscious boy with close-cropped hair.

I remember the Stock and Wool Edition of *The Midland News* quite well: a whole front page of advertisements for various studs; fine pictures of handsome Wanganella rams, with silken chins pulled back into their manifold woolly dewlaps; Friesland bulls, with atlases for hides — white seas with irregular black islands and continents blotched on them. Inside the paper were long reports of agricultural shows, with lists of prizes in a hundred-and-one categories; and advertisements for lucerne mowers, windmills, chaff-cutters, pumps and rakes.

On one of these long trips, from Graaff-Reinet south towards Jansenville, my father was counting his blessings. Chief among these was good health, not only his own, but that of his own generation, and of his wife and children. Not all the wealth in the world, nor brilliance, nor social position, could compensate for bad health. He made great play with the mental robustness of the Butlers and the Colletts, and with regard to the Butlers in particular he said something like this:

'We Butlers have never been rich, and we probably never will be. Whenever I'm tempted to envy anyone for being well seen in this world's goods, I remind myself: there's probably a skeleton in his cupboard. On so many of these great farms, in a back room, looked after by a nurse or a Coloured servant, there's a simple-minded brother or a mongol child. "Elke huis het sy kruis," say the Afrikaners. Give me health and poverty rather than wealth and illness.'

Returning home late one night, Father's one good eye must have been very tired. He stopped the car somewhere near Post Chalmers, and asked me to drive. I felt honoured, excited and petrified. Although there was very little traffic on those roads, least of all late at night, donkey- or oxwagons without lanterns dangling beneath their rear axles could be a danger. Car headlights did not fling beams very far ahead. And as the roads were mostly unfenced, there was always the chance of hitting a sheep or coming to a halt with a black ox astride one's ruined radiator. So I drove with care. Apart from the occasional loping light of a springhare's eye on the side of the road, or a vlakhaas frozen momentarily in the beam, we saw nothing. We got home pleased with each other, I think.

It seems as though disaster announced itself the very next day. Appalling things were happening in a street called Wall Street, New York. Millionaires were throwing themselves off skyscrapers into the busy traffic below. They were doing this because the stock market had collapsed.

The results were felt almost immediately in South Africa. The price of wool dropped, and other agricultural produce followed suit. For farmers in the Karoo, and for the townsmen who depended on them, this spelt disaster, particularly as nature saw fit to aggravate matters by afflicting the land with a searing drought.

Breakfast at The Poplars was a regular family meal like any other, presided over by Father at the head, with Alice on his left. While he ate his porridge or boiled egg, he would slit open the letters of the morning's mail, brought from the post office by the Works messenger, Dohman. He would scan the correspondence, and place it into two or three separate piles in front of him — a preliminary filing; these piles he took up in a folder at the end of his meal, and so strode across to the Works with round one of the day's battle already over. Alice was always interested, particularly in the pile which contained narrow pink slips of paper. They were called cheques, and were as good as real money. Many cheques were a good sign. Against this pile, was the pile of bills. Many bills were a bad sign.

Dad no longer attacked his mail with relish and expectation. One would watch surreptitiously to see if one could catch a glimpse of pink. Alice would ask, with puckered brow, 'Anything in the mail, dear?' And he'd say: 'Not much,' or 'Plenty, but of the wrong sort,' or 'Nothing.'

White bread disappeared from the family table. Soon butter followed it into exile. It was replaced by dripping, which was palatable enough if you managed to get a smear of the brown salty gravy from the bottom of the bowl. Half a sausage, instead of a whole one. And no tasty things, like Marmite or anchovy paste. Cheaper brands of everything.

As soon as we got back from school each day, off came our footwear, to save leather. We did not mind this at all. During holidays on farms — nearly every holiday at this time was a farm holiday — we usually went barefoot, summer or winter, and our feet became resistant to all but the toughest thorns. After our evening baths at Katkop, Uncle Norman would de-thorn us — it was easier after the thick hide on our feet had been softened by the hot water. But in town Alice thought there was something very wrong with a world in which children approaching puberty went unshod, and she would never allow us outside the front gate without shoes and socks. When asked why, she would give one of two reasons.

'You'll get broad flat feet, like ducks. Do you want your toes pointing to all the points of the compass? You'll never get shoes to fit you when you grow up.'

And the other:

'I won't have my children going about in public like a lot of poor-whites.'

Poor-whites were a common enough sight in the Karoo in the early 'thirties. It is estimated that there were 300 000 of them at the time — a very high proportion of South Africa's total white population of 1 700 000. The measures adopted by the State and municipalities indicate the extremity of the position: South African white men in thousands were forced to do what they regarded as menial work — kaffir's work — with picks and shovels. In Cradock they were employed to construct new tarred streets.

From our position opposite the D.R.C. Pastorie we could not help witnessing the frequent visits of poor families seeking the Dominee's help, particularly at the beginning or the end of the school term. Some of them came in wagons, others in buggies from the kloofs in the Agtersneeuberg, or the Tarka — usually dignified in bearing, wearing old-fashioned but spotless clothes — to hand over their children to the free Koshuis; and always, without fail, to leave a token gift for the pastor, maybe a brace of chickens, or, if really desperate, a pumpkin. Others came from the back streets, and had lost their dignity: the urban poor seemed infinitely worse off than the rural. I recall one gaunt lantern-jawed man whose wife had recently died, walking there with his seven orphans, all more or less dirty and ragged — and barefoot.

When The Poplars children needed shoes, Alice would find out from Ernest which shoe-shop in town owed *The Midland News* money for advertising, printing or stationery, and then take her custom there. As much as possible was done *per contra,* a Latin phrase which appears in the trading ledgers kept in the early 1830s by our trading ancestor, James Lydford Collett, who used to go on 'smousing trips' into 'Kaffirland', and later north to Colesberg — selling merino rams in return for cattle, or meal, or cash.

So Dad was following an ancient family tradition of barter when he loaded the Whippet up with samples of butter paper and stationery, and albums of H.M.V. records, plus an older child as gate-opener, and went smousing among the richer farmers. Joan has a vivid recollection of such a trip; and I recall at least two, trying to sell radios to reluctant farmers. It was heartbreaking to see how bad and embarrassed a salesman one's father was.

The manager of one of the biggest stores in town (W.J. Stevens & Sons) was a Mr Allan, whose son Gordon was in my class and in the same Boy Scout Patrol. Mr Robertson was helping Mr Allan with his books — but they could not be made to balance because so many farmers were defaulting. The distracted manager hired a taxi to take him out to Lake Arthur. He alighted, ran along the great concrete wall, and flung himself over into the water.

The town was stunned.

After the funeral Jean Robertson was sent to board with Mrs Allan to help with her finances, and to cheer her up. Gordon returned to school, pale and quiet.

Father used to bring the firm's books home and pore over them at the family table while we did our homework. What if they didn't balance? Would he do as Mr Allan had done? One would raise one's eyes furtively from one's work and watch him. He had a way of sucking the knuckle of his forefinger when deep in thought. Our anxiety increased when he shut himself up with his books in Aunt Jessie's room.

After one of these sessions, he emerged and said, 'Alice, I'm going to Salt Pans Drift to see Uncle Herbert tomorrow. I'll take Guy to open the gates.'

So we climbed into the Whippet, but the atmosphere was not as before.

He did not tell me much beyond saying that *The Midland News* was heavily bonded to Uncle Herbert, and that he could not meet the interest. When we reached the farm, I was sent off to look at the animals. I looked at no animals. I sat out of sight, my back against a dry-packed stone wall begging God to soften Uncle Herbert's heart.

A bell rang for afternoon tea. Aunt Jessie plied me with biscuits. Uncle Herbert gave me a sixpence for liquorice.

Back in the car Father said, 'He's agreed.' I did not know what Uncle Herbert had agreed to; but I presume it was to wait for the interest, and not call in the bond.

The depression did not affect *The Midland News* only: it affected Butler Bros, the shop. Takings fell so low that they did not cover the rent of the premises in Adderley Street. So the shop was moved into a portion of *The Midland News* premises in Church Street, a far less central site. Mother was installed as its manageress. She did her best, and enjoyed talking to all the customers, picking up bits of news for the paper and gossip for her tea parties. As always, she was a social success. But from time to time customers had to remind her before they left the shop that she had not yet charged them for the Croxley writing pad and envelopes which they had come in to buy.

The depression was harder on the blacksmith's wife. The need for blacksmiths and farriers was declining as the invading internal combustion engine steadily drove horses and oxen out of the valley; and her husband could not make the most of the little work that came his way because he had developed circulation trouble in his legs. Nor could her handsome father do much for her, since saddlers and harness-makers were suffering the same fate as blacksmiths and farriers.

So, like several other women, she sent her Xhosa maid from door to door peddling her wares from a basket: netting jug covers, weighted with small clusters of coloured beads of tiny sea shells, or fresh koeksisters, or coconut ice in pretty paper packets.

Local home-made fudge took the place of Cadbury's chocolate on Saturday nights.

It was during these lean years that one of mother's useless wedding-presents justified itself: Mrs Beeton's cookery book, with red leather cover, about four inches thick, lavishly illustrated with coloured plates of table settings and delectable dishes, and hundreds of exotic recipes. Designed for affluent Edwardian households, it was little or no use to Alice — her meals were plain and the helpings as generous as one could wish. While we never went hungry, we began to miss sweet and savoury things so acutely that we would lie sprawled on the linoleum like untidy petals radiating from the book, playing a variety of culinary and gustatory games. The simplest was to take it in turns to open the book blindfold. If it opened at a plate of illustrations, you could choose a dish from that page; if not, you went hungry. The resulting menus might be somewhat unusual, starting with walnuts or dessert, and ending with barons of beef. A more sophisticated game was to work out an agreed menu on sound democratic principles. 'How many for soup?' Five. 'Thick or clear?' Three thick, two clear. 'Thick gets it.' So we would turn up thick soups in Mrs Beeton and decide by vote which it was to be. The fish course always presented us with the greatest difficulty because of our piscatorial ignorance. Unless a Karoo child is taken to the seaside for holidays, the only fish he is likely to know about are small bluegills in the river, and headless sardines in tins.

One of the perpetual humiliations of my childhood — and of Jeffrey's — was our lack of hair. This was not due to premature baldness but to Father's determination to save money. He started cutting his own children's hair when we were still in 60 Bree Street, during the post-war depression. He would place the rounded cover back on to the Singer sewing-machine (which had a stand of its own) and perch us on it, tuck a towel round our necks, and get busy. The girls took quite a long time. He would place a pudding mixing-bowl on their heads like a hat, and use the rim as a guide for his scissors and clippers. Such sophistication was unnecessary with the boys. He simply clipped our skulls to the bone. When challenged by a critical aunt, he told her proudly how much the clipper had cost, and how many times it had paid for itself.

Such a distinctive scalp earned me the nicknames 'Groot Eier' and 'Egg' — until my revolt at the age of 13 was upheld by Alice and Aunt Mary. I was then permitted to grow my hair a trifle longer, and go to Mr Schoonraad's barber to get it cut for sixpence. There one would sit happily for hours, waiting one's turn, listening to the lugubrious gossip of the townsfolk and the farmers.

Small towns turn all places where people meet into open clubs. It took me a little time to get the pitch of the Afrikaans conversations. They were usually laden with grouses against the weather, the government, the new dip, the old show committee, the school board and the railways. But beneath the fatalistic acceptance of their trials was the comfort of mutual sighs of commiseration. Although no one ever laughed, they thoroughly enjoyed these sessions. They did not like the company of optimistic and enthusiastic busybodies, like Mr P.S. van Niekerk, who was so confident that intelligence and goodwill could remove most of their grievances. There are always these officious people in the world who want to change things and take away your pleasures.

It must have been at this time that I developed a passion for what used to be called nature study, which meant the eager and fascinated observation of all things animal, vegetable and mineral, and the collection of examples of as many varieties as possible. Like most boys, I started with the most delicate, the most beautiful: butterflies, and birds' eggs.

I have memories of dreamy, joyous summer days in the lucerne fields and mimosa scrub that fringed the farm furrows, with butterfly net, and box lined with cottonwool for birds' eggs, a dedicated collector and hunter; or high up in a giant poplar tree on Vrede, moving out along a lateral branch towards a bunch of mistletoe in which I thought I had detected a bird's nest; the quivering poplar leaves, and my own trembling limbs as I inched forward; then the dappled shivering-green and silver world suddenly becoming a skywards cataract as the branch broke and I plunged downward, head first. Fortunately my head fell into the fork of a fairly strong but springy lower branch, and my shoulders took the impact and broke my fall, enforcing a half somersault upon my body, so that the rest of my journey earthwards was feet first. I crashed hard into the poplar saplings, and lay there, very still, afraid to move lest I should find some part of me broken.

The pursuit of science was clearly a dangerous business; but my ardour continued unabated. At this time I was determined to become a naturalist, like the Canadian, Ernest Thompson-Seton, and to spend my life studying the lives of animals. I suspected that this was a crazy idea, that the training would be impossibly expensive and that Ernest and Alice would not approve.

So I kept it dark.

Of course the interest was not purely scientific — whatever that word means. Sitting dead still, watching the behaviour of beetles (water boatmen) on a slow, gently rippling stream; or freezing, lest any movement should betray one's presence, in order to watch a woodpecker assaulting a rotten branch, furiously scattering scraps of bark and capturing the exposed insects in its beak — at such moments one experienced an intensity of attention very close to certain religious states of mind.

It was in 1930 that my sister Joan began to emerge from her shell. 'I was not happy at school until standard Five,' she says. 'Then I woke up as a person and responded all of a heap to Anna Rabie (later Anna Coetzee), our beautiful Afrikaans mistress, and Miss Stone, quiet and dignified. Mother once told me that she and Dad completely misjudged my capability as a small girl, and it was a miracle when I suddenly cheered up.'

I can recall the great interest and excitement of my sisters in these two teachers and in their engagements. How long would their engagements last? What was an engagement for? And I can remember Joan's increasing sense of appropriate behaviour in public. Romping that might be perfectly proper in The Poplars garden was not proper in the Town Hall. I had to learn this fact about times and seasons the hard way, at the Junior Red Cross Ball. I was simply not interested in dancing. The big attraction for me and my ilk was the interval between the dances. Then we would take the floor and use it as a skating-rink; we would do a short sprint, and then let the impetus carry us over the borax-polished surface. Then some bright spark would shout, 'Sweepstok!' Six or seven of us would form up at one end of the hall in descending order of size and hold hands. At a given signal, we would all sprint up the ballroom together; about halfway, the biggest fellow who acted as the whip handle would stop dead in his tracks, then the rest, forming the whip-lash, would race through an arc at a speed which increased in ratio to the distance they were from the 'stok'. The boy at the end had to let go to save himself from being flattened against the wall. He would then sail an independent course, like a launched satellite. When it came to my turn, the fates decreed that a group of parents should decide to cross the hall just as I had reached my maximum velocity. I ended up among a small forest of adult ankles and knees. I clambered erect saying, 'Ekskuus, sorry, jammer,' and ran back to claim another turn, as mine had been spoiled by unforeseen circumstances. But halfway down Joan, erect and blushing with shame, hissed, 'Stop showing off!'

It is difficult to convey just how misjudged I felt. There was only one place and time in the entire year to play this sort of sweepstok, and here was my dear big sister, looking suddenly grown up, stigmatising me as a show-off.

Joan took a great interest in my museum. At this stage it consisted of a set of grey open shelves on the back stoep, with shoe and other boxes containing hundreds of treasures: birds' eggs; sea shells; exotic seeds and pods; coloured pebbles from the Fish River and from the Orange — how different they were! Butterflies, shards of Bushman pottery, beads made out of ostrich-egg shells, crescents and arrowheads. Larger items were on the open shelves: skulls of various domesticated and feral species; the transparent sloughed skin of a snake; birds' nests; and stones of peculiar shape or colour.

It was a great day for me when Joan came home from school with a small snake coiled round her hockey stick — it was a skaapsteker. Although the girls had damaged him badly in one or two places, he became, when bottled in methylated spirits, a fine addition to my collection.

And it was Joan who unwittingly touched off a great phase of romantic fantasy about our ancestry. One day on her way back from school Mrs T.J. Roberts stopped her, saying, 'Come here my child. Do you know anything about your ancestors?' To which she replied in the negative.

'Well, come inside, and see what I've found in a big book.'

Joan came home delighted to break the great news that, provided every Butler father in our line for a couple of centuries had been the eldest son of an eldest son, our own father could have been a Duke living in a castle in Ireland, but for one circumstance. The King of England had been in great difficulties during a time of civil war, and the Irish Butlers had been loyal to him. When his troubles were over, he wished to express his appreciation by conferring a dukedom on the eldest son. But the eldest son, having come under the influence of Quakers, who regard titles as worldly vanities, declined, and the title passed to the second son. The eldest son left Ireland and settled somewhere in England. Alice turned to Ernest and asked if he knew anything about it? And if so, why had he kept it so dark? Ernest said he had a vague recollection of talk on the matter, but was sure Mary would know. Mary was only slightly less vague. Yes, she had heard the tale. There were other old stories she had heard, about a fine French lady escaping from France in a box and marrying a Butler, but she didn't lay much store by them. And there the adults let the matter rest; the present was far too grim for them to indulge in remote and obscure genealogies. Even Alice, the great romantic, could not even find time to borrow the book from her friend Mrs T.J. Roberts. But if the adults were prepared, for whatever reasons, to abandon their forefathers, we children were not.

The man-who-might-have-been-a-Duke drifted in and out of our fantasies far less frequently than the French lady, whose escaping box we had turned into a coffin. To minds recently primed on *The Tale of Two Cities* and Baroness Orczy's *The Scarlet Pimpernel,* such a hint kindled a fine imaginative blaze. The old Tudor chest in the passage became the coffin, in which my barefooted sisters took turns as the aristocratic escapee, while I had a fine time playing the Pimpernel. My disguise was always that of the undertaker. On one occasion, when the Jacobin agents insisted on inspecting the corpse, I said, 'As you please, Messieurs, but at your risk. The Countess died of the Plague.' That put them off the scent.

Now clearly, such a fine Countess could not exist without a name. Aunt Mary had a family tree going back to the post-Revolutionary period, and there, sure enough, we found an appropriate person: Philippa Norman. We had read of a Philippa of Hainsault in *My Magazine* or *The Children's Encyclopaedia*. Philippa was a French name, without doubt. As for Norman — well, wasn't Normandy part of France, and wasn't William the Conqueror a Norman? So, having found her a firm branch in the family tree, we rejoiced in a fine strain of aristocratic Catholic French blood in our egalitarian Quaker veins.

In 1976 I asked Mary about our female ancestor who had escaped from France in a coffin during the French Revolution. Her first response was an indulgent laugh — 'Oh, that's your mother, that's pure Alice!' Then after a little: 'Mind you, there was something about a French woman escaping in a chest, not a coffin — but not our branch, some other branch.' She had no further help to offer on the Butler-who-might-have-been-a-Duke.

In January 1977 I was lent a dossier of family papers collected by Aunt Emmie Fear, my grandfather James's sister, from which it appears that there were Butlers with a proper reverence for titles: Cephas Butler II of Birmingham, the lamp maker, had a son with an interest in such matters, who called in the assistance of the College of Heralds. The following extracts from a letter of Cephas II to Aunt Emmie, dated 17 June 1916, remove every pleasurable taint of Catholic, aristocratic, Gallic blood from our veins. Philippa Norman was after all a good English lass and no foreigner. The French lady belongs to Cephas Butler's branch, by virtue of one Peter Butler's (second) marriage to a Mary Busvine in Bristol in 1833. By this time, however, the Busvines had been in Britain for well over a century; the forefathers had not been aristocratic Catholics flying from atheistic Jacobins, but devout Protestants flying from aristocratic Catholics. 'What I am most proud of', says Cephas, 'is that I come of a stock who lost all for Christ at the Revocation of the Edict of Nantes, my great-great-grandmother fleeing to England after hiding at one of the farms in Normandy, and coming over in a seaman's chest, bringing only her French bible and a china bowl, made by Pallaisy, the Protestant potter. This bowl I now have.'

History always seems to conspire to bring our plebeian branch of the Butlers back to earth. Still, before the Quakers and History recaptured her, our version of Philippa Norman was as fine a French lady as ever escaped a guillotine.

Cephas Butler's letter is less damaging to the Butler-who-declined-a-dukedom. 'In the times of George Fox, the ancestor of the present Marquis of Ormonde (whose seat is near Kilkenny) had done some service for the country, and was offered a marquisate, but, being a follower of George Fox, he felt he could not accept such an earthly title; and so it passed to his next brother.' Cephas then goes on to discuss the family crest: the Marquis of Ormonde's consists of three plumes; the eldest, the title-decliner, is entitled to five. But, I ask, would a man who has risen above the flattery of a marquisate descend to the frippery of a five-feathered crest? Cephas continues: 'My son wrote to the present Marquis about it, and the Marchioness wrote somewhat confirming the matter and sent him a signed photograph of herself.' Cephas, however, has not quite convinced himself, as he ends, 'You must take these particulars for what they are worth, but I think they are correct.'

And Aunt Emmie, after quoting an impressive paragraph on the Ormonde lineage from *Burke's Peerage,* closes her Cephas chapter with a few hard facts: 'In The Bristol Monthly Quaker Meeting, the dates of Butlers go back to 1666' (which would be about right for the self-denying Duke-who-might-have-been). 'But there is a missing link in the chain between William Butler, born 1734' (our ancestor) 'and the earlier date of 1666, which has not been explained.'

To revert to Philippa Norman, who turned out to be an English lass after all. Our French-countess-in-the-coffin fantasy would never have come into flower had we been slightly more observant when attending Quaker Meet-ings at Aunt Eliza's: for there on the wall hung a framed sampler, consisting of very simple black lettering on plain linen, beautifully stitched by Philippa at the age of 7. I saw it recently in the home of one of her great-grand-daughters, Joyce Fear of Cape Town, and it is reproduced in the illustrations in this book. How many 7-year-old children today make samplers? And how many of any age are brought to contemplate such fine stoic sentiments? 'Virtue is that perfect good which is the crown of a happy life, the only immortal thing that belongs to mortality . . .'

12

Mainly among Mountains

Mother used to stand on the kitchen steps and sing out in a melodious voice loud enough to reach me at the bottom of the garden:

'Guysie, do you want a piece-ee?'

And I would drop whatever I was doing in order to fetch a thick slice of her home-made brown bread laden with Adam fig jam, soaked with its juice.

Suddenly the affectionate diminutive and the singing voice made me wince. Telling my friends to follow, I ran up to the house and pleaded, 'You're never to call me Guysie again! I'm not a kid any more.'

She looked at me with one eyebrow raised, and proceeded to spread six slices of brown bread and fig jam for my friends.

Mother was pleased I had so many playmates, but Father remarked drily that my popularity and the grapes matured at the same time.

I believe that 1930 was the year of the N.O.S.F., a secret society founded by John Adan, the science master's son. I was initiated at an impressive oath-swearing ceremony round a single candle in a dry stormwater drain somewhere under Carrington Street. I had to sign my name in a mixture of my own spittle and blood. All the members swore to perform noble deeds of masculine heroism, as unquestioning and unflinching as assassins. The name of the society caught its temper well enough, 'The Noble Order of Schoolboy Fanatics'; its flag sported a skull and crossbones — white on a scarlet background.

It was an exciting society, but in retrospect not commendable. Had 'pot' been available we would almost certainly have smoked it. To break any adult taboo was a noble deed. We encouraged each other's fantasies and swopped dirty stories, but our main concern was our enemies. Enemies were essential; without them whom could we hate, and plot against, and fight?

The town had several rival gangs, most of which we dismissed as beneath contempt. Our only serious rival was Tokkie Verster's gang. Our secret service informed us that they took no oath, had no book of rules, and kept no register of attendance; yet we knew that in spite of this pathetic absence of professionalism, they could fight with a fanaticism equal to our own.

Fights could happen any time, anywhere — during break at school, in the streets on Sunday evening after church, out in the veld. One day we captured a prisoner, blindfolded him, and carried him bound hand and foot out into the veld, where we debagged him, and rubbed his belly, his buttocks, and the back of his legs with the juice of a certain bulb which stung the skin most painfully when it dried. We then released him. We spent much time working out original tortures of this kind.

Our headquarters tended to move at frequent intervals. Parents are so intolerant and uncomprehending.

Our greatest battle was in defence of our den, at that time in the old loft of the Magistrate's disused stables. The heat under the corrugated-iron roof was offset by a thrilling atmosphere of gloom and decay: spiderwebs hanging in dusty beards a yard long, old bits of harness so dry they snapped like twigs, and genuine Dracula bats squeaking intermittently. The ground floor was partially filled with unused items of furniture.

Verster's gang, tired of casual encounters, decided to seek out the enemy and destroy him in his stronghold. We had hoped this would happen, and had stockpiled our weapons of defence: reed peashooters, with peppertree berries for ammunition, and buckets of mud ('potklei') of the right consistency. Our secret weapon was to be hot water.

As Verster appeared in the driveway, Adan instructed Phelps to light the Primus, which Mrs Phelps had supplied without being asked. The enemy attacked and, much to our consternation, were not mown down by the withering fire of our peashooters. We also learnt that it is difficult to fling mud through a small window with any degree of force or accuracy. It tends to backfire. The enemy soon reached the old stable doors and tried to force them open. The seriousness of Verster's intentions was indicated by the tommy bar he was carrying. The time had come to employ our secret weapon.

Adan, standing on the hay-loading platform, poured hot water on the attackers. They retreated, very angry indeed, shouting that we were 'playing dirty'. We replied that they *were* dirty, and needed a hot-water wash anyway. Verster retired to a nearby building-site and borrowed two six-foot sheets of new corrugated iron. Under cover of these they approached the stable door and, having established a penthouse, gave the signal for the battering-ram to be brought into play. Two of his men dashed from the cover of the quince hedge carrying a sneezewood pole. The first blow loosened the screws in the hasp and staple. With the speed and strength of desperation we moved an old-fashioned stinkwood dresser against the doors, and then wedged it there by means of packing-cases all the way back to a manger post. If Verster's gang should batter through the door, they would still have to make matchwood of the furniture.

This crisis had brought the entire N.O.S.F. on to the ground floor. A loud banging on the roof of the loft caused me to clamber up the ladder at the very moment when Verster, tommy bar in hand, slewed one of the roofing sheets aside. The sunlight poured in like flame.

But Verster did not jump into the loft. One of his supporting troops had put his hand on his shoulder, and pointed into the yard below. Verster hissed down to Adan:

'Yerrah, hier kom die Magistraat!' and disappeared.

We were trapped. Outside, the Magistrate was giving instructions to a constable. A thick voice commanded, 'Now come on, you oukies, open up now.' Adan showed great presence of mind.

'All into the loft,' he said. Once there, he pulled the ladder up after him, and then thrust it through the opening which Verster had made in the roof.

'Follow me, quietly,' he said. We did so, out of the loft, down the roof, over a row of water tanks, along a dividing wall, and down a wistaria creeper into Mrs Levenstein's backyard. She was very surprised to see us, but we did not have time to stop and help her hang up her washing. We made for the street, and scattered.

Neither Adan nor Verster was worried about the damage to the Magistrate's property. We all escaped scot-free except the Magistrate's son, who nobly refused to divulge our names. I wonder whether Mrs Phelps ever recovered her Primus stove. It may still be in that loft.

Fortunately the organised savagery of N.O.S.F. was offset by the Boy Scout Troop. It has become customary in some quarters to sneer at this movement, but it played an entirely beneficent role in my boyhood. Within a gentle discipline to which the voluntary members responded because they were expected to behave well, it opened horizons in almost every direction: one had to learn the Boy Scout doctrine of man, to be prepared for any eventuality by land or sea, day or night; it taught us how to handle string and rope, the difference between a reef-knot and a granny, the various uses of the clove-hitch and the sheepshank; how to light a fire with one match; how to make an Irish stew; the importance of keeping a shine on one's boots and one's teeth; how to read a map and follow a trail; how to be thoughtful and polite; to do a good turn each day, and not only to old ladies who needed help in crossing a road; above all, it encouraged us to hike, to climb, and camp in the open, and to observe the tricks of weather, animals, trees, and stars.

I learnt very early that our mountains were made of two kinds of rock: sandstone and ironstone. Uncle Norman's mason, old Barter, explained the difference. 'Sandstone is like white bread samidges. Comes in layers, you see. Get your chisel on the right spot, and she cleaves open clean and flat. But ironstone is like "doodgooi": solid and same all through. It don't cleave open clean. You've gotta shape it, chip by chip. But it's hard, man, and blue, and it's got iron in it. That's why it rusts red and brown with the rain.'

The contrasts observed by the old mason received further elaborations from Mr W.W. Lidbetter, in reply to a question: 'Why are Tafelberg, Doornberg, Spekboomberg and Salpetersberg all flat topped?'

'The whole Great Karoo and southern Free State', he said, 'was once an enormous lake. Rivers from mountain ranges which no longer exist drained into it from several directions, and gradually it silted up. Sandstone is made out of river or seasand that has solidified. That's why you find ripple marks on it so often. That's why you'll find fossils in it — mainly fish and reptiles who lived hundreds of millions of years ago — depending on how deep you go. Most of the fossils here are between 200 and 300 million years old. A great change took place about two hundred million years ago when the lake broke up, and its bottom became a huge plateau exposed to the weather, which has since been eroded into the shapes you see. If the flat mountaintops and the parallel cliffs look as if they've been laid down with a mason's level, it's because they were laid down by water — silt, in fact.'

'What do you mean, the lake broke up?'

'Enormous earthquakes made great cracks in the earth's crust, and through these cracks the molten ironstone was forced up. The cracks run criss-cross through the sandstone. Stand on a mountain, and you are likely to see a ridge of ironstone koppies running in a more or less straight line — that's a dolerite dyke. Sometimes the lava would force itself between layers of sandstone, or pour out and cover large areas. So ironstone is a very young sort of a rock. It is being weathered for the first time. But as it is harder than sandstone it weathers more slowly. Many of our mountains are only there because they have a protecting cap of ironstone.'

There is hardly a farm in the Eastern Cape that hasn't got its koppie or its mountain. And hardly a holiday would pass on a farm but we would climb one or more of them. It was always a progressive adventure, to pause periodically, and see how much more of the world had come into view. Gradually one got to know the mountains by name, and recognise their shapes by their profiles, even though these changed with each eminence one climbed. It was fine, later, to cast one's eye round, and say, 'I've looked at this mountaintop from that mountaintop, that pale-blue silhouette sixty miles away; and from that one; and that, and that'; and to trace the course of the rivers — mostly tributaries of the Fish or the Sundays rivers — marked by dark mimosa bush and tiny patches of cultivation.

I had the great good fortune to be a member of the Rhino patrol, whose patrol leader, Rex Moys, had a passion for camping and a talent for organising expeditions.

There was, for instance, the expedition to Elandsberg. Elandsberg consists of two mountains — one like an enormous rough scalloped shell, the other like a lion couchant — connected by a saddle about half way up.

The plan was to walk there across the veld, and sleep at the foot of the mountain the first night; climb to the saddle, and establish our base camp at the cattle dam which would supply our water; then climb to the craggy top of the lion's head. There, we would light a fire at nightfall. Our parents were to be on the lookout for it, seven miles away in Cradock.

Our first halt was at Egg Rock, an enormous ovoid dolerite boulder supported on a small koppie. It was the first time I had packed a kitbag. I had placed a bunch of bananas at the bottom, together with some extra-strong peppermints. When I opened it in the shade, the heavier and harder items, like tins of condensed milk, were sinking in a yellow pulp. Rex reminds me that, once we had extracted the banana skins, the paper wrappings of the peppermints and bits of canvas thread, we enjoyed a most unusual fruit salad.

McEwen also had his difficulties. Each of us was responsible for his own water supply. He connected two ordinary glass bottles by a piece of string, which he hung round his neck. The string galled his flesh somewhat. The climb to the saddle on the second day was very steep towards the end, and one had to lean forward, and use one's hands to grip the rocks ahead. Just as he reached the top, McEwen's two bottles collided, breaking each other.

Rex consoled him by saying that there would be water at the dam. At last we reached it. It was no more than a muddy pool about six foot across, thick with paddaslime and alive with mosquito larvae, tadpoles, red wriggly worms, and other goggas. Following approved lore, we strained this fluid through two layers of none-too-clean handkerchiefs, added a few drops of iodine, and boiled it for twenty minutes. No microbe, we had been told, could survive twenty minutes' boiling plus iodine treatment. We then made tea. The flavour was certainly unusual, but it did quench our thirst.

Having pitched base camp, we climbed the lion's head. It was marvellous up there. I crawled to the very edge of the great cliff, and lay looking down, elated by red hawks riding the wind with ease and daring. I also gathered succulents such as I had not seen before, for my rockery, and scrub wood from stunted bushes for our fire.

The sun sank over the Wapadsberg sixty miles to the west, and the cool dusk set in. Then the great game — who would be first to see a star? Then the gradual invasion of the deepening space above us by millions of points of light, some of which were in configurations we already knew: Orion and the Southern Cross.

High up, there, we lit our fire in the midst of the sky. It was a glorious blaze, the flames leaping ten or twelve feet from the rock, sending up strings of sparks and even small embers. One such ember lodged in the back of my scout scarf, which provided everyone with an excuse to slap and pound me on the back, to put it out. The air grew cold, but we were conscientious, and would not leave until the last ember had died.

It was a moonless night. We had not thought how difficult the descent would be in the dark. We knew that if we kept our heads there was no real danger of falling over the cliff, but the mere thought of its unspecified proximity in that vast darkness was awesome. The sounds of our boots on the rocks seemed very loud. Far away, a jackal cried. I have never forgotten that jackal cry. It was desolate, but the fact that it meant death to some creature that night appealed to a small, guilty, non-Quaker tiger in my subconscious.

To the south-west of Cradock lie the Bankberge, a massive mixture of sandstone and sills and domes of dolerite, stretching south to the Bosberg at Somerset East, and then westward to the Tandjiesberge near Graaff-Reinet. At one point from the south a tributary of the Sundays River called the Vogelrivier penetrates far into them. Opposite its headwaters, just over the watershed, a tributary of the Paulsrivier runs north, before that river swings west to join the Fish.

Old James Lydford Collett once had two farms on the Paulsrivier, one called 'Waterkloof' deep among the mountains. There was a steep wagon track over the watershed, connecting his valley with the valley of the Vogelrivier. He decided to use this track during the war of Mlanjeni, in 1852, to get his wool to Port Elizabeth, via Uitenhage. But he discovered that loaded wagons could not negotiate its roughness. So the resourceful man rolled the great wool bales down the mountainside, took the empty wagons down, and reloaded them at the bottom.

On other occasions he rode east over those mountaintops, over the Skurweberge, and then descended into Swaershoek, to buy a horse or borrow ten pounds sterling from Mr Malan.

There is a laconic entry in the diaries describing his return home from some such outing: 'Lost all night in the mountains.'

One of those mountains is Spioenkop, on the Cradock side of Swaershoek. Among its massive buttresses and flanks lay the farm of the old Boer War general called Kritzinger (1870-1935). He had been one of De Wet's Commandants, and led three daring raids into the Cape Colony from the Free State, on the last of which he had been seriously wounded and captured. Thirty years later he was elected member of the Cape Provincial Council for the district he had penetrated as an intrepid guerilla raider.

Kritzinger was a gentlemanly general of the old sort. When his commando raided a farm for supplies, he did not allow his men to take whatever sheep they liked. He would ask the farmer for slaughter stock. In later years he had a soft spot for Rooinekke and a gently patronising air towards their sons, particularly those who liked the veld.

On our way up to the windmill deep in one of his kloofs, we would stop at the oasis which was his farm. There he would show us some marvel — such as a swallow's nest built on the point of one of the kudu horns on his stoep; and then he would allow us to pillage his enormous Adam fig tree, and send an instruction to his bywoner to sell us goat's milk if we wanted it.

Like most country-bred people, he had a long memory for families, and he knew and respected the Colletts, particularly that old bachelor, Herbert of Salt Pans Drift.

On the second occasion we camped at Kritzinger's, we were determined to shoot enough dassies to make a kaross each. To secure ourslves enough free time for this ambitious task, we took Isaiah with us, a Xhosa boy of our own age, who sang Christian hymns day and night, and wore a red fez. Born and bred in Cradock location, he was a total stranger to the country-side, an absolute townee; he was saving money for a bicycle lamp, so that he could ride at night. His tasks were to look after the camp, collect fire-wood, wash up, and skin the dassies. We paid him a shilling a day, all found.

We made our first camp on the clean sand of the sloot as the twilight set in. As there was no sign of rain we did not pitch the tent. We sent Isaiah off to collect firewood. Suddenly that magnificent resonant sound, the bark of a male baboon, exploded in the still air. Its echo seemed to stagger from cliff to cliff, all up the kloof. Then again, and again, salvo upon salvo of angry abuse. Isaiah reappeared at high speed, terrified.

'It's only baboons,' we said, with more confidence than we felt.

The great cursing died, and we crawled into our blankets, Isaiah on his own, on the other side of the fire. We did not sleep well. The night wind made lonely, thin noises, and the nightjars called forlornly to each other. And then we heard the soft padding of feet round us. Our camp was being inspected by the baboons. At last they disappeared and we fell asleep. When we awoke, we found that Isaiah had transferred his sleeping-place: he was curled up between the dead fire and our feet.

My turn to be frightened came a few days later.

We pitched our permanent camp in a thicket of mimosa trees, which pro-vided wood for our fire and shade in the noon day. A few hundred yards farther up the kloof was our source of water – a windmill, which filled a small concrete reservoir, which in turn supplied the water troughs for the stock. After a day's clambering over the mountainsides under the Karoo sun we would take a cleansing and refreshing dip in the reservoir.

I had climbed, alone, with a .22 rifle on to one of the parallel sand-stone cliffs so characteristic of Karoo mountains, and lay down, waiting for the dassies to re-emerge. It was warm, pleasantly so, and I dozed off. I woke up with the uncanny feeling that I was not alone. It wasn't the pres-ence of the dassies on the ledges below me that gave me this feeling, how-ever; it was a slight, busy, convivial and conversational noise. Without moving my body, I slowly turned my head – and found myself to be in the line of advance of a pack of foraging baboons. Right in front of me was a magnificent male, on his haunches, examining some small object struggling between thumb and forefinger – possibly a grub or a scorpion – which he had discovered by overturning the large stone before him. A

little to one side was a female, also squatting, tenderly suckling a diminutive baby. Farther off, another female was strolling along, with her child
clinging for dear life to her fur with finger and toe. Two young adolescents
were indulging in a very impolite exchange of views. Once an exasperated
parent cuffed a too-inquisitive or greedy child, who let out a painful and
apprehensive squawk. Towards the back was another large male foraging
but, like the old gentleman sentinel near me, looking up and about every
few seconds. It was an extraordinarily happy scene.

Suddenly — had the wind changed and betrayed my presence? — the large
male fixed me with his eyes, dropped on to his forefeet from his squatting
position, and let out a single, vast bark, his two-inch canine teeth showing
white in the cavity of his mouth. I grabbed the rifle and leapt up in terror.
He braced himself but did not budge, merely continued barking. Behind
him there was a second or two of pandemonium of shouting mothers,
screaming kids — but, in less time than it takes to say this, the whole troop
were scrambling for the distance. There were no abandoned babies. The
sentinel, joined by two larger males, brought up the rear; they paused and
turned round at frequent intervals to bellow their anger and disgust. In a
very short while the mountain silence re-established itself, but I could hear
my heart thumping in my head and throat.

One day I returned to camp to find Isaiah sitting at some distance, crying,
'The bees, she got the jam.' He had been stung in many places. While he
was up at the windmill doing the laundry and swimming, a bee had discovered an open tin of fig jam in the tent. She had made a beeline for her
hive, and returned with several hundred of her co-workers. On the principle
of finders keepers, they believed that that fig jam was theirs, and had
made this quite clear to Isaiah. As I had been guilty of leaving the jam in
the tent, I felt in duty bound to get that tin of jam out of the way before
the others returned. Fortunately most of our clothes were in the second
tent. I borrowed a pair of long pants, and tucked their ends into the first
of two pairs of socks. Over my shirt, I put Rex's leather lumberjacket, and
kept his leather gauntlets for my hands. My only problem was my head:
there was no gauze available, otherwise I would have draped it round my
Scout hat. A large brown paper packet, which had contained our onions,
supplied the answer. I made two small slits in it through which to see, put
it over my head, and tucked the edges all round into the collar of the lumberjacket. I felt that, unless a bee were to find its way through one of the
eye slits, I was as safe as a knight in armour.

It was when I started moving that my admiration for Sir Galahad, Sir
Launcelot and the rest suddenly escalated. It is extraordinary how one's
confidence dwindles when one's range of sight is limited. Because my eyes
and indeed my head moved independently of my vizor slits, which responded only to a re-orientation of my shoulders, my movements were some-

what zombie-like. But I slipped on the gauntlets and entered the lists un-
daunted, the aroma of onions sharp in my nostrils.

The tin was black with greedy bees. Even before I reached it, I could
hear them dive-bombing my helmet. Worse, it was impossible to grip the
tin without crushing several. As I turned round carefully, and started
moving for the tent door, I had a premonition that disaster was upon me.
An uncontrollable sneeze was building up in my nostrils. I got outside.
The sneeze exploded just as I hurled the tin as hard as I could. This was
a mistake. The combined bodily contortions of sneezing and hurling dis-
connected the packet from one side of my neck, and the waiting bees
zoomed in. I swept them off with my gauntleted hand, and clumsily tucked
the packet back. The eye slits were now slewed to the left. Still, I was safe
inside my armour once more, with only a few stings in my neck. All I had
to do was to wait until those bees discovered that the jam was elsewhere.
So I stood still.

Then I heard a sound which I hope I will never hear again: the resonant
sound of a bee inside a brown paper packet which smells of onions. As the
paroxysm of the second sneeze went through me like a bolt of lightning, I
did not feel her plant her dart under the right eye. The second sneeze
jerked the packet free once more, on the other side. As I tried to tuck it
back, another bee crawled under the gauntlet, darting her sting right
through my shirtsleeve into my wrist.

I decided to make for the windmill dam, and dive into it. By now my
vision was so limited — to a narrow strip of earth to leeward — that I had
to move sideways, with my gauntleted hands feeling the air for possible
obstacles. Finding one's way through thorn scrub by braille is not the
simplest of operations.

When you have just come down a mountain, sweating but triumphant, with
two dassies over your shoulder, you will naturally stop short when you see
a figure with a brown paper packet over his head, wearing two pairs of
thick woollen socks, heavy boots, lumberjacket, and great black starfish
hands groping to left and to right through the blinding hot noon. Such was
Arthur Moys's case. He stopped short, and shouted:

'What you playing at?'

I stopped in my tracks.

'Bees. Have they gone?'

He drew closer.

'I don't see any bees.'

I removed my helmet. My upper lip was protruding like a giraffe's, and
my right eye was almost closed.

Arthur began to laugh.

Quakers do not believe in holy places or holy times. The divine Friend may

37 John (son of James Lydford Collett) and Mary (née Trollip) Collett,
Grannie Lettie's parents.

38 'Grassridge', home of John and Mary Collett. Water-colour.

39 The Collett family before it really got going — at the Golden Wedding of John and Mary Collett at 'Grassridge', 1905.

40 John and Mary Collett with their sons- and daughters-in-law: James Butler and Charles are cold-shouldering each other in the back row.

41 Uncle Herbert Collett of 'Salt Pans Drift' in the 1930s.

42 Uncle Norman Collett of 'Katkop'.

43 The Collett uncles. Back: Norman (Katkop), Gervase (De Keur), Dudley (Grassridge), Bertie (Speelmanskop). Front: Walter (Groenkloof), Herbert (Salt Pans Drift), Owen (Rooispruit).

44 Uncle Norman's sons, Neville and Godfrey Collett, at 'Katkop' in the mid-1920s.

45 Guy, Aunt Mary Butler and Joan on Elandsberg, 1930.

46 'The Poplars', with tennis court, 1929. The verandah has been removed. The old stone-lined furrow runs on the right.

47 Boys' High School, Cradock.

48 'Buggie' du Toit and Standards 4 and 5: the author is second from left, front row.

49 Egg Rock, near Cradock.

50 Sampler by Philippa Norman, 1806 (see page 139).

..... VIRTUE .....
is that perfect good which
is the crown of a happy life,
the only immortal thing that belongs to mortality: it is an invincible
greatness of mind, not to be elevated
or dejected by good or ill fortune: it is
sociable, and gentle, free, steady and
fearless, content within itself and
full of inexhaustible delights.

Philippa Norman
Ackworth School
1806.

51 Guy, Joan, Jeffrey, Christine and Dorothy, as Scouts and Guides, 1931.

52 Kritzinger's camp, 1932: Rex Moys, Arthur Moys, Rae Trollip, Guy Butler.

53 Cronwright-Schreiner on Buffelskop with the coffins of Olive Schreiner (with laurel wreath propped against it), their baby (on top) and their dog. He is holding the van Dyk baby.

54 Inscription on Oukop by an unknown hand.

choose to speak anywhere, any time. Where two or three are gathered together in his name he is in the midst of them. It follows that they set small
store by Christmas or Easter or Pentecost; the incarnation, the resurrection,
the coming of the Spirit, are possible everywhere and always. They also set
small store by birthdays. Alice would have liked to give us birthday parties
and presents, but economy vitiated her attempts; so that at least two of us,
Christine and myself, were confused as to the exact dates of our births, and
on more than one occasion remembered our birthdays after they had passed.

Nor do Quakers believe in saints and pilgrimages to shrines. Quaker gravestones are simple slabs with a minimum of lettering, without panegyric,
elegy or epitaph. Such vanities are out of place in death's universal democracy of dust, let alone in the eye of God.

Yet it was Aunt Mary of all people who took us on our first pilgrimage,
to a grave containing the remains of a woman, her baby and pet dog. It was
in a lonely place, on top of a mountain two thousand feet above the plain
— about five thousand feet above sea level. The mountainsides were steep
and rough underfoot, and not easy to climb because the stones were loose,
or the shale brittle. We would pause to rest every so often, and she would
tell us about the last time she had climbed the mountain — in 1921, when
the burial took place.

Olive Schreiner had died in 1920 in Wynberg, Cape. Her husband was in
England at the time. They had drifted apart. He returned in 1921, and took
Mr Schooling the Cradock undertaker up Buffelskop, and instructed him
to prepare a tomb large enough for four coffins. If the dolerite proved too
hard to cut, he was to build the dome-shaped tomb on top of it from loose
ironstone boulders.

The ironstone had indeed proved intractable. While cement, sand and
water were brought up the steeps on pack donkeys in bitter winter weather,
the mason, Mr Mann, wielded his hammer and cold chisel, shaping manage-
able boulders, and cementing them in place, one by one.

The day before the funeral (12 August) Schooling and ten Coloured and
African men carried the three coffins on to a plateau about halfway up the
mountain, and camped there for the night. The next day, a small funeral
party set out from the homestead of Mr A.S. van Dyk, the present owner
of Krantz Plaats — where the Schreiners had started their married life. It
included Mr Lidbetter the photographer and Aunt Mary, Mrs van Dyk, and
her three-month-old baby daughter. When they joined the men carrying
their boxes of dust towards their exalted sarcophagus, Mr Cronwright-
Schreiner asked them to walk informally; it was not to be a funereal procession. He quoted the opening lines of one of Olive's favourite poems, Browning's 'Grammarian's Funeral':

Let us begin and carry up this corpse,
Singing together.

One newspaper reported how, near the top, a lordly lammervanger sailed overhead, its white and black wings outspread against the blue.

Why all this expense, this laborious vanity? How explain Aunt Mary's acceptance of it?

Shortly after her marriage in 1894 (at the age of 38), Olive and her husband had climbed Buffelskop from Krantz Plaats.

'Olive had never stood there before and never stood there again, for her asthma grew rapidly worse and soon we had to leave the farm forever,' writes Cron in his *Life*. 'Olive stood and gazed . . . in an ecstasy; her great eyes, glowing with intensity of feeling and showing it with a depth and absorption that made you still, seemed not so much to look at the scene as absorb it. . . . She was looking on the veld where she had been a poor little governess nearly twenty years before, while far down below lay the farm house to which she had come as a happy bride only three months before. . . . I have never seen her so rapt. . . . Before we went down she said: 'We must be buried here, you and I, Cron. I shall buy one morgen of this mountain top and we must be buried here.'

A year later she gave birth to a baby girl, which died after sixteen hours. She never got over her sorrow. Another child might have given her fierce and frustrated maternalism its proper focus, but none came. As in her girlhood, she had to make do with a pet dog.

Mr W.W. Lidbetter photographed the coffins in front of the tomb. Olive's large box has a laurel wreath propped against it; the baby, who had lain on her breast only once, flesh of her flesh, is in a box stacked on top of her: the separate geometrical shapes deny all mother-child relationships. Poised on a small boulder, the dog's box seems to be sewn into a striped blanket such as tribesmen wear. Behind them, but in front of the dome of the expectant tomb, stands the chief mourner, the grey-headed widower and bereaved father. His left leg is lifted high, and rests on Olive's coffin — 'just like a victorious hunter's on the head of an elephant he has shot,' as one humorist has said. It looks utterly bizarre, until one asks, 'Why?' Superficial people might say: 'Well, she gave him a terrible life; a most difficult, neurotic woman. The foot on the coffin is an unconscious assertion of victory or survival.' But they would be wrong. It is quite clear from his diary of these events that Cronwright, for all his limitations, was trying hard to reach the symbolical and allegorical dimensions so dear to his wife. Hence the Browning quotation.

His leg is on Olive's coffin in order to make a seat for the van Dyk baby, whom he holds on his thigh tenderly, with both hands. He is not looking at the clumsy coffins. He is looking at the child in her most unfuneral frilly baby's cap, and I think he is smiling at it. She is the future.

Before the boxes were slipped under the dome, Cron spoke. He thanked Joe Mann, the mason, and the Coloureds and Africans who had carried the coffins. He reminded them that she had 'always been their champion, as indeed she had been of all subject and suppressed peoples and classes'.

It was surely Olive's tireless crusades on behalf of the poor, despised and afflicted that made Aunt Mary her devotee.

The Midland News endues the interment with the qualities of a Quaker meeting.

'There was as little stir in nature as there was in the world of men . . . there was not a cloud; and the great panorama stretched away in all its exquisite beauty and grandeur . . . Mr Cronwright-Schreiner, speaking with obvious strain, said it was not Olive Schreiner that lay in the largest coffin; it was but a time-garment which, for a brief space, had been the dwelling of that holy and exquisite spirit . . . He ended by repeating, with almost breaking intensity, a verse from Tennyson's *In Memoriam:*

Thy voice is on the rolling air,
I hear thee where the waters run,
Thou standest in the rising sun,
And in the setting thou art fair.

'There was no other ceremony. The coffins were then placed in the sarcophagus, together with a laurel wreath from Dr and Mrs John Brown, to whom *The Story of an African Farm* was dedicated. No fence encloses the morgen of land on which the sarcophagus stands; it is surrounded by the wild life she loved and in view of the mountains that appear to have no end.'

The report in *The Midland News* was Aunt Mary's work.

Roy Campbell must have read a newspaper account of the burial. There is no evidence that he ever visited Cradock or climbed to the grave:

BUFFEL'S KOP (OLIVE SCHREINER'S GRAVE)

In after times when strength or courage fail
May I recall this lonely hour: the gloom
Moving one way: all heaven in the pale
Roaring: and high above the insulted tomb
An eagle anchored on full spread of sail
That from its wings let fall a silver plume.

13

A Chapter of Failures

Good South Africans who have managed to read so far may be a little restive at my neglect of our national religion: sport in general and rugby in particular. At the risk of losing their sympathy, my uneasy conscience insists that I own up like a man, and confess that I am not a sportsman and never have been one. I attribute this not so much to physical idleness, a poor eye, bad co-ordination, flat feet, a lack of the team spirit or the killer instinct, as to sheer bad luck. From the start Fate made it perfectly clear that she disapproved of my ambitions to shine as a sportsman.

True, at one time we played tennis on the court which Father made, and I was moderately good at the game; how moderate became apparent when David Biggs came to board at The Poplars and wiped the court with all of us. Whenever the old racquets — there were some vintage items with almost square tops — lost their tension, Ernest would restring them for us. We had to keep the court rolled, and mark it ourselves. To save on the cost of lime, Father provided us with old used carbide from the works, which we sprayed on the lines with a stirrup-pump.

We had arranged a tennis party for Saturday afternoon. I had practised my service, and my forearm and backhand drives. I had even blancoed my tackies. I was going to dazzle the world; but on Friday afternoon, while spraying the lines, the nozzle of the pump slipped from my hands, and I received a spurt of carbide in both my eyes. It was agonising. Hardly knowing what I was doing, I ran about feeling for the water tap, and collided instead with the trunk of the locust tree. Then I was captured and forcibly led screaming inside, to live in darkness for three or four days.

When I was still in the junior school I developed a keen interest in rugby. I had spent two holidays on Blighty with Uncle George and Aunt Hilda Collett. Whenever Derrick and I returned from our adventures on the fringes of the lucerne lands or the river, we would sit listening to the adults talking earnestly about serious matters, viz. sport and religion. The sport was rugby and the religion British Israelism. I found both absorbing. I returned home with my head full of the measurements of the Great Pyramid, drop-kicks, Armageddon, fly-halves, the Valley of Jehosaphat, and scissors movements. I knew all the names of all the Springboks, Old Testament prophets, All Blacks and the Twelve Apostles.

There was no organised sport at the B.H.S. except for obvious stars; but
I was told that interested boys could go along to the sportsfield on Wednesday afternoons. The problem was the usual one: money. I knew that my
parents could not afford to buy me a jersey let alone a pair of boots, but,
such was my keenness to prove myself a man, that I borrowed these items
from a bigger boy who had outgrown his. They were far too big for me.
The jersey came down to my knees, and the shoulders to my elbows. I had
to slip garters round my wrists to prevent the sleeves from dangling beyond
my hands. I put on two pairs of socks, and filled the toecaps of the boots
with newspaper, but felt a trifle uncertain about my ability to sprint in
them.

When I arrived at the sportsfield some of the fellows thought I was trying
to make fun of the game. One of the bigger boys said I was too small. He
was, in fact, right. I was the smallest there, by about three sizes. But they
were short on numbers, so they put me as full-back on the stronger side,
confident that I would have nothing to do. They were wrong. The left-wing
made two successful breaks. On the first occasion I made a desperate
attempt to catch him, but tripped over my big boots and fell on my face in
the dubbeltjies. On the second occasion I had time to anticipate his movements, and was right in his path as he stormed down the line for the left
corner. I knew nothing about tackling an oncoming man slightly from the
one side. The result was that he ran over me like a rhinoceros over a small
aardvark. I woke up with some chaps splashing water in my face. I tried to
resume my duties, but my neck and shoulder were so painful that I collapsed. I was helped off the field and told to go home when I felt better.

I sat there, defeated, watching the game. It was not at all what I had
expected. I knew that if you tackled a man you might get winded or otherwise hurt. I had been prepared for that. But I had expected that I would
do what I had seen others do — get up after a moment, shake my head, and
stagger back to my position to an appreciative ripple of clapping from the
spectators. So I rose to my feet and tried to get back on to the field. But
one of the Matrics shouted angrily:

'Bugger off home, Butler. Yerrah, man, do you want to break your blerry
neck?'

So I buggered off home, never to return. My blerry neck ached for weeks.
The great game was the loser, not I.

Swimming was cheap — one penny only. We swam all summer. I was merely
an average performer at the short races, but good at the backstroke and
long distance. When fit, I could manage twenty-one lengths without undue
strain. My *forte*, however, was diving. I came second at a gala, and was com-
mended by the judges for my fine performance in an exercise called the
swallow dive.

Aunt Flo from Vrede visited Cradock, and drove us all out to the Warm

Baths. As the water was being changed, it was not as deep as usual. Determined to impress my dear aunt, I took small count of such trifles. I climbed on to the high board, and did the most beautiful swallow dive of my life.

Thus it happened that within five minutes of driving up to the Warm Baths, Aunt Flo was driving back to town with a half-conscious nephew whose head was streaming with blood from a large Y-shaped split in his scalp.

Dr Scholtz sat me in a chair and, having staunched the bleeding, tested the reaction of my pupils by shining a torch into them. Then he crossed one leg over the other, and tapped it below the knee to test my reflexes. They were in order. He then pressed and prodded my skull to see if it made any suspicious crunching noises, but it seemed as solid as usual. Aunt Flo drove me home. I was in a very humble frame of mind — a humility which my sisters found so refreshing that, whenever I got too uppish, they would say, 'Stop swallow-diving.'

My determination to be a normal South African survived these discouragements. Unfortunately my heroic but futile adventures as hockey half-back and welter-weight boxer fall outside the scope of this book. I mention them only to reassure my readers that I continued in my efforts to meet the manly norms long after lesser youths would have lapsed into decadence.

To save on the electricity bill the frugal churchwardens of St Peter's saw to it that most of the lights in the chancel and choir were switched off during the sermon. This meant that the choir inhabited a belt of shadow between the glimmer of the seven altar lamps, and the lectern light on the pulpit. This suited the choir. Mr Evans, a Welsh fitter and turner from the Railways, who sang a good bass, could now fall asleep, and zizz away quietly like one of his own steam engines whose fires are low. Mr Baker, the bottle-store keeper, a tenor, who read the lessons almost as well as the bank manager, Mr Immelman, could anxiously stroke his fine white moustache, like an old Indian mutiny colonel who, having kept himself going all week on brandy and discipline, had now to consider how he stood with his Maker. The thoughts of the boys wandered from the sermon, in and out the windows; in fantasy they shone before their girlfriends; or they got up to mischief.

The cemetery of St Peter's was hedged with quinces and pomegranates; and, fallen creatures that we were, we plucked the forbidden fruits in season and ate them in God's very house. Pomegranate pips and quince cores presented us with a disposal problem. The organ tuner complained that the instrument suffered from a surplus of foreign vegetable matter.

One evening during the sermon I heard the unmistakable squeak that a quince makes when you wrench a chunk out with your teeth. I soon detected who it was, and cupped my hands, inviting him to lob the fruit across the aisle. He did so, and I sank my teeth into its crisp, juicy flesh. I lobbed it back again. Soon there were two quinces of ever-diminishing size being juggled across the aisle.

The boarders of Rocklands Girls' High School gave the show away, by nudging each other and displaying other signs of interest. The Rev. Charles Gould was intelligent enough to suspect that his sermon, good as it was, was not the cause of their animation. He spun round in the pulpit. I fumbled a catch, and the quince thudded on to the organ keyboard. The organ complained with a discord in *vox humana*. Then silence, as Gould's large eyes pierced each of us in succession. He returned to his sermon, and began, 'My house shall be called a house of prayer, but ye have made it a den of thieves.' He spoke of the anger of Christ, how he overturned the tables of the money changers, and drove them out with a whip.

As the choir with its peculiar sailor's roll egressed in the wake of the crucifer, I caught the eye of a girl on one of the aisle seats: black dancing eyes under a straight black fringe, and a slight, wicked, covert smile. It was a case of love at first sight. My mind absorbed little of the Rector's second sermon to us in the Sunday school, where we donned and doffed our cassocks and surplices. I have forgotten how we were punished for our crimes of theft and blasphemy.

I now found myself joining a group of bigger boys after church whose custom it was to trail the crocodile of girls all the way back to Rocklands. Occasionally we would do something really enterprising. We would overtake the croc on the opposite pavement at a brisk pace, then hide behind someone's macracarpa hedge, allow the croc to pass us, and then overtake them again. On the third time round, the croc would collapse into hysterics. This gratified us. We had made our presence felt.

My most daring act as Romeo was to run ahead one night and climb a pepper tree in Hospital Street. There I sat, in my serge Sunday suit and Eton collar, sticky with the gum of that tree, like a leopard waiting for a gazelle to come down to the waterhole. Well, my Juliet approached, indistinguishable in the phalanx of two dozen others, followed by a tweedy teacher. The raft of girlhood and subdued gossip floated past below me. I could have created a memorable effect by letting out a Cherokee yell, but nothing was further from my doting thoughts; I simply wanted to get closer to the sacred object, and I had succeeded.

I think Caroline and I exchanged one or two letters. Then came the holidays; and during these holidays the Boy Scouts (unkindly nicknamed 'broomstick warriors' because they carried six-foot ashen staffs wherever they went) held a Jamboree in Port Elizabeth. Father approved of Scouts, and somewhere the necessary seventeen shillings and sixpence was found to send me on this adventure to the big city.

It was a great experience, and the Cradock Troop, in their grey uniforms, were singled out for smartness. We camped on the Show Grounds. We were taken over factories, including a biscuit and a sweet factory, from which we were not sent empty away; the museum; the snake park. On Saturday morning we visited the *Kenilworth Castle,* and played quoits on its deck. But it was Saturday afternoon that I was looking forward to. On Saturday afternoon I would be free to visit Caroline in her home, alone.

The great hour arrived. The house was one of a row of double-storey doll's houses in a terrace, with wooden lace-work verandahs, overlooking a stupendous view of the Bay. The stoep was a cave of ferns and aspidistras, with a polished red granolithic floor. The knocker shone like a fireman's helmet, and seemed almost as big. Everything was magical about the palace of my princess — until I entered the front door. Enchantment withered almost at once.

Not only was her mother there to meet me, looking excessively smart in high-heeled patent-leather shoes, ropes and ropes of pearls, earrings, a perm, and a la-di-dah accent which didn't seem entirely at home, but there was another boy there, about two years older than I, in cricket togs and a Grey sports blazer with a fancy badge on its pocket. And it was quite clear that he was not her brother.

But, I said to myself, any pretty girl is entitled to have more than one gentleman caller per afternoon, and this oaf could have dropped in uninvited and unexpected. I tried to be as relaxed and grown up as he was.

Something in Caroline's manner made me suspect that she was more impressed by the cricket togs than the Boy Scout uniform.

Her mother did her best to maintain a polite peace by keeping our mouths filled with biscuits, but I soon had to face the possibility that, while I might be someone in Cradock, I was no one in Port Elizabeth; worse, this elegant, potential Don Bradman soon sensed that I could be made a fool of with impunity, if not approval; which he proceeded to do, asking me how the tribal gathering of the broomstick warriors was getting on next to the Portland Cement Factory. Other pleasantries followed, at all of which Caroline sniggered. So, not for the last time in my life, I suddenly remembered that my next engagement was an hour earlier than I had led my hosts to believe.

Once in the street I picked up a stone, and put all my pent-up frustration into hurling it at the horizon. An irate pigeon-fancier yelled at me to leave his birds alone — what harm had they done me — call myself a gentleman — he'd have the cops on me next time, fancy uniform or no.

Port Elizabeth prides itself as 'The Friendly City', but that afternoon I don't think I would have endorsed the epithet.

For quite a time after this I did not focus my interest on one love-object, but on many. I went to every 'hop' possible, and my three dear sisters had the challenging task of teaching me how to dance the foxtrot, the slow foxtrot, and the waltz. Though this last step is the very devil, they insisted that it was quite easy. 'Count *one*-two-three, *one*-two-three, to the music, and relax.' That is all very fine in theory. I found no difficulty in counting *one*-

two-three, with Joan, Dorothy or Christine in my confident grasp; but with a strange girl held tentatively at arms' length, like a charge of T.N.T., who is expecting you to make intelligent conversation?

But the Postmaster had two sensible daughters whom my sisters knew well, and who did not scare me in the least. A crowd of teenagers used to meet at their house and dance. No cheek-to-cheek nonsense; and it was simply unheard of to dance twice in succession with the same girl: we moved from partner to partner, talked little, and concentrated on a strict obedience to the beat, as energetic and serious.as commando troops in training.

14

Complications

Nothing contributed so much to my growing awareness of Africa and the world as stamp collecting, a hobby which my father encouraged, within his means. He handed on to me his own and his father's collections — neither was large, but between them they contained some early South African, Australian, Canadian, American and New Zealand issues — an ancient Stanley Gibbons catalogue, and all the stamps I wished for from each morning's mail. But I had no handsome album such as my friends had, and a new one was too expensive, so Father instructed Mr Terblanche, the compositor at the Works, to print me three hundred uniform pages of empty oblongs, and to bind them in a cardboard cover. Mr Terblanche did a shoddy job, and I was always ashamed of my album.

The range of items which *The Midland News* correspondence could provide was limited and soon exhausted. I did not have sufficient pocket money to buy stamps from dealers in England as my friends did. My envy was intense, particularly of one friend who had everything: silver tweezers, a looseleaf of double transparent sheets which kept the stamps in mint condition, and up-to-the-minute catalogues. Father did not believe in boys buying stamps. There was no fun in that, he said, it was tantamount to cheating. Swopping and penfriends were the only legitimate means. As for the superiority of mint stamps, that was bogus: a stamp needed to be franked to prove its authenticity. Why, there were little tinpot states that balanced their budgets by bringing out new issues every year to sell in mint condition to gullible collectors all over the world!

We knew that we were lucky and privileged to be born white. We took the superiority of the European races for granted. Not only was this spelt out in the patterns of our society, but history and geography demonstrated it beyond question. The coloured map of the world showed it: there was hardly a country on the surface of the globe which was not part of the British, French, Belgian, Dutch, Russian or Portuguese empires. (The Germans had deservedly been deprived of theirs.) True, most of the vast continents of North and South America consisted of independent republics, but the white man was in control there too. We were conscious that Europeans were of many different kinds, and unfortunately given to distressing rivalries which resulted in terrible wars; but, as the outcome of the recent Great War had shown, the British, although supported by the French, and, alas, those slightly comic, boastful Americans, had emerged as the true leaders of the human race. They had achieved this by their superb courage, by their qualities of statesmanship, by their industry and daring as explorers, inventors, scientists, pioneers and colonists; and wherever they went they brought the blessings of efficient administration, impartial justice, economic development and the encouragement of democracy — to an infinite variety of peoples.

More than any other race on earth, the British were endowed with a concern for the underdog. It was they who had taken the lead in the abolition of slavery; it was they who had sent more quietly heroic missionaries than any other people to bring the great light of the Gospel to people sitting in darkness. But glorious as their calling might be, it was often thankless and burdensome.

Proud phrases like 'The Empire on which the sun never sets' gained in glamour by a knowledge of the price paid: 'There's never a wave rolls shoreward yet but marks our English dead.'

My stamp album supported this view of the world as Europe's extended estate. Apart from the anomaly of Abyssinia, the entire vast continent of Africa seemed to be under her direct or indirect control. So was most of the Middle East, all of India and Australasia. Here and there were enigmas: clever Japan, who had gone some way to becoming European by learning from her; China, who hadn't, and was full of starving millions; and above them the great Russian empire, stretching from the Aleutian Islands right into Europe, ruled over by Bolsheviks, a sinister, atheistic breed who had conducted a bloody revolution, murdered their Tsar, and established a Communist regime. But like Abyssinia, these were anomalies. The Commonwealth, with the help of the League of Nations, was leading the human race into the pastures of peace.

I specialised in stamps of the Commonwealth and Empire. I admired the foresight with which Great Britain had secured those essential (usually unwanted or neglected) islands, capes or promontories from which her fleet could control the ocean lanes, thus ensuring the freedom of the seas: Gibraltar, Malta, Cyprus, Suez, Aden, Ceylon, Singapore, Hong Kong — and of course, Zanzibar, Mauritius, St Helena, and the Cape of Good Hope. I found it hard to understand that some members of this glorious family had objected to being adopted into it: our own Afrikaners, for instance, and right on Britain's doorstep, some of the Irish, the Catholics, had been objecting to the British embrace for centuries, which was proof of their feckless, backward but curiously lovable nature: the difficult child of the intimate family circle. The Irish were inordinately fond of their moribund language, trying to revive it by using it on their stamps, and renaming the country Eire, just to be different.

There must be Russian boys today who are subject to the same nonphilatelic fantasies as I was. Is not their empire the largest the world has ever seen? Of all the great nineteenth-century empires it is the only one to have survived; indeed, it has liberated most of eastern Europe from Capitalist and Democratic darkness into the pure light of the gospel according to Marx, and protected it from lapsing into decadence by a necessary iron curtain. Its missionaries, who are not interested in converting souls, but in capturing political and economic systems, are active everywhere, and vast areas of the world now dance to the tune of an empire of doctrine on which the sun never sets. He will be puzzled, as I was, by the graceless behaviour of some states close to home: those jaunty Yugoslavs who call themselves Communists; the unreliable Poles, still benighted, like the Irish, by an irrational devotion to the Pope, that arch-obscurantist; and Red China, who, far from showing gratitude for philosophical and material help, casts covetous eyes on our happy eastern Soviet republics. But these are anomalies. Russia, he will be confident, is leading the world into the pastures of universal peace.

I believe it was about this time that I was introduced to the elements of biology. We were told the differences between categories of plants: lichens; fungi; mosses; ferns; conifers; monocotyledons; dicotyledons. I saw to it that my rockeries — I had three in all — were well supplied with examples of each, except fungi, which demanded such specialised conditions, and lived so briefly, that I gave up.

Perhaps more important were the categories of animals. Our distances from the sea made it difficult to become familiar with many molluscs. Apart from garden slugs and snails, this damp variety of life had given the dry Karoo best — although there were thousands of white mussel shells in the alluvial soil along the banks of the river, as evidence of a different time. Here and there, as on an ironstone koppie overlooking the Fish River on Katkop, one found stacks of them between the boulders where the Bushmen had piled them after eating their soft interiors. Of the crustacea, I found the insects most interesting, and spent hours sorting my specimens into Lepidoptera (butterflies and moths), Diptera (flies), Coleoptera (beetles), Orthoptera (locusts, stick-insects, cockroaches, crickets), and Hymenoptera (ants, bees and wasps), etc.

When in the grip of this collecting and classifying mania or enthusiasm (how does a young boy distinguish?) I would hunt new specimens with an intensity close to passion. In search of insects, I would root among thickets like a warthog, reckless of thorns, and my path across the veld would be strewn with upturned boulders as if a scorpion-hungry baboon had been there.

Thousands of small animals died to gratify my fascination with life. Occasionally I would think of this mortal aspect of collecting, but not for long. My hunting was not introducing anything new into the internecine insect world, nor likely to upset the great balance of nature, which, after all, permitted the magnificent deadliness of lions and tigers.

One day when I came up to the homestead of one of the Biggs farms with my specimen jar full of newly dead wonders, one of my cousins laughed and said, 'Here comes old Janfiskaal.' I was deeply if briefly hurt by this pleasantry. The habits of the butcherbird, Jacky Hangman, or Jan-fiskaal, were well known to me. Roberts in his *First Guide to South African Birds* tells us: 'They live largely on insects, especially on the bigger kinds of grasshoppers and large beetles, but some of them are more predatory and take lizards, small or young birds and mice. The true Butcherbirds have a habit of impaling on thorns any of their prey that they do not want to eat at once.' Though my farming cousins had described a butcherbird's pantry or larder to me, I had never in fact seen a thorn tree thus garnished with insects and small animals.

Did I differ much from the bird? My specimens were also impaled – on steel pins, not mimosa thorns. We were both killing to gratify an appetite. Was not he less culpable? He hunted to provide food for his stomach; I hunted to provide food for my mind. Were not his hunting and collecting necessary, my hunting and collecting a luxury, a sport?

Fortunately, for two or three years to come, the predatory element in nature and in man caused me no more than an occasional twinge. It was only during my matriculation year that I began to wince at the universal war of mandibles, claws, teeth and beaks in the grass and the trees, in the soil and in the sea.

If our horizons were being stretched by stamp collecting, biology and holidays on remote farms, Aunt Mary was seeing to it that our knowledge of Cradock itself grew in depth.

In the late 'twenties she left the room she occupied in Dominee Malherbe's Pastorie opposite The Poplars and took rooms a mile to the south with a warder's wife in the oldest part of Cradock, below the top furrow. The rooms opened on to a swept space under a vine and a fig tree; they looked on to an expanse of oats and lucerne, where the gaoler's goats ran. The goats provided her with her milk.

As more and more blacks moved to the towns, Cradock location grew in size, and with growth came all the problems of poverty, bad housing, malnutrition. A committee of concern was formed to educate the white ratepayers and power wielders as to their plight. That public-spirited man, Alfred Metcalf, paid for the erection of a small building set in the middle of a wide sandy street that ran through the location, and Aunt Mary worked there. It was known as the Dispensary or Baby Clinic. Her father had devoted much of his spare time as a young man to work in the East End of London; she went one better – she became a full-time worker in the Cradock location.

At the very time that the Nationalists in collusion with Labourites (whites only) were passing laws to reinforce the industrial colour bar, the Society of Friends threw its weight behind those enlightened 'kafferboeties' who saw the need to abandon it. They saw that such protection was unjust and would reinforce those racial prejudices which they believed to be irrational and destructive, and not in the long-term interests of the whites themselves. So in the 'twenties, when the Nationalists were pressing ahead with their tragic policy of legislating in the interests of whites only, the Joint Council movement was launched: committees of Africans, Coloureds and whites were set up in several towns in South Africa, Cradock being one.

Growing up 'on' a newspaper and with a Quaker Aunt in the location, the Butler children could not avoid a measure of political and social awareness. Aunt Mary would discuss her work in a dispassionate manner as she tried to solicit the paper's help on some issue or other.

If The Poplars and white Cradock had been hard hit by the depression, what was happening in the location? When accused of being sentimental or of exaggerating, the superintendent of the clinic would produce figures for infant mortality such as these:

In the year 1 April 1929 to 31 March 1930 — before the full impact of the depression on the economy was felt — there were 204 births and 83 deaths, i.e. 406 out of every thousand babies died. The following year the figure had risen to 744 per thousand. But the appalling deterioration of an already appalling situation was not attributable entirely to economic factors. There had been a severe epidemic of measles.

There had also been a severe epidemic of politics in the location. Blacks were not deaf or blind to what whites were saying and doing about them. Their leaders had witnessed the Hertzog government's appeal to anti-black prejudice to ensure victory at the 1929 elections; they had seen the success of that appeal; and they were now having to endure the effects of the government's civilised labour policy — a remarkable piece of social engineering which virtually solved the poor-white problem at the cost of removing the minimal black rights and aspirations, and of driving African leaders to anger and despair.

In 1931 two campaigners for black rights, Mr Plaatje and Mr Tongeni, visited Cradock, and made inflammatory speeches. They were duly arrested. 'The severe depression and the consequent unemployment gave such extremists their opportunity,' said Aunt Mary.

'Human kind cannot bear very much reality,' says T.S. Eliot. Aunt Mary could bear more than most, and patiently attempted to bring whites — her own relatives and officials — to face the facts and responsibilities of privilege. We are all happy to bring, or to hear, good news; but who has the courage to bring, or to listen to, bad? Aunt Mary was a walking conscience, fair minded, deliberate, factual, unflinching. She received little or no thanks from whites, and she experienced the usual liberal fate of opposition from politically conscious blacks. Her loneliness at times must have been extreme.

A child is acutely conscious of his peers, and is always measuring himself against them.

Almost every English family in the town and district who could afford it sent their sons to boarding-schools. The draper, T.J. Roberts, sent his sons to St Andrew's; the surveyor, Otto Reitz, sent his son to Bishop's; Uncle Norman sent his sons to Kingswood.

One missed them when they left, envied them the adventure, and was hurt by the airs they gave themselves when they returned for vacations, gorgeous in cheese-cutters and blazers. The B.H.S. had no uniform.

The Gould boys were sent to St Andrew's. For a few days at the beginning of the vacations they would try to impress us with their new status, but did not always succeed. At a tennis party at The Poplars, Astley, having failed to dazzle us with his racquet, started boasting of his prowess at wrestling — apparently a St Andrew's specialty. He named and described several cunning and deadly grips. Christine, whose build was as substantial as his was slight, pooh-poohed them all. This annoyed Astley, who said he would tie her in knots if she wasn't careful.

'Just you try!' came the tart reply.

It was over very quickly. In two seconds, Christine had him flattened on the tennis court. He could not budge; she was sitting on him. He cried 'Pax', and tennis was resumed.

In spite of concessions to parsons' sons, the Goulds found it almost impossible to meet their educational bills. The St Peter's coffers were empty as parishioners put less and less in the plate. The churchwardens interviewed their Rector: it would be a great saving if he were to withdraw his sons from such an expensive school and send them to the Boys' High, where their own sons were.

Mrs Gould's response was: 'I'll take in washing first.'

An English aunt played fairy godmother, whisking the eldest daughter, Phyllis, away to be educated in England. The youngest daughter, Imogen, was sent to Rocklands. The boys continued at St Andrew's.

Rocklands at this time enjoyed an excellent reputation: girls came from Port Elizabeth and other remote centres to be under Miss Borrow or Miss Stoops. The same could not be said of the Boys' High School.

Mother would have loved to send me to St Andrew's, but I doubt whether Father would have footed the bill even if he could have afforded it. He disliked Anglicanism. If only there were a Quaker school; if only he had the money to send me to England, to his old school, Sidcot.

But he had no money. Indeed, he was deeply in debt. By the end of 1930 he had borrowed £600 from Aunt Jessie Collett, £875 from Uncle Norman, £300 from Uncle Bertie, and £500 from Uncle Dudley; and there was the interest on the long-standing inherited debt for arrears in rent of several thousands to Uncle Herbert.

Quite contrary to her father's advice to keep her little money religiously separate, Alice had pledged The Poplars as security to Aunt Jessie, and her small Louisvale property to Uncle Bertie.

At a meeting of the shareholders of The Midland Printing & Publishing Company held on 28 April 1931, the Chairman (Ernest Butler) had a grim tale to tell: 'Never before in the history of the company had such losses been incurred.' He had retrenched staff; the editor, the secretary, the two senior journeymen had all consented to a 10 per cent reduction in salary. He himself was taking £10 per month less. He had approached Mr Herbert Collett, who, while 'refusing to increase his guarantee of the firm's over-draft from £875 to £1 500', had agreed 'to the postponement of reductions on his guaranteed overdraft' for the time being.

But far more drastic measures than these had to be taken.

One of my most painful memories concerns the visit of an expert from Johannesburg (an accountant? a manager of a big paper?), who was to advise Father on the finances of *The Midland News*. As it was midwinter, and the weather bitterly cold, the discussions took place in the drawing-room of The Poplars. It was my duty to look in periodically, and put more coal on the fire.

Mother insisted that I should wear my Sunday best for this menial task. While she was preparing cucumber sandwiches for the men's morning tea, her anxiety, seldom expressed in words, came out in a flood. 'What will we do if we go bankrupt? What will we do? Your father's got no qualifications, not even a matriculation certificate.'

This came as a revelation. Up to that moment I had regarded my father as a man who could do anything, from 'keeping the books' to tending or mending a machine, from writing an editorial when the editor was on leave to doing the layout for a booklet. And I said so. 'That is all very well,' she said, 'but he's served no apprenticeship and has no paper qualifications that will help him to get a job in a printing-works or a business. My son, what will we do?'

When I entered the drawing-room with a bucket of coal, the gentleman from Johannesburg was asking questions. I took a very long time with the tongs, but could understand never a word. They did not even notice my presence.

By 4 December 1931 bankruptcy seemed inevitable. Ernest pointed out to shareholders that 'the falling-off of turnover for the six months ending June 30 1931 was over £1 000' on *The Midland News,* and a comparable loss on Butler Bros. His unsecured debt to Dudley Collett had risen to £1 000. He 'explained the possibility of saving money' by making *The Midland News* a tri-weekly paper, doing without Reuter service and wireage, reducing his own salary by a further £10, while Mr Cursons, the editor, had agreed to work for £25 a month. 'The abandonment of The Stock and Wool Edition would save £6 per month.'

But in spite of all economies, the fall-off of business was such that he estimated a monthly loss of £155.

'Mr Butler proposed laying the position of the Company before Messrs Herbert, Norman and Dudley Collett, who have lent money without security to the aggregate of £2 275, and to offer them his shares, and to ask them to decide whether they could see their way to rendering further assistance.'

Four days later, on 8 December, the three uncles arrived at The Poplars. The only shareholders present were Ernest, Alice, and Aunt Mary. The editor, Mr Cursons, and the auditor, Mr Phillips, were there by invitation. Aunt Mary's letter reporting the deliberations to the other shareholders — her mother, her brother and sisters — provides a summary of what transpired: 'The meeting took the form of an informal discussion and I wish you could all have been there to have seen and heard what happened. I wonder where else three uncles would be found so unostentatiously and frankly to face such a position. Ernest stated the case, and said he was not asking for help on a business footing, but simply help. He said he and Mr Cursons had discussed the position and proposed to run the paper as a tri-weekly . . . it would cost £150 a month to produce it as a tri-weekly after deducting revenue.'

Norman asked the editor whether it was advisable from a business point to continue. 'Mr Cursons said "No", but followed with a long speech pleading for a further three months . . . basing his plea on the value of the paper to the farmers and Cradock generally, and also for the sake of the staff.'

If the value of *The Midland News* was so generally recognised, asked Uncle Herbert, would not those who benefited be prepared to share the burden of its production? The accountant scotched all hope of a positive answer by saying that times were so bad that people were nervous of investing even in profitable paying concerns. Uncle Herbert nevertheless said that he would not like to see the town suffer, and thought that they should do what they could.

'Norman said emphatically that he had done enough, and was not prepared to do any more.' (For one thing, his position was radically different from Herbert's or Dudley's. He had four sons and a daughter to educate and launch into the world, whereas Herbert was a bachelor, while Dudley had but one child, an adopted daughter.)

At this point Uncle Herbert suggested that the attorney be called in. Mr Metcalf 'put some pointed questions: "When did you discover that you were losing so heavily?" and "Has the loss been progressively greater?" He expressed the opinion that a tri-weekly would suffice for Cradock, and paid high tribute to the value of *The Midland News*. Uncle Herbert then repeated his question: "If the value of *The Midland News* was so great, would not those who benefited be prepared to share the burden of its production?"

'This brought from Mr Metcalf an offer to finance the scheme if the three uncles were willing to guarantee the money, and that he would not charge any interest for six months . . .'

'Dudley in his quiet way expressed his willingness to stand by . . . There was not a word of criticism throughout. Ernest thinks the most notable thing was Uncle H's strong advocacy after all he has done for the paper.'

Of this long tale of borrowing, bonding and finally begging, we children knew little beyond the firm's and the family's general indebtedness to our Collett uncles.

Father was very keen on inculcating frugal habits in his children. Soon after we moved to The Poplars he provided us each with a small silver money box, which took exactly 40 'tickeys', which amounted to ten shillings. On the fortieth tickey the lid would leap off. Victory! He would then add five shillings; and the fifteen shillings would buy a Union Loan Certificate, which would mature into a pound in due course. As we received pocket money of only one penny each per week, these money boxes filled up very slowly — usually as a result of cash presents of a shilling or so at Christmas, or an English postal order on one's birthday, or something from a Collett uncle or aunt in town for stock fair. I believe the best saver was Christine, the worst Dorothy; myself, like my position in order of birth, in the middle. Father kept all the Union Loan Certificate booklets in his roll-top desk.

We knew things were grim, grimmer than usual.

One evening after supper, Father cleared his throat, and said: 'Tomorrow I have to pay the wages. I've been to the Bank Manager, who can't help me. I can't borrow more money anywhere else. I want to know if you will lend me your savings. I will pay them back as soon as I can.'

A long pause followed. He was staring at his hands.

'Joan, do you agree?' Joan nodded.

'Dorothy?' She nodded, biting her nether lip.

'Guy?' I nodded.

'Christine?' She nodded.

'Jeffrey?' He said, 'Yes!'

Ernest then took a sheet of paper, and wrote our names on it, and the number of certificates which each child possessed. He then read out the names and the amounts.

Dorothy burst into tears.

Mother put an arm round her shoulder, and told her not to cry; she was sure that it would not be long before Ernest would repay her.

'I don't want them back! It's because I've got so few!'

Years and years later, we each received a cheque for the proper amount, plus interest due.

Joan's case filled us with envy. When she was born, Uncle Dudley Collett had given her a heifer calf which was to run with his herd, free, on Grassridge, and all its progeny was to be hers. In this crisis, Joan's cows were converted into cash, which she lent to Dad to keep the family raft afloat.

At the beginning of 1932 Christine went on strike. She refused point-blank to go back to school in a frayed gym which had served both Joan and Dorothy before her, and was now a strange shade of purple, not the regulation navy-blue. Poor Ernest went through his books and discovered that he was just sufficiently in credit with T.J. Roberts & Sons to afford a new gym for his youngest daughter. The household breathed again.

At this point the quiet Quakers dropped a bombshell into my life.

The Natal Friends, led by the enthusiastic Maurice Webb, persuaded the yearly meeting to establish a Quaker school in Natal. They set about it with uncharacteristic haste and insufficient caution in the selection of staff. In England, Joseph Butler, grandfather James's brother, worked hard and effectively to raise money for a school to which his South African relatives could send their children.

But what would, what could Ernest do in the depths of the depression? His financial position was no better. To save the salary of a clerk Dorothy was removed from school at the end of 1931 to work behind the counter in *The Midland News* office.

Discussion of the Quaker school was exciting: it was to be something new in South African school education. It would take both boys and girls; it would, in due course, be multiracial; it would abandon outdated classroom techniques and work on the Dalton plan, which aimed at individual rather than group tuition. Pupils would be given assignments; and teachers would be friendly advisors as to how to complete them. Each child would advance at his own pace and explore his own interests. It all appealed to me enormously.

Aunt Mary was curiously unenthusiastic about the project; fences were being rushed, she said. The Natal Friends were in too much of a hurry. But it appealed to Ernest and he was on the committee. It was unthinkable that no Butler child — the Butlers, who were so much part of South African Quakerism — should be a foundation pupil; and all over the country were grandchildren of James and Charles Butler, several of whom, such as Honor Biggs, might be enrolled. There was a harvest waiting to be reaped.

Then one day he said, 'My boy, someone has found the money, and we're going to send you to the Quaker school.' I was dazed with delight.

I could not guess where that money had come from. Under the influence of Dickens, I looked for a remote avuncular benefactor, and decided that it must be Uncle Joe in England.

Uncle Joe had recently lost his wife Sophia, and Aunt Mary had gone to visit him in London, where she says she was 'very tempted to stay in order to look after the dear old man. Although I shouldn't say it, I was his favourite niece. But my heart was in South Africa.'

I was wrong in casting Uncle Joe as my benefactor. Today (2 January

1977) I interviewed Aunt Mary (92) and asked her whether my guess was correct. 'No,' she said, 'I paid £300 for you to go to the school.'

And so in July 1932 I was sent by a doubting Friend to a new Quaker boarding-school established in an old hotel, at Inchanga, halfway between Durban and Pietermaritzburg, Natal.

15

Inchanga

The railway connection between the East Cape and Natal was poor and involved a twenty-four hour stay at Bloemfontein. I was accommodated by some relatives of the Cradock Methodist minister. They entertained me by showing me the sights, including Naval Hill and the Zoo. In the centre of the latter was a large baboon enclosure, with an artificial koppie in it and, as it seemed to me, scores of baboons of all shapes and sizes.

That wild baboons had a high degree of family organisation I knew from my observations on General Kritzinger's farm. How much of that free-ranging family life survived on the koppie in a zoo enclosure, subject to the incessant curiosity of visitors, I do not know; but there were no male sentinels barking in magnificent anger and contempt while their families retreated from the smell of humanity; merely a greedy mob, dashing to any point on the perimeter of their prison where a human might be casting peanuts or bananas through the fence.

I noticed one who did not stampede after food. She seemed to be in a daze. She hung on to the outer fringes of the troop as if from habit rather than need. Every so often she would glance with solicitude at something she was dragging about with her — it looked like a dirty scrap of sisal sacking. Just as we were leaving, I saw her hugging it, a dead baby baboon, already rotting. A little cloud of flies hung over her.

My hostess had seen it at the same moment. We returned to the car in silence. Before she pressed the starter she looked at me and said, with a nuance only South Africans employ: 'Shame.'

And I said, 'Yes.'

We were six in the second-class compartment: two Hilton boys about my own age, two hulking men aged about 30, a medical student from the University of Cape Town, and myself. In order to see as much new earth as possible I had secured a window seat; but my attention to the scenery was distracted by the medical student, a doctor's son, who was explaining sex to the fascinated Hilton boys and me. His exposition had a strong physiological bias. He had read it all up in his father's library. And, naturally, it was female physiology that he specialised in. He told us of the strange cycles of ovulation and menstruation; of the adventures of the spermatozoa seeking the ovum. He asked me when I was born. I told him. He then

said that at a particular moment in April 1917 a particular sperm had found
a particular ovum which eventually resulted in me — me, sitting there, on
the hot green S.A.R. leather seat, looking at the great landscape slowly
wheeling by. He did not have a smutty mind. That dimension was provided
by the two men. They came in before supper, breathing beer fumes, to
spruce themselves up. At last they had picked up two women who had a
compartment to themselves. The prospects for the night were good, said
one. The other was not so sure. 'Bet you ten bob I make it,' came the reply.

Puberty is seldom easy. As a child I had accepted the man–woman,
husband–wife, parent–child relationships as part of the nature of things; I
was aware that there were physiological differences between the sexes,
hidden and yet symbolised by particularities of dress. I knew the differences between bulls and cows, rams and ewes, dogs and bitches, and had
been the startled and fascinated witness to a stallion mounting a mare. But
that I should have had my origins in a similar act filled me with shuddering
incredulity, a frantic mental censorship encouraged by the lack of openness
on this topic in our home.

Now Secrecy was being stripped away by Science, and Puberty was being
forced to face the Facts of Life. Puberty would have found the lesson easier
if the confined space of the compartment had been his and his instructor's
alone; but the presence of raw adult Lechery and Drunkenness dragged the
lesson into miasma, mixing clinical medicine with nightmare.

It was an appalling night for me, on the middle bunk. I lay there wondering what was happening among that adult foursome, my mind awash with
fascinating, guilty images. When at last the Don Juans returned, they moved
about in the dark compartment with the stumbling deliberation of drunks.
The confident one clambered up on to the top bunk above me. Half an hour
later he started heaving. He puked, buckets of foul-smelling stuff, over the
bunk side, on to the floor. Had he, had he of all people, just experienced
the intense intimacy without which no one is conceived?

In the morning the doctor's son found that his shoes were almost full of
vomit. The two men thought this was the best joke in years.

The seminar on sex was resumed. Our tutor turned his attention to the
emotional dimensions of mating. There was something which he couldn't
quite understand, which girls insisted on, called romance: an expensive,
slow ritual, of taking them to dances, giving them chocolates and flowers,
writing them soppy letters; yet even after weeks, some would still hold off.

No wonder there were prostitutes. They were so much cheaper. He had
not been to one yet, not because he thought it wrong but because he was
scared he would catch V.D.

'What's V.D.?' I asked.

'Venereal diseases. Syphilis is the worst. Eats your flesh away.'

And I remembered a horrifying old beggar woman in Cradock, with a
strip of filthy cloth covering her face from ear to ear, to hide the cavity

where her nose had been.

Fascinated as I was, I knew that there was something important missing in the medical student's version of sex. It did not account for the faithfulness of lovers and husbands and wives, nor for the sacrifices they made for their children. It did not even account for that baboon in the Bloemfontein Zoo, cradling her dead child.

The dozen pupils who gathered at Inchanga in July 1932 were a very mixed bag, from a wide social and geographic spectrum. Several were problem children from problem homes. There was a wet of a boy, the son of a sentimental, wealthy, liberal divorcee; he was so nervous of any coltish rough-and-tumble that he spent most of his time with the girls. There was Morgan, the son of a theosophist police official in Durban, who had been expelled from Durban Boys' High for smoking and other misdeeds — as tough, dim and criminally inclined as they come. Because he was senior in years and experience, we tended to take our cues from him. As a Natalian, he had the advantage of being on home ground.

Among the girls, there was one poor fat pimply creature with a perpetual cold, who found the simplest sums too difficult, and seemed always to be weeping in odd corners. I overheard one of the teachers say to the Head, 'The poor child is simple-minded,' and the Head replied, '*You* try to convince her parents, I can't.'

But there were some perfectly healthy young people, far healthier in mind than myself. There was stocky Charles from Harrismith, agile in body and mind, and sunburnt Sally, a farmer's daughter from Griqualand East, with a nose freckled like a partridge egg.

The Head was G.H. Calpin, a tall, elegant man, who had done the mathematics tripos at Cambridge. His manner with us was engaging and relaxed, and most of us warmed to him. He never spoke down to us. His political and educational views were advanced, but he was not what Aunt Mary calls a convinced Quaker. As no convinced Quaker had felt called to offer himself for the post, he had been appointed, much against the will of certain Friends, including Aunt Mary. He must have been a courageous man to come to a strange country to found a pioneering type of school, with a staff which had already been appointed by a committee whom he did not know.

The second master was an older man, called Horrocks, a highly experienced teacher, which Calpin was not. He had a dry voice and drier manner, did not seem to like children, and kept his distance. Miss Thompson, on the other hand, was intense and emotional about every child in the school.

I believe the only real Quaker in the school was old Mr Warner, the odd-jobs man, with a sweet and sad face, and a droopy moustache. 'You look exactly like Thomas Hardy,' said the Head to him one day, as the old man sat in the rustic summerhouse staring towards the distant hills.

On arrival, we were interviewed by Mr Horrocks, who set us intelligence tests. The next day he told me gently that I was far below the average for my age. He was at great pains to speak slowly whenever he addressed me, to give my slow wits a chance to comprehend. Miss Thompson, who did not believe in Mr Horrocks's tests, and said so, launched me straight into *Hamlet.* My first assignment from her was to learn Polonius's advice to Laertes, and the 'To-be-or-not-to-be' soliloquy. Good at explaining metaphors and images, she balked at occasional lines such as

> *. . . Ay, but to lie*
> *In the rank sweat of an enseamed bed,*
> *Honeying and making love over the nasty style.*

I made good her reluctance, drawing on my memories of the lechery I had encountered on the journey to Inchanga.

Miss Thompson also taught me the rudiments of scansion and stanzaic structure, and suggested I might try my hand at a ballad or a sonnet. This invitation resulted in my first attempts at making verses.

I did not find it easy to fit words into a pattern, or to match sound and sense. I found it very difficult, but fascinating. It is still difficult, and the fascination lives on. Most of our triumphs and frustrations are the results of struggles between fascination and difficulty. Sometimes, suddenly, briefly, the outcome is assurance and mastery. Then both fascination and difficulty disappear; the authoritative utterance or act arrives with ease and grace.

Most memorable, possibly because they reminded me of Saturday nights at The Poplars, were discussions and readings held in the drawing-room in the evenings. Calpin loved Dickens, and read *The Christmas Carol* to us with appropriate panache.

Miss Thompson and Horrocks (who played the piano) buried their hatchets in the rich loam of English folklore, ballad and song, teaching us to sing 'Widdicombe Fair', 'Early One Morning', and 'Robin Adair'. During one of these sessions I was disconcerted and excited to find that my voice could no longer be trusted to hit the higher treble notes.

Puberty expressed itself in other ways. Among the books which had been donated to the school was a magnificent eighteenth-century folio of *Paradise Lost,* with fine full-page steel engravings. There I encountered Eve before the fall, fair, naked, with rounded breasts, totally unconscious of the adolescent whose fall into guilty voyeurism she was encouraging. My puritan background filled me with dread and shame, as if I were taking a pornographic meal off those chaste plates. If I heard footsteps I would whip over the page and read the text.

Calpin walked in late one afternoon, and found me there. He glanced over my shoulder.

'By Jove, Butler, you are coming on. Switch on the light, you'll ruin your

I did so.

'Now read me a passage which you particularly like.'

On a previous occasion, when I could bear the naked beauty of Eve no longer, I had encountered a passage which had reminded me — such are the tricks of association — of that quiet evening at Vrede when Uncle Frank had called Aunt Flo from the kitchen to look at the new moon.

> *With thee conversing I forget all time,*
> *All seasons and their change, all please alike:*
> *Sweet is the breath of Morn, her rising sweet,*
> *With charm of earliest birds; pleasant the sun,*
> *When first on this delightful land he spreads*
> *His orient beams, on herb, tree, fruit, and flower,*
> *Glist'ring with dew; fragrant the fertile earth*
> *After soft showers; and sweet the coming on*
> *Of grateful evening mild; then silent night,*
> *With this her solemn bird, and this fair moon,*
> *And these the gems of heav'n, her starry train:*
> *But neither breath of Morn when she ascends*
> *With charm of earliest birds, nor rising sun*
> *On this delightful land, nor herb, fruit, flower,*
> *Glist'ring with dew, nor fragrance after showers,*
> *Nor grateful evening mind, nor silent night,*
> *With this her solemn bird, nor walk by moon,*
> *Or glittering starlight, without thee is sweet.*

Paradise Lost was not the only source of temptation.

Eden was all about us: trees everywhere, laden with forbidden fruit; Eve and Adam maturing in each of us; God real but remote; and Satan close, but usually in camouflage.

The Karoo, once you have been given the hint, is the eroded ruins of a world, the great lake and its giant reptiles gone but for a few bones and ripple marks, gone like Sodom and Gomorrah in earthquake and fire, epochs of reptilian life abolished, stone scorched and purged, and then sculpted clean and bare into noble shapes, the tactics of the elemental artist spelt out in the fine sand of the watercourses, his signature clear in the cirrus clouds. You can see all this because the air is dry, distances clear, and scarcely a shrub grows higher than your knees. In that vast semi-desert it is difficult to forget your smallness; the colour and size of the shrubs is shy; growth slow and stubborn; the dinosaurs seem to be saying, through the small swift lizard, the camouflaged snake, the armour-plated tortoise: we've learnt our lesson, we'll stay small. The extremities of the seasons, from snow to blinding sun, drive the lesson home: no luxury here; every year frost and fire will search you and find you out.

But in sub-tropical Natal between Pietermaritzburg and Durban, grand as the scenery may be, the heights are seldom set in enough space to register: great pieces of sculpture need to stand on spacious floors. The slow-continuing cataclysm can be forgotten, so thorough is the protective camouflage of grass. That is what struck me most: the Karoo can only be appreciated if you develop a feeling for stones. Mountainsides are exposed shale and loose boulders; the plains are covered with soil so thin that rock is for ever reasserting itself. But in Natal the steepest slope is covered in dense vegetation. You rarely encounter rock except in the bed of a stream or in a cliff. Even in the streams, the roots of the vegetation clothe the stones; and many tall cliffs are half hidden by the trees and creepers growing from their bases. There is so much life at your feet and in the foreground, and the air is so humid, that distant views are rare. For someone from the Karoo the scale of Natal is that of a garden.

It was a wonder to me: the ubiquitous lush green, hillsides waving with seed grass as if planted with wheat, dense copses of trees with palms and plantains and other vegetable strangers; new butterflies the size of my hand; new bird calls; new flowers: a paradise to explore or be idle in, just as we chose.

Three images remain with me from those long free afternoons.

A group of boys and girls, moving over an upland steeped in heat, drop suddenly down to a stream. The temptation to strip and plunge is strong. The stream is a succession of treeless pools; in one of these, three young Zulu girls are bathing, laughing, splashing each other. They look very beautiful against the blue and green, the sun transforming the wet on their brown skins to quicksilver, highlighting all that is feminine about them. They are not embarrassed, as we are. Are they still with Eve in Eden, unashamed of their sex?

Old Warner told me of a large iguana that haunted a certain treelined pool. I stole down carefully, making sure not to put a foot on a brittle twig. Each time another stretch of the pool came into view I paused, slowly scanning every rock, every branch. I would not have seen him had he not moved his head — four feet of primeval reptile, bizarre in a football jersey of black and yellow bands. Clearly a giant first cousin to the likkewaans of the Karoo, who had toned their colours down to match the grey of the veld, he had developed this colour scheme as the best camouflage for the tropics: he looked like a branch, blotched and banded with sunlight and shadow.

Quick lizards and snakes, slow chameleons, armour-plated tortoises, all camouflaged — reptilian survivors of the largest animals the earth had known. He had seen me, the upstart, upright monkey. At my next move he slid off the branch into the stream, and swam, creasing the mirror of water in his wake. Had one not seen his entry into the stream, one could not have suspected that the silver lines of the fine ripples were caused by so strange, so sinister a creature.

We climb to the highest point across the main road above the school, and, from a cliff's edge, look down into the Valley of a Thousand Hills: successive gauzes of heat-haze hang in each valley, progressively smudging rather than etherealising the receding ranges. In the near distance a headland rides high, a firm promontory thrusting into a troubled sea. On its crest is a mission station, like a lighthouse, built by Christians of the extreme opposite end of the religious spectrum to Quakers, the Roman Catholics.

We can see clearly enough into the valley at our feet. It seems dry, rough and stony by comparison with Inchanga. Through the late afternoon air voices reach us, the clear primary vowel sounds of Zulu.

'How their voices carry,' I say.

'They live in the open all their lives — mouths like megaphones,' says Charles. 'Look — there they are!'

Four men in tribal dress are walking in file along a footpath, deep in friendly converse. The footpath forks; two take the left hand, two the right, without a pause in their steady pacing or their speech. Their conversation continues even after a great hill has intervened. They speak more slowly, more musically, tossing their phrases high, like balls, confident they will be caught, and tossed back. The echoes applaud the sport.

The angelus starts ringing at the mission station — we watch to see if we can catch the stilling effect that has so impressed us before. Yes, a man ploughing with two oxen in a distant field stops his team; a moving file of schoolchildren on a contour path are frozen into a frieze; but the musical valley-to-valley conversation goes on. Why should it stop? Why should they hail the Virgin? And pray for heavenly grace, 'now and at the hour of our death'? Like the girls in the stream, they seem pre-lapsarian.

'They have no sense of sin,' says Charles.

'You mean they don't feel guilt?'

'No, man, they've got consciences, just like you and me; but they don't believe in original sin.'

The concept of original sin had been debated in The Poplars with vehemence. Dad rejected the notion as insulting to God. Would a just and loving Creator condemn a child, before it could speak or think or act, as guilty? But Mother said: 'People are imperfect. There is something wrong with us, with every mother and father. How can an innocent child come from guilty parents?'

And then the debate would swing on to the relative influences of heredity and environment.

In my adolescent ignorance and arrogance, the inheritance of the pagan Zulu seemed to me preferable to my own. I had discovered an imprisoned noble savage in myself, and would have liked to liberate him, to go bathing naked with black girls in a brilliant pool. Though I quickly repressed the fantasy, I knew that there was something naked and disobedient deep inside me.

These dark turbulences produced no more than little eddies on the surface of the moving stream. We performed all the superficial pranks of schoolchildren. As a firm believer in customs and rituals, however, I find myself compelled to recount how we fulfilled the two great infernal injunctions to children in boarding-schools: 'Thou shalt feast at midnight,' and 'Thou shalt steal fruit.'

The sleeping-quarters of the boys and girls were upstairs, separated by a buffer strip of staff accommodation. No one dared use the linking corridor by night, but a single-storey verandah, which went right round the building, provided a safe, though sloping, cat-walk under all the windows.

On the night of our first midnight feast it was my job to wake Sally, who would rouse the other girls. Having pulled on my socks and laced my tackies, and having tucked my pyjama trousers into the socks, I slipped through my window, traversed the long verandah top, and arrived outside what I took to be Sally's room. There I lost my nerve. What if it was not Sally's room, but Miss Thompson's? I went back to my room, and woke Morgan. Which did he think was Sally's window? He wasn't sure. Nor was Charles. No one was. The whole boy population was now awake; my honour was at stake.

I tiptoed back across the corrugated iron, tapped on the window three times and ducked. No response. Slowly I lifted my head, and peeped in. It was Sally's room all right. The full moon fell on to her profile, and the unmistakable, adorable bird's-egg nose. So I lifted the sash, which slid with surprising ease.

'Sally!' I whispered hoarsely.

She did not respond. So I stretched my arm through the window and, as though plucking a ripe grape, gripped the nose between thumb and forefinger, and gave it a tweak. That did the trick.

Five minutes later four boys and four girls filed across the verandah roofs to the tank at the corner, against which we had arranged a scaffolding of old packing-cases that afternoon. Thence to the old disused stables, where we climbed into two ancient Overland motor cars, down on the rims, and now the abode of hens, hornets, rats and fleas. Each car-load was lit by a single candle.

I had brought a packet of Marie biscuits and a tin of Norwegian sardines, and Sally, a small tin of golden syrup. The Marie biscuits went well with the sardines or the syrup.

It was Sally's idea to combine the sardines and the syrup. She dipped the fish into the tin, drew it out, allowed the surplus syrup to drain off it, then, throwing her head back, slipped it into her mouth like a stalk of asparagus. She assured me it was delicious. But I found it was not.

We then shared one of Morgan's cigarettes. Sardines, syrup and nicotine leave the taste buds dry and outraged.

Pretending to be Sir Malcolm Campbell at the wheel, I proceeded to drive that stationary fossil of a car across the Verneuk Pan of the Natal night. Having broken the world land-speed record, I felt tempted to blow out the candle and put my arm round my co-driver's jerseyed shoulders and kiss her treacly lips. But she suddenly exclaimed, scratching her legs — 'It's fleas! Or tan pans!' — and leapt out of my reach.

The party was over. We filed back, across the moonlit lawn, up the boxes, on to the tank, across the verandah roofs, through our proper windows into our own beds.

The fruit stealing was less of a success. There were only four of us involved — two boys and two girls.

Nearby was a small farmer who owned an orchard of naartjie trees surrounded by a daunting fence.

The plan was simple. Charles and I were to climb the fence, and pass the fruit to the girls, who would put it into small suitcases; when full, they would take them to the old hotel's wood-and-iron billiard room, dump them behind the sofa, and return for more.

The naartjies were ripe, sweet and juicy.

While the girls were away with the first load of loot, the farmer's fox-terrier started to bark. Charles and I had small piles of naartjies at our feet. Practical genius that I am, I said, 'Stuff them into your pyjama pants' — which were tucked into our socks.

It is amazing how many naartjies can fit into the space between your pyjamas and your legs, but I cannot honestly recommend it as the best means of transporting them. It has at least three serious handicaps. First, there is the difficulty of climbing over a barbed-wire fence, particularly when there's a fiendish fox-terrier barking, and a shouting man has caught you full in the beam of his Eveready torch. Second, it impedes the normal movements of running; sprinting with one's feet wide apart is not easy. Third, ripe naartjies need gentler handling. By the time we reached the old billiard room, each pyjama leg was a leaky sack of Tomango squash.

Sally and her friend laughed at us, laughed till they cried.

I don't think I recovered my affection for Sally, freckled nose or not.

Meanwhile Aunt Mary had returned to South Africa with Uncle Joe. Recently she has shown me a little diary of his six-months' visit. He celebrated his eightieth birthday in Cradock, with his sister Eliza, his brother James's widow, Lettie, and Ernest's family. In Cape Town he saw his brother Charles and his sister Emmie (Fear), and elsewhere their children and grandchildren; and Quakers, wherever he could find them, or others interested in education and social betterment: Louisvale, Rooispruit, Kroonstad, Vryburg, Durban and Pietermaritzburg, Johannesburg, and Port Elizabeth, East London, Lovedale and Fort Hare. His lucid mind and charitable concern shine through the text.

Like most Quakers, he takes pleasure in recording interesting facts. He is fascinated by the engineering feats he encounters. At Louisvale he admires the Wal or embankment: it is over a mile long, from 12 to 22 feet high; it is 9 feet wide on top and up to 70 feet at the base.

Mingled with close attention to measurements are human observations.

'Yesterday Dan (Biggs) took Lettie, Josie, Mary and me and two boys to the weir a few miles up the river — a very pretty spot where a comparatively small weir diverts sufficient water to irrigate 1,000 morgen of land. Josie and Dan have 5 children. Honor is the eldest and Pat, who is the youngest, is 7. All but Honor live a very open air life and are generally barefooted, barelegged and bareheaded.'

He is pleased to hear that Dan is in correspondence with Mr Calpin with a view to sending Honor to Inchanga in 1933. Uncle Joe had been one of the few English Quakers to put his heart and soul into raising money for Inchanga — a thankless task at the best of times but doubly difficult in the midst of the Great Depression. He must have looked forward to visiting the place during its infancy. In November 1932 the Natal Quakers held a meeting for worship under the trees in Maurice Webb's garden in Manning Road, Durban. 'H. Calpin had motored over, bringing Guy with him. I got Guy to give me the names of all present.'

I remember my aged, gentle but alert relative very well. I never experienced a moment's reservation or irritation in his presence. He may have looked old, but I could not regard him as such.

On 17 November he began his week-long visit to Inchanga school. 'Guy Butler is v. interested in his stamps, his lessons, his school and the individual method of teaching, which he likes v. much.' But it is clear that the tensions between the Head and the committee had crystallised into a crisis. 'Reynolds brought Howard Pim here today (18 November), and the latter has interviewed different people individually and afterwards discussed matters privately with me, after which he returned to Durban to meet some of the Executive Committee. We now await the report on the difficulties which have arisen.'

On Sundays parents and other interested people would visit the school. Amongst the latter were the Durban Quakers, who seemed to defer to the rotund and loquacious Maurice Webb. Meeting was held on one of the lawns. It was quite unlike the listening, silence-saturated Cradock meeting. Everybody seemed to be waiting for his turn to speak. At the Sunday meeting held with Uncle Joe all the loquaciousness had disappeared. They were in the presence of a sage and waiting for him to speak. He kept them waiting in frozen silence for over half an hour.

Close by, a shrub called 'yesterday-today-and-tomorrow' was in bloom, and we breathed its scent. Uncle Joe started by expressing his delight that such a shrub should exist at all. He gave us its botanical name, and told us that it came from the East. He then turned it into a parable. While Yesterday's flower is withering, Today's rejoices in the present. It knows that it is also doomed, but that Tomorrow will take its place. Different as they are in their conditions, Yesterday, Today and Tomorrow accept each other, are part of one and the same shrub. The application of the parable to Inchanga school was not spelt out, but obscurely hinted at. Could children be Tomorrow, the staff Today, and the committee Yesterday? Or was it that everybody was always living through this sequence? Towards the end of his homily, Uncle Joe became quite specific. People in institutions like this school, who could learn to accept change, and to live in hope and charity with each other, would surely be granted moral beauty and exude an attractive spiritual scent like the shrub.

But the committee, and the staff, and interfering parents found it impossible to live in charity, and soon abandoned hope. After every weekend children would swop items of scandal which they had picked up from their parents about the staff and the school committee. No one saw moral beauty in anyone else; and, far from detecting attractive spiritual scents, angry parents on visits sniffed the corridors to find the bad drains which rumour said were poisoning the systems of their children.

Though I never smelt those bad drains, the air of the school was so infected by adult rancour as to release savagery and fanatacism in the children. On what evidence I do not know, we cast Horrocks for villain. He and Webb were trying to oust Calpin as head. Big, dim Morgan now came into his own. He said that it was our duty to teach old Horrocks a lesson. He should be ambushed on the landing after supper, and be beaten to pulp with cricket bats. He was prepared to do it, but only if someone would volunteer to help him.

I had spent a very enjoyable weekend in Durban as the guest of the Morgans; had been shown the harbour, and been given my first experience of sailing; but it was not gratitude that made me volunteer. I hated Horrocks, and the prospect of 'laying him out cold' appealed to the savage in me.

We waited in the shadows at the top of the stairs, cricket bats in hand. Footsteps warned us to be ready to strike. But it was Calpin, not Horrocks, who appeared.

'What are you doing with that bat, Butler?' he asked.

'It needs oiling, Sir.'

'Curious time of day to oil a bat,' he said with a shrug, continuing on his way.

I turned round to speak to Morgan. My fellow crusader had fled.

After leaving Inchanga, Uncle Joe returned to his brother and sister, Charles and Emmie, in Cape Town, where he heard that a full meeting of the Inchanga school council was to take place in Johannesburg on 11 December. The Cape Town Friends desired him to attend. 'Conditional on an invitation from H. Pim, I agreed to fall in with their wishes.' It says much for Uncle Joe's stamina and devotion to the cause of the school, and the respect in which he was held, that he should have made that long journey to attend what must have been two harrowing meetings lasting from 2.30 to 10.30 p.m. on Sunday, and from 10.30 to 5 p.m. on Monday. No final decision was reached. That was to be left to a general meeting of the whole Society, under the chairmanship of Howard Pim.

The holidays came and the twelve Inchanga children returned to their homes, dimly aware of the adult agony our education was causing.

Uncle Joe and I reached Cradock about the same time. On 18 December he 'attended Meeting for Worship at the Poplars, including Guy who had got home from Inchanga on Friday evening'. I recall him saying to me, 'My boy, walk me down the garden.' There he proceeded to ask gently searching questions about the school. I did my best to give fair answers, but my bias must have been obvious to him.

The general meeting of Friends took place in January 1933 and Uncle Joe and my father attended. The decision was reached that the school should close. It must have been a wounding experience for Aunt Mary, Ernest, and Uncle Joe.

The failure of Inchanga school was a minor tragedy for South African education: a good Quaker school on the Dalton plan might have encouraged our teachers to question the effectiveness of their methods. Dr Will Fox, a Johannesburg Friend, who was involved in the long deliberations, has kindly sent me the following comments:

'Whether the early collapse of the venture was due to internal or external differences I do not know, but suspect the latter. Howard Pim, well known for his efforts to improve race relations, was the only Friend that I knew at all well and deserves much credit for the patience and energy he showed in getting the scheme off the ground, surely a difficult task for a peppery Irishman accustomed to get his own way. My own reaction was a sense of shame for so ignominious an end to our first corporate effort and for the parents who had removed their children from other schools and had then been let down so quickly and so badly.'

16

The Deepening Stream

The Midland Printing & Publishing Company was in deeper waters than ever. At a meeting of the shareholders in April 1932, the chairman had reported a loss of £1792. 9. 6 for the two years 1930 and '31.

He also reported that his sister Mary Butler had given her shares to him.

By 28 November a further big fall in turnover had necessitated additional salary cuts. The editor was now working for £15 per month, and Ernest had reduced his own drawings to a similar figure. He was receiving less than his senior journeymen, whose salaries were fixed by the Typographical Union.

So it is not surprising that, when Joan completed her matriculation at the end of the year, some senior relatives should have thought that she should get a job and bring some money into The Poplars. Among these was Aunt Mary 'who felt that Dad and Mom had struggled enough for the children and it was time they helped their parents. It was suggested that Joan should work in T.J. Roberts & Sons, the Drapers', says Christine. But Joan's examination results had been good enough to ensure the award of a Cape Education Department scholarship for primary school teaching. This financial support strengthened Alice's determination to do better for her daughter. She should become a teacher, as her mother had been. Alice won the day and Joan was sent to the Grahamstown Training College, Grahamstown, then flourishing under the headship of Sister Frances-Mary, C.R. It was the beginning of 1933 — a time of general education shuffle at The Poplars.

Dorothy, after a year in *The Midland News* office, returned to school at the Convent of the Sacred Heart, where she could learn shorthand and typing to improve her usefulness and to escape the rigours of Latin. Ernest, and to a lesser extent Alice, were very disturbed when she showed Catholic proclivities.

'Guy came home from Inchanga full of hero-worship for the headmaster and scorn for the committee. My father tried to temper Guy's violent partisanship but he was in no mood for compromise, and condemned the committee with scornful indignation.' Thus my sister Dorothy. And Christine adds: 'You were always somewhat unapproachable — reading your set books on the back stoep, or doing something to your museum, or helping Dad in the workshop. After Inchanga I tended to keep out of your way.'

Rex Moys, the leader of the Rhino Patrol, had won the Alfred Metcalf

Scholarship to Rhodes University.

Honor Biggs, from Louisvale, who might have gone to Inchanga had the school survived, came to Rocklands instead, and boarded at The Poplars. We were all a little in awe of Honor: always impeccably groomed and neat; deft and efficient, and so conscientious and self-disciplined. She had a quiet and self-contained manner, and a sparkling sense of humour. She seemed to us to score about 80 per cent on Aunt Mary's scale of values for the young. However, Dorothy and I were by now inured to limping by on a mere 50 per cent and Christine was a stubborn non-achiever. As for Jeffrey, he was already showing signs of not giving a damn where he came on anybody's scale. He was growing tall and rangy, with no hips worth speaking of. As he insisted on wearing a belt (the right to wear one having been conceded after a long fight with Father) he experienced some difficulty with his pants; and his socks were usually round his ankles. He was nicknamed 'Sigaret-beentjies' or 'Lappy-legs'.

'At mealtimes,' says Christine, 'especially supper, Dorothy was the one who would start a discussion on any subject under the sun, or on a book she was reading. Dad would join in freely, provided we were only family. He could be so charming when he was at ease, but would freeze up when strangers were around. His efforts to keep Jeff in place were not always successful, especially when Mom used to hide her laughter behind her table napkin, while her blue eyes twinkled over the top of the cloth. Jeff would be sent out of the room. No sooner had he gone than we would all collapse with helpless giggles at Jeff's parting sally. I don't think he was ever cheeky. Dad wouldn't have stood for that.'

Joan reminds me of a family ritual which I had forgotten. At the end of each term we were all sent home with our school reports, issued on the same day from both the high schools.

'At lunch time we passed them up to Dad to read aloud. Guy always did well and Dad was so proud of him. Jeff was always too talkative and his work untidy and, like his pants, always falling down.'

Jeff was naturally beginning to resent this big brother with whom he was always being unfavourably compared at home and at school. It must be confessed that at this stage the Big Brother, deeply self-absorbed, hardly noticed his, or anybody else's existence. Christine says that I was 'very grown up and distant'.

I certainly recall the distance. I was nervous about going back to the Boys' High School (January 1933). Would I not be treated as a deserter? — an abnormal freak who did not attend cadets?

For three years of cadet periods I sat alone in the classroom, finishing off my homework, dreaming, or reading. I don't believe that it strengthened my pacifist leanings, and my non-conformity drew no one closer to Quakerism or questioning. I am sure that it damaged my relationship with my father.

One image survives of all those hours of reluctant protest against school militarism. The new Boys' High classrooms had a few pictures in them inherited from the previous occupants, the defunct Cradock Training College. I would spend hours in fantasy staring at three girls walking towards me along a boulevard on a river's edge. There is a picturesque bridge behind them, and the architecture is medieval. One, on the left, a redhead, in a light, long, coral-coloured robe which clings about her body revealing its intoxicating femininity, is leaning back slightly to look past her companion at a dark-robed man on the left, who has one hand clutched to his heart, the other leaning on the parapet of a bridge. Her fair face seems to be smiling; his is tense, but he is not looking at her. Between them, but noticing neither, looking slightly away and ahead, is another gorgeous girl, in gold and lemon yellow. Is she rapt in some interior vision, or is she snubbing him? The third girl, in dark blue, a little to the rear, is also looking at the man. I knew the picture of old, it was in one of Mother's little art books: Dante and Beatrice, by Henry Holiday.

I knew just enough about Dante and about the nature of true love, sometimes to subdue my excitement at the red-haired girl's body, to brood over the nature of the drama between the man and the other girl who would not look at him, and to wonder about the girl in blue, the least involved of them all. I was forced to conduct a Quaker meeting for myself alone: my thoughts were not on heaven and holiness, but on poetry and love.

I need not have been worried about my reception: my old friends — Keith Cremer, Ted Diesel and others — took me back without reserve. Keith had discovered Dickens. I remember slowly strolling to his boarding-house room after choir practice while he spoke of the wonderful descriptions of stage coaching in *David Copperfield*. I rejoined St Peter's choir and the Scouts, where I became leader of the Antelope Patrol. Within a month it seemed as if I had never been away.

Inchanga, that brief exposure to educational stimulus, had been a holiday from the depression. On my return, I found that the state of economic siege had intensified. September's first job each morning was to clean the kitchen and dining-room grates, and sieve the ashes from the cinders. The cinders, mixed with a little new coal, would be burnt a second time. When a farming relative brought us a gift of butter, we had to choose between butter or jam. To have both was forbidden.

When he came in for stock fair, Uncle Norman would leave something behind for Ernest and Alice: an ostrich egg, which contains as much yolk as two dozen hens' eggs, and could keep us in omelettes for a week; a four-gallon tin of crystallised honey; or, during the shooting season, a whole springbok.

In winter we all felt the cold: no one had a coat. The girls were so short of clothes that they wore their 'gyms' during the holidays.

Mother was growing lettuces and cut flowers for the market. Father was selling off some fine items of Africana which he had inherited from his grandfather.

He was having a most difficult time at the Works. Not only did he have all the anxieties of manager, but also those of mechanic. Whenever a machine went wrong, no matter how tired he was, he would have to repair it after hours, labouring far into the night. One of the older children would accompany him to hand him tools and act as an intelligent lampstand, moving the bulb and reflector to illuminate the machine without shining it in his eyes. It was boring yet exacting, and sometimes freezing cold, in those draughty concrete-floored spaces among the unfeeling iron monsters. One night, about ten-thirty, an anxious Alice appeared.

'Ernest, dear,' she said, 'isn't it time you stopped? The boy has school in the morning.'

Barely turning to look at her, he said with a rare touch of impatience: 'Alice, you know I'll come as soon as I can.'

We finished hours later. A full moon shone from the remote zenith on to the frost. The Dutch Reformed tower struck two. It was a desolate but beautiful world.

One night it was Joan's turn to hold the lamp — perhaps during my absence at Inchanga. She was so tired that she fell asleep on her feet and collapsed on to the concrete floor. Conscience-stricken, Ernest abandoned his problems and brought his daughter home.

Ernest was always buying what Mother called 'job-lots', 'junk' and 'rubbishy secondhand bargains'. The smaller items were stored in his enlarged workshop in the outhouses, in dozens of Laurel Paraffin boxes stacked against the walls to form pigeon holes. The larger items were kept in what he hoped were invisible corners of the yard or at the back of the house. Alice got used to living amongst Ernest's 'precious treasures', and trained her eye to see no farther than her hollyhocks, foxgloves, shasta daisies and roses.

One day he would come home from a sale with a dozen Singer sewing-machines of indeterminate vintage; another with four nineteenth-century typewriters and three ancient telephones — all acquired 'for sixpence'. There were old mahogany cameras with fine brass fittings, primitive gramophones with horns, a complete electric-bell system from an old hotel; in fact, enough items to stock a small museum. These provided him with a stock of nuts and bolts, washers and screws of steel or copper; small cogs and levers, cams and castings — which, with infinite ingenuity, he would use to repair the machines of the Works or to make machines of his own. He manufactured a complete drillpress out of them — apart from the chuck and the electric motor, which he bought second hand. His motto was 'Make do with what you've got', and we all did our best to oblige.

He then hit on a way of saving on lino-metal — a simple alloy of lead, tin and antimony. He set his sons to collecting old motor-car batteries, breaking the bakelite cases, and melting the lead down. We were paid a couple of pence a pound for the metal, to which he would add the necessary proportion of antimony and tin. Jeffrey was more assiduous at this task than I was. His smelting-works was behind the old workshop.

One day, returning in high spirits from tennis, and espying a large Lyle's Golden Syrup tin lying in the garden path, I submitted to the natural urge to kick it as far as I could. It was half full of Jeffrey's lead and I was lame for a week.

This form of economy was brought to an abrupt halt. Jeffrey had gone off to the municipal rubbish tip on his bicycle in search of old batteries. The surface crust gave way and one of his legs sank knee-deep into the secretly smouldering cinders. Somehow he extricated himself. The place was deserted. In anguish he made his way to the water furrow and sat down on the bank, immersing his legs in the muddy water up to his knees. There a passing black man found him, and lifted the whimpering child home on the bar of his bicycle. By the time Dr Scholtz arrived Jeffrey was nearly demented with pain, Alice was pale and trembling. He was rushed off to hospital. It took weeks for the burns to heal.

One of my few triumphs at Inchanga had been winning the competition for a cover for the school magazine. We had been encouraged to draw and to paint. There was a weekly clay-modelling class, presided over by dear old Warner. My assignment was to copy a fifteen-inch heraldic lion by Landseer. Warner was encouraging, but disapproved of the amount of clay I got on to my shoes and into my hair. Quakers are such terribly tidy people.

Back in the aesthetically arid atmosphere of the Boys' High School, I hankered for Inchanga's art sessions. I asked Mother if I could take up a correspondence course with the Strand School of Art, London. I have forgotten exactly what the cost per lesson was. I knew it was the sort of extra that we could not normally afford, but my need was great. With a wistful look, Mother said no. Desperate, beginning to show symptoms of artistic amorality, I wrote off for the first lesson, and waited breathlessly. There was no airmail in those days. Five weeks later the big envelope was delivered with the morning letters, so everybody knew I had received a big envelope, and from London. I had not calculated on such an exposure of my plans.

'How are you going to pay for this course?' asked Father.

'My birthday and Christmas money.'

He looked at the cost of the course. He knew what birthday and Christmas money would come to.

'You'll still be paying for the course when you're 36,' he said drily.

I made the most of lesson one, going over and over the exercises that it prescribed.

When I began to receive a succession of increasingly frightening letters, demanding payment, Mother smuggled me the money for a postal order, but for lesson one only.

A dead springbok arrived from Uncle Norman. It was placed under the shelf in the pantry pending skinning the next day. I sat there, curled up on the cement floor, drawing the head, and particularly the beautiful eye. So engrossed was I that I took no notice when Dorothy entered the pantry to cut herself a slice of brown bread. She proceeded to cover it with whole fig jam — whole figs in syrup. She did not notice me.

I was one of those horrible boys who loved giving people surprises.

Her serge school skirt was just above the line of my sight; and below it the long black columns of her stockinged legs plunged into her shoes.

With my sharp pencil point I pricked her, gently, in the sensitive area behind the knee.

A scream of terror. Then a cry, 'You! You beast!'

And there, bang, was the piece of brown bread on my beautiful drawing, fig-jam-side downwards.

I tried to keep up my stamp collecting, but found it impossible to progress on my father's principle of swopping only. Then salvation dawned. I found a dealer who was prepared to grant credit in return for used South African issues, duly floated from their covers, dried, sorted, and tied into bundles of one hundred. It was a sticky, finicky, laborious task; but the mail of *The Midland News* provided ample raw material. My collection prospered as fast as the round trip between England and South Africa would allow. Without knowing it, I was engaged in barter, almost trading *per contra*, as my father had been driven to do.

My enthusiasm died one afternoon when, having spread over a thousand stamps to dry on sheets of paper on the back stoep, Father called me to help him in the workshop. He kept me there a long time. By the time I returned a hot wind had risen, and the stamps, not yet quite dry, had been blown into the dusty backyard, which turned them into diminutive sheets of curly sandpaper. The final turn of the screw was the command to pick them all up 'as they looked so untidy'. I deposited them in the rubbish bin.

Three times a week the galley proofs would be sent across to The Poplars for proofreading. Alice did most of it, but any child might find his home-work interleaved with a column or two of proofs. It was soon discovered that spelling was not my forte. (I am still an erratic speller. Whenever I interview a prospective typist I ask her if she can spell, as one of her tasks will be to correct my spelling. She usually smiles at this question — she takes it to be a pleasantry. A Professor of English who can't spell? Really! I thereupon remind her that there are economists who cannot add up their cheque-stubs. One of them was kind enough to console me with Mark

Twain's quip: 'I have no respect at all for a man who can only spell a word in one way.')

But far more important was Alice's role as social reporter for *The Midland News*. She had a nose for news. Many small items of gossip would be turned into copy — particularly for a column called 'Here and There's'.

'Mr and Mrs Jim Metcalf have left by car for Cape Town to spend some time with Mrs Metcalf's parents, Sir Carruthers and Lady Beattie. Sir Carruthers is Vice-Chancellor of the University of Cape Town.'

'A severe hailstorm last Saturday destroyed most of the apple crop at Swinside, the farm of Mr Harold Bladen. It is the worst he has experienced. For some time the countryside under the thick layer of hail looked like a scene in the Lake District.'

'Miss Phyllis Gould, daughter of the Rev. Charles and Mrs Gould of Cradock, has returned from England, where she has completed her schooling. She has become very proficient in French, and is prepared to give tuition in it. Parents should consider the advantages of introducing their children to this great and useful language.'

(No parents responded. The matter was discussed at The Poplars, but where was the money for the fees to come from?)

There were, of course, greater challenges than finding 'Here and Theres'. Most regular among these were Weddings and Balls. It was quite impossible to attend all; and when she could, she was, to begin with, reluctant to go around, pencil and pad in hand asking personal questions and writing answers down in public. She much preferred to join in the fun, and be free to talk, and rely on her memory. But her memory was not always reliable. At home she would sit over her pad frowning.

'What on earth did that fat Mrs Knowles wear? She looked awful, but one has to say something nice.'

So she would phone one of her friends who had been at the wedding, and eventually produce something like this:

'Mrs Knowles, the bride's aunt from King William's Town, looked very dashing in a dress of niggerbrown crepe cut on the bias.'

Sometimes she wrote her report in advance. She would spend hours on the phone, talking to ladies likely to attend.

'Is that you, Mrs Figgins? It's Mrs Ernest Butler, *Midland News*, speaking. About the Ball tonight, my dear, what will you be wearing? You're not quite sure? — Oh, I see. — Yes, it must be difficult to make up one's mind between so many. — Of course, I quite see. — But you do think it will be the black velvet? I'm sure that would suit you best. So smart, black.'

And so the whole report might be handed to the lino-operator before the band had struck up. There were occasional disasters, as when Mrs Figgins changed her mind and went in her floral silk after all. These errors would raise Ernest's mildly expressed ire.

'Alice, my dear, the essence of good journalism is accuracy. Bad reporting does a paper no good.'

'My reporting is not bad,' she retorted with spirit. 'People love my reports. They say it's the first time the paper has had such lively social reporting.'

'My dear, that is true. But an error is an error.'

At which point one of the children would say: 'Is what-Mrs-Figgins-wore really important? Who is she anyway?'

'Mrs Figgins is the most important person in the whole world to at least one person: Mrs Figgins. And she might send old Figgins to complain and waste a lot of my time.'

Throughout the depression we were made dimly conscious by Mother's excited talk after the English mail was in, of our English cousins and aunts and uncles. There was Uncle George, and Aunt Frances, who lived at Stoke, or nearby; he was in a pottery firm and she was a Cambridge graduate, and immensely clever; no, George was not clever; and they had two children, Guy and Barbara. And then there were Harold and May in China, also with two children, whom we did not hear about so often. There was Aunt Dorothy, who had married Jim Goddard, who was also in a pottery firm (Mason's Ironstone China); and they had two children, Jim and Patricia.

We saw them from time to time, in photographs, sent us at Christmas. Every two years or so Mother would dragoon us all to W.W. Lidbetter for a family photograph, the main purpose of which was to keep in touch with her English folk. Never was the grooming and scrubbing more thorough. We had to keep up with those toffs, so beautifully dressed and groomed. Particularly the dressed part. We knew, because parcels of vast proportions, with 10s. and £1 stamps on them, would arrive, crammed with clothes that were no longer of any use to Jim or Patricia, or Guy or Barbara. They were great days, particularly for the girls I think, looting those parcels; though Christine says many of the garments were too woolly and thick for South African use. She recalls acquiring a very fancy petite pair of snakeskin shoes into which she crammed her colonial feet for a dance, nearly died of anguish, and walked home barefoot at midnight.

Mother would look at the letters and photographs, and frown, and say, 'Harold (or George or Dorothy) has only two children. I'd hate to be stuck with a pigeon pair.' The five of us, aware that she found some difficulty in clothing and feeding us all, were puzzled but reassured by this sentiment.

1933 was my Junior Certificate year, and the year in which my haphazard interest in poetry, already stimulated by Miss Thompson of Inchanga, began to deepen into a passion. It is difficult to say whether this would have occurred but for my sister Dorothy's consistent and unabashed love of poetry, the occasional passing comments by my mother, and my English master's unaffected appreciation of verse.

One day Mother and I were out walking past the cemetery, and paused to glance at the tombstones. Several of these were most un-Christian, consisting of proud Roman columns, broken before reaching their full height: a kind of tragic declaration, almost an accusation of the Almighty for cutting short the promising career of this or that farmer or townsman. There were others consisting of imitations of draped funerary urns.

With sparkless ashes load an unlamented urn,

said Mother suddenly and followed it with

Can storied urn or animated bust
Back to its mansion call the fleeting breath?
Can Honour's voice provoke the silent dust,
Or Flatt'ry soothe the the dull, cold ear of death?

She was a trifle surprised that I had not yet encountered Gray's *Elegy*. 'What *do* they teach you at school?'
Then by association her mind moved away from funerary urns to Grecian urns with no ashes in them.

Thou still unravish'd bride of quietness,
Thou foster-child of silence and slow time —

I did not know what the words meant, but asked her to repeat them until I had learnt them by heart.

Aird was an excellent schoolmaster and a lovable man. In that most unpromising climate he managed to give me some feeling for, some insight into the nature of poetry. The methods of practical criticism had not yet penetrated South African schools, and poetry was taught less as a sophisticated form of comprehension than as something you got to know by heart.
True, we learnt a little about prosody, and the definitions of dozens of figures of speech, so that we had a kind of spotter's guidebook to the more common usages; and we were encouraged to find out the 'prose meaning' of a poem. This involved a few old-fashioned precautions, like detecting the main verbs, looking up difficult words in a dictionary, and getting a firm grip on whatever elusive classical or biblical allusions were complicating the issue. But — because our teacher, Aird himself, loved poetry almost as much as he loved bees — this information, so frequently abused, fell into its proper place. Our poetry setbook in J.C. was called *Poems of Action* and there they all were, the good anthology pieces, of various lengths, from thumpers like Tennyson's 'The Revenge' to ghostly evocations like De la Mare's 'The Highwayman'. Aird read so well that one soon gathered the importance of the music of the lines.

At Flores in the Azores Sir Richard Grenville lay

sounds as if it means business of a rugged kind; whereas

> *'Is there anyone there?' said the Traveller*
> *Knocking at the moonlit door.*

is clearly in a very different key. But, more important, he was sensitive to atmosphere and emotion, and, although no sentimentalist, not afraid of being moved by what he read, and showing his feeling in his voice.

There was, however, one occasion when feeling almost got the better of him. It was shortly after one of his trips to Scotland, during which he had visited, among other things, the field of Culloden. He had given us a factual and impartial account of that appalling battle, in which kilts and claymores and dour Highland heroism went down in the sleet and mire before muskets and bayonets. He mentioned, almost in passing, that there was a lovely Scots lament for the fallen called 'The flowers of the forest are all withered away' (he gave us the Anglicised pronunciation), which was still, from time to time, heard on the pipes, through the mist and over the rocks and the heather.

A few days later we came to Sir Walter Scott's poetic account of the Battle of Flodden from *Marmion*. He started the lesson with a few words on Scott himself: his heroic probity — standing security for friends who then went bankrupt; his acceptance of his responsibility for the debt; and his writing year after year, until the royalties of the Waverley novels had cleared his honour. That done, he gave us a brief historical background to the poem.

For me it was unforgettable.

He sketched in the strategic features of the battlefield, and the importance of attacking the English, under the command of Lord Surrey, when their forces were split, one half on either side of the river, or strung out along the highway and ill organised; of the opportunities lost by the Scots King, a dandy more interested in the fair sex than he ought to have been. Then he began to read.

> *What checks the fiery soul of James?*
> *Why sits that champion of the dames*
> *Inactive on his steed,*
> *And sees, between him and his land,*
> *Between him and Tweed's southern strand,*
> *His host Lord Surrey lead?*
> *What 'vails the vain knight-errant's brand? —*
> *O Douglas, for thy leading wand!*
> *Fierce Randolph, for thy speed!*
> *O for one hour of Wallace wight*
> *Or well skilled Bruce to rule the fight*
> *And cry — 'Saint Andrew and our right!'*

Another sight had seen that morn,
From Fate's dark book a leaf been torn,
And Flodden had been Bannockbourne!

He paused, to tell us something about Douglas, the great knight, about
Wallace, about Bruce and the spider; how one of them, lightly armed on a
pony called a palfrey, waited calmly as a heavily armed English knight on
a huge charger came thundering down upon him, his lance pointed at his
heart, calmly waited until the very last moment, then jerked his pony aside
and, standing in his stirrups, twisting from his thighs, felled his foe with a
single stroke of his battle axe as he hurtled past.

But Aird had, alas, to return to the Scots at Flodden, badly led. The
Scots set fire to their camp, and the smoke acts as a screen under which
they attack. As Aird proceeded, phrase by phrase, line by line, moving
inevitably, controlling and containing the violence of the story and the
mounting disturbance of his and our emotions, a spell gripped us all. The
clouds of smoke lift partially to reveal the chaos of a battle in progress, an
old-fashioned battle where the warriors are named, and the encounters
personal.

In this clash on the right wing the English knights go down, one by one;
but, alas, the clansmen on the left, instead of turning to help their country-
men, fall to looting and plundering.

In the final section Aird's voice continued its measured march, catching
the nuances in rhythm, from verse paragraph to paragraph:

The English shafts in volleys hail'd,
In headlong charge their horse assail'd;
Front, flank and rear the squadrons sweep
To break the Scottish circle deep,
 That fought around their King.
But yet, though thick the shafts as snow,
Though charging knights like whirlwinds go,
Though bill-men ply the ghastly blow,
 Unbroken was the ring;
The stubborn spearmen still made good
Their dark impenetrable wood,
Each stepping where his comrade stood,
 The instant that he fell.
No thought was there of dastard flight;
Link'd in the serried phalanx tight,
Groom fought like noble, squire like knight,
 As fearlessly and well;
Till utter darkness closed her wing
O'er the thin host and wounded King . . .

The victorious English commander, Lord Surrey, withdraws from the field, and under cover of darkness the remnants of the Scots host scatter:

Tweed's echoes heard the ceaseless plash,
  While many a broken band,
Disorder'd, through her currents dash
  To gain the Scottish land . . .
Tradition, legend, tune and song
Shall many an age that wail prolong:
Still from the sire the son shall hear
Of the stern strife, and carnage drear,
  Of Flodden's fatal field,
When shiver'd was fair Scotland's spear,
  And broken was her shield!

Although there had been no hint of any loss of control, it had been clear to me, and to others, from a certain quality in his voice, that Aird was crying. When he finished, he took off his spectacles and with total lack of self-consciousness, wiped his eyes, then blew his nose, sat down, and said:

'I think that will be all for today.'

As we filed out of the classroom in silence, he rose, crossed to one of the windows, and stared at the distance.

Years later, in one of Yeats's poems, 'Lapis Lazuli', I came across the line about tragic figures, who 'Do not break up their lines to weep.' Aird, the exile, the man, had found in Scott's comparatively simple words an agonising, unexpected liberation of spirit — his own and ours. His eyes might fill with impertinent fluid, but he would not break up his lines.

'I am certain of nothing', wrote Keats to Bailey (22 November 1817) 'but of the holiness of the heart's affections and the truth of Imagination.'

What about my future? The eldest son, the heir? There were no vocation-guidance officers in those days, no aptitude tests. While parents might consult their children, they believed that they knew what was best for them. They also knew what they could afford.

Opportunities open to others were closed to me. At one time I thought I would like to farm, but that notion was ridiculous: where would the capital come from? Seeing Aunt Mary at work in the location dispensary, I thought of becoming a medical missionary, but that was also laughable: who would keep me at university for seven years? Father thought of engineering, but dismissed the possibility when he heard of the cost of the course and of my mathematical incompetence. How did I feel about serving an apprenticeship as a fitter and turner on the railways, and becoming a skilled man at the lathe and the milling machine? But Mother would not hear of it. Her son an artisan? Never. Besides, machines were her sworn enemies, and she would put no son of hers into their service. Architecture?

Almost as expensive a training as medicine.

Then Ernest would come forward with the career he had abandoned at his father's behest — the bank. A bank clerk might not be impressive, but a manager was not to be sniffed at. Alice was caught: was not her father, Frederick Septimus, a retired bank manager?

All these debates skirted round the real issue — was the heir apparent to *The Midland News and Karroo Farmer* to be permitted to abdicate? Let him matriculate, certainly; then let him serve an apprenticeship as a lino-operator, so that he could deal with apprentices, journeymen and the typographical union; then, if his talents drew him that way, he could move on to reporting, and ultimately move into Ernest's editorial and managerial chair, equipped as his father and grandfather had never been. The claims of succession and tradition were clear. The paper had been founded by a Butler, and it had been run for the better part of two generations by Butlers, with a humane and generous policy. But Alice would not hear of it.

Jeffrey tells how he once boasted jokingly to her:

'When I'm big, I'm going to be manager of *The Midland News,* and I'll let Guy be editor.'

She responded with an asperity so unusual that he never forgot it:

'Don't ever mention *The Midland News* and either of you in the same breath again.'

What kind of life had *The Midland News* given her beloved Ernest, his wife, his children? The enormous bonds, the financial precipice, anxiety, indignity — did Ernest really want his son, and his son's family, to inherit these?

Then Mr Aird assured Alice and Ernest that I was university material. That settled it as far as Alice was concerned; to university I must go. Let me become a teacher, like Joan; arts or science, it didn't matter; a teacher received a regular salary and a pension; a teacher's family was secure from the great curse of her life: anxiety.

But Ernest asked: Where would the money come from? There were no generous state scholarships to university in those days. There was, however, the Alfred Metcalf Scholarship awarded every fourth year from the Boys' High School to Rhodes University: fifty pounds a year for three years. It had just been awarded to my old Rhino Patrol leader, Rex Moys; and it would fall due again when I wrote Matric. If I won it, the impossible might become probable. But I seldom topped the class; I was usually third or fourth.

What did I think of all this long-range planning? A future three years away was difficult to grasp. I had the vaguest idea of what universities were, although I liked several men who had attended them: Papa Aird, Charles Gould, Harold Bladen, B.J. Kaggelhoffer. My interests were many, my mind a chameleon changing colour with a rapidity which I myself found disconcerting. I gave myself enthusiastically to this and to that, delightfully and frighteningly free.

An end to this freedom came in mid-1933 when my father took me into a partnership with him, to foot the bill which my future education might cost.

We were working together in the workshop. I was tinkering with my bicycle, he was making furniture. Pausing in his preliminary sawcuts for a dovetail joint, he asked:

'Would you like to go to university?'

'Yes.'

'Are you quite sure?'

'Yes.'

We exchanged a long look; he returned to his sawing as though nothing else were on his mind. Then he put the saw down deliberately, and turned to me.

'Well, then, you'll have to earn the money to get there. We certainly cannot afford to send you.'

'Earn the money? But how?'

'First and foremost, you must win that scholarship. Without it, there's no chance at all.'

He paused to let that point sink in.

'Second, you must make furniture for sale. I'll find the orders, supply the timber, and supervise; you'll do the making. We have the best part of three years to do it in. We'll work Wednesday and Saturday afternoons, and during your holidays. If you make enough, and if you win the scholarship, we might be able to send you. I can promise nothing, of course; you must remember the two "ifs". If you don't win the scholarship, the savings will be useful to you in some other way.'

To sacrifice Wednesday and Saturday afternoons, the favourite 'gang' times! To spend my holidays in the workshop! It was a long sentence, and I regret to confess that I served it with minimal grace. True, my holidays were never entirely swallowed, but there were periods, long periods over the carpenter's bench, when I bitterly resented my isolation and, in the illogical manner of the young, blamed my father for it as if I were doing forced labour for him, and not for myself.

Whenever I encounter one of those pieces of teak furniture, usually on a farm in Graaff-Reinet, I admire the craftsmanship in them — made in a workshop which at that stage had no machine tools, by Ernest Butler and his son, a volcanic adolescent, some time in 1933, '34 or '35.

17

Mother goes to England

Alice was cheerful and charitable by temperament and from choice. Her terms of praise were 'saint', 'angel', 'darling', 'dear', 'brick', 'plucky', 'kind', 'elegant', 'well bred' and 'an absolute scream'. Her terms of disapproval were few: I can recall people being referred to as 'tyrants' and 'bullies', or 'poor fish'; very occasionally she would say that people had no background or behaved in a common or cheap way. Her most deeply felt disapproval was reserved for the lugubrious, the gloomy, the self-pitying, the pessimistic, and the prophets of doom. 'Oh dear,' she would say, 'I've just endured an hour of Mrs X: she's such an old misery.'

There were, however, times when even Alice succumbed to bouts of general anguish of spirit. These usually occurred late in the afternoon when the light was fading. She hated the close of the day. She would move about restlessly, and say, 'I wish Ernest would come.' She would go outside, and stand at the front door, or patrol the front stoep, back and forth on an irregular beat, looking this way and that. 'Where is Ernest?' Once he was home, the gloom would lift, as if the family circle, once complete, generated a power potent enough to exorcise all demons.

Or almost all. There is no doubt that one of the causes of her anguish was longing, the specific and generalised hunger for her own people, her father, her brothers and sisters, for England, its countryside, its villages, cities, a whole world of loved people and places, cut off by six thousand miles of 'salt, estranging sea'.

Then in mid-1933 Frederick Septimus, aware that he had not much longer to live, wrote asking whether she could not visit him. He would pay for her fare. The offer threw her into a turmoil. Could she, should she, leave Ernest and her family for a few months? It seems that she poured out her many anxieties to him in a long and somewhat confused letter, his reply to which she kept. It is written from 'Greystones', Stone, Staffordshire, dated 30 November 1933.

'A drought such as you speak of — I have had accounts of many droughts from you — is hard to bear: that piled on top of your other back-breaking troubles. However, it will pass, as the poor-white and the native problem will pass no doubt in some way — it is not a new one, is it?'

From South Africa's anguish, she had apparently passed on to the future of her eldest son, but had not been sufficiently articulate. 'I don't understand your reference to "Guy and Rhodes". Explain, will you?'

It seems from his next comment that there had been a passage of arms between father and son on this matter, and that his dear daughter had been caught in the crossfire. His reservations about his son-in-law betray themselves.

'It gives me great satisfaction to hear you speak so loyally of Ernest, who, no doubt, deserves all you say of him. As you state, it would be quite natural and easy to understand, with all his troubles, if his temper had got frayed, that he should expend it on yourself. . . .'

He then puts her mind at rest on the cost of her projected visit to England.

'I can well understand your dreams of England, and I trust everything will go well to enable you to come. Understand, my dear, that we shall send you something beyond the mere fare, and your personal expenses when here will be more or less negligible.'

He ends: 'Cheque for £1 enclosed, as usual, for the children for Christmas, which I hope will be a happy one for you all.'

Alice was very uneasy about abandoning her husband and teen-age children; but it was twenty years since she had last been in England. The only members of her family she had seen in the interim were Janet and her father. Janet was dead, and it was clear that her father was ailing and did not have much longer to live. And the trip would be paid for by him. I have no doubt that Ernest insisted on her going.

But Ernest had not had a break for four years, and was at the end of his tether from overwork and anxiety. He needed to get right away from *The Midland News,* its machines, proofs, personnel; right away from Cradock, relatives, and the shop. But the Butlers could not afford an hotel holiday, particularly if any of the children were to accompany them.

'Why don't we go camping at the sea?' asked Alice, game for anything that would give her husband a change of scene. Port Alfred on the Kowie River, as the closest point on the coast and the cheapest to reach, was chosen. As the Whippet was too small to take seven, Christine and Dorothy were quite literally farmed out. Joan, back from her first year at Training College, was to be given a chance to see something of her parents.

It was a disaster.

The small car, overloaded with five people and mountains of camping gear, boiled on the steep hill between Baviaans River and Bedford. Jeffrey leapt out eagerly to top up the radiator. A geyser of boiling water and steam erupted on to his hands and forearms. After a wild paroxysm of crying, he subsided into a low feral whimper which ceased only when a doctor in Bedford applied oil and lint. Throughout the holidays his bandages had to be changed. The oil did not have a pleasant smell.

When at last we reached Grahamstown it seemed splendidly bigger and greener than Cradock. As at Cradock, a steeple formed the visual focus, one possibly taller than Cradock's Dutch Reformed Church. Whereas Cradock's church was of a beautiful grey-white stone and owed much to Sir Christopher Wren, this Anglican Cathedral was a mellow brown, and owed everything to Sir Giles Gilbert Scott and the Gothic revival. 'It's about the only town in the Eastern Cape dominated by an English and not a Dutch Church.' said Father. He was, however, more interested in another church, also in stone, also Gothic in character, without a steeple: the Methodist Church, which he called 'Commem.', short for Commemoration. It was built, he said, to commemorate the landing of the 1820 Settlers.

But we were all too tired and hungry to take it in. Had I known that I was destined to spend most of my working life in Grahamstown, I might have spent less time over my scrambled eggs in a cool cave called the Ramona Café. Alice would have liked a glimpse of the interior of the Cathedral, but Ernest said there was no time for sightseeing. We pressed on to Port Alfred.

We were to pitch our two tents (which, together with the mattresses, had been forwarded by rail) on a sandy stretch among the Port Jackson willows near the West Beach Café. There was a considerable delay before Father found someone willing to transport the equipment from the station to the site, where Alice sat courageously smiling among the suitcases. Pitching the tents took some time in the high, hot wind.

That wind never stopped blowing. The tents were suffocating. Alice's romantic notions about camping withered as she prepared meal after meal for a tired husband and three fratchety children. She was mystified by, and afraid of, the 'beastly' Primus stove on which she had to cook. All meals seemed to be salted with sand, sand, sand. Poor Jeffrey, who could not swim because of his arms, was bored to tears. Insidious sand grains found their way under his bandages and inflamed his burns. Joan and I found no congenial company. Father, who spent most of his days dozing on a mattress on the tent floor or flipping through endless copies of *Popular Mechanics,* would say cheerfully after each evening meal, 'Perhaps the wind will drop tomorrow.' And at lunch time he would say, with less and less conviction as day followed abrasive day, 'A change is as good as a rest.'

Grannie Butler took charge of The Poplars during Mother's absence in England. She ensconced herself in Alice's seat on her son's left hand. Jeffrey sat on Ernest's right, directly opposite her. After one day of Bedlam, she rearranged the seating, moving Christine, the most amenable, into Jeffrey's seat, and placing Jeffrey under the shadow of her left wing.

'Do you see this?' she said, lifting a dessert spoon and wagging it in his line of vision. Jeffrey nodded, and she nodded back.

Before the end of the meal Jeffrey started playing up and shouting down the table. Quick as a flash the spoon descended on his cropped head. Total surprise. Instant silence. A slight knob on Jeff's head ten minutes later. Absolute control from then on.

Except over Dorothy's mind.

Dorothy's mind was incomprehensible to Grannie. 'That girl's a real dreamer.' Which was tantamount to being mentally deficient among the responsible Biggses and Colletts, who didn't stand for nonsense of any kind.

We all had household tasks to perform, sometimes by rota. The evening I am recalling was Dorothy's turn to make the tea. Guests came, not quite gentleman callers, but interesting people, including some young men.

'Make the tea, Dorothy,' said Grannie, presiding at the long table. 'Let the pot warm a few minutes at the side of the stove before you bring it in.'

Dorothy left the company but kept returning at intervals in order not to miss anything. The kettle wasn't quite on the boil.

'Is the tea ready, Dorothy?'

'It's drawing on the side of the stove like you said, Grannie.'

The cups were on the tray, the cake cut.

Chatter, chatter.

'I think you can fetch it now, Dorothy.'

Dorothy swept in triumphantly, placing the teapot next to Grannie.

'How do you like it?' said Grannie to the senior person present.

'As it comes, please, Mrs Butler.'

It came out pure, steaming water.

Grannie looked at Dorothy. Dorothy's hand flew to her mouth to stifle a scream. She grabbed the pot, and fled weeping with humiliation to the kitchen.

'Joan,' said Grannie. 'Go and see she doesn't forget her head this time.'

Grannie had less time for telling stories than she used to have, but she was not entirely without them. I was reminded of one of them recently by Aunt Mary, and I tell it for a number of reasons: it establishes that The Poplars had been built by 1843; that it was then a double storey; that it was the home of Mrs Hockly, an 1820 Settler and one of the first redoubtable school-ma'ams of the Eastern Cape; and that at least one of my ancestors had been to school there, long before James Butler spent his first night in Cradock in Mrs Rhoda Saunders's boarding-house. Also the ambivalent moral drift of her tale may indicate what effect the undisciplined Butler brood were having on Grannie's tidy mind.

'When my Mother, Mary Trollip of Doornberg, was a little girl of seven, she was sent into Cradock for her schooling with Mrs Hockly, who ran her school in this house. She ran it well because she was strict.' Pause. 'Before saying goodbye to Mary, her mother set her daughter a little task: to make a small dress for her baby sister. Fancy that, a girl of seven making a dress.'

She paused to let the point penetrate Dorothy's and Christine's consciousness. Grannie's hands were never idle. Neither Christine nor Dorothy was sewing.

'The dress had to be ready by a certain day, when the Doornberg wagon would be passing through Cradock on its way back from Grahamstown. Well, by the evening of the day before the wagon was due, she had it all complete, except for the sewing in of one of the sleeves. She thought she'd leave that for the morning, and went out to play.'

There was another pause, as if to say, 'Don't put off until tomorrow what you can do today.'

'The next morning when the child came to finish the task she couldn't find the sleeve anywhere. She was very distressed, the poor child, because in those days children were dealt with very severely if they lost anything.'

Under Alice's régime things were always getting lost in The Poplars. We must have given Mrs Hockly's ghost nightmares. But the way Grannie said 'the poor child', indicated that her sympathies were not totally alienated by the loss of the sleeve.

'Well, about midday the great wagon pulled up outside The Poplars to pick up the parcel. The poor child had to confess to one of the junior mistresses that the dress was not ready. The wagon left for Doornberg with a humiliating message to Mrs Trollip that her daughter Mary had failed to complete her allotted task. The young mistress then turned her mind to finding the sleeve, and started with Mary's own small person. Sure enough, she found it in the child's own pocket. She sent her upstairs, where she had to wait all the long, long afternoon for the return of Mrs Hockly, and for the hiding she knew she would get.'

My hope for another paragraph, in which Mrs Hockly would be shown to have an understanding heart towards little girls of 7, was disappointed. There was a long, long pause. It would have been easier if Grannie had ended her story differently '. . . upstairs, where she had to wait for Mrs Hockly, who gave her a hiding when she returned.'

Then someone swung our attention away from the child to the house.

'How could she be waiting upstairs? We've got no upstairs.'

'There used to be one, and the front door was upstairs,' she stated flatly.

'How does one get to an upstairs front door?'

'There were big outside stairs of stone, which led up to a balcony. They took them both away when your father was a small boy.'

'Why, Grannie?'

'I think the upstairs had been badly built,' she said.

I did not quite like the thought that The Poplars had once been so utterly different from what it now was. I felt uneasy, wondering in which now non-existent upstairs room that little girl had sat waiting, waiting, all alone.

The Poplars was to endure many other changes in the next forty years.

A vain and brash young accountant took Dorothy to a dance. They won the prize for the waltz.

'I'm sure it was my dancing and your dress,' he said.

He said a great deal more: that judging from the number of *per contra* entries in the books which he audited for various businesses he would hate to do the books of *The Midland News*.

Father went into a cold fury at this unprofessional exposure of one of his survival tactics.

The pressure of the depression and my priggish bias caused me to assume a high and hectoring moral stance on such issues as hard work, religious observance, and seriousness of purpose. The previous year I had taken my father to task for allowing Bible reading after supper to lapse. He revived the practice, but it did not continue for long. In 1934, at the end of the first term, Christine's report was worse than usual. I took it upon myself to reprimand her. She burst into tears. I apologised, and, almost crying myself, pleaded with her to consider how hard our parents struggled to keep us clothed and at school. The least we could do was to work hard.

I had forgotten this episode until Christine reminded me of it:

'I will be eternally grateful to you for jolting me out of my slothful ways when I was in J.C. and Mother overseas. The changed attitude towards my school work brought unexpected blessings; no more "rowings" from Mom and Dad; a word of praise from teachers, and a change in class position from thirty-second out of thirty-six to fourth or sixth.'

Spare parts for the printing-machines were very expensive indeed, and Father lived in dread of having to order them; so that when the *Queenstown Representative* buildings burnt down in July 1934, he decided that it might pay him to buy some of the scorched machines as scrap and pirate his spare parts from them. Mr Robertson, the retired Scots engineer from Limebank, volunteered to accompany him on a reconnaissance; and I was taken to open the gates.

It was my first trip to Tarkastad and Queenstown, and I enjoyed the new scenery greatly. The gravel on the roads was rich purple. Mr Robertson had brought his steel straight-edge which he applied to various shafts and surfaces of the flame-blackened machines to see if the heat had buckled them. Beneath the coatings of soot, and of rust produced by the firemen's hoses, the metal for the most part was sound.

The real difficulty was the cost of transporting the scrap to Cradock. As there is no direct railway line between the centres, the cost would have been quite prohibitive.

Father sought out Mr Gunning, one of the last transport riders, whose three ancient wagons rested among the pepper trees on the river bank, and whose thirty-six donkeys grazed on the commonage.

The Gunnings were a happy-go-lucky family. So expensive was rail cartage, however, that they made a living for some years carrying forty-four-gallon drums of petrol from Port Elizabeth to Middelburg, returning loaded to the skies with wool bales. They always took shelter under their wagons when it came on to rain or if they outspanned in the heat of the day. And they would make a fire there, under the wagon, no matter what the freight, even if it was petrol. From these feckless folk my father sought a quotation for fetching his heavy bargains from Queenstown.

One of the Gunning boys was very bright. He was two years older than I was, and was reputed to be a near-genius at mathematics. He was not one of those mean hoarders who clutch the candle of knowledge to themselves: he brought light into the darkness of any idling group of younger boys he encountered. He was always at pains to reduce difficult concepts to easily comprehensible and familiar examples. It is to him that I owe all my knowledge of Einstein. One afternoon over at the stock-fair pens, which are just across the road from the goods yards, I was privileged, with a few friends, who had come to watch some cattle being loaded, to be introduced to the theory of relativity. According to Okkie Gunning, who had a thin face, white eyebrows, carrot hair, and silver-rimmed spectacles, relativity was all about firing bullets from moving trains.

If a man stands on the station platform near the signalbox, and fires at the watertower, four hundred yards away, the bullet will reach the watertower at the normal speed of a .303 bullet, will it not?

That seemed reasonable enough. Of course.

Now if the man were sitting on the cowcatcher of the 8.45 express travelling at 60 miles an hour, and if he were to fire at the watertower four hundred yards away, just as the cowcatcher was in line with the signalbox, at what speed would the bullet be travelling?

At this point some realist simpleton, incapable of appreciating an allegory, would say:

'It would never happen. How would he get on to the cowcatcher with a loaded .303? He'd fall off, man — trying to aim at the watertower and see the signalbox at exactly the same time, he'd miss the watertower for sure.'

Our explicator of Einstein would sigh, or throw his eyes up to space, and try again.

'Well, let's try another example.'

'Yerrah,' someone even slower would say. 'That chap Einstein had better watch out. The Railway Police won't stand for shooting holes in the watertower.'

'Forget about the watertower, man. It's only an *example.*'

'Of what?'

'Relativity.'

'Oh, I see.'

Nobody saw.

The populariser of science tried once more.

'Take a cow standing in the corner of a camp. There's a tick on this cow's back, next to the tail. The tick is stationary, sucking blood. Got it? Now the cow starts moving, at two miles an hour towards the water trough. At what speed is the tick moving?'

'Two miles an hour, of course!'

'Rubbish! He said the tick is fast, sucking blood.'

The bringer of wisdom to the benighted smiled complacently, and said, 'You're both right. Relative to the cow, the tick is stationary; but relative to the water trough it is moving at two miles an hour.'

Some were beginning to grasp; but at least one got up and walked away in disgust. How could a tick be a relative to a cow, let alone a water trough?

'Now,' said the descendant of Euclid, 'while the cow is moving towards the water trough, the tick starts moving along the cow's spine, from the tail to the horns, at the rate of one mile an hour. Remember the cow is moving at two miles an hour. At what speed will the tick be moving towards the water trough?'

Pause.

'Man, a tick could *never* travel a mile in an hour. Have you ever seen a tick's legs?'

If new ideas about the nature of space and time were slow to penetrate the popular mind of Cradock, new political ideas, or old ideas in new guises, found a distressingly fertile soil.

Our family in almost all its ramifications approved wholeheartedly of the fusion of the South African and Nationalist Parties into the United Party, which won an overwhelming victory at the polls in May 1933. It rejected with equal impatience the purified Afrikaner Nationalists under Dr D.F. Malan and the conservative Dominionites under Colonel Stallard. What worried the Quakers of Cradock, however, were the indications that fusion would have to be paid for by those people of colour who enjoyed the vote under the old Cape franchise.

All over the world the darker doctrines seemed to be gaining converts. During 1931 and 1932 Japan had invaded and conquered Manchuria in defiance of the League of Nations — which protested, but did nothing. Not surprisingly, the World Disarmament Conference had failed. Early in 1933 Hitler had come to power in Germany, and his poisonous racial theories were spreading with frightening speed. Many of my Afrikaner friends were ardent listeners to Zeesen radio. Some of them, and some English-speakers, welcomed the herrenvolk myth with joy: it corroborated their ancient belief in the superiority of the white man. Zeesen also encouraged us to be anti-Semitic — and by extension anti-Asiatic. The small communities of Jews, Syrians and Indians in Cradock had no business in Aryan South Africa: let them be sent back to Palestine, the Lebanon or Madras. Nationalist politicians picked up certain powerful visceral appeals from Nazism;

Afrikaners were encouraged to think with their blood, and to reject every-thing foreign. Some clamoured for stricter immigration laws. They did not want any more Jewish refugees from Germany, and wished to revise Dr Malan's quota acts of 1930 in order to ensure this.

The impact of this propaganda was borne in on me one sultry afternoon, when one of my fellow Scouts, a second-generation South African of Catho-lic Syrian extraction, a gentle fellow called Joey, asked me round for a game of chess. Halfway through the game he started to tell me how afraid he was of Dr D.F. Malan and Adolf Hitler.

'I know I'm not a Jew,' he said, 'but it doesn't help. I look like one. The chaps at school say Syrians are Asiatics, and Indians are Asiatics, so I'm no better than a coolie.'

'But you're white, and you're a Christian,' I said.

'It doesn't help,' he said. 'For Doctor Malan a Catholic is not a Christian at all but anti-Christ. Chaps at school say the Lebanon is right next to Pales-tine, so the Lebanese are just Jews in disguise.'

I tried to reassure him by pointing out that Hitler was a long way away, and that Dr Malan was no longer Minister of the Interior, but he kept on saying, 'It doesn't help. The chaps at school say . . .'

My vision of the world had expanded painfully beyond the gardens below the furrow in Bree Street. Great generalisations about Mankind challenged me on every corner in our polyglot little town.

'God has made of one blood all the nations upon earth.'

'Man is born free and everywhere he is in chains.'

Under many pressures my vague awareness of the relationship between history and the geography of our town would sharpen into moments of acute critical consciousness and then dissolve once again into a liberal optimism that time would gradually abolish injustice. In spite of all evi-dence to the contrary, our parents maintained an ambience of hope. They had inherited the Victorian belief in progress. Good would prevail.

Cradock society demonstrated the hierarchy of conquest, the legacy of battles won and lost. On top were the whites, English and Afrikaner, and a few Jews and Syrians. There was a slow civil war between the first pair, which the Afrikaners were winning, but both sides were in substantial agreement about 'White supremacy'.

In the white town the houses had large plots, gardens, individual sanita-tion, light and water; and all white children were compelled to go to school, which was free. Whites had the vote, could own guns, and had free access to liquor. Almost all officials, all people in authority, were white. Whites gave the orders, the rest obeyed as servants and labourers. The few exceptions, like Coloured and African school teachers, small shop-owners, tradesmen and craftsmen, were looked at with suspicion by most whites, and kept a low profile.

To the south of the white town was an area with indeterminate frontiers, with no particular focal point: on the one side it merged with the white town, and on the other with the location. Here lived the Coloureds and Asiatics. The men still had the vote under the old Cape franchise. They also had free access to liquor, a liberty which many whites thought ought to be denied them for their own good. Some had skilled and semi-skilled jobs in the town; many dressed well, and were generally devout and respectable. They sometimes tried to dissociate themselves from the Coloureds from the farms as backward and uncouth; in many cases these were pure Hottentot, without any admixture of white blood. I don't think the Coloureds were as large a community as the whites or the blacks. The houses they inhabited were mostly solid little brick buildings, with laid-on water, fronting on to streets which were part of the normal municipal grid.

Beyond Hare Street (except for a narrow strip close to the river, below the irrigation furrow as far as that bastion, the Gaol) a gradual change overtook the scene — the 'streets' became dusty, stony deserts between straggling rows of shanties; all habitations were small, a few were of unplastered brick, most of mud or constructed out of junk such as rusty flattened paraffin tins; and here and there, reminding one of a different way of life, were neat round huts, with hard plastered walls and thatched roofs, but these slowly disappeared, the builders finding it difficult to come by thatching materials in the Karoo. At long distances rose single street-lamps; and every mile or so, a standard tap, with a patient queue of black women and children with buckets or four-gallon paraffin tins, standing in the blinding February sun, the August dust clouds, or the bitter winds of June. Many were ragged. Nearly all were barefoot. No trees in these streets. No pavements. And at intervals, communal latrines. And starved 'kaffir' dogs.

Here and there on the outskirts of the location, in dongas or in the lee of patches of 'wolwedoring', were the really lost: vagrant Hottentots and rare Bushmen sheltering behind a 'scherm' of ashbush; their flesh the colour of dust, they were desolate, resigned, pausing as they drifted up and down the valley, in and out of jobs, on and off the farms, flotsam and jetsam on the currents of their ancient migratory rounds and the white man's whim.

Across the river from the location was the cemetery for blacks. Tombstones were unknown. Here or there was a cement slab with a name, a date, a text, in a hand not used to writing in capitals in wet cement. But the whole place, from a certain aspect and in a certain light, could glitter like gossamer — from the hundreds of glass bottles, large and small, which had been brought to hold the precious tribute of a bunch of flowers. Flowers! Where did they obtain them? At what cost? A new grave there — with the long, damp mound of earth, and a fading wreath of marigolds on it — was the sight which made a line of Virgil's, which I had seen discussed out of context, become a final formulation of one of my sentiments — *Sunt lacrimae rerum, et mentem mortalia tangunt.* (There are tears for our lot, and mortal fortunes touch the heart.)

At the other extremity of the town, on the other side of the river, beyond the green park and the sports stadium, lay the white dead, by denominations, weighed down, many of them, by tons of Paarl granite with gilt lettering: a fascinating, stony archive. In their efforts to demonstrate piety, affection and family pride, these memorials somehow exorcised poetry and sublimity. Small human vanities and concerns were stamped on the place; whereas among the bottles, Mexican poppies and wild tobacco plants a few miles away, one felt the liberation of death.

The blacks had no vote; were not allowed to own firearms, or assegais, or knives with blades more than three and a half inches long; and they could not buy liquor or brew beer. Police raids on shebeens and illicit brewers were a perpetual source of racial grievance. The main bootleggers between the white bar-owners and the blacks who liked alcohol were, of course, the Coloureds.

Curious as it may sound, indeed almost incredible, we were seldom aware of the oddness, the difference, the injustice. How should we be? We grew up into it, almost unquestioning. It was all we knew — we had no standards of comparison. It had always been so. It would change for the better, of course, gradually, particularly for the blacks and Coloureds, who would slowly, and at a pace which would not make a single white ever feel threatened or uncomfortable, become civilised like us. So most of the grown-ups would say, if ever a white child's conscience got out of hand, or a black politician or white liberal shook an angry fist or prophesied the wrath of God. There was all the time in the world. History was a slow business. Like evolution. A favourite argument was: It took us (whites) 2000 years to get where we were. And we were a clever lot. The blacks must be patient, particularly with themselves. After all, they had only just met civilisation — a mere 200 or 300 years ago.

I don't know how rare or typical The Poplars climate was, but I did not grow up in mortal dread of the black man. Relations were perhaps paternalistic and patronising, yet genuine care and some affection was the rule and not the exception across the class and colour line. Our servants stayed with us for long periods. In all my first twenty years, The Poplars had but two cooks: Chrissie, and then Susan, and they ruled the kitchen in more or less happy amity with Alice.

Chrissie was Mosotho, I suspect a descendant of those Mantatees who for generations, first as refugees from the Difaqane, and later as voluntary migratory labourers, came from north of the Orange River into the old Colony in search of safety, then food, then cash to buy cattle, then guns (until the 'Gun War'), umbrellas, top-hats and wagons. Many had espoused Christianity early, under the influence of missionaries like Edwards. There was a sufficiently large colony of Sotho-speakers in Cradock for the Methodists to erect a church for them — a 'tin temple', above the furrow.

Chrissie was short and very fat. Her skirts were long and her centre of gravity low. She was cheerful, and smiled and laughed a great deal, revealing a few very lonely teeth in a large red mouth. She was infinitely patient with our endless demands. She died very suddenly during Mother's absence in England. One day she was there, the next she wasn't.

Christine, who was sleeping on the verandah, was woken at first light by Aunt Mary with the news that Chrissie had died in the night of a heart attack. Christine burst into tears. After comforting her for a few seconds, Aunt Mary told her to pull herself together, to get up, and prepare breakfast for the household. She, Aunt Mary, had to go to the hospital about another very urgent case. Life must go on.

It was very strange. It was the closest death had yet come to us. What was death? It was strange to hear Aunt Mary tell Ernest at lunch-time that she thought we should all attend the funeral the following afternoon. Ernest demurred (he was very busy stocktaking) but only for a moment. It was stranger still for the Butler children to be putting on their Sunday-best in mid-week, arriving at the tin church filled mainly with black women and girls dressed in black dresses, white blouses, and black shawls; and being led right up to the front on the right. I was on the aisle standing next to the coffin. I could have touched it with my hand. I was not afraid but mystified. How could Chrissie be in that black box? How on earth did they fit her bulk into it? Were her eyes open or closed? Where was *she?*

The minister made a reference to the presence of the family she had served so long and so faithfully. It was the first time that that had occurred to me. She had served us so long and so faithfully.

It was hot and suffocating in that iron building, and the service was long. The hymns dragged mournfully. Whether because there were not enough male voices or because there were not enough traditionalists, the music did not have the disturbing organic quality I had experienced while listening to communal chanting at river baptisms — not until the very end of the service.

On the other side of the aisle was a group of some twenty young girls — aged about 15 to 18, belonging to some guild or class which Chrissie had taught. When the pallbearers lifted the coffin off the trestles, they burst into song. Suddenly one of them started to sway and move, and her voice rose, wild, totally alien to the spirit of Messrs Sankey and Moody; and others followed suit, until the building shook with a human cry that was part lament, part exultation, and so uncontrolled as to make the hair on the back of my neck bristle. To their cries we filed out after the coffin.

'It's a pity those girls behaved in that hysterical way,' said Aunt Mary.

'Weren't they just crying for Chrissie?'

'They weren't as sorry as they sounded. They were enjoying themselves.'

I wish I had known then the little I know now about the African feeling for their dead — their izinyanya, their amadhlozi — they do not forget them, lose touch with them, neglect them, as we do. The Communion of the Saints is real to them. I think those wild girls were trying to get through to Chrissie in a way that both Methodists and Quakers had lost.

Chrissie's successor as cook was Susan. She was Xhosa, slender, erect, dignified, ageing, slightly withdrawn. If the kitchen wasn't quite the children's club it had been in Chrissie's time, that was not altogether surprising. We were all growing up. Adolescence was harrying us, one after the other, into isolation and individuality.

Nearly every overseas mailday brought a picture postcard from Mother: Big Ben; the new theatre at Stratford-upon-Avon; King's College, Cambridge; Oxford's dreaming spires; and then — as a result of old Septimus's generosity — she took a trip up the Rhine, to her beloved Nuremberg, to see her old friends the Falks. The picture postcards of great half-timbered Gothic houses were mingled with others of a different kind. I recall a beautiful Nordic youth looking confidently into the future, with a swastika flag draped over his shoulder. Ernest gave it a disapproving anti-military sniff, but admired the quality of the printing. I envied the German youth: both the idealist and the tiger in him were apparent and unashamed.

Mother's stay with the Falks was not easy. As all four Falk sons — two of whom she had taught — were members of the Nazi party, and held high posts in the government or army, the two women could not speak freely in the house. They would escape to the safety of a public park. What did they discuss when there? In a letter some months previous to Alice's visit poor Frau Falk had complained that she did not like the new ersatz acorn coffee. Alice had responded by sending a pound of best coffee beans through the mail. The parcel was confiscated, and Frau Falk received a nasty reprimand from a German post office official for unpatriotically revealing her preference for genuine coffee to a foreigner. While sharing such confidences in the park one day, two Nazi policemen approached.

'Now Alice,' said her unfortunate hostess, 'if they stop in front of us, you will stand up and say "Heil Hitler" with me.' Fortunately Alice was not put to the test.

She brought home a large parcel of German delicacies and *objets* for our Christmas at The Poplars: pumpernickel, and other strange foods; and tinsel decorations for a Christmas tree, among which was a glittering papier-mâché angel — which delighted us, but caused Ernest to wrinkle his nose in anti-Popish disapproval, almost as if he smelt incense.

Alice returned sooner than expected. To our utter amazement, she explained this by saying that she couldn't bear to be away from us any longer. I am sure that Grannie was relieved at the premature return of her Anglican daughter-in-law. I have the impression that they respected each other, those two, but across a little distance. As different as chalk from cheese, in my recollection. The severities and simplicities, the Methodist pieties and pioneer stoicism of three generations in the frontier regions of the Karoo did not produce a heart sensitive to all the vibrancies of a turbulent, cultivated urban woman from a late-nineteenth-century, middle-class family from Stoke-on-Trent.

It was expected that Alice would do the adjusting to Ernest's people. She did, and she didn't. Both in what she did, and in what she didn't do, she followed her instinct, a blend of profoundly deep convictions about the Church and the Family, with a carelessness as to detail; a slapdash, amateurish approach to housekeeping, bookkeeping, gardening; a sporadic indulgence of her own wishes, a refusal, a failure — a victorious failure, if you like — to fit herself to the Butlers, the Colletts or the Biggses, no mean people, as she herself acknowledged, all Quakers, Methodists, or Baptists, nonconformist, hard-headed, for the most part responsible, all teetotal — or almost all. And yet apparently without offence she had won them over, staunch Anglican as she was, romantic, inefficient, teetotal under duress. I think she came back from England strengthened in herself.

There were times when she allowed herself a moment's rebellion against the consistent stoicism, patience, and moderation of her husband and his sister, Mary. She fancied that she would find relief in flaming rows with business and other opponents, in giving people a piece of her mind, or turning a frigid shoulder on avowed enemies in public — though she never did any of these things. Ernest, and particularly Mary, believed in turning the other cheek, in loving your enemies, and in 'the soft answer that turneth away wrath'. She knew they were right, of course, and that made it worse. I recollect a debate among the three of them about the proper way to handle a senior employee who had behaved in what she thought was a despicable fashion. Ernest was all for allowing him time to ponder his misdeeds and come to his moral senses; Alice was for putting him on the carpet at once, and giving him a rocket. Mary thought that before anything was done, they should ensure that the trouble had not sprung from a simple misunderstanding. Alice flushed and cried:

'Oh, you Quakers! You're such spiritual aristocrats.'

Father's protracted negotiations with the Gunnings, over transporting the rusty printing-machines, had broken down, but he heard of a Queenstown African who was an efficient wagon master. He went across to Queenstown to conclude the deal, accompanied by Jeffrey, whose account illustrates the difference in *lingua franca* between the two districts. Father having given his instructions as a Cradock man always would, in Afrikaans, the tall African asked: 'Where is the material the master would like to be conveyed?'

No sooner had Mother returned than she had to witness the arrival of the trek from Queenstown — three wagons, creaking under the weight of soot-blackened, rust-reddened printing-machines, dragged across the Market Square towards *The Midland News* by four dozen dusty donkeys. Some people, who had always thought the Butlers were odd, were convinced that economic anxiety had robbed Ernest Butler of his wits. Alice caught the infection, and confided her horror 'of all those starving donkeys and mountains of rusty old iron' to me.

But it proved to be one of Ernest's better buys. The whole exercise — machines, transport and hotel expenses — cost him £61. Not only was he able to save considerable sums of money on spares, but he managed to bring an expensive German printing-machine, a Miehle, back into commission at the nugatory cost of a few spares ordered from the manufacturers in Leipsig. The Miehle greatly increased the jobbing capacity of the firm, and was sold at an astronomical profit during the war.

18

In the Open

In the autumn of 1934 I spent a few days' holiday at Vrede. It was memorable for two experiences.

To provide shelter for his mountain shepherds Uncle Frank had built a stone hut on the plateau that almost encircles the final knoll of Vrede Mountain. He organised a camp to inaugurate it: John and his sister Ruth came with friends from their schools, and there were others I have forgotten; but the mountain, the sense of space, remains with me, and of stillness, linked curiously enough with rhythmical movement, the movement of horses. We took turns at galloping across the fairly even terrain above the kranses. I was not much of a horseman, but suddenly found the knack of riding: it was quite intoxicating moving over that bare upland with vast plain and mountain scenes opening up as one moved – particularly when Ruth galloped beside me. I have a vague recollection of her horse getting out of control, and of not knowing what to do; of riding up alongside, catching its bridle, and bringing it to a halt miraculously, without falling off my mount – perhaps not exactly so, but there was some little incident which made me feel six foot tall.

The other experience was also of movement – not the half-conscious, half-instinctive integrated rhythm of man and horse, but the blind, brutal movement of a river in flood.

After an exceptionally fine overture of thunder at midday, a dense rain drummed on the mountains for most of the afternoon. It stopped after supper, and a great moon poured its light intermittently through the gaps between rapidly racing fragments of cloud. About nine o'clock Uncle Frank said, 'I think we'll just go up the river to inspect the new intake.'

The 'intake' was at a weir some miles upstream which diverted the water into a furrow feeding the lands and orchards on the homestead-side of the river. Uncle Frank had recently made alterations to it and wished to see how they were standing up to the test of this first flood.

John and I and one or two others accompanied him. We followed the furrow, already carrying a full freight of scented, silty water. When the moon hid her face we moved slowly, and stumbled a little; but when she was free with her light, our pace was close to a run. At times we could hear the grumble of the river. As we drew near to the intake it grew louder, and we caught glimpses of its silver turmoil between black rocks and trees. The heavy continuous thunder of the weir increased until it silenced us utterly. Uncle Frank inspected the new sluices with care, and we started our journey back, well pleased.

Before long we reached a point where a boundary fence crossed the river, in the form of a 'mat', a wire curtain or mesh which fits the deep gully of the stream, suspended from strong wires stretched at some height above. As no mat can stand the pressure of a river in flood, it is not anchored at the bottom; it yields to the weight of the stream upon whose surface it floats, subsiding as the waters subside. Uncle Frank decided to cross the stream by means of this mat, and by another farther down, to reduce the distance of our return journey by two or three miles.

Uncle Frank crossed first — hand over hand on one of the upper strands, his feet thrust into the fence at intervals. It looked simple enough, except that waves of the torrent rose and fell unpredictably: now he would be clearly visible, all of him; the next moment he was up to his thighs in water.

The next man had a frightening experience. When he was in midstream an uprooted tree came slowly floating down towards him. What, I asked myself, if the tree, and the water behind it, put such pressure on the mat that it snapped? But all it did was lift the mat higher than usual, then ducking the passenger correspondingly deeper.

My crossing was comparatively dry. To begin with I was rather taken with the magnificence and excitement of it: the torrent of dense, muddy water quicksilvered by the moon; and I, a little spider crossing it on my ingenious web. But the combined effect of the stream rushing towards me and the unsteady, swaying undulation of my hand and footholds induced a state of incipient nausea — or was it sheer funk? Worse was to come, however. When I was half way across, where the movement was most violent and uncertain, and the noise of water loudest, the moon blacked out. I stopped moving, and hung there swaying in dense oblivion just above the gabbling, hissing surface, waiting for the moon to appear again. It failed to oblige, and my fingers were beginning to feel tested by the wire. There was nothing for it but to continue by the dimmest of vision and sense of touch.

A curious longing overcame me in the dark — if only I had no shoes on! If only my toes were free to help my fingers to cling on! At this distance in time, I can muse upon, and laugh at, this survival of the twig-grasping instinct in me, but it was no joke at the time.

This adventure, which the farming folk thought nothing of, worked on my imagination. What if a really large tree had come heaving downstream and snapped the suspension wires? I imagined myself flailing, drowning, wire-entangled in black and silver water, saturated in the worst terrors of my darkest, most suffocating dreams.

Her name was Eve; she was a friend of Christine's, she was tall, she was shy; and, added to her other charms, she did not come — as Caroline had — from

Port Elizabeth. She came from a farm near Schoombie — which is near
Teebus and Koffiebus, unmistakably distinctive mountains that mark the
point at which the waters of the Orange River now emerge from the long
tunnel and enter the upper reaches of the Brak River, which flows into
Grassridge Dam, and from thence into the Fish River valley. And she had
a whole string of sisters, and two brothers. I didn't get to know the brothers,
who went to Grey College, but the girls, Joy, Eve and Kathleen, were all at
Rocklands at various times, more or less contemporaries of Joan, Dorothy
and Christine.

Eve didn't make me feel that there was anything odd in painting or trying
to write poetry. Her own dream was to become a violinist. She replied to
my long letters with sufficient promptness and warmth to transport me
into the realms of agonised bliss. At last it seemed that the full meaning of
life was revealing itself to me, the dark secrets of the universe were unfold-
ing.

I suffered the torments of the damned if I thought that she so much as
smiled at another male. I took an unaccustomed interest in my appearance.
I read and declaimed swathes of love poetry in secret. I read all Jeffrey
Farnol's novels. I blushed when her name was mentioned. No glancing
blow from Cupid this time, but a real bull's eye. Separation was intolerable.
Company was impossible. So afternoon after afternoon I spent hours 'enjoying' remote views of tennis and hockey games in which she was playing.
There were very few chances of speaking to her: boarders were not allowed
to receive phone calls. And the holidays loomed ahead — she would be removed to another world, fifty miles away. The thought was intolerable. So
I developed a sudden desire to cycle up to Uncle Owen Collett at 'Rooispruit' near Middelburg, which is near Schoombie.

Why this sudden interest in Uncle Owen? asked Alice. It appeared that
I had longed for years to visit Rooispruit. Would Father let me off furni-
ture-making for a week? Having secured his consent, I asked if he would
mind if I took a detour via the Torr's farm on the return journey. Everyone
saw through the subterfuge; the family visit was mere camouflage for a
courting jaunt. Ernest and Alice knew of my affliction, and approved of
Eve in a way they had not approved of Caroline: not that they said a word.
And the Torr parents were quite agreeable for me and friends to visit their
farm.

My companions were to be Godfrey Collett and Gordon Allan. Their
attitude and their preparations were off-hand and light-hearted. I prepared
as if the expedition were a matter of life and death.

About a week before we were due to set out a letter arrived from Eve.
The envelope — lavender-coloured — with my name in a clear and enviably
legible hand — was picked up in a pulsing palm, and torn open in the
secrecy of my room. It read:

55 Teebus and Koffiebus, two koppies near the Torrs' farm.
56 The Location, Cradock. Pencil sketch by C.C. Andries.

57 Aunt Mary Butler
in nurse's uniform,
which she wore at the
Cradock Location baby
clinic, 1934.

58 Cradock Location:
women and children in
front of mud huts.

59 Cradock Location: at the water tap.

60 Washerwomen at the Warm Baths sulphur springs, three miles north of Cradock.

61   The author's parents: Ernest and Alice Butler.

62   'The Poplars' garden, January 1933. Back: Guy, Dorothy, Honor Biggs, Christine, Ernest. Front: Alice, Uncle Joe Butler, Jeffrey. Note Ernest's junk against workshop wall.

63 Disastrous holiday at Port Alfred: Jeffrey, Alice and Joan with the Whippet.

64 The family in 1934. Back: Christine, Guy, Joan. Front: Ernest, Alice, Grandma Lettie Butler, Jeffrey, Dorothy.

65 View from the Salpetersberg.

66 Aerial photograph of Cradock about 1938. The dark area indicates the old town below the furrow. Across the course of the river, note the road, the rail-track and station, and the winding irrigation canal. The location is top right. The town has expanded up to the ridge, and the first houses have been built on it (top centre).

67 The Mountain Hut at 'Vrede'.

68 'Vrede' dam.

69 Flood waters on the Great Fish River.

70   Sundown on Salpetersberg.

'Dear Guy,

I'm afraid you can't come. We've all got measles. See you next term some time.

Yours ever,

Eve.'

Devastation. Anguish. Despair. Suspicion — were the measles real? Self-hatred: How dared I even let such a thought into my head? Let me die, now, at once.

My sisters rallied round. I provided the cash, and Christine phoned Schoombie from the public callbox. Yes, they all had measles. Which posed the question: why go on the trip at all? Merely to see relations? But as the plans were complete, and as Gordon and Godfrey were eager to go, I hid my disappointment as best I could, and went.

It turned out to be a magical week in which I grew in awareness of Karoo spaces and silences. Cycling is almost noiseless motion. Free-wheeling down an incline on a good road, you may seem to be witnessing a slow drifting apart of the closer landscape — the boulders, the wolwedoring clumps, the anthills, the fence posts, the windmills, the cattle, the sheep, all flotsam on the incoming tide of veld. Because your coming is so quiet, you hardly disturb the Stanley cranes or the grazing springbok.

By mid-morning we arrived at Hough's, a desolate enough place set on a slight irregularity in the plain; but Mrs Hough took us into her cool, scrubbed kitchen, where we all but emptied a calabash of delicious sour milk.

One of those high, hot winds which my Grandfather James had found so trying came up, so that by the time we reached 'De Keur', our skins were parched and our throats dry. De Keur, which had until recently been farmed by Uncle Gervase Collett, was deserted, and its windmill out of order. So we left the bikes on the stoep, and made our way down to the deep river bed. Sheltered from the wind, we found a cool pool and swam, which left us refreshed but ravenous. The unpeopled house — which we discovered was still partly furnished — seemed both sumptuous and inviting. The doors were locked but the window catches unfastened. This was as good as an invitation to enter, in search of something, anything, to eat. If only there were a little meal or flour or some potatoes. No such thing: instead, a cupboard full of preserved peaches in ball jars.

We drew up our chairs round the table and did complete justice to two of the jars, and then washed up. Just as we were about to leave we were smitten in our consciences. Should the owner discover the burglary, he would be almost bound to get the police to harry the people in the neighbourhood. As we had no writing materials for a note, we wrote THANKS FOR TWO JARS PEACHES in salt on the table top.

De Keur seemed even quieter on its knoll as we departed. It seemed to be following us.

Whether our revived sense of guilt or the stolen peaches themselves were responsible I cannot say, but on a quiet stretch of the road Gordon turned his bike into the rooigras, shouting, 'I can't go another yard,' and rolled on to the ground, hugging his abdomen. He was soon joined by Godfrey and me. We spent about an hour there trying to be sick, but in vain.

Two hours later we rode up an avenue of trees in the dark towards a glimmering window. Godfrey knocked at the door, and a man in a dinner jacket appeared. Behind him we glimpsed the glitter of silver and candles: a dinner party was in progress. We were turned away without so much as a cup of water, and very bad directions as to how to find Rooispruit.

Our road petered out into bare veld as flat as a billiard table under the beautiful but icy stars. After pushing our bikes through the dark for some time we came up to a stark barn of a building, which we found to be a small airplane hangar: we were on an airstrip.

Perhaps two hours later we knocked on another door: a tall bearded man appeared. As the organiser of the expedition I cried cheerily, 'Good evening, Uncle Owen,' to which he responded, 'My name's Gilfillan.'

His directions weren't very good either. We soon found ourselves lost in a vast stubble of new-mown lucerne lands. They smelt delicious but we were too tired to notice that very much. At one point we almost gave up and slept among a troop of hamels with which we had collided in the dark.

When we did at last knock up Uncle Owen, he came to his door in his dressing-gown, and told us that we were to camp a little farther down the road on his son Leslie's place. It wouldn't be a good plan, he added, to wake Leslie at this time of night, and shut the door.

Farther down the road we went, and as soon as the silhouette of the house appeared, we turned off, lifted our bikes over a fence, found a flat piece of earth, crawled under our blankets, and slept.

We were woken very early by Cousin Leslie, who wasted no time at all on pleasantries – 'Get out of this camp, double quick. It's the bull's camp.'

Sure enough, a massive, surly beast was lying not many yards away, glowering at us over his shoulder, his horns black against the red dawn.

We camped under some trees along the fountain furrow. Each took his turn to do the chores for an entire day, thus releasing the others into total freedom. When my turn came round, I completed my tasks early, and had a long afternoon to myself. I drifted up towards the main house. Uncle Owen, seeing me at a loose end, said, 'There's some spur-winged geese in the corn-stubble land; and guinea fowl in the dry dam. Would you like to take a crack at them?'

I answered positively, but was slightly unnerved when he handed me, not a .22, but a .303, with three cartridges.

So I set out, very conscious that I was carrying the rifle awkwardly. I couldn't find its point of balance at all.

It was one of those hot still afternoons when everything vibrates with heat and life; the stones and the hills seemed to be trembling with quiet excitement, the birds seemed to fly faster, and the stag beetles dashed about as if they were running to fetch the police, or fleeing from them.

I approached the stubble cornfield and scanned it with care. Yes, there in the far corner, sticking out of the stubble, were two geese heads. I did a little careful stalking and got myself to within a hundred yards. Between me and them was a barbed-wire fence, so I rested the front of the barrel on one of the strands, having first set my sights. I was shaking with excitement and apprehension. I had heard that a .303 kicked like a mule.

The two geese suspected that something was happening in my direction, and started moving about. As soon as I had one of them lined up and was taking the first pressure on the trigger, he would move towards or away from the other. It was infuriating. And the more calm I tried to remain, the more the front sight seemed to draw circles and figures of eight round the birds' heads. So, at last, when it seemed to me that the sights were more or less on the space between the two birds' heads — they were at that moment very close together — I pulled the trigger.

I had been so apprehensive about the kick of the rifle that I had forgotten there would be a bang. It was terrific. I expected to see the whole field in front of me blown open as if by a six-inch naval shell. Instead of which the two geese took off. And then, suddenly, while the echoes were still clashing, one started dropping. It fell into the stubble not far from me. There was a moment of intense silence and utter immobility. Then I shouted and moved.

I don't know how I managed to get over that fence as quickly as I did, leaving the rifle behind me. I dashed across the stubble, and found the bird, still alive, pathetically twisting its neck, and flapping its wings. I seized it, and wrung its neck, feeling the neck-bones crunch in my palm. I then stooped over it to see where it had been hit. My bullet had half-severed its neck, including the windpipe. Of all the fluke shots, I said to myself. Still, a hit is a palpable hit. I felt buoyant with success.

I picked up the rifle, and started with my prize towards the river, but noticed Uncle Owen at the lucerne stacks not far away.

I strolled across and laid the bird down at his feet. He turned a twinkling eye on me: 'Crack shot,' he said. 'I see you don't believe in spoiling the body of the bird. Aim for the head and the neck. That's the stuff. Try the river now.'

And he chuckled. But I was not inclined to treat my first shot with a big rifle so lightly. I went off towards the river, with the second cartridge in the chamber, and the catch on safety.

Uncle Owen certainly knew the habits of game on his farm. I came upon the river suddenly and, looking down from its perpendicular, red earth banks, saw the green pools caught between the hard lower layers of ochre earth and the silvery-blue sand. At that very instant, emerging in single file

from the scrub on the opposite bank, came the neat grey shapes of the
guinea fowl, their tall necks carried erect on their diamond-shaped bodies.
I lay flat behind an ashbush and took steady aim. The bird I chose could
not have been twenty-five yards away. I pulled the trigger. Nothing happened. I had left the safety catch on, of course.

I tried again, and missed hopelessly. My bullet hit the water. Before the
ripple rings had got half way to the bank, the last bird had disappeared.
They had risen in a panic in all directions, but now they were gathering
over on the left towards the old dam.

Why had I missed such a sitting shot? Was it the angle? Or was it that my
sights were still set for a hundred yards?

A family of meercats, ma, pa, and all the children, gave me a critical and
inquisitive once-over before ducking into their burrow. A lizard lay on a
hot blue stone, breathing quickly. I moved. A flash of its tail and he was
gone.

I felt embarrassed at this evidence of nature's fear and my lordship. We
take it for granted, we accept it without thought, this universal homage of
fear.

It would be worse, though, if the wild animals were not afraid. There
would be no fun in hunting then. It would be quite cold-blooded, like most
of our killing is. Perhaps farmers like hunting because on a hunt their victim
has chance; whereas their pigs and sheep and cattle have none. They are
bred for death. Perhaps the reason why I was out here enjoying myself in
spite of myself was that an instinct as old as man was having its say. When
you shoot you are without hatred, you are simply being as skilful and as
clever as you can be.

I moved between the mimosas towards the old dam. A few yards ahead
of me on a high twig sat a butcherbird, singing. I stopped, looked and
listened: neat and dapper in black and white, imitating the calls of half a
dozen other birds; very clever at it too, like a chap showing off at a party,
doing impersonations. If his pantry had been in evidence I would have
spent my last .303 cartridge on him. Somehow he got me on the raw.

I bungled my approach to the dam badly. I should never have approached
it from the wall end, where the blindest bird could not help seeing me in
silhouette, there being no cover or camouflage on the earth wall. As soon
as my head came over the top, the birds started sending frantic alarm signals
to each other in that harsh Morse code of theirs. I could see them moving
among the Mexican poppies which grew in a grey-blue belt at the silted end
of the dam. The poppies had their pods already, and it was impossible for
me, in that heat, to distinguish at any one moment between pods and birds'
heads.

I tried stalking those birds. I must have spent an hour at it. I followed
them half round the farm, only to end up once more trying to distinguish
between them and the poppy pods. So, losing patience, I took a pot shot

where the heads seemed densest among the pods. Once more the birds disappeared rapidly, some running, some flying.

'You're wasting your time,' I said to myself as I walked through the poppies to where the birds had been.

'You never know', said another voice in me.

And you never do; for there, among the light green-blue of the poppies, lay the polka dots of a guinea fowl. Its head was missing, completely.

Two flukes out of three.

No one quite knew how to assess my marksmanship: although Godfrey and Gordon pulled my leg about shooting birds in the head or not at all, we all enjoyed the guinea-fowl stew.

The climax of the holiday was to be a jackal hunt. Would my luck hold?

The morning star was still a shimmering fleck of silver when we were woken. By the time the east had turned a pale grey-green we were moving over the stones and bushes, and being shown our positions by Cousin Leslie. We were to lie in ambush while the jackals were driven from the other end of the camp towards us by a host of beaters and their dogs.

Our positions were in dips along the chain of ironstone koppies which stretched due west for three miles before sinking to nothing. In this light it looked like the long scaly tail of an enormous fire-dragon, which, having reared itself through the level lake of the plain, was now slowly sinking back into it.

I had been up and about early before, and alone in the veld; but never on a hunt, never with a rifle in my hands. Perhaps it was my previous elation over the death of the goose; or was it that I remembered the jackal on his way down the kloof that night during the Elandsberg camp, on his way down to kill a lamb: a jackal, a small incarnation of the burning tiger that haunted me? I don't know, but sitting there alone with the cool wind blowing up my shirt sleeves, feeling my flesh, I was soon in that disturbed state in which bushes begin to burn and stones to speak.

Tafelberg and Doornberg were glowing purple and pink at the far end of the valley, their parallel cliffs in horizontal bands lending them an architectural repose and strength. How different the rock on which I was sitting: not the product of wind and water, but of violence and fire; volcanic; igneous; not built up granule by granule, but injected as smoking liquid from the hot heart of the earth, vertical through the buckling sandstone towards the sun.

I gripped the wedge-like face of the boulder in front of me. This was pure, unspoilt, primitive, original. It has never compromised. The soils and the sandstones are second- and third-hand, resting on top of older rocks; but an ironstone koppie is a nail driven up from the centre of things, piercing layer upon layer of laminated stones.

Hunting to kill: that is letting the dolerite thrust through the crust of custom and sentiments and morals, through layer upon layer.

And to make love must be the same: a shedding of disguises, of custom, of caution, letting the stifled instinct sing.

That was it. Or something like that.

I ate my sandwiches, watching the red grass heads pulsating to the wind. From this angle, the whole hillside looked like a curled-up jackal, because of a trick of the sunlight on the feathery grass; yet when I raised my head a little higher, the boulders abolished the illusion, and the grass was nothing but a delicate film, a spider's web spun over insensitive stone.

I heard a soft footstep behind me. It was Cousin Leslie.

'The jackal,' he said, 'if he comes this way will come up the dip, along that little sloot; and he will break into the open over there, where those biesies stop.' And he flung a stone in the direction of the biesies.

'How many yards do you think that is?' he asked.

'About a hundred.'

'A little less. Well, now get yourself into a good position, and try following him in your mind's eye.'

I did this. He showed me a better position, and how to grip the rifle as though it really belonged to me; as if it were built-in.

'He might, on the other hand, come from this side.' And he repeated the lesson.

I now gave my undivided attention to the narrowing strip of veld between the beaters and the foot of the ridge, but could see nothing, except a single hare far over on the left. Then I saw him, a big red jackal, running diagonally across my front. He was obviously not going to come up my way, and was much too far away to shoot at . . . I watched him disappear, then swung my eyes back.

There, exactly where Leslie had said, was a silver jackal, sitting on his hunkers, panting slightly, like a dog that has just enjoyed a run. He had turned round and was looking back, down the hill at the approaching beaters. He looked a little amused. He was so much himself, his very own self, as he sat there.

But before I had got him properly in my sights someone opened up on my right, presumably at the red jackal. My victim stood up. I fired. He jerked his head up, and fell over sideways. I leapt to my feet elated, shaking with excitement, but waited in case another jackal should appear.

The other rifles were crackling along the ridge. The air was banging like Guy Fawkes. Once a ricochet bullet whined overhead in an eerie curve. The beaters were now close, so close that it was futile to expect anything else to break cover, so I decided to examine my prey. I went up and knelt over him.

He looked extremely beautiful there among the brown boulders in the sun, as if asleep. There was no snarl on his lips. The wind was in his fur as it was in the overhanging grass. And, malachite-green and bottle-blue, two large flies were dipping their probosces into the blood round the bullet hole. Even while I watched, a third buzzed past my left ear and joined them.

But I did not leave him to the flies and crows: at least, not all of him. At that moment a Coloured beater appeared, and seeing the dead animal, shouted:

'Mooi so, my basie.' Lifting his kierie, he struck the dead animal a hard blow on the head. He then did a ritual dance of triumph round the jackal as if he had killed it. Well, he had in a way. I would never have got a glimpse of him unless he had done his part of the job.

'Skin him, please,' I said. I would nail his pelt to my museum wall.

'Yes, my basie, later on.'

And he burst into song, joined by two other beaters while a triumphant dog barked and leapt and snapped his jaws at his dead distant cousin. For a moment, I seemed to be in the heart of the ancient hunter's world.

19

A Thirst for Knowledge

The five or six days of this jaunt to Rooispruit were quickly over. I spent much of them writing interminably long accounts of our adventures to Eve, and to composing my first long poem, called 'The Karoo'. I submitted this to my English schoolmaster in place of an English essay. He handed it on to the Head, B.J. du Toit, who returned it to me with the comment, 'Interesting: read Cilliers's "Die Vlakte".' This was perceptive. My poem was inspired by Shelley's 'The Cloud', which critics accept as the metrical model for Cilliers's poem. The main non-English poetic influence on me at this time was, however, Leipoldt, as mediated by our Afrikaans master, B.J. Kachelhoffer.

B.J. Kachelhoffer, 'Klaf', as we called him, was a broad-shouldered, red-faced, clean-shaven man, with very blue eyes; he walked with his feet wide apart, like a sailor — sometimes wider than at others. Some unkind people said this was to keep himself steady as he returned from the Club. There was certainly never any indication of alcoholic interference with his mind, which was bell-clear, nor his speech, which was deep yet crisp. He was fluent in English and in Afrikaans, and he taught me Afrikaans to matriculation level, and History until standard 9, when the new Principal, B.J. du Toit took over.

'Klaf' had been born, or had his earliest education, in a Free State concentration camp; but he never displayed any bitterness or anti-British sentiments. Rumour had it that he had originally intended to go into the church, but that — as so often happens — he lost his faith at university.

He was a good teacher of Afrikaans, which had been a school subject for no more than a decade I suppose. It was clear that he also liked Hollands. In addition to their Afrikaans set books the Higher Grade pupils had one or two in Hollands. 'Klaf' took the Lower Grade through them as well, thus giving me an introduction which helped me with Nederlands at university, and in a subsequent visit to Holland in 1960.

But I will always remember him best for his teaching of Leipoldt's *Uit Drie Wêrelddele* — a volume of poems remarkable for its interest and range. 'Voorspel vir 'n Afrikaanse Heldedig', for instance, started my interest in the Portuguese exploration of our coastline, by Diaz and Da Gama; while sonnets like 'Multatuli' or 'Krakatoa' swung my mind to the Dutch East Indies. It made me aware of our historical and geographical co-ordinates as

I had not been before. Then there were poems, many poems, which made one acknowledge one's familiar world consciously for the first time. 'Oktobermaand', for instance, made me take note of what happened in the veld around me during that month, and sharpened my vague awareness into knowledge and possession. And in 'Op my ou Ramkietjie', in the image of the crazy coloured beggarman strumming his one-stringed, improvised guitar under the moon, one found a prototype of the poet; so that when one encountered Orpheus in 'Lycidas' and 'Il Penseroso', and looked him up in a dictionary of fable, the lonely musician figure was not totally strange. And then there were individual lines that have never left me. A little while ago, returning from Cape Town down the Langkloof through a thick mist, we stopped for a moment under a tree to change drivers. The tree was heavy with ethereal drops — ' 'n pêrelbesaaide witdoring met sy bas en sy blare nat'.

'Klaf' as historian gave me an interest in two great periods of history: Athens and Florence at their peaks. Of course he was working on soil thoroughly composted by Alice's art books and photographs of classical figures from the Louvre, the Vatican and the British Museum. Ancient Greece, however, was more than a gallery of handsome marble men and beautiful marble women with a predilection for nudity. 'Klaf' introduced us to names like Aeschylus, Sophocles, Euripides, Aristophanes, Socrates, Plato, Aristotle. And for the first time one heard it enunciated, as a sort of natural law, that too much democracy led to chaos, and that the way out of chaos was tyranny. One heard, with distress and surprise, that the Athens of Pericles had been a slave state.

Then, the Renaissance: the great magical names. For class after class 'Klaf' did a completely unprecedented thing in the Boys' High School — he brought books, other than set books, into the class: encyclopaedias and art books. Here was the Sistine Chapel; these were the frescoes painted on its ceiling by Michelangelo. And these three ladies, in diaphanous robes, are the Three Graces, by Botticelli; and this demure girl, standing on a seashell, with no clothing whatever except her own golden hair, is Venus, by the same artist.

Images, images, of marble and paint, human figures carrying a burden of meaning, of mystery, joy, tragedy. Artists were embroiled in an agonised and joyous love-affair between the Gods and men.

I am in 'Klaf's debt for ever.

One of the great good fortunes of my life was The Poplars out-buildings which contained a large variety of rooms. One of the smaller rooms had for years been the store-room, particularly for the garden tools and the chicken feed; but when we abandoned keeping chickens because it proved uneconomical, this room was given to me — on Grannie's suggestion, I believe — as a quiet place to study. What incredible luxury! I converted it into my museum, alchemist's den, library, art gallery, hermit's cell, sanctum, tiger's lair — but also the place where I was reduced to the size and shape of a common-or-garden schoolboy by the necessity of having to open my textbooks and do my homework.

My passion for collecting blew hot and cold.

I had an inarticulate suspicion that the marvellously various sub-human world would never be enough; that collecting and classifying, arranging into logical order and sequence might be very important, but that it left the most important, the unpredictable, out of the picture. Somewhere I acquired an old pack of cards (in themselves highly suspect — no card games at The Poplars that I can recall). On a bare piece of wall, below the jackal pelt, I pinned them, arranged in the following artful wise:

A somewhat disordered deck at the top, with the backs towards the beholder, from which, higgledy-piggledy, a rain of cards is falling, cards of all suits and all denominations, the two of spades taking precedence over the king of diamonds and, needless to say, the joker in the most obvious place, and upside down, of course. And then, under this odd confetti, two pictures of men with noble, lowering features, fine foreheads and pursed lips, the one with sparse dark hair, the other with the hair-do of a maenad: Napoleon Bonaparte and Ludwig von Beethoven. I knew virtually nothing about either but they were clearly symbols of man, of energy and genius, and of Destiny with a capital D.

But though their glorious scowling was reinforced by Dürer's Melancholia, which Mother brought back from Germany for me, science emerged triumphant in a new form — chemistry invaded my museum, and the collections of insects, eggs, leaves and feathers were left to the attentions of fishmoths, ants and other tiny creatures which soon reduced them to dust. I remember the shock I received on opening my box of most precious butterflies to show to a visiting friend — most of the wings had fallen from the bodies, which seemed to have been consumed.

I don't know why chemistry should have fascinated me so: I suppose it was more exciting than collecting; you could make things happen, you could see them happening, and you could explain the process by playing about with wonderfully satisfying formulae, in which one could 'see' by changes in colour and consistency, a compound molecule shed an atom and take in another in its place.

I took the precious jackal skin to the Divisional Council, and got ten shillings for it, and turned other treasures into fluid capital, altogether some two pounds five shillings. This I invested in some rudimentary chemical equipment and a few basic chemicals, supplied by the firm of Heynes Mathew of Cape Town. The chemistry master's son assisted with small stolen quantities of more esoteric elements such as phosphorus (to be kept in paraffin) and sodium (to be kept in water) — or is it the other way round?

Chemistry proceeded in a subdued, scholarly climate until the nature of unstable compounds caught my fancy; that, and certain varieties of extremely rapid burning, whereby a small quantity of matter in the solid state is suddenly, very suddenly, converted into a vast volume of matter in the gaseous state. Both these transformations are accompanied by violent disturbance of the atmosphere, so violent that they set up shock waves, which register themselves upon the diaphragm of the ear as loud bangs; and such is the energy released that objects in the immediate neighbourhood may be badly disturbed, damaged or destroyed.

As an example of an unstable compound, let us look at iodine nitrate. (Nitrogen generally seemed to be a tricky customer and to specialise in unstable relationships.) I have forgotten the exact mixture, but you get some iodine in the solid state, dissolve it in strong ammonia, and leave it to evaporate. In due course you will find a sprinkling of small dark crystals. These are very sensitive to the slightest pressure or warmth, and disintegrate with a sharp crackle. *Use:* Sprinkle a few at the entrance of the classroom and watch the effect. If you are very brave and don't much care about your academic future, leave a few on a highly strung schoolmaster's chair.

With rapid burning, it is essential to limit oneself to the smallest possible quantities. There is no use in conducting experiments which are so successful that you do not live to record your observations.

Sulphur is a good oxidising agent, and easy to acquire. It also has an appropriate infernal stench.

Not all my experiments with sulphur were successful. For instance, the occasion on which I mixed sulphur with potassium chlorate crystals, thus making an explosive mixture. Taking an old .303 cartridge case or 'doppie', I filled it with the mixture; then closed the case in a vice.

All I now had to do was to start the burning process, which would be so rapid as to smash the doppie to smithereens with a most satisfactory bang. But this was easier said than done, as there was no means, such as a fuse, to introduce rapid oxidisation into the cartridge. All I could do was to apply heat from the outside, and hope that the metal would conduct sufficient heat to the mixture to start the process. I tried placing it on a small pyramid of burning match sticks, but without success. With the reprehensible impatience of an impetuous experimenter I went into the kitchen. Susan the cook was nowhere about, so I slid the kettle aside, popped the doppie into the inferno of coals, slipped the kettle back, and disappeared into the dining-room. Here I was overcome by those second thoughts which always come too late in this particular field of scientific research. What if Susan should return, and the stove blow up in her face? What if . . . ?

Fortunately I didn't have time to be tortured by third or fourth thoughts. The stove exploded. That's what it sounded like; but on dashing through to the kitchen, I found it intact, except that the plates, and the pots on top of them, were in great disarray. I managed to fit them together before Susan returned.

I went and sat under the pear tree in a cold sweat, confessed myself to heaven, and made a good resolution not to be impetuous and impatient, ever again.

There was one experiment which I could never make up my mind about — was it a success, or not? It impressed my friends, who were watching from the cover of the dry furrow; but as I could not satisfactorily describe the event in terms of unstable compounds or rapid burning, let alone show the formula for the reactions, I felt that I had fallen somewhat from the position of a true scientist to that of mere showman.

Take a large beer bottle, introduce a small quantity of zinc. Add dilute hydrochloric acid. Wait two minutes. Introduce a small piece of sodium. Run like hell for cover in the furrow.

One of the friends likely to be in the furrow was Paul Michau, son of Piet, of Braemore. Paul had suffered a mild breakdown at Grey College, and was now attending the Boys' High School for his senior certificate stint.

In spite of the Fusion between the South African and Nationalist parties, English–Afrikaans relationships remained difficult. Moderates felt that extremists were introducing politics into every committee and organisation. The Boy Scouts had been found to be foreign in spirit, and Die Voortrekkers movement started in Cradock under the energetic leadership of Buggie du Toit. The Red Cross was supplemented by Die Noodhulpliga. Buggy had a strong ally in Max du Preez, and Max had a beautiful daughter.

It was a difficult time for the Montagues and Capulets of the Dorp. Saps were becoming Nats, Nats Saps. But Max du Preez remained firmly Nat and Piet Michau of Braemore firmly Sap. They differed in temperament as well as conviction. Piet had the advantage of a voice as big as his body, and a knack of knocking fine issues off their theoretical perches on to the floor of practice.

Dr D.F. Malan was on a visit to Cradock to get support for his Purified Nationalist Party. Max du Preez took the platform to introduce the great man. In doing so he made vitriolic remarks about the English, their language, and the corrupting effects of their foreign ('uitheemse') culture. He was stopped in mid-sentence by the big bass voice of Piet Michau from the body of the hall:

'Ou Max, dis net jammer dat die Here vir jou 'n Engelse skoonseun gestuur het.'

Max's daughter had crossed the language line.

I have already written in this book about Piet's eldest daughter Marie — my senior by a few years, and therefore a star out of my reach. She struck up a friendship with Mother, and they corresponded for years. When her marriage to a diplomat failed, her parents took extreme positions. Life in South Africa became unbearable, so she determined to return to the U.S.A., which she had come to like during her period there as a diplomat's wife.

When I was in the United States in 1958 I saw her twice: first at her flat about twenty kilometres out of New York, and the second time in New York itself. On both occasions we talked about Cradock, and about ourselves. She held a senior P.R.O. post with the *Reader's Digest*.

We had come out of a show on Broadway, and she was about to drive home. There was a slight fall of snow. The flakes were sprig-muslin-ing her hair. She put out her hand, and watched them melt slowly on its warmth.

'It reminds me,' she said; 'when I left Port Elizabeth on that cargo boat — the sun was blistering hot on the Bay. I was the only passenger. I watched them loading bales of Cradock wool into the hold. At the end of the voyage we tied up in Boston. I had lost my nerve completely. I wanted to go back, to die, anything rather than follow the course I had chosen. Then they started unloading the wool. It was snowing, just like this. When the Cradock bales came swinging out past me, I wanted to hug them — I could smell the sun, Guy, I could smell the Karoo. When they touched down on the wharf side, I found I could leave the ship.'

She climbed into her car and was gone. I walked to my hotel through the dirty snow, moved and elated. We carry our childhood with us wherever we go.

20

Quakers, Xhosas, Cats and the Cosmos

Shortly after the turn of the century Aunt Eliza Butler, who had spent many years as the youngest unmarried daughter looking after her aged parents, came to join her colonial brothers; and, at about the same time her sister Emmie and her husband Bert Fear arrived to help on *The Midland News*. He had been quite high up on the staff of a paper in the West Country, and apparently was so unimpressed by the Cradock plant and the poor climate, which, whatever it had done for other people's lungs, did nothing for his, that he did not stay for very long. After a few years he went to Cape Town, on to the staff of the *Cape Argus*. But for a brief period before he left, no less than four of old Philip John Butler's children were in Cradock, C.P. — James, Charles, Emmie and Eliza.

Up to this point, James and Charlie had managed their religion by affiliating with the Methodists, of whose puritanical standards they could approve, and they had of course married into a stalwart Methodist family, the Colletts. For a time James and Lettie had sent their two eldest children, Mary and Ernest, to Sidcot, the Quaker school in Somerset, an experience from which Mary returned a convinced little Quaker. She found life in Cradock restricted, particularly as her parents never permitted her to go to dances or parties where there was alcohol or cards. And the mainly Anglican uppercrust of the village did not mix much with 'Chapel'. She worked in *The Midland News* office, but was a failure she says, because she was not quick enough at figures. I suspect — but I have no reason to assert — that she was the catalyst that made these children-in-exile of Philip John Butler set up a Quaker Meeting in Cradock. From outside the clan came only one couple: W.W. Lidbetter, the photographer, and his wife.

They had no meeting house, and used to meet in each other's drawing-rooms at eleven o'clock every second Sunday, rain or shine, icy blast or berg wind. Religion was never a matter of choice, of 'I don't feel like it.' It was one's duty, and one did it. We realised it was important, because obviously nothing could be more important than God, whom we took as seriously as our small brains and souls permitted.

The Quakers believe that God is man's Friend, because He said so. 'Henceforward I call you not disciples but friends.' Thus the name 'The Society of Friends'. They also believe that when man listens God speaks. 'Be still, and know that I am God.' So a Quaker Meeting is a gathering of friendly listeners.

And God apparently speaks more readily to a group than to an individual. 'Where two or three are gathered together in My name there am I in the midst of them.' No sermon. No lessons. No hymns. Silence. Occasionally — perhaps once during a meeting — someone would feel moved to speak out of his or her experience, or to pray aloud, or to read a short passage. Quakers did not — as we understood the tradition — come to Meeting with prepared pieces like Anglican priests or Methodist ministers. They came to listen to God rather than speak to each other.

By the time I came on the scene the membership of the Cradock Meeting was as follows: Ernest and his wife Alice, and their five offspring — all more or less reluctant but dutiful (Ernest never spoke or prayed aloud, he was too shy; neither did Alice, let alone any of her brood); Aunt Mary, without whom I think the meetings would have died; the Lidbetters, Wilfred and his New England wife, an unenthusiastic American Quaker (they never said anything either, although he might read a Quaker meditation); grandfather James Butler having died in 1923, I have no recollection of him at a meeting, but of that generation Aunt Eliza was still very much alive (occasionally she would speak, very simply, in the high sing-song of a deaf person); then there was her boarder, the round-shouldered London Scot called Thomas, a bad asthmatic whom she had 'taken in'; and in 1934 her brother Charles, who retired to Cradock from his post as Secretary to the Y.M.C.A. in Cape Town, and bought a house in Dundas Street.

The Quakers had another kind of meeting, called Reading. They would gather of an evening in a house and read a 'good book' together, and discuss it. They were predictably keen on pacifist literature. I can remember them eagerly discussing an article or a book by Bertrand Russell. From England came a monthly magazine called *The Friend,* which was not much read at The Poplars. Father preferred his *Popular Mechanics,* and Mother her *Ladies' Home Journal;* she would also get *Country Life* and *The Illustrated London News* from the library, and pore over glimpses of Royalty.

In the early mid-'thirties, Aunt Mary ran a kind of young people's club or seminar: picnics, mountain-climbing expeditions, and serious discussions on matters of the day — the Butler children, Louis Gerber, Keith Cremer, Rex Moys and a changing spectrum of visitors on holiday, frequently university and training-college students, such as Ted Floweday. Her ability to gather young people round her and to get them talking on matters of moment was remarkable. She salvaged many hours from adolescent and youthful inanity. Add to this Alice's warmth and her interest in art and history, and one can see why many young people in Cradock regarded The Poplars in something of a special light.

The young have a touching conviction that brothers and sisters of any generation previous to their own get on well together. They believe this in spite of having been taught about Cain and Abel. Our elders carefully censored from their talk any suggestion of rifts in the family or of any failure of sisterly or brotherly love. Simply by a determined habit of turning a blind eye to failures and by always mentioning one another's good points, they kept their relationships sweet.

Alice was particularly good at family loyalty. When she married Ernest, she married about another thousand people — all the Butlers, the Colletts and the Biggses, plus lesser clans, past, present or to come. So that one of our first tasks (nobody questioned that everybody of whatever age had tasks), on returning from a holiday or college or university, was to visit Aunt Eliza, or visit Uncle Charlie, or visit Aunt Mary. Dorothy mentions that Jeffrey and I would delay calling until the last day of the vacation.

We were 'naughty' about Uncle Charlie. It is difficult to say why he irritated us, but if ever a young look-out dashed down the passage on a Sunday saying, 'Uncle Charlie's calling!', the Butler children would scatter for the bottom of the garden, where they would stay until spies informed them that the coast was clear.

Uncle Charlie, shortish, upright, grizzle-bearded, was full to overflowing with good works. So was Aunt Mary, but Uncle Charlie seemed more aware of his, in a manner which made us too conscious of our abysmal half-Anglican, half-pagan enjoyment of life. I think that was it. The fun-and-games of the harum-scarum Poplars brood was not approved by Uncle Charlie. His wife, Aunt Emma, struck us as a very quiet, slightly forbidding woman. Still, we were polite, and really quite fond of him; he was part of the family, and that was enough for tolerant acceptance.

Uncle Charlie was a walking compendium not merely of virtues but of knowledge. He had the scientific interests of that generation of Butlers, and he had their excellent disciplined habits. I believe he took the maximum and minimum temperatures every day of his long adult life; and no shower of rain was allowed to fall to the earth without being measured and recorded. He kept voluminous scrapbooks, and was generally intelligent and very public-spirited. He eventually became Mayor of Cradock.

He also stood for old-fashioned Victorian puritanism. Alcohol was piped straight from Hell itself to the 'Vic.', the 'Masonic', and the other hotels of Cradock.

Sunday in Cradock was holy. You could never go to enough services on Sunday. You dressed suitably, in your dark, best, most expensive clothes, so that church became a modest fashion-and-wealth parade, though none would admit it. And you didn't play games, or make an unseemly noise, or even move too fast on a Sunday. In this, Uncle Charlie was at one with most of the Methodists, the Baptists and the D.R.C. Only Anglicans and Catholics of the laxer sort would ever be seen in tennis flannels on the Sabbath, and then seldom in town. They would play their pagan games on remote farms in valleys unseen.

Aunt Eliza lived in the upper part of the town, and to attend Meeting at her house we would have to walk across the dusty market square with its old circular cast-iron horse trough — exactly like the one that has survived at Rondebosch, Cape. Her small cottage was one of a row set cheek by jowl, 'as if space was an extremely limited commodity in the Karoo', says Dorothy. 'One entered the small front verandah, and then dived into a narrow, dark linoleum passage which had a disconcerting step down somewhere along its length, which we had to feel for, because our eyes were not yet adjusted to the gloom. The contrast with the outside glare was extreme.'

Aunt Eliza was short, plump, pink-cheeked, white-haired, blue-eyed, and dressed in garments long out of fashion. As far as we children were concerned, her sitting-room was the best sitting-room for a Quaker Meeting: there was so much to look at; it was a museum of Victoriana. In the centre was a round table draped in a port-wine velvet cloth fringed with bobbles, which bore a variety of fascinating *objets,* such as glass paperweights, with the most beautiful floral or formal coloured hearts to them. All round the walls were cupboards and cabinets containing and supporting treasures: cut glass dangling ornaments; a superb brass clock under glass; Victorian paper cutouts; daguerrotypes and other portraits of ancestors; a beautiful sampler; brass candlesticks and lamps with painted china shades; and a cuckoo clock. No two chairs were the same. Aunt Eliza's throne was a rocking-chair (with springs) orientated towards the window which looked out on to her small walled garden. Our favourite object was an unusual musical box under a glass dome: a little model sail- and steamship on a painted, pliable paper ocean. A pull on a brass knob in the base would wind it up. The still ocean then woke into rhythmical life to a most delightful tinkling shanty and the ship would seem to be sailing. In all that room with its hundreds of items there were only two which bore any relation to Africa: a diminutive set of dolls' furniture made out of porcupine quills, and a small, smooth, beautifully grey-green Bushman digging stone on the table among the coloured glass paperweights.

The cuckoo clock would start calling eleven, and before the bird had stopped popping in and out of his cubbyhole, we would all have sunk into silence. 'Our mother, worn out by early attendance at St Peter's, and five unruly children,' says Dorothy, 'would sometimes fall asleep — to our shame. Aunt Mary would sit quietly, her head bent, in attentive silence. She was the focal point, the essential core, who held the small group together by her dedicated life and conviction. We children spent the time as best we could. Sometimes Guy and I used to try to see the time on Aunt Mary's wristwatch and mouth the words or signal with fingers if the adults were sufficiently absorbed in their thoughts. Christine would heave protracted sighs, which would bring a twitching smile to the corner of our father's lips.' I used to count the knots in the pine ceiling, or the bobbles on the tablecloth.

Yet it would be wrong to leave the impression of mere tedium. There were moments of unforgettable hilarity, and of moving religious experience.

Uncle Charlie had come to deliver a prepared piece, a little sermonette — which was not really Quaker cricket as we understood the rules; worse, his text was not from the Bible or the Book of Quaker Saints, but from that journal of the radically self-righteous, *The New Statesman and Nation*. Cradock must not be weak-kneed in its support of the ailing League of Nations.

Well before he had finished, Aunt Eliza started on one of her rare contributions. I doubt if she was aware that her brother was speaking. How could she have been? She did not have her ear-trumpet plugged in.

Uncle Charles raised his voice. 'As I was saying' — cough — cough.

But Aunt Eliza continued, oblivious.

'I've been thinking a lot lately about the virtue of patience,' she said.

'It seems to me our clear duty to support the League of Nations,' shouted Uncle Charlie, very impatient indeed. Aunt Mary frowned. So did Mr Lidbetter. Mother looked worried — she hated things going wrong for anybody. I was secretly backing Aunt Eliza.

'Patience', continued Aunt Eliza, 'is a virtue.' At this point Uncle Charlie shrugged his shoulders with an expression of grief on his face, and gave up.

'One must be patient. That is easier said than done, particularly for me, where there is so little to be patient about. My life is very quiet, very little happens. But one must put up with it. I was thinking of this, feeding my hens the other day, and I thought I could learn from them. Hens are not sufficiently respected.' At this point Mr Lidbetter blew his nose, loudly, to cover up a guffaw of laughter I suspect.

'Consider my hens,' continued Aunt Eliza in a high wail. 'How patient they are. Uncomplaining. Year in, year out, in the same small run, on the same monotonous diet. They lay eggs, and the eggs are taken away; and they never complain.'

My father had a fit of sneezing, and also had to blow his nose, at intervals for the rest of the meeting.

'Why,' Aunt Eliza sang on, 'they live and they die, never seeing a chicken, just a lot of hens together.'

If we thought she had reached the end we were mistaken.

'And', she added, 'there's not even one rooster to cheer them up.'

By this time everyone was in stitches, except Uncle Charlie, Aunt Emma, Aunt Mary, Mrs Lidbetter and Alice.

'So, whenever I get impatient with my lot,' said the little Victorian lady, 'I think of my patient hens.'

I suppose the meeting might have recovered its Quaker calm, and some higher thoughts been thought, had not those paragons of patience, the hens themselves, taken a hand. They started a most unseemly, indignant brawl. It died down; but just as the great laughter-geyser inside me was becoming more easy to suppress, one of them started signalling her success in producing another infertile egg.

'Pok-pok-pok-*paw*-pok; paw-pok-pok-*paw*-pok.'

By this time Father was wiping perspiration off his brow.

At last that other bird, the cuckoo, popped out of his nest and announced the hour of noon. Meeting was over. All the way home from Market Street to The Poplars we young folk were in fits, Jeffrey crying out at intervals:

'Pok-pok-pok-*paw*-pok!'

'We shouldn't laugh. Patience *is* a virtue,' cried Dorothy, trying to be respectable, but collapsing into helpless splutters.

Then there were times when all of us would find ourselves possessed by infinite stillness, a calm that had no limit. A presence more than human seeming to be amongst us, both reassuring and awesome in its mystery.

'As we grew older,' says Dorothy, 'the meetings became more meaningful and worship a reality. None of us became Quakers in our adult years, but those periods of silent attentiveness and heart-searching made an indelible impression on us all.'

My own growth into a deeper religious awareness was touched off by the tragi-comedy of disposing of a cat surplus at The Poplars.

About this time we had twenty-three cats of all ages, temperaments, sexes and colour schemes.

Mother didn't exactly collect cats, nor did she breed them. She wasn't even fond of them. I don't remember her ever stroking a cat, but she just couldn't help feeding strays. Word got around the cat underworld that Mrs Butler would never turn away a stray cat.

Things were just tolerable when we reached the number of eight; in fact, it was rather a pleasant sight to see eight cats sleeping in close proximity and amity in the sun presided over by a big black tom, who wore a dress shirt and white cuffs, whom we called The Caliph. But when, in rapid succession, three of his harem produced large litters, things became critical. The milk bill soared, and the bird, mice, rat and locust populations of our garden simply disappeared. Mother left it to Father to drown the kittens, but he forgot until they were too big.

What got the cats into trouble was not merely their rapid multiplication, but their strange idea of music. It was natural and right that a male cat should court his feline sweetheart, and that she should be coy about his advances. But the lovesong of a male cat is the most tragic and heartbreaking sound in the world. And it goes on for so long, particularly on a moonlight night.

When the two lovers did get on to speaking terms, their language was a series of hisses, sudden explosions and piercing shrieks that were quite a revelation to me. It demolished my theory that cats were unemotional.

My bed was on the verandah, and I used to lie awake listening to their serenades and duets. It was funny, of course, but at times, particularly when the moon was up and the town quite still, it was also disturbing and mysterious. I felt sorry for them, and I envied them.

The tempo of the nightly caterwauling increased intolerably when one of the younger generation, a magnificent tortoiseshell tom, whom we called Curry, challenged the Caliph. It was an all-or-nothing contest. Their fights were frequent, violent, and I suspect, dirty. All's fair in love and war, and in a love-war no holds are barred. They tore each other to pieces. By day they licked their wounds, fed copiously, and lay in a scheming silence; but when the sun went down they stretched themselves, sat up with smouldering eyes, and tested their claws in the bark of the pear tree.

The life of sheer instinct. Not immoral, simply amoral. Never to have to worry about right and wrong. Driven by your desires until you were fulfilled or out of your misery: Curry coming into his own; The Caliph, the old king, fighting to the death to maintain himself.

Then Father, having had his night's rest disturbed by their caterwauling, gave instructions that all the cats, except one, were to be taken to the chemist, who, by arrangement with the S.P.C.A., would put them to a quick death with a touch of cyanide.

The next day was Saturday, and I overslept. I awoke to the murmur of the African beggars, queuing up outside the kitchen door.

There was some written or unwritten law or regulation in Cradock which allowed the old men of the location to go begging in the European quarter on Saturday mornings. They soon learnt that there were certain households where they were sure to get a penny, and certain others where the copper rainfall was erratic, and others where conditions of perpetual drought prevailed.

They worked to a strict time schedule, to which their benefactors had to adhere. By eight-fifteen on a Saturday morning they would be lined up outside our kitchen door; some of them blind, led by little boys, with a short smooth stick as connecting link; some with wonderful bearded old faces, surprisingly Arab-looking. Some of them were white-haired; and white hair on an old black head looks especially venerable. For the most part they chatted while they waited, but their patience was short; they had many calls to make. If Joan, whose task this was, wasn't there within five minutes, they would start knocking at the door, and a resentful, complaining murmur would arise. For a long time the number stayed at about twelve, and Mother always saw to it that there was a shilling's worth of copper in the house. A penny may not seem much, but it was equal to the weekly spending-money she gave each of her children.

'Now here you all are,' I heard Joan say. There were mutterings as each old gentleman came forward for his dole, received it, and made a shuffling dash for the next generous door.

So that morning I woke up to help choose the lucky survivor among the cats. Mother preferred not to have anything to do with the miserable business. It was left to the children. It was strange, choosing which one of those trustful creatures, placidly waiting for their breakfast outside the kitchen door, should survive. We eventually settled on Curry, and left September our gardener to catch the remainder as they came for their milk.

No one was quite as miserable as September, because, although he was a good practising Christian, he had a superstitious fear of cats. He was filled with dread at having a hand in the death of almost two dozen.

He put them into a large packing-case, which in turn he placed on the wheelbarrow. Sorrowful but fascinated, we watched his progress up the street.

It so happened that there was a bazaar in the Town Hall that day. Outside the hall, on the pavement, stood a little group of organisers, waiting for His Worship the Mayor and his wife to drive up; and on the steps behind them was quite a crowd of people, not waiting for His Worship but to rush at the stalls the moment he had opened the bazaar.

His car approached along Beeren Street. He and his wife (looking like a sack of mealies in danger of splitting at the seams) were both no doubt preoccupied with the task of being dignified. And so was September, approaching along the pavement, with his barrow.

There wasn't a collision. September did pull up in time. In fact he pulled up so suddenly that the box slid off the barrow and the lid jarred open about three inches in one corner. The effect was unexpected. From this gap spouted an artesian fountain of cats of all colours, who shinned up the beefwood trees, on to walls and roofs, or down stormwater drains, or into the bazaar itself. Every dog in the neighbourhood had a momentary thrill. The crowd collapsed and rocked with laughter. But the Mayor was not amused, nor was his wife.

Later that day, one of the old beggars crossed my path on his way back to the location. He wore a bandless old hat, and an army greatcoat without buttons, almost reaching to the ground, under which his bare feet took small jerky steps. According to Father, many of the Cradock Xhosa had arrived as a result of the Cattle-killing of 1856, so he might have been a boy when his deluded elders killed all their cattle, to turn the white man's bullets into water. Was it so ridiculous? Faith shall move mountains, even such faith as a mustard seed. They had much more faith than that, and it hadn't worked. Because it was faith in false gods? They were pagans; his father, no doubt, wore skins of wild beasts, and had no masters except chiefs and headmen of his own colour. And here he was in discarded European clothes, begging from door to door. How are the mighty fallen. He passed close to me, emitting a faint familiar smell of sweat and mimosa smoke.

Aimless, I followed him. About a quarter of a mile along the river bank the beggar sat down and, leaning against a boulder, took out a long-stemmed, deep-bowled, bead-decorated pipe, and stuffed it with black tobacco. He started smoking, happy in the sun. As I walked past he raised his hand in salute, and mumbled, 'Molo.' I replied in the same fashion. The strong smell

of his tobacco reached me at the same moment. It pleased me, the son of
the conquerors. And my mind went back to Thomas's fight with the Bushman goatherd at the drift close by so many years ago.

Indeed, that had been a long time ago, but all the insecurity I felt then was
suddenly in me and in the air itself; also something new, a sense of guilt, of
a sword hanging over my head.

I tried to reason with myself. What had happened then, and what I was
now finding out about the world and myself, was all a result of the Fall.
All the bullying, all the hatred, the violence, the lust, they all came from
man's corrupted will. So did the fascination of these things for my imagination. Only the grace of God could cleanse my will, or could save mankind. There, among the ashbushes and the mimosas, I prayed with a passionate earnestness. Perhaps for two minutes. It might have worked better
if I had actually knelt there in the open, but my vanity was too great for
that. I simply sat on a big smooth stone brought down by some ancient
flood.

No assurance of grace came, no feeling from outside. But I knew that
prayers were not necessarily answered in an obvious manner. God moves
in a mysterious way. One prays on the understanding that He is listening,
but one leaves the time and place and method of the answer entirely to
Him.

But I did get an answer. It was so shattering that it turned me into an
atheist for about two months.

When I got up, I was able to dismiss my broodings and introspections, and
take some note of the world about me. It was, in fact, a beautiful, blue day,
with the newly arrived swallows chasing each other over the pools, or sailing
and drifting, high, high up; a lazy day, when even the engines over at the
railway station seemed unable to puff either loudly or quickly. I started
walking back home.

Then I saw him, the butcherbird, stocking his larder. His hooks were the
long white thorns of a medium-sized mimosa, on which he had already impaled several insects. At this moment, however, he was busy with something
special. Dapper in his customary suit of black and white, he balanced on a
bouncing branch, a baby sparrow in his beak. The little bird looked particularly helpless and exposed because its feathers had not yet covered its ugly
nakedness. It flapped its almost bare wings, and uttered tiny screams which
seemed to tear the afternoon in two. Adjusting his footing, the dandified
butcher at last got into the right position. Then he tugged his victim towards
himself, impaling it through the neck on to a long white thorn. He chirruped
with gratification and flew away for more.

I didn't know what to do. His pantry was right out of my reach. I couldn't
knock the creature down. And what would be the good? It was a butcher-

bird's nature. It was not wrong for a butcherbird to hang young sparrows like that, and to leave them in the sun, their huge mouths still open, emitting soundless screams into the unhearing afternoon.

On a thorn to the sparrow's left was a large locust, and to his right a painted-lady butterfly. Even as I watched, the locust pulled in his great hindlegs and kicked desperately to free himself from the long white thorn through his thorax; kicked, and kicked nothing but the beautiful, still, blue air.

Most of the cats had returned home by that evening. Having sacrificed one of their nine lives, they seemed to find it necessary to celebrate in orgiastic fashion.

I experienced a complete revulsion against the whole process of life, or rather the aspects of it which then obsessed my emotions and mind: sex and violence, love and war; the mating cats, the African beggars, the butcherbird, the young sparrow, the locust. Henceforward I would have as little part in it as possible.

I stopped eating meat. My vegetarianism was noticed at once. I tried to explain my revulsion, ending with an incoherent account of the butcherbird's pantry. Mother turned pale, and Father looked at his hands.

'There are many things we don't understand,' he said.

'I can understand it, as long as the Creator is not a God of Love,' I said.

Mother asked if I would be prepared to talk my difficulty over with the Rev. Charles Gould, the Rector. I agreed. She fixed a time for the next week.

I spent much of the afternoon with a very bright matric boy, an avowed atheist, who read widely in dubious and forbidden books. He started telling me about Darwin, and evolution, and how it was much more sensible to regard ourselves as highly developed animals who had certain difficulties with our instincts, than as the corrupt offspring of God, living in the shadow of perpetual failure and guilt. He lent me a fascinating book on biology which I spent the rest of the day reading. It revealed far more to me than the Book of Revelation ever did. I was quite enthralled.

It became more and more apparent that Man had won and maintained his position in the world by his superior cunning only; by his ability to destroy, or to breed, what lesser animals he chose. But the result was that I liked the idea of Man less, rather than more.

So when Monday came, I faced the destruction of the cats with a certain bitter satisfaction. It was a cruel, irrefutable illustration of Man's necessary inhumanity to the lesser creatures. After all, human life would be impossible if Man did not kill millions of cats every year.

September took no chances the second time. He pinned the packing-case lid down firmly with a nail at each corner, and set out for the chemist.

September was very polite, as always, but desperately in a hurry; insistent, and not to be delayed. He carried his huge box in among the polished display cabinets, among the photographs of smiling Kolynos toothpaste girls, and the ladies buying cosmetics, and placed it at the foot of the main counter. It was too large a box to get through the narrow opening that led to the dispensary, so the unfortunate cats had to be handed over the counter one at a time.

When they were all dead, their still, limp bodies were handed back over the counter to September, who placed them in the box, neatly side by side, like sardines. By this time the poor fellow was trembling and sweating with terror, and the chemist's staff anxious for him and his box to be gone. But he would not move until he had noisily hammered that lid on to the box with several three-inch nails. He was less terrified of those cats living than dead. When he got home, he dug a pit about five foot deep and buried them, box and all.

Home (the garden in particular) was not the same without the cats. But the sole survivor of the holocaust, Curry, lamented not at all. He took it all in his lordly stride. He simply stepped out a bit farther at night. He really was a magnificent beast. His coat was thick, glossy and gently tigerish. The deadly delicacy with which he stalked doves was utterly admirable. The completeness with which he gave himself up to sleep, or to purring in my lap, was proof-positive of his unfallen state. He was wholly himself. He was not a divided creature.

Contemplating Curry made me think that there was perhaps something in the notion that the lower forms of life, like rats and insects and birds, could quite properly be said to be giving life to higher forms of existence when killed and eaten by such creatures. Life feeds on life, all the way up from plankton to Man.

I was progressing quite well with this theory of life as a pyramid of lower forms carrying higher forms on their backs, as it were, when I saw a stunt photograph showing what an average European family eats in a year: hills of vegetables and fruit, whole crates of poultry, a small herd of cattle, several pigs, a fair-sized flock of sheep, a small aquarium of fish, vast hogsheads of milk, mountains of butter, pyramids of eggs; and also in my mind's eye I saw the antelope and wild birds, the unspoilt forests and plains which had disappeared to make room for the farms which had produced all that food. I seriously wondered if Man could really justify such a wholesale sacrifice and disturbance of the natural world.

I confided my doubts to my atheistic friend. His answer was quite unconcerned.

'Myself, I'm worth any amount of sacrifice of the animal, vegetable, and mineral kingdoms.' He looked at me appraisingly, nodded and said, 'And so are you. But I have my doubts about half the chaps in school, and at least ten of the masters. They're not worth the cabbages they eat.'

That was the sort of remark that made me hero-worship him. He was capable of contempt. It's something I have not been effective at. And he knew how to curl his upper lip and sneer. I used to practise in front of the mirror, but with little success.

I had hoped to shock Aunt Mary with my new views, but she surprised me instead. I put forward the idea that Man had evolved from the higher apes; that less than a million years ago certain baboons who had been tree climbers took to the open, staggering about in a more or less erect position.

Once he didn't have to use his forelimbs for walking and climbing, Man could use them for other things: throwing stones for instance, or breaking off sticks, and using them as clubs. Then later he learnt how to make tools out of stone. And because he used his hands, his brain developed and his skull grew bigger. In the last resort it is his bigger skull that makes him superior, because it enables him to invent more deadly weapons than any other animal. He became the fittest to survive, because he was the best at killing.

I found myself emphasising the notions of death and violence as the very basis of Man's manhood, because it was so completely anti-Quaker. But I think Aunt Mary was shrewd enough to realise this.

She said she didn't know very much about biology, but she knew the cost of a child to its mother in energy and suffering. It was all very well to say that human advance depends on a big brain-box, but before a species could develop a big cranium, it had to develop other characteristics. Why? I asked. She took some time to reply. The bigger the skull, the longer the child remains helpless and in need of the care of its parents. Intelligence grew in Man, because Man had the patience to look after his young far longer than any other species. By animal standards, human children are backward and retarded.

I thought a moment, puzzled.

'Backward and retarded?' I asked.

She laughed. 'Most animals can fend for themselves after a year or two at most. Here you are, seventeen, and you haven't earned a single meal in your life.'

That sent me off in a chastened mood. My parents had had seventeen years of me. A lifetime of me, in fact. I felt suddenly, genuinely sorry for them.

Patience and compassion. What I needed was some sort of toughness to feel the pain in nature and men without impatience: to endure it; to be a Stoic.

I looked up Stoic in the encyclopaedia, and learnt with grim fascination that Stoics were permitted to commit suicide if life became intolerable.

So when I visited the Rector, I was prepared with questions about suicide, and had a dozen shocking propositions to fire at him. But somehow he steered the entire interview away from religion. At one point I thought, 'He doesn't know the answers himself,' at another, 'He's not prepared to

discuss my problems. He thinks I'll grow out of them, smug old duffer.'
He sat in his armchair, endlessly lighting a very dandy little pipe, and talking about poetry; and about figures of speech, particularly paradoxes; and how much of the best poetry in the world was built on paradoxes. The solitary Wordsworth, walking alone, sees a host of dancing daffodils. The dying Keats listens to the immortal voice of the nightingale. The imprisoned Lady of Shalott longs for the broad world outside. Did I know Donne by any chance? Mad about paradoxes, he was. Yes, all things considered, I could do a lot worse than spend a little time on William Blake: 'The Marriage of Heaven and Hell', and *Songs of Innocence* and *Songs of Experience*. He presented me with an Everyman edition.

I found Mother waiting for me anxiously.
  'How did you get on with the Rector?' she asked.
  'He talked about poetry all the time,' I said. 'He gave me this to read.'
  Mother opened it. 'Blake! But he was supposed to be a little mad, wasn't he? I suppose the Rector knows what he's doing.'
  I read *Songs of Innocence* before supper. Frankly I felt humiliated that the Rector should have fobbed me off with such pretty-pretty kid-stuff. I could imagine those little pieces being a great success with the toddlers in the Sunday school. Some of them sounded well enough, while others seemed to have a deliberate amateurishness, enough to make you think they were written at the dictation of that unconvincing little child sitting upon a cloud laughing. If that is what Innocence is like, it is not for me.
  But after supper I settled down to *Songs of Experience,* and from the very first poem I was gripped:

Hear the voice of the Bard!
Who Present, Past & Future sees,
Whose ears have heard
The Holy Word
That walk'd among the ancient trees.

  I heard his voice, and have listened to it intermittently ever since.
  When I came to 'The Tyger' I was shocked and excited by meeting on the white open page a beast that had been secretly prowling round my interior night all these many years: the awful symmetry of the Tiger, of the animal world, of instinct, of sheer energy, made by the God who made the Lamb.
  And then 'The Proverbs of Hell': my eyes grew wide as I saw it proclaimed that passion and energy were good, that the body was good, that everything that lives is holy.
  'The roaring of lions, the howling of wolves, the raging of the stormy sea, and the destructive sword, are portions of eternity too great for the eye of man.'

Aunt Mary had talked of sacrifice. Yes. All life depended on it, but in the vast majority of cases the victims had no choice in the matter. They were like that poor scapegoat the ancient Jews used to drive into the desert, or like the Xhosa beggars, or the poor Bushmen in our own history. They had to bear the sins of the whole people, whether they wanted to or not.

At every meal we consume life bought by death; every day there is death and birth, life dying and life beginning. That's why, I suppose, all religions have sacrifice at their centre.

So my diet reverted to normal, and I went back to church. But my notion of God and the Crucifixion changed. Religion ceased to be a series of moral stories. It was a dark mirror that answered every question by a paradox: it flung the words and actions of the characters in the Old and New Testaments at me like bombs. The whole, dreary, safe surface of Cradock was blasted open before my gaze and I walked down Bree or Beeren Street as down an avenue of flame. I began to stare at the later pictures of Van Gogh, and enter great whirlpools in the sky.

Sometimes, kneeling in church, I would say: There's nothing, nothing under my knees. I have no weight at all.

And all the movements of Curry the cat, the deadly delicate stepper, were a delight to me.

'Energy is Eternal Delight.'

Yes, and no. Everywhere in the world one encountered energy in terrible and terrifying forms void of delight.

Father came in one evening shaken and miserable. The police van had stopped outside the South African Hotel to pick up some rowdy drunken Coloured men. Two constables, standing one a side, each gripping an ankle and a wrist of a drunk, would swing him back and then release him on the forward swing so that he crashed into the van as if he were not of mortal flesh and bone. Father remonstrated. 'Do you want us to treat them like gentlemen?' was the sneering reply.

And then there were the newsreels. On the rare occasions we went to the cinema there were always soldiers marching, marching, and great men making violent speeches. There was also talk from Germany of 'Strength through Joy'.

If Uncle Charlie's well-meant attempts to teach me morals and manners fell on barren ground, his statistical and scientific observations did not. His years as an editor of *The Northern News* in Vryburg had taught him how to help the lay mind grasp the meaning of figures.

One day before Meeting began at his Dundas Street house he was trying to assist a visitor from England to understand the human emptiness of the Karoo. The visitor came from Yorkshire. Uncle Charlie disappeared into his study for a moment to look up his works of reference, and returned:

'The district of Cradock', he said, 'is only slightly smaller than the entire West Riding — 1,400,000 as against 1,700,000 acres. The population of Cradock, town and district, is 21,800; that of the West Riding, one-and-a-half million, which is not much short of the entire white population of the Union of South Africa. In Cradock the density of population is approximately one person per sixty-five acres; in the West Riding one person per one acre.'

Like Mr Kissack and Mr Lidbetter, Uncle Charles was an amateur geologist, and I believe it was from him that I learnt something important about the nature of the stone from which the Bushmen made their arrowheads, crescents and scrapers, which we found on dozens of sites up and down the valley. I had always imagined that they were made of igneous rocks.

'Not at all,' he said, 'though lydianite is always found in close conjunction with them. You find lydianite where dolerite and mudstone meet. What happened was this. When the molten dolerite forced its way through the sedimentary rocks of the Karoo system, the great heat of the new material from the earth's centre transformed the old rocks — fused the fine particles of mud and sand rather as they are fused in kilns in the making of pottery or glass. The result is a material different from either dolerite or sandstone; something that can be chipped and flaked into various shapes, and take a keen edge: a very useful material indeed. It was, in fact, a great moment in Stone Age history when men discovered this stone, and learnt where best to look for it — in the neighbourhood of dolerite intrusions.'

It was a great moment in my mental history. Up to this point much of my thinking tended to categorise experiences as 'sandstone' or 'ironstone': sandstone stood for experience, for tradition, for raw materials that had been through great chastenings of wind and weather, growth and decay, and then been laid down in workable strata, vast laminated books of knowledge; ironstone stood for raw instinct and energy tapped from the molten heart of things, still defiant and resistant to wind and weather, primordial, difficult to work, innocent of secrets and knowledge. There was much sandstone in my parents, and much ironstone in myself. Sometimes it seemed I was a small, untidy dolerite outcrop surrounded by great, level, sandstone mountains of ineluctable authority and poise. Growing up seemed to be an inevitable weathering process — ironstone being broken down, granule by granule into sand, and levelled out into beds.

But here, at the interface, was lydianite, neither sandstone nor ironstone: something comparatively rare, a product of two worlds, partaking of both, belonging to neither; something which lent itself to shaping, neither philosophical nor instinctual, sophisticated nor primitive, traditional nor original, but essentially between, exposed on both sides, a useful, bastard, frontier stone.

Of course I could not have formulated the matter so at that time, but a symbol had been implanted in my imagination of a possible integrity and function for the mind, or the moment, or the mood, which, while owing its origin to highly contrasted sources, is different from either.

Something similar happened to my thinking about Karoo plants, which I had collected for many years, and transferred to my rockeries at The Poplars. A visitor with more botanical knowledge than anyone I had yet encountered smiled wryly and said:

'Everybody collects succulents. They are interesting enough, but I don't care for them. Nearly all are surface feeders. Like stone plants they survive mostly by disguise, or by thorns, or both. In one way or another they have distorted themselves in order to keep on living: stems become leaves, leaves disappear and become thorns, as in the prickly pear.'

For himself, he preferred the shrubs and bushes of the Karoo, which alone made life possible for man and animal. They did not hoard water in the manner of succulents. Instead, they sent their roots down deep. True, their leaves were for the most part small, but nevertheless abundant. Drab they might be — a characteristic caused by a thin coating of gray wax, which minimised evaporation. If you take a few leaves in your hand, and rub them, they emit the clean, unsentimental scent of the aromatic oils, which also inhibit the loss of moisture. The most famous scents in the world come from desert plants — frankincense and myrrh, and 'all the perfumes of Arabia'.

If he did not like succulents for being useless surface feeders, he had some sympathy with what he called the opportunists. Every time one put one's foot down on a bare piece of veld one probably trod on hundreds of seeds of a variety of annuals awaiting their chance. Given a good season they will leap into swift life and cover all the bare soil between the respectable deep-rooted stoics, recklessly green, then go rainbow-minded, before withering into abundant seed.

Indeed, there were seasons when the veld was thus glorified and transformed by flowers; when, for instance, the 'tulp' came out in such abundance as to turn the grey flats into purple lakes. But even in dry seasons, in the right places, such as the shadows on the south side of great rocks, one would find pretty opportunists such as nemesias.

And walking across the Karoo scrub, after rain, inhaling its sharp ascetic smell, one might be assailed by a scent which did not speak of strength, endurance and age, but of delicacy, tenderness and youth. In that stripped, hard, clean landscape it might seem like a seductive heresy: the scent of freesias, milky and golden white, smooth as a girl's cheek, with a hint of blue vein beneath a fine skin.

The freesia is neither a surface feeder nor an opportunist; its beauty and sweetness derive from moisture stored in almond-shaped bulbs buried deep in the loam.

21

Turmoil

It was during standards 9 and 10 that I became a semi-nocturnal animal. When afflicted by insomnia I would do the strangest things. I remember climbing barefoot and in nothing but pyjamas on to the top of the outbuildings. It was full moon. The air was dead still and ice cold. The frosted iron of the roof seemed to cling to my feet. To be alone, very cold, motionless, absolutely quiet in a moon-blanched world, was to put oneself in the proper ascetic posture for prayer. Or to rise half an hour before first light and sit on the side of the old Graaff-Reinet road which ran through Moordenaar's Nek; to watch the slow change in the eastern sky over Elandsberg, thinking one's own thoughts (who was the Moordenaar? whom had he murdered?). To sit there so still among the ashbushes that neither the touleier nor the driver of a wagon loaded with firewood for the morning market guessed one's presence. To sit there till the first small birds stirred, and the Stanley cranes spiralled slowly into the still grey light, their hoarse cries a desolate intercession to the coming day.

This desire to expose myself to the universe, to get to where nothing could give God the excuse for not revealing himself to me, drove me to strange almost Faustian lengths. Late one hot afternoon in early summer the sky blackened from an unusual quarter, and a huge mass of dark cloud seemed to steady itself over the ironstone hills near Egg Rock. As the mutterings of thunder grew louder and more frequent I cycled towards the storm across the old race track. When the large first drops began to smack down like hail, I abandoned my cycle on the footpath and climbed an ironstone eminence. There I lifted my face so that the descending drops stung it, and shouted into the thundering sky: I am nothing; I am weak; I am wicked. If you don't intend to cleanse me and strengthen me, strike me dead, now. The rain came down dense and drenching. Wet to the skin, tired of playing the unwanted lightning-conductor, I descended, and ran, elated with my strength, along the watery footpaths through the thundering, flashing atmosphere.

How do I explain such weird behaviour? Or was it so weird? I was, perhaps, living out the religion I had dimly discovered in Shelley's 'Ode to the West Wind'. Adoring his 'Angels of rain and lightning', I abased myself before

  . . . *the congregated might*

Of vapours, from whose solid atmosphere
Black rain, and fire, and hail will burst . . .

and through identification with them sought to share

The impulse of thy strength, only less free
Than Thou, O uncontrollable!

Is it not understandable that a frustrated, guilt-ridden boy should seek
liberation in this mystical way?

. . . Be thou, Spirit fierce,
My Spirit! Be thou me, impetuous one!

Twenty-four hours later I might with equal devotion be lost in wonder at
Christ's refusal to use his energies, his obedient submission to the errant
powers of the world he had created.

In January 1935 Honor Biggs's brother, David, came to board at The Poplars
and attend the Boys' High School. He was in standard 9. A larger table was
found, and he joined me in my den. Like his sister, he was a well-organised
person, whose disciplined habits of work and recreation were a perpetual
accusation of my improvised, temperamental and experimental mode of
existence.

Dorothy, having matriculated at the end of 1934, went to Cape Town to
try her vocation as a nurse. She was back after four months; that practical
profession was not her metier. For a time she went to Vrede to test her
proficiency as secretary to Uncle Frank: her commercial matric and her
experience in *The Midland News,* however, proved insufficient preparation
for completing his income tax returns. Uncle Frank required her to add up
each column of figures three times. She got three different answers. 'What
must I do now? ' she asked in desperation.

'Take the average, I suppose,' he said, with a grin.

Joan, having completed her two-year course at the Grahamstown Training
College, was in charge of the farm school at Langfontein — a beautiful place
between Vrede and Westbrook, where she was to stay two years. It belonged
to Uncle Frank, and was being run by Uncle Boy Vorster. She seemed to
enjoy it, and regaled us during holidays with endless stories of classroom
crises with children, which led to subsequent confrontations with parents.
One began to appreciate the problems of teachers.

At The Poplars, Christine and Jeffrey were left to endure their big brother,
his moody presence mercifully diluted by cousin David. David was quite
baffled by the effect that 'my girl' was having on me. He watched with
growing concern my neglect of my studies as I wrote long letters and longer
poems, most of which were torn into confetti and flung into the wastepaper
basket.

My habit was to strap my schoolbooks together with a broad leather belt. I preferred this to packing them into a leather bag. For three nights running I had not opened a book.

On the fourth night I was busy — all apprentice poets have to tread this slough of despond — trying to write a Petrarchan sonnet but, after a splendid first three lines, had ground to a halt, appalled by the moronic limitations of a language which had so few viable rhyme-words for the most important word in all the world: *dove* and *above* were worn threadbare; *glove* had possibilities, but not for the volcanic material I was working on; *shove?* — hopelessly unromantic.

At this point David tapped my strapped-up schoolbooks and said, with a mixture of anxiety and impatience:

'Isn't it time you undid this buckle?'

I then indulged in one of the few poetic gestures in my life. I hurled the parcel of books through the open window into outer darkness. They lodged all night in an old valencia orange tree. They smelt of orange blossom throughout the first period next day.

My long interrupted friendship with Paul Michau blossomed. He stayed in Mrs Nel's boarding-house in Beeren Street. One night he begged me to come to his room because he was being frightened by noises. He was being spooked. I went and sat with him.

'Listen!' he cried, clutching my arm, his eyes wide with terror.

I could hear nothing, and said so.

'Are you sure?'

Stretching my ears for a long second or two, I said:

'There's nothing, Paul. Let's play chess.'

By eleven o'clock he seemed much calmer, and I left.

It was my first contact with someone suffering acute nervous strain. He was 'frightened of nothing' as we simpletons say.

He became a doctor, and died of cancer a few years ago.

In Cradock the only white visitors who knocked on the back- or kitchen-door were villainous-looking but picturesque knife-grinders and tinkers, hobo-artisans who reminded me of old Barter, the Katkop mason. So it was something of a shock to find a tall, handsome white man in an elegant if crumpled suit standing at the foot of the stone steps next to the cat's saucer, and to hear him ask in cultivated English if he might see Mr Butler.

'My father's having his lunch,' I said.

His eyes were bloodshot, and his expression tortured.

'Tell him it's Captain Abercrombie,' he pleaded.

I relayed the message to my father, who flared up.

'He's got no business to come begging here. It's bad enough when he comes to the Works. In any case, I told him yesterday that he'll get no more from me.'

But he rose from his seat, and went to speak to his military mendicant. Mother explained: 'Poor Captain Abercrombie, he's an alcoholic. It's quite pernicious, really. He used to be wealthy, owned two farms, but he drank them both. He used to be everybody's boon companion at the Club, but now that he's down and out no one will help him. It's ironical that he should pester your father, of all people.'

Father stayed away so long that Mother sent his lunch through to the kitchen to be kept warm. When he returned, he spoke in an intense voice, as though he disliked every word he spoke but could not do otherwise.

'Alice, the man's been thrown out of his hotel room. Typical of the liquor trade: fleece you, then kick you out. None of the other hotels will have him. He wants money, of course, to pay for a couple of nights' lodging "until his remittance comes through". But I can't give him money — he'll just use it for drink. Would you mind if we allowed him to sleep in the un-let garage for a few days? The boys can take him his food. It'd be better if the girls had nothing to do with him.'

And so it came about that alcoholic Captain Abercrombie lived in an un-let garage at The Poplars, enjoying the strictly limited hospitality which his teetotal Quaker host could see his way clear to giving him. A camp-stretcher was found, an old table, a spare chair. At mealtimes I would be sent to him with a tray, for which he was always formally grateful. I longed to get into converse with this strange, afflicted man, but he kept our relationship on a strictly official basis: he was the officer and gentleman, I was the batman, the flunkey. Then one day — how soon was it? — I found him trembling from head to foot, and looking quite wild.

'Malaria!' he cried. 'A spot of the old anopheles, you know,' and began to giggle. 'Yes, the anopheles — he's the mosquito who parks with his posterior elevated into the air like a howitzer.'

I left the tray on his table, and reported to Father that his guest was suffering from malaria and behaving in a dotty manner. Ernest groaned.

'Now the poor devil's got the shakes,' he said.

I can only assume that Father phoned the Medical Officer of Health or the District Surgeon, because Captain Abercrombie's billet was empty by suppertime. We never heard of him again. In a strange way I missed him.

The more I brood on alcohol and its abuses, the less critical I become of my father's attitude. Two anecdotes may show how others viewed him.

At the height of the depression, when it was doubtful whether the firm would survive or not, it must have been an enormous temptation to my father to relax, and accept liquor adverts for the paper. Not a bit of it. Alice, who did not feel as deeply about high principles as she felt about the needs of her children, let me know her mind once, and once only. 'Why *can't* he take the liquor adverts — just until this depression's over?' Then, as though she had caught herself out, she shook her head, puckered her forehead, and said, 'I'm sorry, my boy, one must never be disloyal,' and walked away.

Years later, in the 1960s after my father's death, while trying to raise funds in Johannesburg to establish the Institute for the Study of English in Africa, I was having lunch in the Rand Club with one of the directors of a powerful printing and publishing concern. He was an impressive example of financial efficiency and success, with a handsome, strong face.

'Are you by any chance the son of the Ernest Butler of *The Midland News*, Cradock?'

To the great man who moved in orbit with massive papers like *The Star* and *The Sunday Times*, *The Midland News* must have been something of a curiosity, a doomed still-struggling Darwinian survival, having already shrunk in status to a mere bi-weekly. I expected some amusing anecdote: instead I received a glimpse of my father as an eccentric yet wholly admirable man.

The great director of companies went on: 'I can never forget him. Year after year, at the annual meeting of the National Press Union, with virtually no support, he'd propose that the press refuse liquor adverts. We'd all listen, with varying degrees of impatience.'

There was a longish pause, in which we were both remembering a man recently dead. When he spoke, his bass voice had gone a trifle hoarse.

'Year after year. It was heroic,' he said.

Late in February 1935, news reached Alice that her eldest brother Harold had committed suicide. The terrible phrase was not used, however. We were given the briefest details. While his wife (Aunt May 'China') was in England with her two sons, Harold, second-in-command of the Shanghai waterworks, had suffered so severe a nervous breakdown that he was sent home, via the Trans-Siberian railway, in the charge of a friend and a male nurse. They boarded the steamer *Vienna* at the Hook of Holland for Harwich. During the night he eluded his caretaker. A smoking-jacket and a pair of slippers were found on the promenade deck. This was the news delivered to his wife and sons, and to his brother Uncle George and his wife Aunt Frances, who had gone to Liverpool Street station, London, to meet the boat train.

Our tentative inquiries and awkward utterances of sympathy produced only one response from Alice: it was all too sad to speak about. Ernest was even less forthcoming.

But the fact that two of mother's family had died tragically weighed upon my mind. Why did people succumb to 'nerves'? Why did other people drink themselves into 'the shakes', into disgrace and into ruin? The stories of Aunt Janet, Uncle Harold and Captain Abercrombie had certain common elements: they were all exiles, and had all experienced a great failure or breakdown of love: Aunt Janet who never found a second lover; Uncle Harold with half the world between him and his wife and sons; and Captain Abercrombie with no one anywhere caring whether he lived or died.

These tragic people would walk side by side in my imagination with the afflicted souls I found in my reading: Maggie Tulliver from *The Mill on the Floss;* Magwitch, the returned Australian exile, from *Great Expectations;* King Richard the Second, Brutus, and many others. No one, it seemed, could escape being injured, hurt, wounded. The centrality of the Crucifixion in the Christian scheme began to make better sense. Affliction is one of the great facts of life.

St Peter's Church displayed no cross with the suffering Christ upon it. Such crucifixes were regarded as Popish. Mother confessed to having owned one when she first came to South Africa, but had quietly buried it out of deference to the family into which she had married.

There lay about The Poplars for many years, an old leather-bound ledger known as great-great-grandpa's diary. It was, in fact, only a portion of the remarkable diary kept by James Lydford Collett, the settler, covering some fifty years of his hard life, with only very short breaks. It was in the main a matter-of-fact record of his farming operations; his flocks and crops appear in it far more frequently than the members of his family; but every so often history would thrust its fist through the pastoral and agricultural rituals, break them, and bring them to a temporary halt. I used to dip into it casually, and read a few of the laconic entries to my friends, such as:

'Sat. 7 March 1840. Experienced great difficulty as well as exposed to much danger in crossing Fish River this morning at daylight, having our wagon and oxen carried past the Drift, and upward of 2 hours toiling in the water before we were able to get out. Arrived in Grahamstown about sunset. . . .

'Thursday 30th April 1840. Rode to Salem with my two sons John and James (to attend school there). Sheep doing extremely badly about Salem and mortality great. . . .'

On the second flyleaf was an entry: 'Arrived at Elephant Fountain with my family February 15th, 1834.' This was followed by many pages of accounts — he was trader as well as farmer — before one came to a great Job-like cry of anguish written down in the midst of disaster — dated 31 March 1835, just a century before I read and re-read it: 'O Lord my God in the bitterness of my soul do I cry to thee this night. O save me, for I am passing through deep waters which threaten to o'erwhelm me. Thou dost indeed move in a mysterious way Thy wonders to perform, but who am I, that I should demand of Thee "What doest Thou?" Nor dare I attempt a reason why or wherefore Thou permittest such a fearful calamity to come upon me.'

During the Frontier War of 1834–5, unlike most of the farmers in the neighbourhood of the Koonap near Fort Beaufort, James Collett had refused to abandon his homestead, in spite of a previous attack. This prayer is written during the night of the second attack. He begs to be saved 'from infidelity and unbelief. Strengthen my staggering faith in the over-ruling Providence of Thee my God.' He has cause: he has lost a faithful Hottentot servant, and much of his beloved stock. He pours into his prayer what has just happened during the attack, with concrete details which evoke the living relationships of men and animals on his farm. He asks God why the 'Caffres' should have been permitted to rob him 'of my three span of valuable working oxen (which) I have with assiduity and care been for several years matching and training, and all those choice milch cows which supplied us with butter, and my dear children and People (servants and labourers) with milk in abundance; and also those quiet and useful animals our Horses on which myself and family have so frequently and so safely rode and journeyed; *and,* what grieves me infinitely more than all and is calculated to fill my cup of sorrow to the very brim, to murder, barbarously Murder, my poor faithful Faltein, who had by his incessant labour by Day and watching by Night, been mainly instrumental in reserving and saving my Cattle up to this very day, but whom I have now just left lying in the fields, a cold and lifeless corpse, his mangled body surrounded only by his faithful dogs whom neither the Caffres could drive nor myself succeed in bringing away from the fatal spot.'

He ends: '. . . have mercy upon us and save us . . . from further bloodshed . . . grant that this may be the last victim that shall fall by their blood-stained spears; and while Thou strengthenest my wavering Faith, sustain my worn-out body, and say to my sinking soul, "Hope thou in God for thou shalt yet Praise him." '

Never in his long diary does he express doubts about his right to his farms: he had paid for them. But Elephant Fountain was in the Ceded Territory between the Koonap and Kat Rivers, and this fact worried me, even in my youth.

It was at this time that I became aware of the cry of the Jan Diederick, or Green Cuckoo. Dee-dee-diederick it cries, so sad a cry through the hot, still air. Dee-dee-diederick, inconsolably all afternoon. For some reason it brought to mind the strange passage in Milton's 'Lycidas' about the helplessness of the Gods themselves to save their darlings from disaster.

What could the Muse herself that Orpheus bore,
The Muse herself, for her enchanting son
Whom universal nature did lament,
When by the rout that made the hideous roar,
His gory visage down the stream was sent,
Down the swift Hebrus to the Lesbian shore?

According to my notes on 'Lycidas', Orpheus had been dismembered by drunken maenads, but his head, thrown into the stream, continued to cry Eurydice, Eurydice, Dee-dee-diederick, Dee-dee-diederick, while all the shores re-echoed Eurydice, Dee-dee-diederick.

There seemed to be an appropriate inevitability in each stage of Orpheus's story: the theft of his beloved by Pluto; his descent into the underworld to recapture her, where the power of his music

Drew iron tears down Pluto's cheek
And made Hell grant what Love did seek;

Eurydice's release, and the injunction that Orpheus must not glance back to see if she is following; his so-fallible turning on the borders of day; her slipping from his grasp: how many times has this been re-enacted? And then the rest of a life spent in a vain search, inconsolably calling for her, turning to the world of beasts, plants and stones for company.

Eurydice, Eurydice. Dee-diederick, Dee-diederick.

Other vague ideas attached themselves to the cry. The diederick is a cuckoo. It hatches among sparrows. Its foster parents do their best for it, but it belongs to another species, and inevitably they lose patience and drive it from their nest. It then begins its restless, migratory life, an exile, like Orpheus, incapable of building a nest or rearing its own family: a sort of parasite too, yet what a lovely cry!

Like many children during periods of parental stress, I indulged in such fantasies: my differences from my parents were so great as to be explicable only by resort to suppositions of adoption, or of babies getting confused in hospital, or of some other such improbability. And with this went other fantasies: that one belonged by rights to a larger, more beautiful and juster world than that into which one had been born. One listened with interest to eccentrics who believed in reincarnation or transmigration of souls. It was a great source of comfort to one old lady in Bree Street, Cradock, C.P., to know that she had been Marie Antoinette in her previous life but two.

During the September vacation 1935, Rex Moys returned from Rhodes University on his ancient A.J.S. motorcycle. Alice and Ernest thought that I needed a break before the all-important matriculation examination. And so it came about that the current holder of the Alfred Metcalf Scholarship and one of the aspirants set out to visit Langfontein next to Vrede. We intended to return via Rooispruit and the Torrs at Schoombie. There were no tarred roads in the Karoo in those days, and any trip was a challenge to the demons of dust and/or mud.

I had never ridden on the pillion of a motorcycle before. The disadvantages were many: one's eyes became bloodshot, one's lips cracked, one's joints grew stiff. The only advantages which the motorcycle had over the pedal-cycle were speed and power.

Our trip to Langfontein went off without incident. Uncle Boy and Aunt K were in fine form. I spent the best part of a day in the semi-darkness of the old mill-house drawing and painting its works. Unfortunately the external waterwheel had already rotted beyond recognition; but the large wooden cogwheels inside were intact. I have remained fascinated to this day by machines in which the skills of the worker in wood and the worker in iron are combined — mills, wagons, carts, old-fashioned threshing-machines.

Much of the energy of Uncle Frank and Uncle Boy was being consumed by the construction of a large dam in an ironstone gorge up one of the tributaries of the Swartrivier. It was an atmospheric spot. En route one had to pass a cairn of stones, the grave of an old Hottentot chieftain. Then one turned left to the site itself. Uncle Frank had painted the outline of the finished dam wall in white on the purple ironstones on either side of the gorge. The manner of construction was most unusual. The downstream side of the wall was to consist of ironstone boulders, dry-packed into rectangular layers of decreasing breadth, held in position by heavy-gauge wire mesh. From that side it would look like a gigantic stairway. On the upstream side the ironstone wall was to be perpendicular. Against it an impermeable seal of shale and then earth was to be packed.

Very few people believed in that dam. The Department of Water Affairs disapproved of the design; an engineer said that, once the dam was full, the valve which Uncle Boy had installed would shoot out like a cork from a champagne bottle. Others said that the project was too big and ambitious for one man.

The night before Rex and I were due to set off on our return journey, it rained. The next morning, although there was cloud about, and the air was crisp, we started off cheerfully enough — but soon ran into trouble. Somewhere beyond Stofhek we encountered mile after mile of slippery and sticky clay. We skidded and slewed on a drunken course until we came to a halt; the back wheel was immobilised by a solid mass of mud packed between the tyre and the mudguard. As this took a long time to remove, and a very short time to fill up again, our progress was slow and our time schedule dislocated. Once we got on to the main road we had less trouble with mud.

As we pulled out of Graaff-Reinet we did not like the look of the sky ahead at all: heavy sagging clouds of that consistency and colour which one associates with snow. We pushed on up the series of passes. On several occasions I had to dismount and walk; we had run into mud once more. Every so often the sky would fling fistfuls of icy raindrops at us. When we reached the top of the pass that opens on the New Bethesda plain, our hearts sank. The cloud ceiling was halfway down the mountainsides ahead, and even lower on the Renoster- and Wapadsberge. I was already gibbering uncontrollably from cold.

In the distance at New Bethesda siding we saw a smudge of smoke. We decided to catch that train wherever it was going — back to Graaff-Reinet, or on to Middelburg.

Just as we drew up, we heard it whistle. We dashed on to the station

platform yelling, 'Stop! Stop!' — and to our great relief, a man with a flag
in his hand made a signal which brought the slowly moving train to a halt.
We explained our problem. The man looked at us, and shook his head in
sympathy. We lifted the A.J.S. into the guard's-van, and climbed in after
it. The train started moving through the deepening twilight and thickening
snowfall. We ate our remaining sandwiches, but were so cold that we had
to do vigorous physical jerks to keep our circulation going. It is not altogether easy to run on the spot in a lurching guard's-van, but we managed to
steady ourselves by holding on to each other and the interior of the van.
Rex and I ran inside that van all the way from New Bethesda up to the top
of the pass. By then it was so dark that we could not see a thing, and had to
settle for rubbing ourselves, and smoking. At one of the sidings we got out
into the snowing air to see if any of the trucks contained sheep. I had heard
of shepherds who kept themselves warm on frosty nights by crawling in
among their flocks. But there were only two draughty cattle trucks. We
returned to the van.

The train pulled into Middelburg about 9.30, by which time that respectable metropolis was plunged in sleep. The remotely spaced street lamps
increased rather than diminished the impression of desertion. There was
only one non-official at the station, a Coloured youth in an old army greatcoat and a pair of very white tackies. For sixpence he undertook to guide
us to an hotel. He trotted ahead in the beam of the headlamp of the A.J.S.,
which Rex kept going in low gear. The colour of our guide's greatcoat
blended so aptly with the darkness that it seemed we were following an
apparition whose white shoes alone betrayed his presence.

The hotel was full. For another sixpence our guide undertook to lead us
to Mrs Vermaak's boarding-house. It was not fifty yards away and in total
darkness, but we hammered on the door until a severe-looking lady in a
woollen dressing-gown thrust her face through a partially opened door.

'Ja?' she snapped.

'Asseblief, Mevrou, ons verkluim van die koue.'

She opened the door. We paid our guide his additional fee, and entered
Mrs Vermaak's establishment. All she had to offer was a double bed. The
stove was already dead, she said, so she could not make us anything hot.

She left a candle with us and shuffled down the dark passage. Rex and I
took off our boots. As we were too cold to undress we climbed straight
into bed in our clothes. To our horror we found that it had one blanket
only. So we unhooked the curtains off the pelmet and lifted the carpets
off the floor, and pulled our pyjamas over our clothes. We slept warm.

The next morning the air was ice-clear and crystal-cold: every bit of
moisture in it had been frozen into snow and frost. The mountains shone
white against the pale horizon, and the veld was bleached with furry frost.
It was one of the most beautiful mornings I had ever seen; and its beauty
was a good omen for my long-delayed meeting with Eve. We expected to

reach Rooispruit for morning tea, and the Torrs before lunch.

We set out after a good breakfast, but took a wrong turning, towards Steynsburg. At last it dawned on us that we were among completely strange mountains. We stopped at a stone building to ask the way — no tree, no garden back or front; simply a kraal and a windmill. I was so cold that I asked Rex if we could not get ourselves invited inside to warm up. A desolate man with a white moustache said he was sorry, but his wife had died the previous day, the undertaker had not yet come for her, it wasn't the time to have strangers in the house. Briefly he gazed beyond us to the snow on the mountains, shook his head, withdrew, shut the door.

By the time we reached Rooispruit just before lunch I could not move from the pillion; my right leg was frozen stiff. I could not talk either; all the right side of my face was dead as if a dentist had injected the nerve of every tooth. Uncle Owen set me down on a riempie stool near the fire to thaw, and plied me with hot tea. By the time we had finished three helpings of each course of the midday meal we felt sufficiently strengthened to proceed. This we did in spite of an invitation to stay until the weather had warmed up. But I would not hear of it. The last time I had tried to visit the Torrs, measles had intervened. A little snow and some cold wind were not going to stop me this time.

Neither Rex nor I knew the terrain we were now entering. The farms were strange to us, and the directions we had received not as explicit as they might have been. But after the difficulties I had experienced in finding Rooispruit on the previous year's expedition on a pitch-dark night, I felt that this would be a piece of sunlit plainsailing — particularly when we came to a gate with 'Torr' written on it, in large clear letters. Within the next few minutes we came spinning up to the front stoep. Jamming on his brakes smartly, Rex skidded the A.J.S. to a dashing halt. We mounted the steps. I had expected the door to be opened by an eager, blushing and excited Eve, but a small, somewhat solemn-looking lady appeared, who seemed surprised to see us.

I said: 'Good afternoon.' To which she replied: 'Good afternoon.'

An enormous Karoo silence took possession of the scene once more. I cleared my throat.

'Mrs Torr, we've come to visit your daughters.'

'What are your names?' she asked with a close look. We introduced ourselves.

'Come inside,' she said.

We sat down in the shady parlour.

'Excuse me, I'll see where the girls are.'

Eventually a girl appeared, who said:

'Hullo, I'm Phyllis.' She seemed very amused. I had not heard that Eve had a sister called Phyllis, but the family likeness was unmistakable. Then two more girls appeared. We didn't know them either. It was getting distinctly embarrassing. Mrs Torr was standing there, watching, suspicious.

'Excuse me, Mrs Torr,' I said. 'We don't know any of these. Have you got any more?'

'Certainly not!' she exclaimed. 'Who *are* you looking for?'

'Eve and Kathleen, for a start,' I said.

Then her girls burst into peals of laughter, and even she smiled.

'Next farm,' she said. 'My brother-in-law. Lots of Torrs around here. Particularly girls.' As I went out of the front door I could hear Phyllis busy on the party line, screaming, 'Is Eve there? Get me Eve!'

When we reached our proper destination, we were welcomed by the triumphant hilarity of the young who were not emotionally involved. It was no laughing matter for Eve and me.

The air was scented with rain. We all spent the late afternoon walking, talking; but by some kind of wordless communication Eve and I would always find ourselves way out in front or far in the rear of the main body.

And after supper we went walking again, by the light of the fullest, yellowest moon that had ever shone on my seventeen years. Eve and I lingered on the homeward stretch. Greatly daring, I let my hand touch hers as we walked. Then I caught it, and we found ourselves swinging our joined hands high, backwards and forwards, moving in a kind of dance-march together. Then by the same magical co-ordination, both came to a halt at the same instant, faced each other, and embraced; simply embraced, without kissing: the feel of her hair, and her cheek against my face, and the sense of our bodies, breathing as deeply as our pulses were pounding loudly. And all inside the scent of rain and silt. Nearby, the brown, earth-scented flood waters were spilling into quicksilver over a sluice; the sound of it; and a night-jar letting out his long, spacious rattle; and over all, that moon, its X-ray light seeming to pour through her dress, through my khaki shirt, on to our flesh.

We stood like that for ever. Neither wished (nor dared) for more. For all our limitations, for that timeless time, we were complete.

When, at last, a voice calling from the house made us release each other, I realised I had not kissed her. I was aching in every limb. And I didn't sleep that night.

I had to wait a year, another whole year, before I kissed her.

What is it about one's first real love-affair? The more words you use the sillier you sound. As Sydney Clouts says, 'One word is too many, many too few.'

22

The Darkening Landscape

My unease about the world, particularly the political world, grew steadily. One of my best Afrikaans-speaking friends had become an open admirer of the German 'renaissance' led by Adolf Hitler. A keen amateur cameraman, he received finely printed photographic booklets and brochures, and sent copies of his photographs for free critical comment to Germany. Two beautiful pictures of the Graf Zeppelin hung on his walls. Tall and blue-eyed, he claimed to feel his Nordic blood respond to the leadership principle far more than to democracy, which was a mere mean-spirited kow-towing to the little man in the street. It needed a Herculean race to cleanse the Augean stables of the world. A committee of pinks or reds would never do it.

I, meanwhile, was dipping into the volumes of the Left Book Club, to which Father had subscribed. So I had some ammunition to use in our debates. The more we talked the clearer it became that there could be no meeting of minds between extreme nationalists, whose appeal was to the will or 'blood' of an ethnic or cultural group, and the Communists, whose appeal was to the workers of the world everywhere.

While we were arguing late one afternoon, we heard a loudspeaker blare an invitation to everyone to meet on the market square at seven-thirty to hear about a Jewish plot to dominate the world.

'It must be the Greyshirts,' said my friend, as we dashed outside.

We saw a van approaching slowly, most dramatically lit by the late after-noon sun; attached to its radiator was a flagpole sporting a large, handsome dove-grey flag, with a pure-white circle containing that black, sharp symbol, the swastika. The driver of the car and the occupants were dressed exactly like Nazi officers, complete with swastika armbands. Images from Mother's visit to Germany, from the illustrated papers, from the Movietone News, had taken on sudden flesh. Mr Weichardt and his crew clouted me into consciousness: Nazism was not a remote European phenomenon. It was stalking Cradock, C.P. I was outraged and fascinated.

We went to the meeting that evening. The crowd was not large — mostly poor-whites, and some Coloured people, whose lack of Nordic purity did not seem to offend the speaker.

The burden of Weichardt's message was: To Palestine with all Jews. Don't buy from them. They are cheaters, corrupters of morals, exploiters of the poor, seducers of Christian girls in their employ. They are great enemies of the Boerenasie because they are international. They take their orders from a secret society of British and American Jews in London; America, France and Britain are, in fact, governed by them, and so cunning are they that Russia, Communist Russia, is also governed by them. Jews are both capitalist and communist, and apart from Germany, they have a stranglehold on the entire world.

One might dismiss it all as a lot of twaddle, as Father tended to do, pointing out the inconsistencies and falsifications; but one could not dismiss it as twaddle when one considered that it was backed by the might of a Germany who seemed to be doing exactly as she pleased in Europe; nor could one dismiss it as twaddle when one went into old Mr Berkowitz's shop opposite, as Mother did, to buy some cloth for Susan's apron, and found a stranger to Cradock, a coarse, hulking man, calling the shopkeeper a filthy Jew; a hulking man who, moreover, turned on her, Mrs Butler, and demanded, 'Are you going to buy from this swine?'

Fortunately the Greyshirts never caught on, but the influence of Nazi racial theories on Afrikaans poets, political theorists and politicians was for a time profound and formative.

I was distressed to hear that Roy Campbell, a South African poet living in Europe, had become a protagonist of extreme right-wing thought. Aird had introduced me to *The Flaming Terrapin* two or three years before, and I had revelled in its metaphors, many of them struck out of the Africa I knew; I had also found myself responding to its many images of energy:

The frailest reed
Holds shackled thunder in its heart's seclusion.
. . . a great machine,
Thoughtless and fearless, governing the clean
System of active things.

I discovered affinities between Campbell's Terrapin and Blake's Tyger.

One evensong the Rev. Charles Gould called for the names of candidates for Confirmation and announced the times of the weekly classes. Joan and Dorothy had already been confirmed. Was it not the turn of Christine and Guy? asked Alice. With reluctance Ernest consented: must all his children become Anglicans? Yet, if they felt their spiritual home to be there, could he stand in their way? If only Inchanga school had survived to saturate at least one of his children in Quakerism. He had, in fact, sold the pass long since with the baptism of Joan, according to whom 'there was a crisis over my baptism. Alice clamoured for an Anglican christening, but Ernest as a good Quaker said the ceremony was unnecessary.' He did not believe in holy water or promises by godfathers and godmothers. Grannie Butler intervened. 'Ernest,' she said, 'your father was a Quaker, but he agreed that all his children should be baptised in the Methodist Church — not because he believed in baptism but because I, the mother, wanted it. Besides, what harm can it do?' So Methodism came to the rescue of Anglicanism, and the Butler children were taken to the font at St Peter's.

If confirmations activated all Ernest's anti-sacramental and anti-sacerdotal prejudices, he had to stomach them, just as Alice had to stomach the periodic visitations of revivalists to Cradock. 'While Anglicans and Catholics held themselves aloof from such soul-searching and dynamic gatherings,' says Dorothy, 'our father allowed us to attend these services in a spirit of fine impartiality, but with perhaps some lack of discrimination as to the effect they might have on his brood. My mother didn't care for them but was loyal to Father and simply continued to be utterly and consistently faithful to her Anglican faith.'

If I remained unresponsive when the evangelist summoned those who felt so moved to walk up to the front of the hall or church, my sisters were 'saved' on more than one occasion. Christine says that they were once so profoundly evangelised as to determine to tidy their room from top to bottom. They started in fine style by emptying all drawers and cupboards onto the floor. Then they felt called to interrupt their work in order to rush off and spread the good news of their salvation among their friends. This seemed to tire them completely. Late that afternoon Alice had to step in, where the Holy Spirit had left off, and tell them they had better forget about being saved, and tidy the room before supper, or else.

The Rector took us methodically through the Catechism, and explained or rather described the sacraments. As always in these matters, I was made aware of the inadequacy of language. I was also convinced that the attempt was necessary. As the word Confirmation itself suggests, the laying on of hands by the Bishop was to strengthen a process begun at the font in infancy. The Rector warned us that it might be accompanied by a very moving experience but, if we were not moved, we should not be worried: God loved the individuality of his children and would do what was right for each. It was for us to understand and learn as much as we could about His nature and the teachings of the church He had founded, and to approach the event with a clear conscience towards Him and our fellowmen.

Gould did not press the question of confession to a priest: if we felt it would help us, he would be available. I did attempt a thorough private self-examination, and was properly appalled at what it revealed: a selfish, sensual, temperamental, undisciplined, proud, rebellious, dishonest and conceited youth. I knew that I was a source of pain and grief to others, and to my Creator and Redeemer. Late one afternoon I stole into St Peter's and, kneeling in a back pew near the font, confessed myself to heaven, expressed my penitence in simple words, and promised amendment of life. It was not an overwhelming religious experience. I did not feel the presence of God. I was not in a profoundly emotional state, but as I walked into the churchyard among the old graves I knew as truly as I knew anything that I had been forgiven.

I remember little of the Confirmation service itself, though Bishop Archibald Cullen of Grahamstown made one point only in his sermon, which has stuck with me all my life, not because he said it, but because it put into words one of the guiding principles in the lives of Alice, and of Ernest, and of Aunt Mary, and of most of my uncles and aunts — the huge family who had been my unofficial godfathers and godmothers since my baptism: be faithful, be true.

I was one of those who experienced no unusual sensation or emotion when the episcopal hands were laid upon my submissive head, and I had quite forgotten the words that the Bishop uses at that moment until I attended the confirmation of one of my sons. As a 17-year-old I had been untouched by them. As a parent they moved me to my depths:

'I sign thee with the sign of the cross, and I lay my hands upon thee. Defend, O Lord, this thy child with thy heavenly grace, that he may continue thine forever; and daily increase in thy Holy Spirit more and more, until he come unto thy everlasting kingdom. Amen.'

It sometimes seems that all the memorable experiences of our lives, but particularly those of childhood, are mysteries whose meaning is progressively unveiled as we grow older. If we have been given a good spiritual inheritance we do not grow away from it, but into it.

Driving home from that service, some fragments from T.S. Eliot's 'The Dry Salvages' kept repeating themselves in my mind:

It seems, as one becomes older
That the past has another pattern, and ceases to be a mere sequence . . .

We had the experience but missed the meaning,
And approach to the meaning restores the experience
In a different form, beyond any meaning
We can assign to happiness. I have said before
That the past experience revived in the meaning
Is not the experience of one life only
But of many generations . . .
Time the destroyer is time the preserver.

Mr B.J. du Toit, the new head, had been principal at Prince Albert before coming to Cradock. This struck Paul Michau as an hilarious antecedent. He had seen Prince Albert, which, he said, was only about an eighth of the size of Cradock. Boys in the bigger Karoo towns are difficult to impress.

B.J. was a short man, who carried himself very erect. His head was disproportionately large, his neck thick, and his eyes bulging. Only later did we learn that he was a chronic sufferer from hyperthyroid, an affliction which may have accounted for his unpredictable temper.

He took the Matrics for history, and there is no doubt that he could teach it well when he chose. The results in his subject had been exceptionally good the year before. He expected us all to acknowledge his excellence. While he won our respect, he did not win our affection. It was not that he was anti-English. He spoke English fluently and correctly, and, if anything, he used it more frequently in class than Afrikaans. And he certainly gave us a far clearer picture of the complexity of our history than we had ever had before — details and personalities not in Fowler and Smit. History was thoroughly exciting when he got going. For instance, he made it quite clear that the Bezuidenhouts, the martyrs of Slagters Nek, were not the simple blonde Afrikaner heroes killed by brutal imperialist British officers in charge of low-caste Hottentot soldiery that one had been led to believe; it was far, far more complicated than that. There was the matter of High Treason, for instance; the heroes had tried to persuade Gaika, the Xhosa paramount chief, to join forces with white rebels against Lord Charles Somerset; and when the final pursuit took place, and the cornered man defended his cave to the end, one of his last faithful companions was his Coloured concubine. Not simple at all, particularly in view of the pure-white stand of many Afrikaner politicians.

B.J.'s difficulties sprang from vanity, a violent temper, and an inability to organise his school. My particular crisis would never have occurred if there had been a system of school prefects or class representatives — some channel of communication between ourselves and the upper deck; but there was none, and we were, after all, the senior boys, perhaps a little vain ourselves, and totally ignorant as to how to make a legitimate complaint.

The crisis occurred three or four weeks before the dreaded final examination — Matric itself. We were supposed to be revising the syllabus. B.J. failed to appear. He missed four classes in a row. He sent no excuse, no message, no instructions, and the class became restive. The anxious and the conscientious — for there were a few such — tried to revise on their own, but it became difficult to concentrate when the couldn't-cares began skylarking in a subdued manner. One daredevil smoked an entire cigarette — taking the precaution of sitting by an open window, through which the draught bore off the tell-tale fumes. But clearly the decibels were louder than we imagined.

Suddenly B.J. was in front of the form, storming. How dared we make such a noise? How dared the senior form in the school set such a bad example? What was the matter with us? Did we not know how to behave? Had we not been brought up properly? What sort of homes did we come from?

To none of these questions did he receive a reply. The class was used to such verbal flagellations, and sat in smug, dumb insolence. He couldn't stand it, so he picked on an individual to humiliate and reduce to jelly.

'Mann, explain your disgraceful behaviour.'

Mann rose slowly to his feet.

'We are worried about our work, sir.'

'Worried? Then why do you behave like a circus? A worried man works and is quiet.' Mann's head stooped. Then, 'Butler, what have you got to say for yourself?'

'It's our history, sir.'

His expression darkened. I had mentioned his subject.

'What about your history?'

'We're worried about it, sir.'

'Why should you worry about it? It's the best-taught subject in the school!'

My reply was not intended to be facetious but factual:

'There are differences of opinion about that, sir.'

'What did you say?'

'There are differences of opinion about that, sir.'

The full fury of his rage now burst. Question followed question like a succession of blows, to which I replied never a word. Finally he cried, 'Why don't you reply? . . . Come to my study.'

I followed him to his study, where I did try to explain: he had been absent for four classes in a row, I said, it was near exams, and we were worried — but it was no use; he began storming again. In retrospect, I suppose he was hoping for an apology, for tears of repentance; but I was completely un-sorry. He then tried another tactic. He left me alone in his study, and went to the staff commonroom next door, and after what seemed like an age, returned with Mr Kachelhoffer.

'Look at him!' he cried. 'Stubborn as a mule. Insolent. You speak to him!' And he left. 'Klaf' sat down, and told me to sit.

'Now, what happened?' he asked.

I told him as best I could. I was beginning to shake all over.

Klaf said I had better apologise. I said I did not know what I had done wrong. I had told the truth. At which point the Head burst back into the room, crying, 'What does he say, what does he say?'

Klaf got up.

'We have just started — '

'I won't have my staff pleading with boys!'

Klaf left the study.

'Well?' cried Du Toit, his eyes bulging out of his head.

I stared back at him. Then:

'Out of my school! Fetch your books, and out!'

There was an awed silence in the class as I emptied my desk, book by book, and, having strapped them together, walked out of the school at the unusual hour of 11.0 a.m. Nothing seemed quite real. For one thing, the unique shakiness in my limbs; and the blank sense that, although I was moving along Frere Street, everything had stopped. No Matric exam. No chance at the Alfred Metcalf Scholarship. No university. Indeed, no job of any kind.

I got home to a surprised Alice, who immediately phoned Ernest, who did the completely unprecedented thing: left his office, and came home at once. I retold my story, over and over. Alice grew angrier and angrier, stamping her foot, and shaking her head, and crying, 'It's simply abominable,' while Ernest got quieter and more and more tight-lipped. The main immediate concern was to establish whether expulsion deprived me of the right to sit the exam. He left, to spend the rest of the morning with his old school friend, the lawyer George Tunbridge, and with the school board officials. By lunch time he had established that it would be very difficult for B.J. to prevent me from writing. He might be able to stop me from writing in 'his' exam hall, but exams could be sat elsewhere, and a plan could, no doubt, be made — for instance I might be able to write at Rocklands Girls' High school, whose principal, Miss Stoops, was a great friend of Mother's. But the idea of being the only boy in a hall full of girls filled me with horror. Still, I was told, beggars can't be choosers. The second question was: would an expelled boy be eligible for the Scholarship?

Dad asked me to go over the details once more. The whole conduct of B.J. came under his cool review. He then started phoning or interviewing the parents of various other matriculants, no doubt seeking corroboration of my version of the event. He then considered for a day or two — should he take the matter to the school board, and to court if need be? But the time factor made him hesitate. The examination was three weeks away. And if I should miss the examination while a case pended, I would miss the chance of the all-important Scholarship.

Meanwhile I started working at home. I had some contact with the teaching staff, through 'Pop' Adan, the Maths and Science master, to whom I was sent for extra classes in Algebra. But it was a lonely limbo isolated from the infectious atmosphere of my friends who were preparing for the common ordeal.

Meanwhile B.J. had had time to cool his heels, and it was intimated that I would be allowed to return to school to write the exams. But disaster struck again. Jeffrey went down with measles.

Such was my parents' determination that nothing should stop me from writing, that they opened urgent negotiations through an intermediary with B.J.: would it not be possible for me to become a boarder in the school hostel until the exams were over? The hostel was run by B.J.'s wife. Within a matter of hours after the measles diagnosis I was bundled off, with a suitcase, and my strapped-up books.

I remember very little about the next three or four weeks, except that Paul Michau had become a boarder to enable him to swot harder; and that we bunked out a couple of times.

Of the actual examinations I remember even less, except that I had no idea how well or badly I had done on any paper.

The ordeal was followed by a blank period of waiting for the results. I spent much time dreaming about my future. In spite of growing up in the years of depression, of earning and saving money, I had little knowledge and regrettably no real interest in exactly how my dreams were to be realised. I inhabited a world of romantic visions many of them alien to the intellectual climate of Cradock: I believed myself to be a poet or painter in embryo, an original creative mind. As my attempts to communicate the nature of my destiny to my parents always broke down in mutual incomprehension, I became more secretive and more arrogant towards them.

One evening Father asked me to help him install a radio set for Mr Nicholson, a devout supporter of Colonel Stallard and the Dominionites.

In the hallway of his house, 'Mafeking', a coloured picture of King George V held regal sway. The vases in the front room were polished brass shell cases, the ashtrays degutted hand-grenades, the doorstop a German helmet with a gruesome bullet hole through it. On three of the four walls were large monochrome prints of soldiers winning V.C.s, and on the fourth, over the mantel, a picture called 'Wilson's Last Stand'.

Mr Nicholson had a very red face, very blue eyes, very white hair and a very straight back. There was nothing semi-, demi-, half, so-so, fifty-fifty, partial or medium about him. Above all, he was very British.

While we went about our business of installing the set, he recounted a recent conversation he had had with one of the hot Nationalists in town. This 'rebel' had advocated cutting all ties with Britain and the Empire immediately. Europe was heading for war. South Africa must stay neutral, and not be dragged into other people's fights.

'Neutral! Can you imagine it, when the mother country is at war?'

'They don't see it like that. Britain is not their mother country,' remonstrated Father.

'Perhaps not,' said Nicholson, 'but do they think they can go it alone, without any allies or friends in the world?'

'Some do. Some think they could find better and perhaps stronger friends.'

'Exactly, the traitors! They're banking on war and a German victory to put Afrikanerdom into the saddle for ever.'

He then repeated his well-known satire on the Afrikaner's claim to be unique and entitled to express his nature and needs in his own way. With variations, it went something like this:

'What is this unique essence that needs isolation from the rest of the world for its preservation? Your language? It is a decayed dialect of Dutch. Your religion? It's the heretical work of a Frenchman, Calvin. Your favourite drink is brandy, also French; so is your surname. Your most typical dishes — yellow rice, sosaties and biltong — are Malay. The mealies and potatoes you plant come from the Redskins; your Angoras and Merinos from Turkey and Spain. Your coffee comes from Brazil, and the cup you drink it from is Czechoslovakian. Your car is American, your rifle Belgian, your wristwatch Swiss; your bluegum avenues Australian, your oak-trees English, and your Bible Jewish. And the game that you spend all your spare time talking about, rugby, is a minor by-product of the British genius.'

Father found this catalogue vaguely amusing, and would add items to it when particularly irritated by Afrikaner insistence on uniqueness. But I found it a little smug, even offensive. Admittedly very little is unique to South Africa, but the peculiar selection of things, borrowed from all the corners of the world, is, as is their configuration and their setting. And so is the structure of the land and the temperament of the peoples, and the sequence in which things have happened. Geography and history do differ from country to country.

So at the very time when I felt increasingly drawn to Europe, to a world elsewhere, I found myself being driven to condemn too slick a sneer at people who felt the need to cry 'we belong here, and nowhere else.'

I found myself staring at 'Wilson's Last Stand': a gloomy, heroic picture; a fatal twilight stitched with the white of bandages, the scarlet of blood, the glint of steel and polished leather. The central background consists of a copse of trees, rising elated out of the sad, level grassveld, only to melt into a twilit distance on either flank and into the wet, sagging sky above. Amongst these trees and slightly ahead of them stand or crouch a small group of soldiers warding off the attacks of an enemy, unseen except for one crumpled black form in the right foreground and several scattered assegais. The trapped band were cavalry, but now all their horses are dead, their carcasses forming a glossy black-brown rampart. Over one of them a dead trooper lies slumped, a scarlet patch on his white shirt. Of the small group still standing, one had just fired into the scrub on the left, another is recharging, a third seems to be scrutinising the field of fire in front of him. Thin wisps of rifle smoke hang over them in an eerie, broken halo. They are doomed, obviously, gloriously. The darkness that is closing in on them is not a normal night.

'Wilson's Last Stand. Fine, isn't it?' said Nicholson.

'Who was Wilson?' I asked.

'Who was Wilson?' he repeated softly, outraged. 'What do they teach you at school? Nothing but Voortrekkers?'

He gave me his version of this event from the Matabele Rebellion. Wilson was officer in charge of a patrol of thirty-nine men sent across the Shangani River to capture Lobengula, who was in flight. Everything went wrong. The Shangani rose, cutting off their retreat, and preventing reinforcements from getting through. Many could have escaped, but they refused to leave their wounded to the mercies of the Matabele. So they fought it out, from dawn to nightfall, entirely surrounded by Matabele armed with rifles as well as spears. Late in the afternoon, in a lull in the fighting, the few survivors rose to their feet and sang 'The Queen'. Soon after that they were wiped out. They had killed over four hundred of the enemy. The Matabele were so impressed that they refrained from their custom of mutilating the corpses of their foes.

By this time Father had finished the installation, and asked if his customer would like to test his set on the late news from London?

Hitler had made another impatient speech somewhere or other, Anthony Eden — or was it Sir Samuel Hoare? — was cutting a dash at a conference. Mussolini's army was advancing victoriously into Abyssinia. There were allegations that they were using mustard gas. When the cultured, controlled B.B.C. voice ended, there was a roll of drums which set the window panes rattling; then a full orchestra blundered into and thundered through 'The King'. Mr Nicholson rose from his chair, and stood stiffly to attention.

Walking home I asked Father whether he remembered anything about Wilson's Last Stand. Yes, a little. He was a boy when it happened. The news came through in bits and pieces. Clearly they had been very brave, but their deaths were quite unnecessary. Like the Charge of the Light Brigade — someone had blundered. Like Magersfontein — over-confidence. Like the Jameson Raid — gambling for big stakes. The whites had just defeated the Matabele at an earlier battle on the Shangani, proudly claiming to have killed six hundred for the loss of one white trooper, one Coloured wagon driver, and six wounded. In Father's view, the laurels for sheer courage should go to the Matabele. The figures speak volumes. The whites had Maxim guns which cut down the blacks like corn.

But the Shangani patrol took no magical Maxims. And as for singing 'The Queen', that was just hearsay. A trader picked up the story among the Matabele when it was all over — the white men had stood up and sung before the end. But was it 'The Queen'? It could have been 'Abide with me', or, since many of them were Scots, 'Scots wha hae wi' Wallace bled'. We shall never know.

But they did sing. That was the gesture that so impressed the Matabele: the doomed men sang.

That was one way of responding to a frontier crisis. James Lydford Collett's prayer was another. But, moved as I might be, I did not see myself in either of these situations or roles. I felt I wanted to paint or to write. And as far as I knew from my very limited experience of South African literature and painting up to that time, very few had tried to do these things in South Africa. There was, of course, the case of Olive Schreiner, right on my doorstep. But the attitude to her was equivocal: a difficult freak of a woman to whom it was proper on occasions to doff one's moral or patriotic hat.

I felt that I must leave the Union, as Roy Campbell had done; get into an old society, where frontiers and civil wars were things of the past; where the landscape bears beautiful cities, centuries old; where princes have left magnificent gardens, green, with flashing fountains and honey-coloured statues; countries whose air has been breathed by long dynasties of artists.

With the Christmas mail came a picture postcard from Aunt May Daniel: Piero della Francesca, 'The Nativity', National Gallery, London.

A group of wingless angels, standing solid as stone statues on the earth, singing for an infant Christ lying naked on his mother's cloak; she kneels on the earth, to one side. I stared and stared. The colouring of the setting and the light reminded me of a sunny winter's day in the Karoo, and the countryside (pale earth colours with dark blobs of green) bore an odd resemblance to the veld itself where the bare earth shows between the shrubs. Behind the angels, the only intermediary between Christ and the landscape, rises a ruined stable, with a leaky penthouse roof. The walls are of dry-packed stone, like so many I have seen.

On one corner of the roof is perched a bird, looking more like a butcher-bird than any I have yet come across in paint. He is in profile. He is not singing. He is not looking at the Holy Child. He is biding his time.

The Angels are not looking at the Child either; they simply tower above him singing. Nor are they, at this moment, concerned with the landscape, the stable, the butcherbird or the kneeling mother. They simply stand there, barefoot, four square, singing: not looking at the infant Creator on the earth, nor raising their eyes or their hands to the heaven that has sent him.

The moment for looking or prayer is past. How could they properly praise, or play those instruments, in a kneeling position? Their eyes are unfocused, vacant, undistracted by the historical accidents about them. They are busy with what they were blessedly sent to do: to transform it all into praise; to play their instruments and sing.

While I dreamily turned pictures into allegories, my father struggled with his ailing business. When he bought *The Midland News* property some years previously, he had converted its large hall into a cinema, called the Plaza, and let it to a Mr Paris; and two other smaller portions on the street were let as shops. Ernest relied heavily on these rents to balance his books. Two blows struck him at once: 'standing' advertisements declined rapidly, and Mr Paris informed him that he would not be renewing his lease for 1936. So Ernest had been obliged to dispense with the services of his editor Mr Cursons, completely and finally; a painful decision, as he had served the firm well for twelve years. The editor's wife was so overcome as to say harsh and unkind things about Ernest. This came to Alice's ears. The effect was electrifying. Our good-humoured mother became a blazing tigress, ready to tear her limb from limb. When Aunt Mary said quietly, 'Alison, dear, be reasonable,' she snorted, stamping her foot: 'Reasonable? I'll be nothing of the kind.' It took hours of Ernest's patient persuasion to prevent her from storming up town to tell her exactly what she thought of her. But the hurricane blew itself out, and Alice was soon having her foe round to an atoning cup of tea.

At last the matriculation results were announced and, shortly after, the news that I had been awarded the Alfred Metcalf Scholarship to Rhodes University College, Grahamstown, for three years. Everyone was very proud of me and I was inordinately proud of myself.

We now turned to the Rhodes University Calendar and Prospectus with renewed interest. Father was very worried. Fees and costs had risen during the past three years, but he said little, apart from pressing me to make up my mind as to what career I wished to pursue and what courses I would take. I shilly-shallied for days. At one meal, I would express a keen interest in Science; I had scored an A for chemistry. At the next, I was all for the Arts: I had scored an A for English — then a very rare mark indeed. In the light of this uncertainty, Father asked: What about Commerce? — still hoping perhaps that I would go into the family business. He clung to the hope that it might in due course recover.

'What', asked Father, 'do you want to become?'

That was, indeed, the question, but Mother, quite sure of the correct answer, had no hesitation in supplying it:

'A teacher — Arts or Science — it doesn't matter which.'

The moment of truth had come.

'I may have to be a teacher, but I want to be a writer.'

There was a puzzled pause.

'You mean a journalist?' asked Father.

'No. A poet.'

There was an appalled silence. Then Ernest said:

'You don't need to go to university for that.'

Alice looked up from her darning, startled. Ernest went on:

'Until the boy makes up his mind what profession he wishes to enter, there's no point in wasting good money sending him to university. As far as I am concerned there is no profession called poet. Poetry butters no parsnips.'

And he got up and left the room.

I banged my fists on the table and cried out, 'I want to write!'

Alice said, 'You be sensible now. You can write in your spare time. Most writers do.'

Explosions were so rare at The Poplars that they left people paralysed.

I got up, and went to my room. It seemed impossible that my father should go back on his word. For more than two years I had made furniture, I had worked hard, I had won the scholarship. I had fulfilled my side of the bargain. How could he go back on his? He had made absolutely no conditions about careers or anything else — all he had asked was, Did I want to go to university? And now he was insisting that I could not go because I wanted to be a poet. If I had said a journalist, or a teacher, he would have agreed. And maybe I should have to be a journalist or a teacher to earn my bread, but that was not what I wanted to *be*. Did they want me to pretend?

In a turmoil, I left The Poplars, banging the wicket gate behind me. The river was down, and I leant over the parapet of the bridge. Watching its familiar display of elemental power might relieve my mind. How many million times had it been in flood? Enough to carve out the entire valley from sandstone measures formed from the silt deposited by other streams four or five hundred million years ago. Where did my troubles belong in that vast geological calendar? What did it matter what happened to me? whether I went to university or not? I would soon be dust, a few bones, less interesting than the fossils in the rocks of the Beaufort series.

Caught in the silver moonpath in midstream the roots of a willow tree appeared above the lurching quicksilver like despairing hands, then disappeared; then the sopping shock of its leaves reared up, only to sink in swirls and bubbles. Eurydice, Eurydice. Dee-dee-diederick. My tears of self-pity and rage fell into the impersonal flood. But the blessed trick of imagination which enables us to transcend ourselves allowed me the consolation of a self-indulgent image: where would my tears be in twelve hours' time? Diverted by the Scanlen weir, soaking into the lucerne fields to make a drop of nectar for Papa Aird's bees; or far downstream at Golden Valley, flowing among the orchards of apricot; or, if they escaped all the weirs, drifting into the Indian Ocean to be the heavy air in which gardens of swaying seaweed spread, through which fish flew and hovered like mysterious birds; where the silt even now was settling into beds of sandstone which other storms and streams would sculpt. I was beginning to enjoy my desolation. It was no mean thing to be conscious, to suffer and to think.

But a pain in my stiffening elbows and shoulders brought me back from this flight of Darwinian pantheism, to the problem of my immediate historical, not my remote geological future, and to the awful emptiness of spirit which always overcame me after conflicts with my parents.

I made up my mind as I walked up Church Street from the Gilfillan Bridge: I would enrol for either a B.A. or a B.Sc., depending on the expert advice the university would no doubt offer; and I would undertake to become a teacher or a journalist. This would be my contract with the world as represented by my parents. But I had another contract with myself, not necessarily in conflict with this, but deeper and more determined.

As I reached The Poplars corner I was appalled to see my mother alone on the front stoep. She was on one of those anguished look-outs which she usually conducted in the late afternoon before Father returned. But this time it was me — me she was waiting for. Since she was gazing down Bree Street, she was not aware of my approach until the wicket gate clicked behind me. She spun round and walked quickly towards me. There was an anguished pause in which I tried to speak, to say, 'Yes, I'll be a teacher,' but could not. When she spoke I realised that she had been driven to keep watch less for my sake than for her beloved Ernest's. Gently but very firmly she said:

'You've no business to stalk out like that, my boy. Your father always has done his best for you. He always will, and you know it.'

Then she took me by the hand and spoke with a blend of authority and pleading which I had never heard before. The choice of my career had dwindled to nothing before the threat it posed to the sacred family bonds. 'Your father is very hurt. Go and make things right with him.'

I opened the dining-room door. He was sitting in his accustomed seat, at the head of the family table, without any work in front of him, waiting. He glanced up. As always when tired or under a strain, the cast in his eye was more noticeable than usual. I sat down slowly in the nearest chair, which left the whole length of the table between us.

'I'm sorry,' I said with difficulty. 'I'll become a teacher or a journalist.'

'Thank you,' he said very quietly. 'It's the money; you see, even with the scholarship and the furniture, there's not enough.'

My heart sank.

'You mean I can't go?'

'No,' he said. 'We'll have to borrow, that's all. The university has a limited loan scheme. You'll have to pay it back when you can. As for the rest, well, I phoned Joan. She's saved steadily these last two years, and she'll lend you what she's got. I think we'll manage.'

I could stand it no longer. I put my head on to my arms. Great dry sobs shuddered through me, from somewhere infinitely deeper than my tears on the bridge.

Ernest got up, and briefly, clumsily, put his hand on my head.

'Few people know how much they are loved,' he said, and left the room.